FAMILY SYSTEMS

within

EDUCATIONAL CONTEXTS

Understanding Students with Special Needs

Rosemary Lambie
Virginia Commonwealth University

Debbie Daniels-Mohring
Private Practice, Richmond, Virginia

LOVE PUBLISHING COMPANY®
Denver, Colorado 80222

Page 198 poem: From *The Prophet* by Kahlil Gibran, Copyright © 1923 by Kahlil Gibran and renewed 1951 by Administrators C.T.A. of Kahlil Gibran Estate and Mary G. Gibran. Reprinted by permission of Alfred A. Knopf Inc.

Library of Congress Catalog Card Number 91-077050

Copyright © 1993 Love Publishing Company
Printed in the U.S.A.
ISBN 0-89108-223-9

CONTENTS

INTRODUCTION

Your authors came to the field of family systems from very different directions. The first author, Rosemary Lambie, became interested in family systems after years of being a teacher in the area of emotional and behavior disorders. She had reached the conclusion that these children and youth came from families with substantial challenges and that, unless those challenges were faced, the students would not make significant gains. In 1982–1983 she attended monthly seminars led by Murray Bowen and Michael Kerr. During that year she also attended a three-day workshop conducted by Virginia Satir. In the summer of 1983 she attended one of Satir's month-long institutes in Crested Butte, Colorado. It was then that she realized the field of family systems offered much to the challenges of families having children with behavioral disorders and other disabilities. The following year she began the first of six pivotal years of training offered at the Family Institute of Virginia.

"The Person and Practice of the Therapist," co-led by Joan Winter and Harry Aponte, met two days each month during the academic year. What Lambie learned about her own family of origin (one that included a chronically physically ill parent, a child with a severe learning disability, and a child with other special needs) taught her much. She wanted to translate for school professionals, especially teachers, family systems learning that has made a difference in her life and the lives of children and youth with disabilities.

Rosemary and Debbie Daniels-Mohring met when Debbie joined the family systems training group. Debbie had come to the field more directly with degrees in psychology and majors in family therapy and child clinical studies. She originally obtained her master's degree in a program that taught psychodynamic psychotherapy. After three years of working in a rural mental health center, she felt that individual long-term therapy was not the answer for most of her clients. As soon as she was introduced to the ideas of family systems theory, she believed that this was the new approach that would make a difference in working with clients with severe problems.

Debbie returned to graduate school to study for a Ph.D. in clinical psychology in a specifically designed program with a major in family systems therapy. Over the next twelve years, she worked with families in a variety of settings, including a mental health center, a psychoeducational center, a juvenile detention center, an inpatient facility, and private practice. She often consulted with teachers, counselors, and other school professionals who expressed interest in understanding and working with families.

It is from these two paths that this book was conceptualized. Our hope is that the blending of our experiences will make a difference for school professionals reading this text.

WHY WE WROTE THIS BOOK

Drawn to family systems approaches from the experience of being a sibling of a child with special needs, both of the authors found a deeper level of understanding about their respective family experiences by studying family systems approaches. Rosemary was the daughter of a chronically physically ill father and gained also from that experience with disability. Both authors also feel a deep commitment to sharing their insights and understandings as well as methodology with school professionals.

In the summer of 1984, Debbie Daniels-Mohring consulted with Rosemary Lambie on a project funded by the Virginia Department of Education. Lambie and others trained trainers to conduct workshops for school professionals that included a day-long module in family systems principles. The personal response of the participants was so positive that the two began discussing writing this book.

As we have talked to school professionals, we have found that most people who enter the field of education do so out of a desire to affect the lives of children and adolescents. They begin working with lots of energy and a sense that their commitment can and will make a difference. Often, after only a few years, this enthusiasm is dampened. Educators have told us how they use programs within the school that seem to be effective but do not carry over into the family life of the child. They are searching for some ways to be able to extend their influence into positive, long-term change for their students. We believe that this text addresses the need to include families in making decisions and changes in the lives of children and adolescents. The potential for affecting students, with the addition of family systems knowledge, is tremendous.

ACKNOWLEDGMENTS

My family of origin has been my greatest teacher about family systems. Being the sibling of a child with a severe learning disability and daughter of a father with severe, chronic physical illnesses has provided many opportunities for growth and affected my choice of careers. I also acknowledge the gifts that my extended family have presented. Helen Miles affected my view of life and family at a critical time in my childhood, and I am most appreciative.

I also acknowledge Joan Winter, the director of the Family Institute of Virginia, for the gift of sharing her views of family systems approaches. Harry Aponte is the second most influential person in my learning process. Harry has been a father figure and, like Joan, crucial in my personal growth and development. The gentle guidance and keen vision of these two family systems specialists provided insights and understanding that allowed me to approach writing this text. I am deeply grateful.

Virginia Satir died in 1988. I truly appreciate the continued impact she has on my life. I am grateful to her for her gifts to all of the people of the world.

Murray Bowen's vision of family systems has greatly affected my personal and professional life. He is the individual who truly started me on my journey to understanding family systems concepts and approaches. The unexpected side benefit is that I have a deep sense of connection to my extended family on the Ryan side.

Debbie Daniels-Mohring's willingness to co-author this text when she has a new baby was a godsend, and I value both her perspective and work. George Lambie, my brother, edited and provided crucial assistance. He is a fine, gentle teacher and gifted writer. John Seyfarth has been masterful in providing feedback and suggestions. Fred Orelove and Howard Garner have also been supportive. My division head, Paul Gerber, influenced me to strike out on this path. Patsy Hemp has provided valuable feedback. Katty Inge made tables and charts that are readable. Dale Bateman, Lisa Mayhall, and Beverly Frye have provided positive feedback and encouraged our writing. Beth Ayn Stansfield also provided feedback on two chapters, encouraged me to write, and carted heavy books. With the help of these individuals we were able to do what would have been impossible alone.

I thank Dianne Connelly for helping me keep myself in balance, bringing life to life, during this time. I appreciate Elisabeth Talbot for her emotional support and encouragement. Christen McCormack's shared vision has made a large impact on my life at this time. Susan Thesenga's gentle empowerment and understanding of the child within has made a vast difference in my sense of self and connection with spirit. My thanks and blessings to all of these individuals.

RAL

My first acknowledgment is to my family, source of much happiness and pain, who have taught me about giving and sharing and provided me with a legacy of caring and commitment. If not for them, family systems thinking wouldn't ring so true for me.

Secondly, I would like to acknowledge Martha Foster, Michael Berger, Carrell Dammann, and the staff at the original Atlanta Institute for Family Studies. For two years they led a consultation team at our mental health clinic in rural Georgia. They were responsible for introducing me to the ideas of Sal Minuchin, and life hasn't been the same since. They also had the vision and commitment to organize my graduate program in family therapy at Georgia State.

Next I acknowledge Joan Winter and Harry Aponte, who co-led our family therapy training group for five years of my attendance. They are both talented therapists and have a warmth that helps gently guide you through the pitfalls of family-of-origin work. They were able to take a technician and help mold her into an explorer and guide. Thanks.

Thank you to all of my friends and colleagues who have provided support and assistance throughout the process of writing this book. My husband, Chris, was the ever-ready babysitter, editor, and, in the final hour, writer who ultimately made my portion of this text possible. Kathy Byrnes provided encouragement and constructive criticism of the final product.

My co-author, Rosemary Lambie, sustained the foundation upon which the book was built. Without her stamina and attention to detail, this dream would not have become reality.

Finally, to the families who have come to me for assistance, thank you for sharing your stories and your trust.

DDM

We both thank Hannah Huszti, a former VCU student and now a teacher in special education, who was a miracle worker copying material and carrying books from the library.

Our publisher, Stan Love, has been very encouraging, and we are grateful for his input and support. His low-key style and warmth have been invaluable in the process of writing this text.

In order to protect the identities of families, names and significant data
have been changed in the case examples within this text.

To Grace Ryan Lambie, favorite mother, gifted teacher and professor, model of equanimity, and the greatest gift of my life

To George William Lambie, Sr., my loving father

To my older brother, George Lambie, Jr.

To my younger brother, Tom Lambie

To my sister-in-law, Karen Lambie

To my Aunt Gladys Ryan and Uncle George Ryan and other Ryan relatives whose love and support provide a net of safety

To my surrogate child, Beth Ayn Stansfield

To the families and children with whom I have worked, especially Tom and Jan Hallin, their son Robbie and his siblings Julie, Linda, Stephanie, and John, for allowing me into their home that I might open my heart and eyes even wider

RAL

To my husband, Chris, whose emotional support and love have given me the time and strength to complete this project

To Jamie, teacher and guide, and Kelsey, Merry Sunshine, who makes everything in my life more important

To my parents, Helen and James Daniels, who taught me the importance of family and raised me to believe in myself and to follow my dreams

DDM

PART I

DESCRIPTION OF FAMILY SYSTEMS

INTRODUCTION 1

The purpose of this book is to provide practical and useful information about family systems approaches. It is written for the school professionals who work with at-risk and special needs students and their families. *At-risk students* are those who are likely to fail either in school or in life. Because their numbers are increasing (Frymier & Gansneder, 1989), this book offers substantial information for the general educator. We define *children with special needs* as those who have been labeled and found to be eligible for special education or related services. ("Currently, federal law refers to them as children and youth with disabilities.") Thus the book also speaks in very particular ways to the special educator. In addition, this book addresses the other people—parents, and professionals—with whom the general and special educator collaborate. Specifically, administrators, psychologists, social workers, and counselors may all find family systems approaches useful.

Family systems theories and approaches provide techniques that can be used with children and adults. Specific problems are viewed within the context of an individual's life experiences and relationships. Based on the assumption that changes in one part of an individual's life reverberate in all other areas of that person's experience, interventionists deem all aspects of the person's experience to be inseparable parts of a whole. A family systems approach is especially appropriate for use by professionals who have responsibility for the care and instruction of children and youth because their experiences are determined and shaped by adults, especially their parents. This approach, unlike some others, does not attempt to remediate a student's performance in school or improve his or her adjustment without attention to the student's interaction with family members and others.

It is not necessary to know family systems theory in order to understand this book. If you are well versed in individual psychology and the currently prevalent explanation for behavioral and emotional problems, you may find this book brings you new and different ways of looking at your background. You do not need to discard your current beliefs and opinions when reading this text. It simply provides another slant, one that is systemic in nature. You might consider systems approaches as adding a different dimension to your thinking. Systemic approaches are ones that consider the interconnectedness and interrelatedness of all the parts of a whole. In family systems approaches that means the interrelationships of all the members of the family are considered when considering any one member, in our case a child who is at risk or has special needs.

When you have finished reading this book you should have a broad knowledge of a variety of family systems concepts and methods, preparing you to interact in systemic ways with at-risk and special needs students and their families. Reading this text will not make you an instant expert, but you will learn to apply a variety of strategies and methods.

The purpose of this first chapter is to introduce you to systemic thinking as it relates to at-risk and special needs students and their families. To provide a context of understanding systemic thinking, we will initially present the background of the fields of psychology and counseling as they relate to the field of family studies. We then focus on the field of family systems by further elaborating upon its definition. For professionals unfamiliar with at-risk and special needs students, we describe those types of students. We then concentrate on a holistic approach, the logical extension from which we work when focusing on families of at-risk and special needs students. Our objective in focusing on holistic education is to allow you to view a framework that undergirds working with families. We conclude this introductory chapter with an overview of the remainder of the book.

BACKGROUND

Before the 1950s, the fields of psychology and counseling were focused on the diagnosis and treatment of the individual. Psychological and behavioral problems were viewed as originating from some underlying tension or conflict within the mind and experience of the individual. Treatment involved psychotherapy sessions that included the counselor and the patient trying to discover the root of the problem through discussion and association. In addition, the individual might be given medication designed to diminish depression or anxiety that would then help change personal behavior.

In the middle of the twentieth century, the field of family studies began to take shape (Christensen, 1964). Sociologists, psychologists, educators, physicians, and counselors began to think of the individual in relationship to other people, including friends, work colleagues, and family members.

The first data generated regarding families were descriptive in nature (Berardo, 1980). Professionals who worked with psychiatric patients began to observe and write about their patients' involvement with and reactions to their families. Professionals from various fields of mental health, primarily in hospital settings, began to notice that patients who were "cured" in the hospital would be sent home and begin exhibiting their symptoms again. Educators who developed elaborate behavioral programs for use in the home discovered that what worked in the classroom did not necessarily work with the family. For those who worked with these patients and students, the question became "Why do things change when the family becomes involved in therapy?"

The past forty years have witnessed the generation of numerous answers to this question. The early description of family process was followed by experimentation and theory construction. Family interaction has been videotaped and analyzed by sophisticated computer programs. Family theories have proliferated to the point that an article by Holman and Burr published in 1980 listed at least 18 different approaches. Clearly, it is beyond the scope of this book to attempt to discuss the content and impact of each of these theoretical approaches. In their 1980 article, Holman and Burr suggested that the three approaches having the most impact on the field of family studies at that time were interactionist theory, exchange theory, and systems theory. This text addresses systems theory only.

FAMILY SYSTEMS

Systems theory has been the basis for the development of most of the family treatment approaches that have been generated and applied since the 1960s. The generalizations that have arisen from systems theory are useful for understanding not only the family, but other systems such as the school, community, and work place as well. Because of the practical and widespread applicability of systems theory, we have chosen to present three approaches to family therapy that have developed out of this theoretical base. These approaches are transgenerational, structural, and strategic. Each of these family systems theories includes an approach to treatment that has proven effective with families experiencing problems. We also present the communication model of Virginia Satir, a pioneer in the field of family systems, because of its potential impact on at-risk or special needs students.

Appendix A contains an overview of the transgenerational, communication, structural, and strategic theories. You can read and understand this text without reading Appendix A, but reading it will add to your understanding and enjoyment. If you are interested in this background, we recommend reading Appendix A before reading chapter 2.

Again, the basic principle underlying family systems theory is that no individual can be understood without looking at how he or she fits into the whole of the family. When trying to understand a family system, one must consider not only the individuals within the family, but also how they interact and how their history has unfolded. A student who looks distracted or lethargic in the classroom might be viewed differently if the teacher knew that his family was going through a divorce or that her parents just had another child.

A second family systems principle is that families need both rules for structure and rules for change. The rules for structure organize the day-to-day functioning of the family. The rules for change allow for adaptability to new circumstances. For example, all newly married couples have to come to agreement about how to run their household in terms of cooking, cleaning, and paying bills. When children are born or if one or both spouses become highly involved in their careers, the tasks assigned to one or both of the individuals may need to change. If the couple is not able to renegotiate these rules with changes in their lives, the marriage will become more and more unhappy until divorce becomes a possibility. The children of these parents will be at risk for failure in life or at school.

A third principle of importance is that interaction of the family with the school, community, extended family, and friends is essential to the life of the nuclear family. All of these external systems need not be included in the most intimate details of family life. However, family members should interact with some people outside of the nuclear family. Families that remain reclusive and hostile toward outsiders tend to be dysfunctional in nature, and their children are at risk for failure.

Finally, it may be helpful to understand something about how family systems produce symptoms in a family member. All families become unbalanced at times and react to stress with nonproductive interactions. For many people, this process makes sense as a "push my button" phenomenon. Once a particular topic is broached or once a particular action is taken, each family member can then predict how every other family member will react. It is as if everyone is watching a very familiar one-act play but they cannot seem to change their lines to change the outcome.

In healthy families, there comes a point when someone does change his or her lines, and the nonproductive cycle is broken. In pathological families, these cycles continue to repeat over and over for months or years at a time. In these families, the cycles repeat until a crisis ensues. It is at this point that a family member develops symptoms that provide a stabilizing force for the family stress. Just as the old saying goes that people pull together in times of crisis, the family tends to pull together around the member with symptoms, who is usually a child, and avoids making any real changes in the family patterns that caused the initial crisis. This pulling together around the problem member might make it look, to observers, as though the family had changed its dysfunctional patterns and was functioning better. However, the essence of the system has not changed; the dysfunctional process will resurface in another way as the member with symptoms begins to function in more healthy ways.

A deeper understanding of these general ideas by school professionals, which this book can provide, can form the foundation for knowing when, how, and why to apply these principles to families of pupils with special needs. The connection between family experiences and at-risk as well as special needs students takes on a new meaning when viewed from a family systems perspective.

AT-RISK AND SPECIAL NEEDS STUDENTS

The focus of this text is on at-risk and special needs students and their families in both elementary and secondary classrooms. For the professional unfamiliar with these students, we are providing a brief background on both types of individuals.

At-Risk Students

As we stated in the beginning of this chapter, at-risk students are those who are likely to fail either in school or in life (Frymier & Gansneder, 1989). These authors pointed out that:

> "At-riskness" is a function of what bad things happen to a child, how severe they are, how often they happen, and what else happens in the child's immediate environment. For example, a pregnant 14-year-old is at risk. But a pregnant 14-year-old who uses drugs is even more at risk. And a pregnant 14-year-old who uses drugs, has been retained in grade, has missed 30 days of school, and has a low sense of self-esteem is still more seriously at risk.
>
> Moreover, being at risk is not solely a phenomenon of adolescence. Children of all ages are at risk. A 6-year-old whose parents are in the throes of a divorce and who is doing poorly in school is at risk. A 17-year-old whose grades are good but who is deeply depressed because she just lost her boyfriend is also at risk. A 10-year-old whose brother dropped out of school a year ago and whose father just lost his job is certainly at risk. (pp. 142)

Slavin and Madden (1989) indicated that "a practical criterion for identifying students at risk is eligibility for chapter 1, special education, or other remedial services under today's standards" (p. 4). In a study published in 1989, Frymier and Gansneder found that between 25 and 35% of the students in their population were seriously at risk (defined by 45 factors that research had linked to being at risk). Ralph (1989) has indicated that at-risk behaviors are not growing worse, we are simply finding more students who are at risk.

Cuban (1989) offered a new and different explanation for at-risk students. It departed from the old notion that these students are the cause of their own poor performance or that their families do not prepare them for school and do not provide proper support. His alternative view is that the school fails to meet the needs of the child:

> Because the culture of the school ignores or degrades their family and community backgrounds. Middle-class teachers, reflecting the school's values, single out for criticism differences in children's behavior and values . . . .
>
> The structure of the school is not flexible enough to accommodate the diverse abilities and interests of a heterogeneous student body. Programs are seldom adapted to children's individual differences. Instead, schools seek uniformity, and departures from the norm in achievement and behavior are defined as problems. (p. 781)

Slavin and Madden (1989) agreed with this view. They indicated that it was the incapacity of the school to meet the needs of each student, rather than the incapacity of the learner, that caused failure. They saw at-risk students as those in danger of failing to complete their education with adequate skills. In the risk factors they included low achievement, retention in grade, behavior problems, poor attendance, low socioeconomic status, and attending school with a large number of poor students.

Fortunately, there are many programs for at-risk students. Brendtro, Brokenleg, and Van Bockern (1990) have written a thoughtful book about the reclaiming of youth who are at risk. They view this process of reclaiming as our hope for the future.

This text does not focus on the academic programs developed for students who are at risk. What this text does provide is an understanding of, and means of working with, the families of these students. By providing an understanding of families we are hoping to address needs of at-risk students before problems begin.

Students with Special Needs

Skrtic (1991) has also suggested that schools contribute to the problem of students who fail. His thought-provoking examination of schools critiques them by focusing in particular on the schools' impact on students who are or have traditionally been placed in special education classes.

It is this student whom we have labeled as having special needs. In particular we focus on individuals with physical disabilities and chronic illness, behavior disorders, learning disabilities, and mental retardation. This book does not provide examples of working with families of individuals with severe disabilities. However, the background information dealing with family systems concepts can be generalized to all families; therefore, professionals who work with individuals with severe disabilities will find much in this text that pertains to their situations.

HOLISTIC APPROACH

A holistic approach is one that examines all of the various aspects of the whole that is under consideration. Holistic education focuses upon not only the academic curriculum, but also all of the other relevant aspects of education. Thus working with families would be one aspect of holistic education.

Further, the particular approach that family systems contributes to at-risk and special needs students is potent in that, like holistic approaches, it is systemic in nature. A holistic approach is, by definition, systemically oriented. It focuses on the interrelatedness and interconnectedness of all aspects of its subject, be it holistic education, holistic medicine, holistic health, or any other related subject.

Margaret Mead once stated, "There is hope, I believe, in seeing the human adventure as a whole and in the shared trust that knowledge about mankind sought in reverence for life, can bring life." It is this reverence for life that supports our interest in working with families, a crucial part of the life of the child. As Komoski (1990) stated:

> As the idea of holism opens new ways of approaching science, the environment, and our health, educators are beginning to advocate holistic approaches to teaching and learning. This trend signals a growing appreciation of the interconnectedness of things and recognition of the truth of the adage, "the whole is greater than the sum of its parts." (p. 72)

Holistic approaches (Hendrick, 1984; Reinsmith, 1989; Sonnier, 1985) to education reflect a rebalancing of practice that departs from the behaviorist/reductionist view. Most of the writing on holistic education to date focuses on systemically balanced curriculum or whole curriculum. However, in the journal *Holistic Education Review*, Byers (1992) has recommended the inclusion of talking about spirituality in the classroom. We are not far behind in proposing that working with families using family systems concepts and methods is a logical extension of holistic education.

We bring this to your attention as a context for increasing the breadth and depth of your interactions with at-risk and special needs students and their family members. When given the perspective of holistic education, responsibility increases for involvement with families, especially those targeted in this book.

OVERVIEW

This chapter provides background information regarding our purpose and the field of family systems. Part I provides details of family systems approaches that we have found to be of interest and value to school professionals working with at-risk and special needs students. This description of family systems approaches, concepts, and methods forms a background for understanding the more extensive applications presented in Part II. Appendix A also contains a wealth of background information regarding family systems approaches that is valuable prior to reading Part I.

Chapter 2 initially describes the family life cycle so that you will understand how changes in the life cycle of the family affect at-risk and special needs students. We also provide suggestions about interventions to help families be aware of life-cycle shifts and stresses and to know how to deal with them. Our experience with most human services professionals is that they are quite familiar with the individual life cycle from the perspective of Erikson (1963), with his emphasis on phases from birth through death, or Sheehy (1976), with her passages in adult life, yet are not aware of the family life-cycle literature.

The third chapter presents information linked with the structural family systems approach. We supply professionals with specific ways of looking at roles and communication within families. How family patterns can be out of order and techniques for changing dysfunction are also covered.

Chapter 4 helps school professionals understand how the history of a family can affect the day-to-day functioning of students. Family values, unresolved issues, and patterns of relating that change the experience of the child in the family are described. This chapter also includes information on genograms (charts of families) which provide a tool for professionals working with families. These charts encapsulate much information onto one page and can be used repeatedly to refresh one's memory regarding family facts and process.

Chapter 5 is laden with information about socioeconomic differences as well as ethnic differences as they relate to schoolchildren. Certainly we speak to at-risk students with these concerns. We describe differences in values, patterns of relating, and cognitive strategies that may result from cultural upbringing. We present means of intervention that focus upon concrete suggestions for becoming more personally aware and sensitive to the differing backgrounds of these families. We also present specific programs used on the level of school and community, known as ethnocentric curricula, to increase intercultural awareness and connection.

The sixth chapter focuses upon special populations such as families that are the product of divorce and remarriage as well as families with dysfunctional parents. A dysfunctional parent may be depressed, alcoholic, or abusive. This chapter reveals how educators can deal, in a nonjudgmental way, with students who have dysfunctional parents. Suggestions are presented for providing information that can be shared with students and families to help them deal with these situations.

The seventh chapter relates to dysfunctional families of the student with special needs. We focus on physical disabilities and chronic illness, behavior/social disorders, learning disabilities, and mental retardation. Typical family patterns are identified, and suggestions provided for interventions.

Chapters 2 through 7 each contain a case example. The case examples allow you to reflect on the concepts presented as they relate to one family in particular. Each example includes a child in school and focuses on how school professionals as well as other service providers interact with the family. We initially provide background information on the case and then suggest challenge questions for you to answer before reading our answers to those questions. These questions allow you to apply the information learned from the chapters to a particular case. Our hope is that this opportunity will present a bridge between reading this text and focusing on the families of at-risk and special needs students.

The applications in Part II are also focused on at-risk and special needs students and their families. Thus, human services professionals from many fields will find this information useful. Besides teachers and administrators, social workers, clinical psychologists, counselors, school psychologists, nurses, physicians, and other professionals will find these chapters of value when interacting with families having a student who is at risk or has special needs.

Although the first chapter in Part II focuses on family involvement with school teams in the traditional sense, the other five chapters are devoted to more detailed applications of the family systems concepts within school contexts. Those five chapters contain considerable new information that results from a distillation of concepts from the field of family systems, as well as already existing applications from the field of family systems.

Chapter 8 relates to team functioning and family involvement. It focuses on such topics as different approaches to working on teams, who is included on educational teams, and how teams evolve over time. Aspects of planning and implementing team process allow you to formulate ideas that you can use in your specific situations. Means of avoiding problems and facing challenges and a problem-solving process are also presented. The chapter concludes with information on the linking of families and schools.

The ninth chapter concerns planning with family members. Woven throughout the chapter are references to family systems concepts described in Part I. Aspects of intervening with families and joining them in the development and implementation of individualized education programs (IEPs) are highlighted.

Chapter 10 initially covers the process of working to alleviate student problems before the student is considered for referral for evaluation of eligibility for special education. The involvement of family members is one objective. Family conferences as they relate to at-risk and special needs children is the second topic of this chapter, and family systems concepts permeate examples of both topics.

"School Professionals as Family Liaison" is the topic of chapter 11. In this chapter we focus on sharing information with family members. This is not always an easy process, and family members may misconstrue the intention of professionals. Avoiding alienation and increasing involvement and trust are the objectives of this section. We also focus on networking as it relates to the family and their friends, as well as other types of resources. We view families as needing resources on only a temporary basis and as already possessing rich and diverse resources.

Chapter 12 extends concepts of family systems to such previously uncharted waters as academic curriculum as well as instruction. The use of techniques popular in the field of family systems is described for use in the classroom.

The last chapter in Part II provides information regarding overcoming barriers to implementing the concepts proposed in this text. Our hope is that you will be able to prevent the barriers from developing; and, if not, at least be able to lessen the impact of those barriers.

Part III contains a case study that brings the whole text together at one time. Our purpose is to adequately view information presented in Parts I and II of this text and see how they relate to schools.

Appendix B is a reading list that may be of interest. The readings concern functional families and at-risk and special needs children as well as dysfunctional families. Our suggestions are arranged by topics. Although not extensive, we believe you will find them worthwhile. Finally, we call your attention to an excellent resource for using reading as a way to sensitize others to families with a child having a disability. Mullins (1983) has a chapter devoted to the use of bibliotherapy in counseling families who have a child with special needs. She quoted an inscription over a library in ancient Thebes, "The Healing Place of the Soul." We agree that, in reading, we heal. As siblings of individuals with disabilities, we have read many books that have helped us understand and heal ourselves. Mullins not only has provided selected bibliographies, but also has written about the use of books in working with families having a child with a disability.

We are enthusiastic about the possibilities this text presents. You will find that we also invite you to learn more about your own family as you read this book. On many occasions we recommend that you try out methods such as charting your own family life according to a strategy we present. We believe that the better you understand your family of origin and nuclear family, the better you will be able to implement family systems concepts with at-risk and special needs students and their families.

FAMILY LIFE CYCLE 2

P art I of this book presents specific descriptions of how family systems approaches are applied to working with students at risk and those with special needs. The first three chapters include theoretical concepts that are basic to understanding a family systems approach. As mentioned in chapter 1, the student who is interested in a more in-depth theoretical study might like to read Appendix A, included at the end of the book, before proceeding to chapter 3.

Each chapter in this section includes ideas about how specific issues such as family history, sociocultural context, and environmental factors impact family life and thus impact student adjustment. In addition, each chapter contains examples of how educators can use a family systems approach in diagnosing and helping students. A case example ends each chapter; questions and comments about the case are included to help the reader identify how the family systems concepts are put into practice.

One specific area that helps school professionals understand how a student functions in the classroom is knowledge of the day-to-day family life of that individual child. This chapter presents one way to describe the development of the family and how particular issues affect this development during the child's life. By knowing something about the impact of the family's development on the child, the school professional can place classroom behaviors in an understandable context.

The development of the child as an individual has been studied extensively from a number of different perspectives. Piaget (1952) wrote about changes in cognition that occur as the child grows. Motor development was cataloged by Gesell, Leg, and Ames (1974). Beginning with Freud and continuing with Jung, Adler, and other personality theorists, the importance of various periods in the psychological development of the child has been emphasized (Hall & Lindzey, 1978). Erik Erikson's (1963) theory of the tasks of ego development was the first to introduce the concept of continuing psychological challenges into adulthood. The book *Passages* by Gail Sheehy (1976), which was based on the work of Gould (1970), addressed the struggles and changes faced by adults as they age. Although each of these theories acknowledges the influence of relationships upon personality development, the primary focus is on the individual and the ensuing changes and struggles during different periods of development.

E.M. Duvall—a sociologist—was the first to look at development from the perspective of individuals in relationship to one another. Her framework for characteristic tasks of family life included eight stages, beginning when the family is formed by marriage. Her book, first published in 1957 and now, following her death, in its fifth edition (1977), was the beginning of a shift in focus from the individual to the family as the primary unit for the study of development.

Other theorists have followed Duvall's lead and proposed various models to describe predictable events and stages that occur in the development of families. These stages are collectively termed *the family life cycle*.

At each stage in the family's life cycle, a particular nodal event occurs that ushers in the next phase of development. Subsequent theorists have developed many ways of extending this concept. Carter and McGoldrick (1980) proposed a six-stage family life cycle model that includes single adulthood prior to marriage. A six-stage model beginning with formation of a family by marriage was adopted by Turnbull and Turnbull (1990), and a seven-stage model beginning with courtship and ending with the death of both spouses was developed by Hughes, Berger, and Wright (1978). For purposes of our discussion, we have adapted the Carter and McGoldrick (1980) model.

The family life cycle is particularly useful in diagnosis from the family systems perspective known as *strategic therapy*. According to strategic theory, family members are prone to developing symptoms at transition points in the family life cycle. When the family system is unable to adjust its interactions to accommodate to changes in the life cycle, the family becomes "stuck" at a particular stage and cannot move on in its development. Interactions within the family become more and more inflexible and nonproductive until some member of the family becomes symptomatic (Haley, 1980). For a more extensive discussion of the theoretical principles of strategic therapy, see Appendix A.

NORMAL FAMILY LIFE CYCLE

This section describes the specifics of how the family life cycle operates. The challenges and tasks required of the family at each stage of the life cycle are delineated. The six stages of the normal family life cycle are as follows:

Stage 1: The Newly Married Couple
Stage 2: Families with Young Children (ages 0–5 yrs)
Stage 3: Child Rearing Families (ages 6–12 yrs)
Stage 4: Families with Adolescents (ages 13–19 yrs)
Stage 5: Families Launching Children (ages 20 and over)
Stage 6: Families in Later Life

In looking at the stages of the family life cycle, the reader will notice that the family's and the oldest child's development parallel one another. For the most part, developmental changes required of the family are determined by the age of the oldest child because that child is the first catalyst for new demands upon the family. However, as we will describe, the diagnosis of a child with special needs can affect this pattern. Particular focus for the school professional clearly is on stages 2 through 4, from the birth of children through the rearing of adolescents.

Plateaus

Each stage includes a "plateau period" and a "transitional period" (Carter & McGoldrick, 1980). Plateaus are periods of relative stability when the family operates within roles and functions predictably. For example, a young married couple who have worked out the initial difficulties of living together and have settled into a lifestyle pattern are experiencing a plateau period. Plateaus are periods when the forces of homeostasis or sameness are in operation.

Transitions

Transitional periods result when a life event occurs that demands changes in the structure or function of the family. Carter and McGoldrick (1980) list eight normative events that serve to usher in new life cycle stages: marriage, birth of a child, child enters school, child enters adolescence, child launched into adulthood, birth of a grandchild, retirement, and transition to old age. Events that occur "on time" or at expected points in the life cycle are less stressful than events that are perceived to occur earlier or later than expected (Walsh, 1982). For example, an unplanned teenage pregnancy will be more emotionally stressful than a planned pregnancy for a couple who have been married for some time. The early, unexpected death of a spouse will be more stressful and require more family changes than the death of a spouse at an older age.

Other events may occur that serve to change the normal cycle of the family and precipitate a transition period. These circumstances include miscarriage, marital separation and divorce, illness, disability and death, relocation, changes in socioeconomic status, and catastrophes that result in dislocation of the family unit. When these events occur, not only must the individuals within the family deal with their own reactions to the loss or change in circumstances, but the family as a whole must change communication patterns, roles, and functions in order to successfully deal with the change (Patterson, 1985).

Transition periods are often marked by anxiety, uncertainty, and a sense of loss (Olson et al., 1983). Flexibility and adaptability, described in Appendix A, are needed during transition periods. Change events can be a stimulus either for successful adaptation and growth or for dysfunction (Walsh, 1983). Clinical or behavioral problems are particularly likely to appear at transition points in the family life cycle if the basic structure and roles of family members are not reorganized. (Hadley, Jacob, Miliones, Caplan, & Spitz, 1974; Haley, 1980; Walsh, 1982).

Tasks and Changes

As with individual development, there are specific family developmental tasks required at each stage of the family life cycle. In addition, each stage requires a change in the family goal orientation and direction. Successful completion of tasks at early stages builds a foundation for successful completion of later stages. Like a child who must learn to stand before learning to walk, the family must learn to negotiate the tasks of raising children before it can successfully launch children into adulthood. Failure to complete the tasks of early stages may lead to difficulties with later ones.

The primary themes and developmental tasks required at each stage are as follows.

Stage 1: The Newly Married Couple

Primary theme—Attachment (Kantor, 1983)

Primary tasks—Realignment of relationships with friends and family to include spouse and spouse's family; commitment to marriage; commonality of goals and directions for future

An example of this realignment is the decision about where the couple will spend holidays—with her family or his? The successful resolution of this question is a good indicator that the individuals have made the transition to viewing themselves as part of a couple.

Individuals who marry without successfully resolving issues in their own families of origin (see chapter 4) are more likely to experience marital difficulties and adjustment problems (Fogarty, 1976). In fact, a classic study by Lidz, Cornelison, Fleck, and Terry (1957) about families with schizophrenic children found that, in five out of eight marriages in their study, the focus of the spouse's loyalty remained in the parental home rather than in the current nuclear family. These individuals had never successfully transitioned from the role of child in their own families to the role of partner in a marital system.

Stage 2: Families with Young Children

Primary theme—Industry, developing strategies for getting things done (Kantor, 1983)

Primary tasks—Realignment of marital system to include children; changes in the sexual relationship of the couple, coping with lack of privacy; development of parenting style; realignment of relationships with extended family and friends to include presence of children and requirements of parenting

Rollins and Galligan (1978) found that the companionship between spouses decreased with the arrival of an infant. The presence of dependent children in the home places new demands on time, energy, and financial resources of the couple. Thus many couples in their study reported a decrease in marital satisfaction. Other couples who had successfully negotiated the changes brought on by an infant in the home reported that children brought them closer together, giving them a shared task and a common goal.

One example of how this process occurs comes from a study (Pedersen, 1983) of fathers' involvement with their infants. This study found that the father's role was influenced by his involvement with the birth process. If fathers were involved in anticipation of the birth, planning for the child's space in the home, and the actual birth, they were more likely to feel a commitment to and involvement with the new baby. Pedersen described the father's primary role as an emotional support to the mother. He found that the more support the mother felt from her spouse, the more she worked to include him in her relationship with the baby, and the more direct interaction occurred between the father and the infant.

Stage 3: Child-Rearing Families

Primary themes—Affiliation and inclusion, allowing others to be brought within the family

boundaries; consolidating the accomplishments of family members (Kantor, 1983)
Primary tasks—Involvement with peer network; establishing sibling roles; division of family responsibilities

At this stage, parents must begin accepting the personality of the child and the ways in which this personality is expressed both within and outside of the home (Barnhill & Longo, 1978). Interactions concerning the school, extracurricular activities, and families of peers must be negotiated.

The need for parental rules is most clear during the child-rearing stage. Rules provide the structure and identity for family life. McFadden and Doub (1983) have developed a successful training program to teach parents to cope with family life cycle changes. In the first session, they presented guidelines for parents regarding the responsibility for making family rules. These guidelines are:

1. Make rules.
2. Stay in charge.
3. Stick together.
4. Make room to play with your children.
5. Change with the times. (p. 143)

These guidelines put in simple form the need for guidance, cohesion, and adaptability in families experiencing transitions.

For some parents, the need to share authority when their child begins school is a difficult transitional demand. Parents are accustomed to making all of the decisions about their child's well-being and may be reluctant to adhere to guidelines that are proposed by the teacher. In these cases, the teacher would do well to keep in mind his or her knowledge of the life cycle and help the parents make the transition into the child-rearing stage by sharing authority and asking for input. If attempts to elicit parental cooperation continue to fail, it may be an indication of more severe family dysfunction. Two of the classic signs of abusive and neglectful families are extreme family secrecy and a lack of inclusion of people outside the nuclear family.

Stage 4: Families with Adolescents

Primary theme—Decentralization; loosening boundaries
Primary tasks—Managing children's increasing independence; refocusing on midlife career and marital issues; increasing flexibility of roles

This stage of the family life cycle has become particularly difficult in contemporary society. As Quinn, Newfield and Protinsky (1985) argued:

> The accelerated pace of physiological growth (of children)...has stretched the stage we have come to define sociologically as adolescence.... We have not come to a consensus on how to determine its [adolescence] onset or termination. This uncertainty obscures guideposts for defining roles and status of family members and, subsequently, family interactional patterns. (p. 102)

Often, in families, physical maturity of children is mistaken for emotional maturity. It is the difficult job of parents during this stage to develop appropriate and flexible rules for their adolescents, allowing enough room for them to experiment with independence. Parents who are extremely involved with their children often have problems with their own identity and tend to perceive adolescent rebellion as a personal affront. In addition, for the married couple, watching their children's developing sexuality may bring up their own unresolved sexual issues from previous stages.

For the school professional who is familiar with adolescents, a good strategy during this stage is to try to help parents have a sense of humor about their child's attempts at rebellion. Just knowing that struggles for independence are normal and necessary at this stage and need not be taken personally can be a relief to parents who are trying to achieve a balance between control and letting go. An adolescent's constantly dirty room may not seem so important to the parent when seen in the light of alternative forms of rebellion such as sexual experimentation or drug or alcohol use.

Stage 5: Families Launching Children

> *Primary themes*—Differentiation, detachment (Kantor, 1983)
> *Primary tasks*—Negotiating to become a couple again; renegotiating roles with adult children; realignment to include in-laws of children who marry

During this stage, women who have stayed at home with their children have more time and energy to develop themselves in personal areas. Women who have made a deep commitment to motherhood may experience feelings of purposelessness or lack of meaning (Hesse-Biber & Williamson, 1984). At this point, both parents and their children are adults and in some ways social equals. Thus, family members must change communication patterns to include the possibility for equality and differences of opinion among members of two generations (Hess & Waring, 1978).

Stage 6: Families in Later Life

> *Primary themes*—Letting go, dissolving ties (Kantor, 1983)
> *Primary tasks*—Redefinition of roles between aging spouses; dealing with the death of friends and family

Retirement and advancing years may mean a loss of income, loss of occupational status, large blocks of time at home, and loss of roles (Aldous, 1978). Senior citizens may experience the loss of their homes and communities, their physical well-being, or their mental capacity (Brody, 1974). When one spouse dies, the surviving spouse must reformulate a personal identity as widow or widower and renegotiate relationships with children and extended family. If older parents are ill or disabled, children must negotiate care-giving tasks involving caring for their parents (Montgomery, Gonyea, & Hooyman, 1985).

Research by Spark and Brody (1970) showed that, contrary to popular belief, older parents are not usually abandoned by their children. In fact, three-fourths of the senior citizens they interviewed lived within thirty minutes of at least one child and more than four-fifths had seen an adult child in the previous week. Spark and Brody argued for the inclusion of grandparents in family therapy to help with the resolution of multigenerational dysfunctional family patterns.

At this point, we have presented a framework for the developmental demands and changes required at each of the six life-cycle stages. Thus far, we have focused on the progression of the normal life cycle. Equally important are the problems that can arise to make progression through the life cycle more difficult for the family.

FAMILY LIFE-CYCLE PROBLEMS

Families experience each stage of the life cycle with varying degrees of success. The degree of flexibility and adaptability of the family will contribute to how successfully the child develops. The past history of the family, the timing of life events, and the extent of family stressors are all important in determining how the family will adapt to life-cycle difficulties.

Stressors

There are predictable stressors that must be faced at each life-cycle stage. Olson and colleagues (1983) asked 1140 families across the life-cycle about significant stressors they experienced. The authors found that the following factors were the most problematic stressors reported at each stage:

Stage 1: The Newly Married Couple. Work-family: Balancing changes with extended family, dealing with in-laws, and developing dual career goals.

Stage 2: Families with Young Children. Financial strains: Coping with the added financial burden of young children, buying a family home, making decisions about both spouses' careers and the cost of child-care options.

Stage 3: Child-Rearing Families. Intrafamily strains: Dealing with the added stress of involvement with the school, extracurricular activities, families of children's peer group.

Stage 4: Families with Adolescents. Financial strains: Handling the financial demands of feeding, clothing, and entertaining adolescents.

Stage 5: Families Launching Children. Financial strains: Dealing with paying for college, weddings, or helping children begin their own nuclear families.

Stage 6: Families in Later Life. Financial strains: Planning for the loss of income following retirement, paying for medical bills, and health care costs.

Inability to handle significant stress is one factor that can arrest or slow down life-cycle progression. Although each life cycle stage brings a primary stressor, there are many other stresses at each stage. Focusing on the six stages of the family life cycle, you may want to think back to the development of your own family and see what other significant stressors you can identify.

Sociocultural and Transgenerational Impact

Other factors that can influence the family's response to a normative event are the *sociocultural context* and the *family's past experience* over many generations. The significance of a particular life event, the normative timing of its occurrence, and the rituals that mark it vary with different cultures and ethnic groups.

Bowen's (1985) theory, briefly discussed in chapter 3 and elaborated on in Appendix A, focuses on the significance that particular life cycle events can take on over many generations. For example, if a young couple is having their first child at the same time that a grandparent is dying, the birth and death will be woven together emotionally and symbolically. When the couple has another child, we can predict that the feelings of joy and loss from the first event will reoccur at the second birth. If the couple does not make the connection about how birth and death were linked in time at the birth of their first child, they may be confused about their mixed feelings about the second birth. They may feel guilty that their feelings of anticipation and happiness are mixed with fear and sadness.

There will always be some unresolved issues and conflicts at one or many of the stages of the life cycle. A potential problem occurs when, as Barnhill and Longo (1978) described,

> The family must continue to move on if it is to meet the new challenges ahead. The conflicts can then become sealed over, though vulnerable points can be left behind. It is possible then to conceive that under a later situation of stress...the family can regress to previous levels of functioning.... Old unresolved conflicts...can become uncovered and alive again. Thus, as if it is not enough for the family to deal with one difficulty, an old conflict is reawakened, together with the old unsuccessful patterns of coping with the stress. (p. 471)

With this comment in mind, it is clear that professionals may need to look not only at the current difficulty that a family is experiencing but also at what old issues are being reenacted for the family. There might be a legacy of problems from previous generations that occurred at this particular stage of the family life cycle. In many families myths and stories surrounding births, deaths, and other life events are passed down from generation to generation. These myths can and do influence family members on unconscious and conscious levels. For example, in many Southern families, little boys receive their first hunting gun as a rite of passage. The gift of the gun takes on a meaning and intensity born of generations of men sharing the ritual of their first hunt together. What happens in these families when a boy with a disability reaches the typical age to receive his gun? Many issues and feelings will need to be considered before a decision is made about this boy's rite of passage. The school professional who takes into account this type of family culture and legacy will better understand when this boy becomes depressed or confused about his identity. If this boy begins to play with make-believe weapons in the classroom or begins to act aggressively, the teacher can have a much greater impact if he or she is aware of the cultural importance of this transition point in the student's life.

Pile-up

Another important issue in predicting family responses to life cycle adjustments is the concept of *pile-up* (McCubbin & Patterson, 1982). A large number of changes within a brief period contributes to disrupting the family unit and may make life cycle adjustments more problematic. If the family resources are already depleted from dealing with other changes, the family may be less well-equipped to adapt to future changes.

As one at-risk adolescent girl commented to her counselor, "First, my brother graduated in June, so he's looking for a job. Then my father changed jobs in August and we had to move. My mom hates our new neighborhood. Who cares what I'm going through?"

We have presented four different areas in which major life cycle problems can be generated. First are predictable significant *stressors* that are faced at each stage, including financial strains, intrafamily strains, career demands, and extended family demands.

Second are *family myths* that arise due to the timing of life cycle events and the significance that an event takes on for the family at future stages. Third are *cultural demands* from former generations. Last are the problems that arise because of the *pile-up* of numerous stressors within a short period. For the school professional who understands the dynamics of the family life cycle, students' behavior problems can be viewed and managed within a context of possible extended family difficulties. We now turn to the challenges that arise due to the stress of responding to children with special needs.

FAMILIES WiTH SPECIAL NEEDS

The diagnosis of a child with intellectual, emotional, sensory, or physical disabilities is a significant life stressor that will affect the future development of the family at all levels. At each life-cycle stage as the demands upon the family change the family must again accept the child's disability (Wikler, 1981). A number of researchers have discussed the significant issues and challenges that must be faced by families with children having various types of special needs (Blacher, 1984; Combrinck-Graham, 1983; Leigh, 1987; Patterson & McCubbin, 1983; Shapiro, 1983; Turnbull & Turnbull, 1990). As you read about the challenges at each stage, think about how the impact of these issues upon students with special needs and their siblings may be exhibited in the classroom.

Stage 1: The Newly Married Couple

Siblings of children with special needs must address particular issues when they prepare for marriage and for forming their own nuclear family. Is the disabled sibling involved in the wedding ceremony? How are the new in-laws and extended family to be introduced to the exceptionality? Is the sibling's disability genetically transmitted. If so, what impact does that have on the couple's future plans regarding their own family?

Stage 2: Childbearing Families with Young Children

Not all children with special needs are diagnosed at birth, and even for those who are, the question of degree of disability is often unresolved. The new parents face issues of trying to understand the exceptionality and coping with the loss of their "dream child" (Featherstone, 1980). This is a particularly vulnerable time for most couples, even when their child is born normal. When a child is born with problems, there may be an interruption of the bonding and attachment between mother and infant because of long separations at birth (Spitz, 1946). The parents who have dreamed of holding and feeding their baby may be faced with an infant who is maintained in an incubator or respirator with various sorts of tubes attached and who cannot be held or nursed.

For most parents, the diagnosis of their infant brings on a period of depression and mourning (Blacher, 1984; Howard, 1978; Wikler, Wasow, & Hatfield, 1981). The mourning process is complicated by the fact that the child is not really dead—only the image of the dreamed for child is dead. Significant postpartum depression in the mother may be prolonged, and the mother's depression and anxiety can then affect attachment to the baby. The failure of the mother to become involved in the normal nurturing rituals with her developing child, such as gazing, cooing, and smiling, may make the disabled infant particularly at risk for abuse (Schell, 1981).

Trout (1983) has written that grieving for a lost child is complicated by the demands of caring for the needs of a new baby. As any parent knows, caring for an infant is tiring and stressful, even under the best of circumstances. The emotional and financial strain of a child with special needs is even more extensive. Quality medical care and specialized day care may be required. Finding a babysitter for a few hours' respite may suddenly become a monumental task. Beckman (1983) interviewed thirty-one families with an infant with a disability and found that the additional care-giving demands of these children were reported as the most significant stress during the infancy period. In the face of these added demands, parents may feel resentful and angry and may have nowhere to express these feelings. In fact, parents may feel guilty about their anger if they view it as directed at the child, a helpless infant, rather than at the demands placed upon them as parents.

Interventions that may be helpful at this stage include listening and offering emotional support for parents, providing information about resources in the community, and activating family and external support systems (Dunlap & Hollinsworth, 1977). For a more extensive discussion of intervention strategies, see Part II of this text.

Stage 3: Child-Rearing Families

The majority of children with special needs who have not been recognized at birth will be diagnosed during the child-rearing stage of the life cycle. During this stage, the diagnostic process will probably involve the school system in some manner. It is imperative that interactions with school personnel be a support to these families, rather than an added stress. The more knowledgeable school personnel are about the child's disability and the family's life cycle stage, the more positive potential there is in the diagnostic process.

Dyson and Fewell (1985) compared 15 families with handicapped children and 15 families with children of the same age who had not been diagnosed with problems. They found, predictably, that the families having a child with a disability reported greater overall levels of stress and that the experience of stress increased with the severity of the child's condition. Stress in these families seemed to stem from four primary sources: characteristics of the child, such as basic personality style and personal response to the diagnosis; degree of physical incapacitation of the child; parental pessimism about the child's health and future; and severity of the disabling condition. Finally, they found that parents who reported the highest levels of social support were most able to enjoy their parenting role in spite of their child's difficulties.

The Dyson and Fewell study points to several important factors in family adjustment during this life cycle stage. First, families need basic information about their child's special needs. The longer and more difficult the diagnostic process, the greater the potential for negative effects on the family stability. Once the child's difficulties have been established and understood, the family can begin the process of acceptance.

Second, the issue of appropriate services and school placement must be clarified. The better informed the parents are, the more they are likely to become actively involved in the child's school placement and contribute to positive adjustment. Parents who are confused about their child's needs or who have misperceptions about the limitations imposed by a particular disability may tend to try to shield their child from challenges and may actually become overinvolved in school placement decisions, to the detriment of the student. A sign that parents have not adequately made the transition to the child-rearing stage and have not incorporated the themes of affiliation and inclusion is a "we versus them" mentality pitting the family against the school.

An example of the failure to transition was found in a couple who sought help from a psychologist to acquire appropriate placement for their 11-year-old daughter.

Sheronda, now in the fourth grade, had been identified with behavior problems in kindergarten. She was originally tested at 5 years old and had an IQ in the borderline mentally retarded range. The parents did not feel that their concerns were heard by the school system and they were unable to accept the MR diagnosis. When the girl entered first grade, placement in a EMR classroom was recommended. The parents refused to agree to this setting for their daughter, so she was placed in a regular classroom with resource help.

In spite of the test results that were used in the original diagnosis, during their initial meeting with the psychologist, the parents insisted that their daughter was suffering from attention deficit disorder and learning disabilities that had never been adequately evaluated or treated. They felt that the school system had never, in 5 years, listened to their experiences with the girl in the home. They were requesting that the psychologist assist them in pursuing a court case against the school system for failure to provide adequate services for their daughter.

The psychologist reviewed 6 years of evaluations and found that the girl was, indeed, functioning at the borderline mentally retarded range of intelligence. However, she also exhibited many behavioral symptoms of hyperactivity, attentional difficulties, and areas of intellectual functioning that were within the average range. In addition, she was significantly depressed because of her continued failure experiences at school and her perceived lack of acceptance by her parents.

In this case, the parents' failure to feel heard, to receive adequate explanations about their daughter's functioning, and to accept their daughter's dysfunctions and mourn the loss of their "perfect child" had caused the family to be stuck at the childbearing stage of the life cycle. The family had never adequately transitioned into the child-rearing stage by involving themselves in a coalition with the school system and helping Sheronda develop appropriate friends and activities for herself.

One of the major struggles for families with a child having special needs during this life cycle stage is balancing functional and emotional tasks that a family demands. Parents must establish routines to carry out family functions and take care of doctors' appointments, classes, and other needs of the child with a disability, while also managing the needs of the remainder of the family. An area of family functioning that quickly dwindles in the face of the functional demands of caring for a child with special needs is family recreation and relaxation (Shapiro, 1983).

Gallagher, Cross, and Scharfman (1981) found that the major stress reported by families following the diagnosis of a child with chronic illness was the alteration of the family's social and recreational life. In their study, the biggest difference in coping among families was the presence of a strong personal support network between spouses and among friends of the families. When families felt their friends understood their child's disability, did not stigmatize the family, and offered their support with carpooling, babysitting, and recreational activities, the stress was reduced.

Stage 4: Families with Adolescents

When nondisabled adolescents successfully complete this stage they will emerge from this period with adequate self-esteem, a comfortable body image, an established identity, and emotional independence. The presence of a chronic illness, emotional or intellectual limitations, or the struggles of a learning disability cannot help but exacerbate the individual's problems in adjustment through adolescence. Added to the stresses of individual adjustment are the struggles of the family to loosen boundaries and promote independence. Given the variability of the adolescent's special circumstances, it is clear that this life-cycle stage will be most difficult.

During this stage, adolescents begin to know their limitations and compare themselves to their peers (Patterson, 1985). The formation of a personal identity should include the reality of the individual's strengths and weaknesses. Of course, this realization will affect self-esteem. Taking personal risks, assertively dealing with peers, confronting challenges, and increasing independence are even more difficult if the adolescent is starting from a base of low self-esteem or a negative identity.

In addition to emotional adjustments, many adolescents with special needs face issues of physical adjustment. Adolescents and parents must deal with the changes brought about by the onset of puberty and emerging sexuality. Parents, who have been responsible for their child's physical well-being, must now decide how much physical care to relinquish to the adolescent (Patterson & McCubbin, 1983). If no concessions are made to the adolescent's increasing needs for privacy and autonomy, he or she may take control by not complying with medical treatment (Blumberg, Lewis, & Susman, 1984). Refusal to monitor blood sugars and overeating are common rebellion behaviors for adolescents with diabetes. Many adolescents with cerebral palsy or spina bifida stop following their catheterization procedures. Anorexia and bulimia occur even in adolescents who seemed perfectly normal before this period. For all of these behaviors, the common theme is a lack of feelings of autonomy and control on the part of the adolescent.

Finally, the adolescent life-cycle stage brings with it the challenges of planning for the vocational development of the student with special needs. Questions that must be answered include: How much does the disability affect the student's intellectual potential? Are there motivational, emotional, and financial factors that must be considered? What are the student's physical limitations? What are the student's desires and dreams for the future? The task of the family and the school system is to help the student set realistic goals that do not under- or overestimate individual potential. In developing vocational goals it is important to keep in mind the adolescent's need for feelings of control and autonomy. Within particular limitations imposed by school rules and the student's abilities, the student should be given as many choices as possible regarding future plans.

For adolescents and their parents during this stage, the struggle between independence and dependence is particularly heightened. Parents must try to be supportive and available while at the same time allowing for privacy and autonomy when the adolescent is ready. Adolescents may vacillate between needs, sometimes resenting their parents' overprotection and sometimes needing their support. If some balance and resolution are not achieved, this struggle makes for problems in communication and relationships.

Zetlin (1985) studied families of twenty-five mildly retarded adolescents over an eighteen-month period. He divided family styles into supportive, dependent, and conflict-ridden. He found that members of the supportive group were least likely to experience serious behavioral disturbances during adolescence. When there was a disturbance, it was usually one of emotional confusion rather than one of an antisocial or rebellious nature. Those adolescents who were involved in conflict-laden relationships with their parents were most likely to act out and exhibit antisocial behavior including theft, inappropriate sexual behavior, and delinquent or violent behavior. In addition, 75% of the dependent group displayed behaviors reflecting emotional disturbance, including withdrawal, alcohol or drug use, and self-abusive or suicidal behavior. Clearly, the relationships between parents and adolescents that were characterized as supportive but not dependent in nature were most likely to reduce adolescent dysfunction.

Along these same lines, Nihira, Mink, and Meyers (1985) conducted a longitudinal study of 148 families having an adolescent diagnosed as a slow learner and 151 families having an adolescent diagnosed as TMR (Nihira, Meyers, & Mink, 1983). They found that the home environment was the most significant contributor to the child's development of various social, educational, and behavioral skills. Specifically, the factors of harmony in the family and cohesive, quality parenting had a dominant effect on a wide range of adjustment behaviors. Again, family relationships that were nonconflicting and supportive without being smothering were the best indicators of positive adjustment in the adolescent.

Education professionals are in a unique position to be able to provide information about adolescent struggles to families in a nonthreatening way. During high school enrollment, parent information seminars can be held. PTA meetings or discussions can be geared toward adolescent developmental issues and family relationships. If parents are informed, they are more likely to know what to expect from their adolescents and to be able to respond with appropriate guidance and support.

Stage 5: Families Launching Children

During this early adult stage the family faces more challenges in letting go of the child with special needs. Parents and social agencies must help the young adult find a job or enroll in an appropriate vocational program. Depending upon the abilities of the person with the disability, the child might need help finding an appropriate adult residence and learning how to manage financial resources. Socialization opportunities outside the family are particularly important at this stage.

Clearly, each stage of the family life cycle brings particular challenges to the family of a child with special needs.

COPING STRATEGIES FOR FAMILIES

It is also important to be aware of how families can be helped to cope with life cycle stressors and the adjustments they demand. In this section, we discuss research concerning coping strategies for families experiencing life cycle stressors and an educational program that has been successful in addressing the needs of families under stress.

Characteristics of Coping

Figley and McCubbin (1983) have identified eleven general positive characteristics that predict a family's ability to cope with life stresses. These characteristics are:

1. Ability to identify the stressor.
2. Viewing the situation as a family problem, rather than a problem of one member.
3. Adopting a solution-oriented approach rather than blaming.
4. Showing tolerance for other family members.
5. Clear expression of commitment to and affection for other family members.
6. Open and clear communication among members.
7. Evidence of high family cohesion.
8. Evidence of considerable role flexibility.
9. Appropriate utilization of resources inside and outside the family.
10. Lack of physical violence.
11. Lack of substance abuse. (p. 18)

These characteristics can provide a useful diagnostic checklist for the educator involved with families of children with special needs. We advocate educational programs for these families geared toward helping them develop these characteristics, when possible. In addition, each family may be helped to develop its own unique adaptive capacities (Reiss & Oliveri, 1980). Of course, if there is evidence of physical violence or substance abuse, the family should be referred to an appropriate treatment facility. For further discussion of violence and chemical dependency in families, see chapter 6.

In general, functional family coping patterns appear to arise from adequate information about and understanding of the stress; supportive versus conflicting relationships within the family; and adequate social network support. Patterson and McCubbin (1983) collected data from five hundred families with a child with a chronic illness. They found three functional coping patterns within this population:

1. Maintaining family integration, cooperation, and an optimistic definition of the situation.
2. Maintaining social support, self-esteem, and psychological stability.
3. Understanding the medical situation through communication with other parents and consultation with the medical staff. (p. 32)

Coping Workshops

McFadden and Doub (1983) have developed a series of workshops for family survival and coping that could easily be adapted for parent groups within a school setting. They begin the workshop series with a set of rules for survival during hard times.

1. Know when you are in hard times.
2. Face hard times together.
3. Take your time.
4. Ask for outside help when your family is stuck. (p. 155)

These rules express in basic terms some of the coping characteristics mentioned earlier. The professional who is planning a family group may wish to develop, with the families, a personalized set of coping "rules."

The family life cycle is an important concept for use by the educator in understanding and changing students' behavior. If school problems can be diagnosed within the context of family development, interventions are much more likely to be successful.

SUMMARY

Much of traditional psychological thought focuses on issues of development, primarily from an individual perspective. The family life cycle is a logical extension of this tradition into a family systems context.

The family life cycle provides a framework for the developmental aspect of systems theory and, as such, provides the school professional with the same tools that theories of psychosexual, cognitive, or emotional development do for the individual student. The life-cycle model serves to identify patterns of normal development for the entire family and as a basis for judgment about dysfunction when developmental difficulties are encountered.

One of the primary tasks faced by our educational systems is the promotion of healthy development. The family life cycle concept gives an opportunity to extend this task to the promotion of the healthy family as well. Knowledge of the principles of the family life cycle serves each professional who meets with family members, both formally and informally, as well as in phone contacts or written communication with families. Healthy family development can then be promoted, initially through grounding families in the concept of the life cycle and then through information gathering and sharing about each family's experiences. Professionals can provide basic life cycle information to families through both written and verbal interactions that can help them put their own development and struggles in a larger context.

CASE EXAMPLE

Nancy, age 13, was brought to the attention of the school counselor by her maternal grandmother. She was eligible for placement in a special education classroom for children diagnosed with educable mental retardation. She had been receiving special education services since she was 3 years old and had adjusted well until the past 2 years. Her parents, who were stationed with the military in Germany, were requesting that Nancy begin living with her grandmother. Their expressed reason was that Nancy could receive better special education and recreational services in the States. At her age, there were fewer and fewer resources provided for special needs students in the American school in Germany. The grandmother was asking the school for their recommendations about Nancy's living situation and possible placement options.

The psychologist took a thorough family history and discovered the following time line: Nancy was diagnosed with borderline mental retardation when she was 3 years old. The family began receiving early intervention services from their local school system and the parents seemed to adjust well to Nancy's diagnosis and special needs. The maternal grandparents, who lived nearby, were actively involved in Nancy's care and adjustment.

Four years later, Nancy's family moved to Germany following her father's military transfer. Nancy continued to receive special education services through the American school. Up to this point, the parents reported that both they and Nancy seemed to make the necessary adjustments with few problems.

While the family was living in Germany, the mother was not required to work outside of the home. For the first time in this girl's life, her mother was available when she got home from school. Things were going so well for the family that when Nancy was 9 years old her parents had another child, a son. This birth was planned and was anticipated by the family with excitement. Again, the parents reported that the family seemed to make a sound adjustment to having an infant in the home. Their daughter expressed love for her brother and often helped with basic care such as bottle feeding. The parents viewed Nancy as compliant and good-natured about the changes in the family. Now in the third grade, Nancy was actively involved in school and peer activities.

During the following year, the mother's father was diagnosed with cancer. Over the next two years the mother made four extended trips to the United States to help with her father's care and with decisions regarding his treatment. Each time, the mother took her infant son with her but left Nancy in Germany to attend school. Nancy was very close to her grandfather, but when he died during her sixth-grade year, she was unable to attend the funeral and never got to say goodbye.

It was during this period that Nancy began to show changes in mood. The parents reported that their daughter was unhappy about her mother's frequent absences from home. Because of her mother's trips, Nancy was placed in an after-school, day-care center where she stayed until her father got off from work each evening. Nancy's behavior became demanding; she was at times openly defiant of her parents' wishes. Nancy, now 12, refused to clean her room or do basic household chores that had been hers since she was 6 years old. Her school performance deteriorated, and she spent more and more time isolated in her room. When her mother was at home, Nancy reacted to her in an angry and sullen manner. Her father finally stated that he could not handle Nancy alone and work his full-time job. The next time Nancy's mother went to the States to settle her father's estate, she brought Nancy with her. After staying a week with the maternal grandmother, Nancy's mother asked if Nancy could remain with her grandmother. It was at this point that the grandmother sought help from the school counselor.

Questions and Comments

1. *Which life-cycle stages and stressors were Nancy's family able to negotiate successfully? What factors and dynamics supported positive adjustment?*

    This couple appears to have made the transition through Stage 1 (Newly Married Couple), Stage 2 (Families with Young Children), and Stage 3 (Child-Rearing Families) of the family life cycle with adequate adjustment. Even the diagnosis of their daughter with mental retardation at age 3 and the family move to Germany did not appear to cause this family significant problems. The couple had the support of extended family and community services.

    They seemed to be able to share parenting roles while both had careers. When the mother stopped working outside the home, the family made this adjustment as well. In fact, the couple made a purposeful decision to reenter the stage of families with young children when the mother's time was more free. Even after the birth of the son, the family continued to adapt and re-establish a plateau period. They included Nancy in the birth process and allowed her to help with the initial caretaking of their infant son.

2. *At what stage did Nancy's family become "stuck?" What were the contributing factors and dynamics identified as precipitating the disruption of the family life cycle?*

It was not until the family reached Stage 4 (Families with Adolescents) that the failure to adapt and reorganize roles was evident. The concept of pile-up is clearly demonstrated in this family. Parental and marital decisions about the family had been made based on the plan that the family would live in Germany, the mother would be able to stay at home with her children, and the family would have a period of relative stability. However, outside of the family's control, events threatened this stability. Within a short period after the baby's birth the mother's father was diagnosed with cancer. Not only did she have her own family to manage, but she was also responsible for helping with her father's care. This change left her husband trying to manage his own job as well as Nancy and their home.

When the grandfather died, the mother was the only member of Nancy's family who was able to attend the funeral and experience the grief with her extended family network. The family did not give Nancy an opportunity to work through her own grief. In fact, the death of her grandfather was not even discussed to any great degree. The parents were unsure how well Nancy could understand the concept of death and much of their energy was directed toward reinvolving the mother in family life and raising an infant.

Nancy's reaching adolescence appears to be the final pile-up of transitional demands and stresses that sent this family into crisis. The daughter's noncompliant behaviors and sullen attitude were her expression of the distress that the entire family was experiencing, as well as a predictable response to her growing sense of independence and the struggles that adolescence brings. The parents felt so overwhelmed by the changes they saw in Nancy that their solution was to place her outside of the home altogether.

3. *What interventions could be used to help the family move on in the family life cycle?*
   Intervention for this family involved a number of different paths. First, the family was given information about the family life cycle, and their pile-up was acknowledged. Nancy's development as an adolescent was discussed, and the mother was given information about the struggles faced by other families with an adolescent with special needs. The mother was invited to attend a support group for parents with children with special needs. She attended a meeting and was able to discuss the changes in her daughter with other parents who had experienced similar difficulties.

Second, the family was helped through the grief process that had slowed down their ability to make an adequate transition. The mother was advised to talk to her daughter about the loss of her grandfather and to give her as much information as she wanted about her grandfather's illness, death, and funeral. In fact, the family made a visit to the grandfather's grave site so that the Nancy could say her goodbyes and have a concrete way to experience the meaning of death.

Finally, the parents were advised not to leave Nancy with her grandmother. Nancy was able to tell her mother that she did not want to be left behind. She cried and expressed how much she had missed her mother over the past two years. With help from the counselor, Nancy was able to communicate some of her turmoil and confusion about becoming an adolescent. Nancy's mother was convinced that leaving Nancy in the United States at this time would be interpreted by Nancy as the ultimate rejection.

The mother was also advised about special education services that she could receive through the military in Germany. She was able to see that if, in a few years, Nancy was not happy with the situation in Germany, she could always choose to return to the States. By this time, however, the grandmother would have had time to adjust to her own loss, and Nancy would have had time to reconnect with her family.

Upon return to Germany, the parents were also advised to begin to spend individual time with their daughter and time alone as a couple. The family had developed a lifestyle, when they were together of always going everywhere and doing everything with both children. As this daughter's developmental needs were significantly different from those of her younger brother, she needed some individual attention and activities that were geared to her age level. The parents needed some time together so that some of their stress could be alleviated and they could solidify their relationship as a couple.

With information, the parents realized that, even though their daughter was 13 years in age, she was functioning at a much younger level because of her intellectual limitations, coupled with the family's unresolved grief and failure to make transitional adjustments. They were then able to provide more support and work with her in controlling her moods and noncompliant behaviors. When the parents were able to view their daughter's rebellious behaviors within the context of the family stress, they were more willing to help her through this transition.

FAMILY INTERACTION 3
PATTERNS

This chapter introduces the family systems theory known as *structural family therapy*. The structural concepts related to closeness and distance between family members and roles, functions, and distribution of power within the family are elaborated. We conclude with a case example that illustrates these structural concepts and their usefulness for the school professional in understanding how and why families communicate in particular ways.

INTRODUCTION

A key concept in viewing students' school difficulties within a family systems approach is that the individual's behavior is not solely dependent upon what is going on in that person's head. Rather, the behavior is maintained by a complex set of interactions that occur with regularity and can be predicted by observing the family system over time. This basic systemic premise is evidenced in the work of Salvadore Minuchin, a pediatrician turned psychiatrist, and his coworkers (Minuchin, Montalvo, Guerney, Rosman, & Schumer, 1967), who developed a treatment approach known as structural family therapy.

According to Minuchin (1974), the primary job of the family is to "enhance the psychosocial growth of each member" (p. 51). In order to accomplish this task, the family must operate with some predictability and stability. For instance, children should be able to forecast that each time they misbehave they will receive a similar response from their parents. In addition, the family must also be able to respond to changing circumstances with some flexibility. When prolonged stress occurs, if the family is not capable of flexible roles and communication patterns, family conflict and dysfunctional behavior will result. In structural family therapy, the role of the helper is to help families adapt to changing circumstances through changes in the structure of the family. In each family, members have prescribed roles and functions that set up a pattern of behaviors within the family. The trained observer can identify these patterns by watching how the family interacts. The student is only one member of this complex family network. If students' behaviors are to be understood, they must be observed in the context of their families' patterns of relating.

Minuchin and his colleagues have observed and worked with thousands of families over the past twenty-five years. Through these observations, they have been able to describe patterns of relating that occur frequently in families. They developed terms to describe these patterns, including *boundaries*, *subsystems*, and *hierarchy*. In the structural family approach, problems of an individual are viewed as a result of dysfunctional family structure in one of these three areas. For more information regarding the theoretical principles underlying structural family therapy, see Appendix A.

BOUNDARIES

In observing family structure, one aspect of importance is the pattern of distance and closeness between family members. In other words, how emotionally connected are family members? How openly do they communicate with one another? How well is individuality tolerated in the family? This dimension of closeness and distance is defined through boundaries or rules that determine "who participates and how" in the system (Minuchin, 1974, p. 53).

If a system is functioning well, boundaries are described as clear and semipermeable. For example, within a school an example of clear boundaries would be that the teacher is responsible for evaluating and managing the student within the classroom and the school psychologist is responsible for evaluating the student and meeting with families at the request of the teacher. Indications of semipermeable boundaries would be that the psychologist might observe the student within the classroom and ask for the teacher's feedback or the teacher might meet with the family and the psychologist to discuss a particular student's behavior.

Assuming that both professionals are adequately skilled, if the system is operating functionally, the teacher appreciates the psychologist's presence in the classroom and the psychologist will value the teacher's presence at the family meeting because the two professionals will feel as if they are joining their resources for a student's well-being. If the two professionals are communicating openly, respecting one another's domains and contributions and working for a common outcome, then the boundaries in this system are clearly defined.

Boundaries are described as dysfunctional if they are either blurred or too rigidly defined. The extremes of distance and closeness in terms of boundaries are called *disengaged* or *enmeshed*. Table 3.1 is a visual representation of this continuum.

Families with a pattern of relating that falls at either extreme of the continuum are at risk for having a member who exhibits physical or psychiatric symptoms. As we will discuss, children tend to be the most at risk for reacting to family stress and dysfunctional family patterns.

Disengaged

At one extreme of the continuum are families or systems in which boundaries are inappropriately rigid and there is excessive distance between people. Communication between members is limited, and collaboration within the home or with the school is

Table 3.1
DEFINITION OF BOUNDARIES

Disengaged	**Clear**	**Enmeshed**
Rigid	Normal Range	Blurred
Underinvolved		Overinvolved

Source: Adapted from *Families and Family Therapy* (p. 54) by S. Minuchin, 1974, Cambridge: Harvard University Press.

difficult. Nuances of behavior tend to go unnoticed in a disengaged system so that children may go to extremes of behavior such as temper tantrums, fire-setting, suicidal threats, or stealing in order to get attention. Members of a disengaged system will report feeling as if they were required to make decisions or handle problems alone.

Students who come from highly disengaged families are more likely to exhibit behavior problems or problems of externalizing versus internalizing. If appropriate intervention is not given, these students are at risk for becoming involved with legal or court systems in the future. Acting-out behaviors such as speaking with a loud voice, acting the class clown, stealing from other students, cursing or acting belligerent are all possible indications of inappropriate distance and rigidity in the family.

The school professional can observe disengagement by watching the responses and interactions of family members. Do people in the family sit far apart from one another? Do the children have to repeat themselves to be heard? If a parent is called by the teacher or if a note is sent home, does it take a long time for the parent to respond? A particular aspect of disengagement to watch for is inattention to expressions of feeling on the part of family members. Do family members have to escalate in order to get attention for their feelings?

Other aspects of family life may also reflect disengagement. For example, does the family have regular meals together? Are there regular activities in which the whole family participates, such as church, vacations, or sports events? Are parents involved in PTA activities? Do they attend their children's school activities, when invited? Failure of the family to be involved in these types of activities may be an example of disengagement and should be noted by the school professional.

If disengagement is observed, the student's behaviors may be viewed in a different context. A note sent home to a family that is disengaged may need to be stated more forcefully and highlighted as a potential crisis if the teacher is to gain a response. If an initial note or phone call does not elicit parental concern, the teacher may want to ask the principal or assistant principal to sign the next notice in an attempt to signal the importance to disengaged parents.

It is also important for teachers to note that they may feel that children of disengaged families are more resistant to teacher direction than other children. In fact, the child's lack of responsiveness may be a function of the family pattern. In the same vein, a teacher's efforts to provide approval and nurturance may be initially rejected by the child from a disengaged family.

Professionals often have a tendency to want to define disengaged families as "bad" or abusive. It is important to keep in mind the principles of how and why a system operates as it does. Often disengagement is a systemic response to extensive conflict, long-term family stress, or overtaxing of emotional resources. The distancing is an attempt by the family system to gain a balance and to continue to function in the face of these forces. In fact, once these families do notice that something is wrong, the school professional may observe high levels of conflict and verbal reactivity. It is often fear of this out-of-control conflict that leads to the initial disengagement process (Colapinto, 1982).

In families of a child with special needs, there has often been a long history of involvement with special educators, health care providers, or social services. At a particular point, disengagement may be observed between parent and child. However, the distance may be a reactive response to years or months of overinvolvement or overtaxing of the parents in the service of their child. In these instances, understanding the historical context may be useful in understanding and changing the disengagement process.

School Systems

Disengagement can also be observed in many school environments. If professionals feel they each have their domain within the building and if there is little collaboration between instruction, counseling, and administration, this may be a sign of disengagement within the system. Steps to resolving this process may include identifying the fear or conflict that has led to the rigidly defined distance, increasing understanding of the different roles and functions within the school, and experiencing team-building and collaboration exercises.

Family Systems Example

Kevin, an 8-year-old deaf boy, was identified by his third-grade speech and hearing teacher as experiencing a family systems problem when he was absent for three consecutive weeks. The teacher had called Kevin's mother, a single parent, after a week's absence and had left a message of concern on her phone-answering machine. When Kevin did not return to school after another week, his teacher contacted his mother at work and was told that Kevin had just gotten over a bad case of the flu, was being nursed back to health by his grandmother, and would return to school the next week. After a third week, the teacher asked the school counselor if she would contact the mother and invite her to the school for a meeting. Both professionals hypothesized disengagement on the part of this mother due to her failure to respond to two teacher requests about her son's absences. In addition, because this mother was a single parent, they believed that she might be overwhelmed with the demands of parenting and thus relieved by Kevin's being allowed to stay with her mother.

Enmeshed

At the opposite end of the continuum are families or systems in which boundaries are blurred and there is excessive closeness between people. In enmeshed systems, autonomy and independence are difficult to achieve. There is a lack of privacy, and individual differences are not well tolerated. Members of an enmeshed system may report feeling smothered or overprotected. One comment made about enmeshed families is that if one person is cut the rest of the family bleeds (Aponte & Hoffman, 1973).

Students who come from highly enmeshed families are more likely to exhibit emotional problems or problems of internalizing than to act out or externalize their difficulties. Without early intervention these children are at risk for future need for mental health services or psychiatric hospitalization. Child and adolescent behaviors such as sadness and withdrawal, identity problems, and poor social skills may be evidence of an enmeshed family environment. When the child acts out, such as having temper tantrums or threatening to run away, it is usually in response to limit setting where in the past limits have been blurred or nonexistent. This is in contrast to the lack of involvement seen in disengaged families that precipitates acting out behaviors.

Questions that may indicate if a family is enmeshed include: Do family members sit too closely together or inappropriately touch? Do younger children exhibit clingy behavior or acute distress at separation? Do people in this family interrupt one another or speak for each other? For example, if Johnny is asked how he feels about something, does his mother respond, "Johnny feels _____" as if she feels for him? If someone expresses a disagreement, is he or she ignored or talked over?

If the school professional observes signs of a family being enmeshed, certain cautions should be followed. In contrast to the disengaged system, in enmeshed families reactivity and emotionalism are the standard. A note sent home to a family that is enmeshed about a student's behavior may result in frantic phone calls or visits from the parents. Criticism of one family member, such as the student, is perceived as a personal affront to other family members as well and may elicit a defensive reaction. In dealing with the enmeshed family, understatement should be the rule. Rather than needing to "loan" reactivity, the professional dealing with enmeshed systems needs to maintain a calm and nonreactive stance.

For the teacher, children from enmeshed families may be more clingy and attention-seeking than other students. They may have difficulty with self-direction and may request frequent teacher assistance. These children may ask the teacher inappropriate personal questions or make requests for her time that are beyond the regular school structure. In these instances, it is important to view the student's behavior within a personal context. In an overinvolved family culture, these behaviors are seen as appropriate.

As with the disengaged family, it is vital for the school professional to recognize that family enmeshment is also a result of systemic forces in operation. The need for intense closeness and family loyalty is often a homeostatic response designed to avoid extreme levels of anxiety (Colapinto, 1982). Again, the family usually becomes enmeshed in response to chronic family stress or unfulfilled and unresolved emotional needs.

Particularly when dealing with a child with special needs, parents are often fearful of allowing too much independence (Foster, 1986). They may feel that someone who has not "walked in their shoes" cannot understand or comment upon their parenting or attachment to their child. In these situations, recommendations for a support group for families may be beneficial. Even enmeshed parents will often validate the opinions of other parents who have had similar experiences with their children. Keeping this context in mind may help the professional to maintain personal boundaries in a clearer fashion when dealing with enmeshed systems.

School Systems

The enmeshed school environment is easily recognized by its degree of involvement. It is characterized by excessive togetherness. Decisions regarding school policy are often laborious because of the need to involve everyone in a consensus, whether or not they will be affected by the particular decision. These systems frequently have staff meetings where the agenda is never completed because of the focus on expression of feelings versus accomplishment of tasks. If a staff member chooses to leave the school and take another job, this is often viewed as disloyal behavior.

Steps to resolving an enmeshed school system may include clarification of functions and goals for each member, instituting an incentive program for innovative ideas and accomplishment of goals, and focusing on solutions that minimize disagreement rather than requiring complete agreement from all staff.

Family Systems Example

Ranu, a 16-year-old girl with Down syndrome, had begun requesting frequent passes out of her second period reading class. She complained of dizziness and headaches and asked to go to the school clinic. When this pattern repeated itself five times in two weeks, her teacher discussed the problem with her co-workers and was informed that Ranu had been meeting a male student in the hall during these alleged trips to the clinic. The teacher refused to write another pass and sent a note home regarding this problem. The following day, Ranu's parents brought her to school and went to the principal's office, requesting a meeting. The reading teacher went to the meeting prepared to face the forces of an enmeshed system.

Summary

Families and systems can usually be characterized as functioning, on the whole, somewhere along the boundary continuum between disengaged and enmeshed. This terminology is used to describe the overall emotional climate of the system and a preferred transactional style. At dysfunctional extremes, the terms *enmeshed* and *disengaged* will describe the usual patterns of functioning within the family. However, in most families there are examples of both disengaged and enmeshed boundaries. A parent might be overinvolved or enmeshed in interactions with a child with special needs to the exclusion of other children in the family. A highly enmeshed pattern between mother and children may leave the father feeling excluded, and he may disengage in response. A father who is highly involved in his work and excludes his family may find his wife overinvolved with parenting to combat her loneliness. This dysfunctional pattern, consisting of an overinvolved mother and a disengaged father, is often found in families having a child with special needs. For further discussion and details regarding this pattern, see chapter 7.

The school professional may benefit from information regarding the overall family style of boundary management. Knowledge of family boundaries is important in understanding such dimensions of children's behavior as emotional reactivity, degree of need for attention, and parental responses to the identification of problems in a child. Opening the door to communication with an enmeshed family may require appealing to the emotionalism in the family system. A request made to an enmeshed family may begin with, "Since I know how much you love and worry about Cindy, I'm asking that you do _____." The same request of a disengaged family might begin, "Although I'm aware of how busy you are, I'm asking that you do _____." The school professionals' ability to communicate in a way that parallels the family's boundary style may be a key factor in developing a relationship with the family that supports problem solving and efficient partnership between parents and the school system.

SUBSYSTEMS

The primary building blocks of family structure are the subsystems within the family. The traditional nuclear family consists of four subsystems (Minuchin, 1974):

- o Spousal subsystem
- o Parental subsystem
- o Sibling subsystem
- o Extrafamilial subsystem

Each subsystem has its roles and functions that are common to all families. For example, every family has some person or persons who are identified as executives or decision makers for the family, that is, the parental subsystem. In addition, there are aspects of subsystem functioning that are uniquely defined by each family. In single-parent families there is no spousal subsystem. The extrafamilial subsystem may include biological family or friends and neighbors.

In an intact nuclear family, the marital partners constitute two different subsystems. As husband and wife, they compose the marital or spousal subsystem. As mother and father, they are the parental subsystem. These two subsystems have different but often intertwined functions. If there are communication problems between spouses, their functioning as parents will be affected.

Spousal Subsystem

The primary tasks of the spousal subsystem are providing for the functional needs of the family and the individual emotional and sexual needs of husband and wife. As discussed in chapter 2, successful resolution of the first stage of the family life cycle, formation of the marital system, is the framework upon which the entire future life of the family is built. Thus, the initial task of the spousal subsystem is the establishment of a sense of commitment and mutual trust (Framo, 1981a).

Functional Support

Once the issue of commitment is resolved, the couple must work together to build a future for themselves. Basic skills in negotiating and division of labor must be developed. It is essential for healthy family functioning that the marital couple be able to divide chores, communicate about and resolve problems to evolve an interdependent relationship, and accomplish the tasks of daily life. In early marriage, spouses must make decisions about how household tasks will be divided, who will make money and how much, how money will be allocated, how leisure time will be spent, among others. The positive resolution of these questions comes from open, honest communication and mutual respect.

Emotional Support

Equally important is the role that the spousal subsystem plays in providing for the basic emotional needs of the marital couple. It is this emotional foundation that determines psychologically healthy patterns of interaction within the family and with other systems. Friedrich (1979) studied mothers of children with special needs and found that reported marital satisfaction of the couple was the single most accurate predictor of successful coping and family adjustment to the child's special needs. In a follow-up study of 158 families with a child with mental retardation, marital satisfaction was the best predictor of positive overall family relations (Friedrich, Wilturner, & Cohen, 1985).

The happiness and stability of the primary relationship between the couple contributes heavily to the individual self-esteem, motivation, and mood of the husband and wife. Particularly in modern society, where extended family has become subordinate to the nuclear family, the spousal relationship may be the primary source of intimacy and sense of connectedness in the world. With this basic sense of connection as the foundation for the spousal relationship, many life problems may be faced more flexibly and productively.

Families with Special Needs

Marital stability is often threatened by the demands of a child with special needs (Featherstone, 1980). Parents who are trying to make time for their own careers, the needs of their other children, and functional household tasks may take time away from their relationship as a couple to meet these various demands. Love (1973) reported that separation and divorce in families with a child with special needs are three times as high as in the rest of the population. Wright, Matlock, and Matlock (1985) interviewed 48 couples with a child with an exceptionality and compared them with 42 couples with children without a disability. They reported their findings as "parents of the handicapped...were six times as likely as parents of the nonhandicapped to indicate that their children caused marital problems" (p. 38).

In contrast, it is clear that many marriages are able to remain intact and satisfying in spite of the presence of a child with difficulties. Longo and Bond (1984) reviewed ten studies from 1959 to 1981 that reported no differences between the level of marital adjustment, parental friction, or incidence of divorce in couples having children with chronic illnesses and control couples. The primary characteristics that appear to relate to healthy marital response in these cases are strong, supportive spousal relationships prior to the diagnosis of the child and individual personality strength of the spouses (Abbott & Meridith, 1986).

Questions that school professionals can ask themselves to diagnose the functioning of the spousal subsystem include: When was the last time the couple went out on a "date" together? How do they make decisions? When conflicts arise, how are they resolved? Does the couple have common interests and friends? Do they have a process for problem solving? Is communication open, direct, and honest?

In our modern age, there are many variations of the intact, nuclear family pattern. Because of these variations, the definition of the spousal subsystem may need to be expanded to address the functioning of particular families. For example, in most single-parent families, there is no spousal subsystem. The functions of the spousal subsystem may be carried out by one parent and a significant dating or live-in relationship, though not marriage. In these instances, the reasons for the lack of a legal commitment and the impact upon the family must be considered. The basic premise, that the emotional well-being of parents, revolving around their primary relationship, affects their functioning within the family, still holds true.

Parental Subsystem

The tasks of the parental or executive subsystem are primarily oriented around nurturing and teaching or disciplining children. In the intact nuclear family, this subsystem consists of biological or adoptive mother and father. In a divorce situation, the roles of the parental subsystem may be fulfilled by a single parent, by a parent and a grandparent, or by a parent and a stepparent. When the parental subsystem is not composed of mother and father, the emotional issues involved in parenting become more complex.

Nurturing Function

For many parents of children with special needs, the nurturing and protecting functions of the parental subsystem are particularly complicated. As was discussed in chapter 2, the feelings of shock, guilt, and grief that are associated with the diagnosis of a child may initially interfere with the parent's ability to bond with their infant adequately (Trout, 1983). As the child develops, parents will go through many stages of adjustment and many ambivalent feelings about their child (Wikler, 1981). Buscaglia (1983) described some of these stages and feelings when he stated,

> It is normal to want to avoid pain....Parents will find that there will be inordinate demands made upon them....These demands will cause them great frustration and resentment....They will often feel trapped and tied down....Parents will feel helpless, stupid and confused at times. (p. 95)

In the midst of these conflicting feelings, parents must make decisions about how much or how little freedom to allow their children while at the same time insuring their safety. Lack of clarity about the child's developmental progress may make parental decisions about allowing independence even more difficult.

Disciplining Function

An issue of primary importance is the agreement between parenting partners about discipline. If parents divide roles rather than sharing them, children learn how to negotiate around their parents rather than learning to internalize values and responsibilities. For example, a typical pattern in dysfunctional families is for one parent to be viewed by the children as a "softie" and the other parent to be seen as "abusive." In most cases, the abusive parent believes he or she needs to be a strong disciplinarian to combat the partner's permissiveness. The soft parent believes he or she needs to pamper the children to make up for the abusiveness of the other parent. Thus, the parenting subsystem has reached a homeostatic balance. However, the basic tasks of teaching and disciplining children are not being adequately fulfilled.

In the family with special needs, this parental "splitting" is often unknowingly intensified by those offering supportive services. If the mother is the parent who attends all meetings, takes all telephone calls, and schedules all appointments involving her child with special needs, she may have a different understanding of her child than her husband has. Particularly in cases where the child's disability is not physically evident, lack of understanding on the part of one parent may lead to different disciplining styles.

For the school professional, a first step in joining with parents is to acknowledge conflicting feelings and struggles. A second step may be to provide information about child development in general and specifics about the child's particular level of functioning. Finally, the school may serve as a resource for information on parenting classes or support groups that can help alleviate some of the stress of parenting. For further discussion of resources, see chapter 11 and Appendix C of this book.

Sibling System

The primary tasks of the sibling subsystem are the socialization and development of the children in a family. Siblings may provide an identification network in which values are formed, negotiations with parents are carried out, and perceptions of the outside world are supported or clarified (Bank & Kahn, 1982). In addition, crosscultural studies have characterized the sibling group as an important *in vivo* testing ground for the transmission of cultural norms, roles, and functions (Johnson, 1982; Weisner, 1982). Beginning at a very young age, interactions with siblings can teach sharing, negotiation, assertiveness, and empathy.

Siblings with Special Needs

In families with a child with special needs, the siblings must adjust to decreased parental time and energy (Atkins, 1987; Fischer & Roberts, 1983). Where in most families, parents tend to distribute their emotional resources somewhat evenly across siblings, in families with one child who is experiencing special problems, that child will often receive the lion's share of parental focus. Siblings may feel competitive and angry with their disabled brother or sister at times and then may feel guilty about these feelings (Featherstone, 1980). They may also experience a form of "survivor's guilt" about being healthy when their sibling has problems (Trevino, 1979). Siblings may feel they can't express their emotions to their parents, for fear of causing more stress (Koch, 1985).

Finally, children may incorporate having a sibling with special needs into a negative self-concept of their own (Harvey & Greenway, 1984; McKeever, 1982). They may feel that because their sibling is disabled, they are damaged as well.

Awareness

It is important that siblings have information about their brother or sister's special needs that is understandable to them. Parents are often reluctant to discuss specifics about their child's problems for fear that they will distress their other children. Until the disability is clarified, siblings may worry that they will "catch" the problem themselves (Featherstone, 1980; Seligman, 1979). Siblings seem more likely to have these worries if the disability is mild and not physically evident. They may be afraid to tell their friends that this difficulty has occurred in their family for fear of being ostracized. They may then withdraw from the sibling with problems and from their peer network, adding to the family's sense of isolation. McHale, Sloan, and Simeonsson (1986) interviewed sixty siblings of children with special needs and found that when siblings have a better understanding of the child's condition, the sibling relationships tend to be more positive.

Responsibility

Siblings may be asked to take on more personal responsibility than usual when there is a child with special needs in the home. The oldest female sibling in these families is at particular risk for *parentification* (Fowle, 1968; Howard, 1978). Mothers who are overwhelmed with caretaking tasks for their diagnosed child may ask, either covertly or overtly, that their oldest daughters take over more parenting functions. These girls are then at risk for failure to have their own emotional needs met and for problems in later life.

Abilities

As children develop, they may have concerns about surpassing an older sibling with special needs who is functioning at a younger age (Vadasy, Fewell, Meyer, & Schell, 1984). This may result in the younger sibling feeling guilty about surpassing him or her, even though this sibling is diagnosed with special problems. Younger siblings may even try to hide their abilities or may refuse activities where they will likely excel.

Educators should be particularly alert to motivational problems in students with a sibling who has special needs, as the processes of parentification or feelings of guilt may be operating. An understanding discussion with the sibling and the parents about the issues of survivor guilt and the struggles of having a sibling with a disability may provide the information and support that is needed to readjust the family structure.

Positive Aspects

Although siblings of children with special needs are at risk for various types of problems, the extent of these problems seems to depend, most significantly, on the adjustment of others in the home, especially parents (Ferrari, 1984). Given adequate coping skills, open communication, and an environment of mutual support, there are some positive effects of having a sibling with special needs. Siblings tend to have a greater understanding of and tolerance for differences in people (Grossman, 1972). Siblings of children with emotional problems frequently show an orientation toward idealism and humanitarian interests (Cleveland & Miller, 1977). Often siblings, particularly females, will choose careers that are influenced by the disability (Cleveland & Miller, 1977; Farber, 1963). In fact, both authors of this book have siblings who have special needs.

Sibling Groups

The school professional may be in a unique position to provide services to the siblings of children with special needs. One of the authors of this book, Daniels-Mohring, led sibling groups at a self-contained special education setting. The school served children with special needs between the ages of 4 and 16. In this setting, one evening a week was designated as parent night. Teachers and counseling staff were available during this evening to meet with families for counseling, updates on students' progress, problem-solving sessions, and goal-developing sessions. During one quarter, a four-week sibling group was offered. It met on parent night. This group contained eight siblings of children in the school. Activities included group discussion, sharing of information, and role-playing of difficult situations encountered by the siblings. Role-plays were videotaped; at the conclusion of the group, the members elected to invite their parents to view their videotapes. After parents were able to see their children acting out some of their concerns and problems about their siblings, a lively and open discussion followed. Evidently, the group met a need that had previously gone unnoticed.

Meyer, Vadasy, and Fewell (1985) have developed a handbook for sibling workshops entitled *Sibshops*. These workshops developed from their experiences at the University of Washington with brothers and sisters, ages 8 to 13, of children with special needs. Their workshops are held on Saturday mornings for two to three hours, or on two-day overnight camping trips. Workshops include both an informational and a recreational component. Some informational activities suggested in this workbook include discussion groups using problem-focused activities; panel discussions involving adult siblings or other parents of children with special needs who are willing to share their experiences; and presentations by a speech therapist, physical therapist, special education teacher, or other professionals about their experiences with students having special needs. These authors also include an extensive reading list of suggested fiction and nonfiction books for siblings of the disabled. For further information about implementing a sibling workshop, this workbook is highly recommended.

Extrafamilial Subsystem

In addition to the subsystems already discussed, family systems also have an extrafamilial aspect. Not truly a subsystem of the nuclear family, the extrafamilial interactions represent those parts of the family system that interface with the outside world.

Extrafamilial contacts provide assistance and exchange of resources, a source of social and recreational activities, and emotional support (Gabel & Kotsch, 1981). Support for family and cultural values is also supplied by the extrafamilial subsystem. There are particular issues and functions within each subsystem that relate to extrafamilial interactions.

Interaction with Spousal Subsystem

For example, one task in the formation of the spousal subsystem is making decisions about interactions with the extended family. If one spouse continues to be involved with his or her family of origin to the exclusion of the other spouse, problems in the spousal subsystem will result. Likewise, if a spouse is overinvolved with his or her friendship network, the level of intimacy within the spousal subsystem may be affected. In special needs families, if only one spouse participates in special functions or support groups regarding the child, marital distance may result.

Interaction with Parental Subsystem

In the parental subsystem, day-care providers, babysitters, school professionals, and extended family and friends are all part of the extrafamilial subsystem. These persons interact with parents to make decisions regarding their children's care. They provide support and assistance to parents and may also serve as role models for appropriate parenting skills (Kazak & Wilcox, 1984). The parental subsystem must be functioning cohesively and clearly to allow these extended network interactions to operate positively. Otherwise, there may be mixed messages between the couple about which role models to follow in parenting.

Again, in a family with special needs, if one parent is attending special parenting classes or listening to the advice of school professionals to the exclusion of the other parent, conflict in the disciplining function may result.

Interaction with Sibling Subsystem

Finally, the sibling subsystem has extensive extrafamilial involvement. The family must negotiate around school activities with peers, sports teams, extracurricular activities, and daily peer interactions. How many times do parents say, "It's not my child's fault; it's the crowd he[she] runs around with?"

The role of peer relationships in children's adjustment and socialization has been clearly demonstrated (Abramovitch & Strayer, 1977; Rubin, 1985; Sluckin & Smith, 1977). If children have positive peer relationships, they will bring these skills home to share with their sibling network. Likewise, if children are rejected or isolated from peers, the resulting self-image problems and poor social skills will become a part of their sibling interactions as well. In families with special needs, the acceptance of peers is particularly important to both the child with the disability and to the siblings.

Subsystem Dysfunction

Dysfunction in the extrafamilial subsystem occurs either when the family is too inclusive or too exclusive about network involvement. If family members have very enmeshed and diffuse boundaries, they may not be able to make family decisions without input from the extrafamilial subsystem. At the opposite extreme, if family members have very rigid or disengaged boundaries, they may isolate themselves from any social supports.

Questions that school professionals may ask themselves to diagnose extrafamilial functioning include: Do the children ever have peers over to spend the night or go to friends' homes to spend the night? Are the children involved in any extracurricular activities? Is the family active in a church community? Are grandparents regularly involved with the family? Do the parents have their own friends?

If it is clear that the extrafamilial subsystem is not fulfilling the family's needs, the school professional may want to make suggestions about Boy or Girl Scouts, sports teams, Special Olympics, specialized summer camps, or other special activities that are geared to the needs of the particular student. More specific suggestions about networking resources may be found in chapters 10 and 11 and Appendix C in this book.

Families with Special Needs

Families with a child with special needs often feel isolated from their extrafamilial subsystem (Kazak, 1987). Parents often feel they have few sources of support. Extended families may go through their own mourning process when a child is born with a disability. As Gabel and Kotsch (1981) argued, "Grandparents who are angry, grief stricken, or who deny the child's handicap may become an additional burden to parents" (p. 32).

Kazak and Wilcox (1984) compared families with a child with spina bifida with matched control families and found that the friendship networks of the parents of the children with spina bifida were smaller in size. These authors hypothesized that not only might friends withdraw support because of their lack of knowledge about the child's illness and their feelings of fear or inadequacy about providing help, but the parents might also be less receptive to support because of their own fears and anxieties. Particularly with children who require specialized physical attention, parents may be afraid that their friends or family will not know how to adequately respond to the child's needs. In addition, they may feel that asking for help with their child will place too great a burden on their friends.

Another potential difficulty in the extrafamilial subsystem of families with a child with special needs is the required interactions with outside services. Often these families must have frequent meetings with physicians, counselors, teachers, physical therapists, and other professionals to maintain their child's functioning. The majority of these services focus on the child rather than the family (Foster, Berger, & McLean, 1981). Parents often feel overwhelmed with demands from these extrafamilial systems rather than feeling a sense of support in their struggle.

The extrafamilial aspects of the family system are particularly important to school professionals. The most functional view of the family will include the school professional as part of the family's extrafamilial subsystem. When teachers or counselors view themselves as being joined to the family system in meaningful and positive ways, interactions that affect the system will follow. This framework lends itself to cooperation between school and family rather than to defensiveness and alienation.

HIERARCHY

Hierarchy is a term used by Minuchin to describe the distribution of power in families (Minuchin, 1974). The concept of hierarchy involves the power relationships between members of a system. A member at the top of the hierarchy is one who has the most relational power within the system. In an adequately functioning family system, parents and children have different levels of authority that are accepted and respected. Likewise, in a school system the principal has the final authority and accepts ultimate responsibility for management decisions.

There may be different levels of hierarchy within a system. Parents may share authority but at times one or the other parent may be in charge. Parents may delegate authority to a teenage sibling or a grandparent. Sibling subsystems that have children of different ages tend to have a clear sibling hierarchy. Older siblings normally serve the dominant role in interactions with their younger siblings (Dunn & Kendrick, 1982).

In school systems there may also be different levels of hierarchy. Teachers are the ultimate authority in their classrooms. Team leaders may be at the top of the hierarchy with regard to decisions made by their team. Counseling departments may have one person designated as the director of guidance. Finally, there may be a principal and an assistant principal who lead the decision-making process (somewhat like a parental subsystem).

Dysfunctional Hierarchy

When the hierarchy in a family or system is unclear, as with a weak parental subsystem, turmoil and chaos result. In highly stressed families, this lack of management may be evident in many areas. Children may come to school wearing dirty or torn clothing. Messages to the home may be left unanswered and papers unsigned.

At times the hierarchy is clear but inappropriately reversed, with children having as much or more power than parents or teachers. In families where one child's demands take priority over the needs of the rest of the family members, a hierarchy problem is evident. When a child regularly functions in a parental role and assumes an inordinate level of responsibility for his or her age, hierarchy dysfunction is operating in the system.

Cross-Generational Coalition

One type of hierarchy shift is called a *cross-generational coalition.* A coalition was defined by Minuchin (1974) as an inflexible alignment between two or more family members against another family member. When the alignment occurs between a parent and a child or a grandparent and a child, it is crossing generational boundaries.

In families, cross-generational coalitions are seen when a child is drawn into an alliance with one parent against the other. These coalitions typically occur when spouses are disengaged from one another. The child may be expected to assume excessive responsibilities, may be the confidant for a parent, or may be asked to compensate for the absent spouse by providing emotional support.

In schools, a cross-generational coalition occurs when, for example, a student is in an alliance with parents against a teacher or a school counselor is in alliance with a student against the parents or teachers. In either case, hierarchical and generational boundaries have been crossed inappropriately.

Detouring

A hierarchy dysfunction often seen in enmeshed systems is called *detouring* (Minuchin, Roseman, & Baker, 1978) or *scapegoating* (Boszormenyi-Nagy & Spark, 1973). In this pattern within families, parents detour their energy away from potential spousal conflict or distance to focus on a particular child. Detouring may take the form of parents uniting to protect a vulnerable child, as in the case of intellectual deficits or chronic illness, or uniting to blame a child as the cause of family problems, as with the acting-out adolescent. In either case, the family focus is exclusively on the identified child. This child then has the hierarchically inappropriate power to control family interactions by his or her behavior. Boundaries are blurred, and the ultimate result is the temporary avoidance of marital conflict that might destroy the family.

Detouring can be observed within a school system when a particular student has multiple staff members involved with him or her. When making decisions about a particular student causes emotions to run high, this may be an indication that conflict between staff is being detoured through the student. An example of this process might be as follows:

> A teacher and an assistant principal disagree about management of a particular student. The teacher feels blamed by the assistant principal. She and many of her colleagues think that the assistant principal does not provide adequate support for them when they intervene into management problems in the classroom. The next time this student acts out, the teacher sends him directly to the assistant principal's office. The administrator gives the student two days in after-school detention under the teacher's supervision. The teacher, who disagrees with this consequence and has other commitments after school, fails to enforce the detention. The student is caught in a detouring of conflict between the teacher and assistant principal.

Sibling Hierarchy Dysfunction

Daniels-Mohring (1986) conducted an observational study comparing interactions of pairs of siblings in which the older sibling had been diagnosed with psychiatric problems, with same-age control sibling pairs. She found that older siblings who were diagnosed as emotionally disturbed lost some of their relational power within the sibling subsystem. This loss of role disrupted the typical hierarchy organization of sibling interactions where the older sibling is in a dominant position. Not only did the emotionally disturbed youngsters have to cope with problems of identity in dealing with their peer networks, but they also had to adapt to the loss of power within their own family systems.

To diagnose hierarchy dysfunction, the school professional might ask the following types of questions: Do parents defend the student even when the student's behavior is obviously inappropriate? Are parents inconsistent with discipline, for example, threatening to ground the adolescent and not following through? Does one parent act more like "one of the kids" than as an authority figure? Does the student talk back to the parents, exhibiting lack of respect? When parents begin to disagree, does the conversation shift to focus on the student's behavior?

Hierarchy dysfunctions are very common in families and systems, in general. Often the people involved are unaware of the hierarchy reversals in their interactions. The school professional who observes a hierarchy problem may be able to affect the system simply by neutrally commenting on the process. Some examples might be: "I understand Billy's concerns about serving detention, but I think it's important that we present a united front to him to avoid confusion" or "Hey, Leanne, do you always talk to your mom that way? It surprises me because you're usually so respectful in class." Observational comments such as these may be sufficient to help the parent reflect on his or her behavior and take action to reestablish appropriate hierarchy.

SUMMARY

In this chapter we have presented the basic theory of structural family therapy. For the school professional who has a clear understanding of these structural characteristics, the student's behavior will be easier to view as part of a family pattern. We have discussed the three major areas in which observations can be made regarding family transactional patterns: *boundaries*, *subsystems*, and *hierarchy*. *Boundaries* indicate the quality of distance and closeness within a family. The four *subsystems* are subgroups of the family system that provide the building blocks of family interaction. Diagnosis of family interaction patterns must include some assessment of how well each subsystem is sustaining its roles and functions. Finally, the concept of *hierarchy* describes the distribution of power and decision making within a system. Once family interaction patterns have been assessed, the student's behavior can be viewed within the context of his or her family structure and transactional style. Adding these contextual variables to the school professional's under-standing of the student can greatly enhance the use of that understanding toward promoting academic and emotional development.

CASE EXAMPLE

Charles W., a 9-year-old boy, was referred to the evaluation team due to poor school performance during the past semester. Charles was currently placed in a third-grade classroom and received resource help in reading and math due to severe learning disabilities.

He had begun acting out by refusing to dress for physical education. The following week, he began to dawdle during class assignments, frequently commenting that he could not understand the work. The teacher consulted with the school psychologist and confirmed that the work she was giving Charles was within his capacity. After an initial note home regarding this problem, Charles's mother, Mrs. W., had contacted his teacher by telephone each week to check on Charles's progress. In spite of sending assignments home, Charles was falling further and further behind in his studies.

Mrs. W. reported that Charles would get up every morning complaining of a stomach-ache. She would coax him out of bed in spite of the fact that he looked a little pale and reportedly had dark circles under his eyes. Mrs. W., who did not work outside of the home, picked Charles up from school each day. She reported that, since the initial report regarding his missed assignments, she spent every afternoon helping Charles with his homework even after her other two children, ages 12 and 15, returned home from school.

When asked how Mr. W. felt about Charles's performance problems, Mrs. W. replied that he was angry and upset. She stated that Mr. W. worked long hours and had no idea of how Charles really felt or whether or not he was completing homework. By the time her husband returned home in the evening, Charles was usually preparing for bed. In fact, Mrs. W. volunteered, her husband had never understood Charles's problems. Ever since Charles was diagnosed as learning disabled, her husband had been negative and withdrawn in his interactions with Charles. According to Mrs. W., her husband had expectations for Charles that were beyond his capabilities, and he tended to blame her for the fact that Charles was not achieving.

Questions and Comments

1. *Using the information provided, what is your hypothesis about the structural character-istics of this family? What data support this hypothesis?*

   The referral team hypothesizes that there is an unresolved conflict between father and mother, at least regarding Charles and probably more extensively. Distance between father and Charles is indicated by the mother's report that the father is "negative and withdrawn" in his interactions with Charles and that, by the time the father returns from work, Charles is usually in bed. Apparently, Charles and his father have limited interactions. In general, the father is disengaged from the family system and the mother and Charles are overinvolved in their relationship. Indications of enmeshment are the mother's "coaxing" Charles out of bed, her extreme concern about his physical appearance, her picking him up after school each day, her weekly phone calls to the teacher, and her daily help with homework. The marital conflict seems to be detoured onto Charles, indicated by the fact that, in spite of his mother's extensive "help," Charles is still unable to perform at school. Apparently the mother is not willing to make appropriate demands on Charles. This behavior can be seen as a reaction to what she views as inappropriate and negative demands made by the father. According to the available information, the other two children are functioning adequately and do not seem to be the focus of parental conflict.

2. *If the family dysfunction were to be resolved, what would the probable family structure look like?*

The ideal structure for this family would include the mother and father as equals in the family hierarchy. They would make joint decisions regarding their child's school problems and support one another in carrying out plans for helping their child. The adolescent child would be higher in the sibling hierarchy than either of the two younger children. All boundaries between subsystems would be appropriate and flexible, as indicated by open communication, expression of individual identities, and clear roles and functions within the family.

3. *What types of intervention strategies might be appropriate for working with this family?*

In order to work towards a functional family structure, the referral team will want to make certain that the father is involved in any meetings or future communication regarding Charles. Both parents might be brought in to review Charles's records and clarify his functioning level, to decrease the possibility of misunderstanding about Charles's abilities. In order to interrupt the enmeshment between Charles and his mother, the team might want to suggest that Charles be required to complete his assignments during school hours or stay after school for study hall. Another suggestion might be for Charles's adolescent sibling to help him with minor homework assignments to build some cohesion in the sibling subsystem. Finally, the team might suggest that Charles be allowed to ride the bus home from school in order to increase his peer interactions and level of independence.

HISTORICAL FACTORS 4

T his chapter gives a framework for viewing students' problems within an historical context. It discusses a theory of family process developed by Murray Bowen that utilizes historical factors. Appendix A also covers this theory in greater depth. For the educator, the framework of family history can provide information about motivational factors, toxic issues, and family scripts from many generations. Together or individually, these factors can influence students' reactions and performance within the school environment. This chapter concludes with a case example that illustrates the use of historical factors in understanding a student's educational difficulties.

INTRODUCTION

To the same extent that historical information about human growth and development is important in understanding the individual, the family history plays an important role in understanding family systems. It is intuitively appealing to believe that what we are and how we behave today maintains some continuity with a history that extends back several generations. This chapter focuses on the theory of Bowen (1978), who has emphasized the historical aspects of systems theories. His efforts expand consideration of behavior not only from the individual to the system, but also from the present to the past.

There are a number of specific concepts to be examined from Bowen's work that address the notion that personal family history is important in the formation of personal identity and life choices. The concept of *differentiation* addresses the theme of individuality and self-integration. *Emotional transmission* describes the forces by which family prejudices, rules of behavior, and patterns of relating are relayed through several generations. *Birth order* is the concept that deals with how factors within the sibling subsystem affect personality development and relational patterns throughout a family's history. Finally, *triangulation* delineates the process by which historical patterns of relationships are played out in the present.

DIFFERENTIATION

The concept of *differentiation* is the core around which Bowen's (1978) theory is built. Differentiation is the process by which one becomes increasingly less emotionally dependent upon the family and more able to make independent choices and decisions. This process involves the ability to keep intellectual and emotional systems separate.

For example, suppose you were bitten by a dog at a young age and you are now deathly afraid, almost phobic, of dogs. If you see a dog and you automatically run out into a busy street to avoid being chased, your emotional system is in control. If, however, you can see a dog and ask yourself "How dangerous is this dog? Is it a miniature poodle or a great dane? Is it housed within a fence or on a chain?" before you decide whether or not to run, your emotions are being mediated by your intellectual system. When your emotional system is mediated by your intellectual system, your capacity for making choices is increased (Kerr & Bowen, 1988). For further discussion of these concepts, see Appendix A.

Levels of Differentiation

Individual levels of differentiation may show up in a number of factors. Note that these descriptions are intended as a framework for school professionals to increase understanding; we do not wish to suggest that diagnosis of levels of differentiation should be required of the educational system.

Higher Levels

Someone who is well-differentiated from his or her family of origin can make choices about personal behavior based on information as well as feelings. These individuals are not overly dependent in their relationships; they can cooperate and negotiate with others in patterns that may differ from their family experiences. Their behavior is based on a set of personal values and principles that have been derived from their experience and moral development.

Clearly, higher levels of differentiation are not possible until adulthood. Bowen (1978) believed that no one living in the home of the parents could be operating at a high level of differentiation. However, he also proposed that we tend to achieve our personal differentiation at the same or lower levels than our parents, unless some purposeful intervention is attempted to change this pattern. In other words, "like begets like" in terms of differentiation. Therefore, students' predisposition for a general level of differentiation can be viewed in light of their parents' emotional patterns.

Lower Levels

There are several signs of low levels of differentiation.

1. Excessively influenced by other people; dependent upon or reactive to the opinions of others.
2. Difficulty keeping emotions in balance; denial of feelings or outbursts that are out of proportion to external events.
3. Poorly defined boundaries between self and others; feeling responsible for others or blaming others; inability to see self clearly in relation to others; need for intense

closeness to combat loneliness or need for much distance to relieve fear of fusion with another.

4. Definition of principles and values based on emotional reactions or family prejudices rather than well-thought-out personal identity. (Bowen, 1978)

Relational Patterns and Differentiation

Bowen (1978) suggested that we tend to form relationships with, and marry, persons at our same or a similar level of differentiation. There is a connection between the concepts of differentiation and codependency. As defined by Beattie (1987), "A codependent person is one who has let another person's behavior affect him or her, and who is obsessed with controlling that person's behavior" (p. 31).

In codependent relationships, both partners fit into the low level of differentiation. Highly reactive emotional forces control the relationship. Partners describe feeling tied to the relationship even when it causes them pain. Physical or emotional symptoms in one member of the couple develop when the level of stress is too high for the relationship to manage with the low level of personal differentiation.

Aside from personal relationships, degree of differentiation often impacts effectiveness in work or organizational settings (Weinberg & Mauksch, 1991). The ability to maintain appropriate task focus, to adopt suitable organizational roles with peers, superiors, and subordinates, and to sustain productivity may be closely related to level of differentiation.

Applications

For school professionals, the concept of differentiation may be meaningful in terms of evaluating both student behavior and organizational dynamics within the school. In the earlier grades, students who exhibit clingy behavior, excessive dependence on teacher direction, and less well-developed peer relationships would likely come from families in which the level of differentiation is low. In adolescence, low levels of family differentiation may be expressed by intolerance for others, personally loaded rebellious behavior (such as name calling), and limited acceptance of changes in schedule, routine, or expectations. Chemical dependency, teenage pregnancy, and the rigid thinking often observed in adolescents may represent social issues that are related to low levels of family differentiation.

The tendency toward lower levels of differentiation is particularly common in families with a child with special needs. Chronic stress and chronic anxiety strain even a healthy family's adaptive capabilities. When coping with the functional and emotional needs of a child with a disability, personal emotional issues may take control over reasoning and thought. Thus, even when correct information is being given to the parents of a child with special needs, their capacity to use the information to effectively change their behavior may be limited by their anxiety and low levels of differentiation of self.

In schools, colleagues and administrators who exhibit a flexible approach to management of students, instructional methods, and system policy most likely represent higher levels of personal differentiation. These educators are able to understand and relate to a variety of perspectives, to consider multiple factors in decision making, and to engage in healthy and productive collaboration.

Assessment of Differentiation

The degree of differentiation in a system may be assessed by testing the emotional reactivity. To try this out you might find it interesting to take some stands, about what you believe or who you are, that are different from others in the system, and observe the response. If others respond with their own "I" positions, differentiation is high. If they try to engage you in arguments, differentiation is presumably lower.

In family interviews, level of differentiation may be assessed by how well each person expresses a feeling or thought without eliciting emotional reactivity from other family members. Can one person cry or express anger and be comforted or confronted by the rest of the family without everyone else dissolving into tears or displaying explosive temper? In the special needs family, can family members show empathy and understanding for the child with a disability without feeling as if the family were disabled?

A convenient personal assessment of level of differentiation can be based on the degree to which returning to one's parent's home elicits feelings that were familiar and uncomfortable during childhood and adolescence. An indication of your personal level of differentiation can be found in how quickly you revert to feeling like a child rather than an adult in your family or to old patterns of relating with family members.

Differentiation represents the core construct in the Bowen (1978) model. It is a process that extends throughout the life span in which the individual moves from the total dependence of infancy toward increasing independence and self-integration. To a great extent, differentiation represented, for Bowen, the struggle for emotional development in the face of the forces of family history. As such, it represents a major determinant of quality of life in relationships. While differentiation is a concept specific to the Bowen model, it integrates well with other major lines of thought in family systems theory.

EMOTIONAL TRANSMISSION

Just as members of each family tend to have similar levels of differentiation, each family also has its own set of issues that bring intense emotional reactions. For some families, tension focuses around sex role issues with rules about what women *should* do or how men *should* behave. For others the issues of religion, having children, or achievement are deeply rooted in family myths and values. As discussed in chapter 2, family myth and secrets are often attached to a particular stage of the family life cycle. The passing of these issues and ways of relating over generations of family life are known as *emotional transmission*.

Transmission of Family Issues

The process of emotional transmission of particular family issues can be seen in how students react to peers from different cultures or backgrounds. Satir and Baldwin (1983) described families as being either open or closed in structure. Open family systems allow for change depending upon the family's life-cycle stage as well as emotional and relational context. People from open family systems learn values and morals without extreme prejudices or judgments about others. Acceptance of self and others is the theme transmitted through the life of families characterized as open. The process of unconscious and unresolved emotional transmission is low in these families.

In contrast, closed family systems are distinguished by their level of rigidity and negativity. These families are based on control, dominance, and conformity. Children in closed families develop with low levels of self-esteem that are indicated by their judgmental attitude toward others. Prejudicial values are transmitted in closed systems across many generations. Emotional transmission of unresolved issues, family secrets, and inappropriate myths is greater in closed families.

Assessment

To discover which prejudices and family issues have been emotionally transmitted, the following questions may be asked: What topics did your parents never talk about? What can't your children (or students) talk to you about? What things about your life would surprise or shock your parents [colleagues]? Think of a statement that is guaranteed to induce guilt or shame in you. Where did this statement originate?

In terms of the classroom, values clarification exercises will often uncover issues or prejudices that have been emotionally transmitted in your students. A simple exercise such as the following may help identify family issues.

> How would you complete the following sentences? Women are.... Men are.... A wife is.... A husband is.... A mother is.... A father is.... How would your parents complete these sentences? How are the two sets of answers different?

Often the experience of being asked to identify and discuss one's own values will help break the cycle of transmission. For further description and examples of values clarification exercises, see the text by Simon, Howe, and Kirschenbaum (1978).

Family Patterns of Emotional Transmission

Emotional transmission is also responsible for patterns of family relating over generations. Bowen classified family relational patterns as being either cohesive or explosive in nature (Guerin, 1976).

Cohesive Families

Cohesive family systems have extended families that usually cluster together in a somewhat limited geographic area. Frequent telephone calling, visiting, and shared communication will occur in these families. Nuclear and extended family members will be taken into account in making various family decisions such as where the family will live, take vacations, and attend church or school.

At the extreme, cohesive families can be highly intrusive systems that do not allow for personal differentiation or privacy. Dysfunctional cohesive families parallel the enmeshed family pattern described in chapter 2. Typically, in these families, there is extensive leakage or emotional transmission of anxiety from the extended family into the nuclear family.

Explosive Families

Explosive family systems are characterized by extensive fragmentation (Guerin, 1976). The family roots are in one geographic location, and in fewer than two generations the extended family is scattered over a wide area. In this type of family system there are often very few ongoing relationships between members. The nuclear family is on its own, without much support from the extended family. Family contacts tend to be ritualized and predictable, such as holidays or family reunions. In this type of family system, members do not generally share their everyday lives with one another or really know each other at an intimate level.

For the special needs family, this type of multigenerational pattern may leave them without extended family resources for helping with the functional and emotional demands of a child with a disability. Therefore, the stress experienced by the nuclear family may be increased. For families that are historically explosive in nature, the provision for use of outside support services is especially important to the family's well-being.

At its most severe level, the extended family becomes fragmented in response to a dramatic family event that leaves members "not speaking to" one another over many years or even generations. This type of avoidance is known as an *emotional cut-off*. Explosive families that are dysfunctional parallel disengaged families, as seen in the structural model described in chapter 3 and Appendix A.

Although the level of contact in highly explosive families is minimal, the level of differentiation is extremely low. A couple who has moved to another area to take the "geographic cure" from their family may be as poorly differentiated as a couple who lives next door to their in-laws and sees them every day. In both cases, if the decisions about living arrangements are made in reaction to issues stemming from the family of origin, the level of emotional reactivity to the nuclear family is the same. The emotional transmission of family anxiety results in the couple's living decisions being made to reduce that anxiety. In one case, anxiety is relieved by closeness; in the other, by avoidance.

Friedman (1986) discussed how emotional transmission can be important through multiple generations, giving this example:

> ....individuals who have been catapulted out of their families to achieve.... The "standard bearer" usually is the oldest male, or the only one to carry on that last name, or anyone, male or female, who has replaced a significant progenitor two or even three generations back. Such individuals have great difficulty giving emotion or time to their marriage or their children.... Success has the compelling drive of ghosts behind it. They have too much to do in the short span of a lifetime. In addition, failure is more significant, since it is not only themselves or even their own generation that they will have failed. (p. 23)

The process of emotional transmission can be seen in the behavior of many different types of students. Often overachievers are students who feel compelled to make up for some failure or unhappiness in their parents' lives or for the disability of another sibling (Seligman, 1983). They may be pushed by the expectations of their parents or grandparents beyond their level of ability. The aggressive student may come from a physically abusive or aggressive family. Parents who abuse their children or one another are likely to have grown up in an abusive environment themselves (Meier & Sloan, 1984). Depression is also a symptom that is often transmitted through many generations of family life. Severe depression, unexpressed anger that is turned inward, is usually born of a context where the expression of anger is not tolerated. In these families if someone becomes angry, he or she may believe that a crisis will ensue or that someone will be extremely hurt by the anger. This pattern of fear around anger typically has many generations of unexpressed and unresolved feelings behind it.

Realization of the forces of emotional transmission may help the school professional to remain nonjudgmental about certain prejudices, values, or ways of relating that are evidenced by students and their families. When these issues are seen as multigenerational in origin rather than personal, more objectivity and easier problem resolution is possible.

BIRTH ORDER

One of the factors that is often considered when looking at historical patterns in families is sibling position. Much of the literature regarding siblings has focused on the actual temporal order in which siblings are born. Theories of personality related to ordinal sibling position were developed by Freud and Adler in the early 1900s. Since the 1970s, the trend has been to focus on psychological position of the sibling, or *birth order*. This term includes the consideration of additional variables, including family crises, death of a sibling, sibling spacing, family size, and sex of siblings, in the definition of sibling status.

Personality Factors

On the basis of observations, Adler (1959) characterized firstborn siblings as dependable, conforming, and believing in rule and responsibility. He also hypothesized that firstborns, as adults, tend to have a feeling of natural power. Later borns, according to Adler, tend to be more active, aggressive, and nonconforming. Youngest children were described as having a tendency toward dependency and passivity.

Dethronement

Adler (1959) developed a number of different theoretical constructs to explain the process of sibling identification. The first is the concept of dethronement, which is a process affecting firstborns following the birth of a sibling (Schvaneveldt & Ihinger, 1979). The process is one in which the child, who has been the sole recipient of parental caretaking in the past, must lose a certain status within the family and feels rejection. This feeling explains the firstborn's need to conform and excel in an effort to regain the throne or the family status.

Enthronement

Another construct that has been derived from Adlerian theory is that of enthronement (Shulman & Mosak, 1977), which is used to describe the relationships of youngest children in the family. Enthronement is the process whereby parental forces operate to savor the final child and tend to be somewhat smothering. Youngest children are never forced to experience dethronement nor do they need to be competitive in order to gain a special family role. However, they may depend upon the power of the baby role to provide their major sense of identification and esteem, resulting in a passive and dependent personality.

Deidentification

The final construct derived from Adler is that of deidentification (Niels, 1980), which is primarily used to describe the personality development of later-born children. This premise is that later borns observe areas where their older siblings are proficient and avoid competing in these areas. They choose areas of interest that are, typically, nonconforming and different from those of their older siblings.

Birth Order and Relationships

Building on the initial work of Adler, Toman (1976) developed a theoretical framework for the impact of siblings that takes into account birth order as well as the gender of siblings. Toman maintained that siblings are important in the identification process through which children acquire a basic social/sexual sense of themselves and resulting patterns of relating to others. Based on clinical observations, Toman predicted relational patterns with same and opposite gender friends as well as choice of marriage partners and potential for marital success in terms of birth order and gender of siblings.

Duplication Theorem

Toman (1976) proposed the duplication theorem, in which "other things being equal, new social relationships are more enduring and successful, the more they resemble the earlier and earliest (intrafamilial) social relationships of the persons involved" (p. 80). According to this theorem, marital relationships are easiest when a partner is chosen whose sibling constellation pattern is complementary rather than conflicting with one's own in terms of sibling rank and gender.

For example, when an oldest brother of sisters marries a youngest sister of brothers the relationship is complementary. When an oldest brother of brothers marries an oldest sister of sisters, the relationship is conflicting in terms of sibling constellation. In conflicting relationships, the same sibling roles are held by both partners. Thus, they compete with one another rather than having personalities that complement one another or work together.

Other Sibling Factors

Within the concept of birth order, predictions about sibling personality must take into account other aspects of the family constellation as well as ordinal sibling position. Large families may have several sibling subgroups in which, depending upon the ages and spacing between children, there may be several children who function as oldest or only children. For example, in a two-child family in which there is at least a seven-year age difference between siblings, they will both be, functionally, only children.

The psychological effects of sibling status may also be mediated by age spacing between siblings. Peterson and Kunz (1975) surveyed 2200 boys and found that younger siblings were perceived most positively by their older brothers when spacing between them was either less than twelve months or greater than four years.

The gender of sibling groups must also be taken into account in the concept of birth order. Female-dominated sibling groups tend to be oriented around language, accommodation, caretaking, and prosocial interactions (Abramovitch, Corter, & Lando, 1979; Brody & Stoneman, 1983). Male-dominated sibling groups are more physically active and challenging in nature (Abramovitch et al., 1979; Cicirelli, 1972; Johnson, 1982).

Finally, the presence of a sibling with a disability may change the expected birth-order effects in sibling groups. As discussed in chapter 3, Daniels-Mohring (1986) found that emotionally disturbed oldest siblings tend to lose some of their power and position in the expected sibling hierarchy. In families where the sibling with the disability is the oldest, a younger sibling may behave as the functional eldest child. No matter what the actual sibling position of the child with the disability, other siblings may be required to accept responsibility beyond their years if the physical or emotional demands of the child with special needs are extensive.

Breslau (1982) compared 237 siblings of children with congenital disabilities with 248 siblings from a random sample of families. She found that, for males, younger siblings of children with disabilities scored higher on psychological impairment than older siblings. This effect was particularly pronounced for those siblings who were fewer than two years younger than the child with the disability. For females, the effect was opposite, with older siblings evidencing more impairment than younger ones. Breslau concluded that, for girls, the role of oldest female tends to bring with it an increased sense of responsibility for the child with the disability that may bring on depressive/anxious feelings that are more intense than the general stress experienced by other siblings in the family. For males, the impact of being born into a family with an infant having a disability preceding them by less than two years tends to make them at risk for psychological impairment later on in life.

Bowen Theory

The Bowen perspective on sibling position functions as a bridge between the birth-order literature and the conceptualization of the family as an active system. Bowen (1985) proposed that the knowledge of birth order gave one a sense of some guidelines within which to predict a family role assignment. Bowen's therapeutic framework examined the sibling position of people in past and present generations in an attempt to discover family patterns that may have arisen from the particular emotional value associated with one sibling position. For example, if three generations of women are all oldest daughters, family expectations and roles will be passed on about how an oldest daughter should operate. The family pattern might be that oldest daughters take care of their parents and don't marry or leave home until they are well into adulthood. This pattern sets up a family script that may be acted out generation after generation outside of the conscious awareness of family members. The third or fourth generation oldest daughter may have to struggle with her own needs, her present social culture, and the unconscious demands of her family pattern. If she breaks out of the script and marries young or moves away from her parents to pursue a career, she may feel unexplained anxiety that stems from abandoning this standard.

Certain patterns of personality tend to go along with particular sibling positions. In addition to ordinal sibling position, family size, spacing between siblings, and gender of siblings must all be taken into account when attempting to discover the significance of sibling factors in the life of the student. With this information, the school professional may be better able to understand students' personalities and interactions with peers.

TRIANGULATION

According to Bowen (1978), any two-person emotional system is inherently unstable. When two people become anxious about negotiating closeness and distance in their relationship, the anxiety is most easily resolved by bringing in a third person. This results in a lowering of anxiety between the twosome and thus creates an emotional triangle. Individuals who have higher levels of differentiation of self are more able to observe and control the patterns of relating within a triangle. Individuals with lower levels of differentiation of self tend to be reactive to tensions within the triangle. For further discussion of this concept, see Appendix A.

Triangles

The most stable relational systems are composed of three-person emotional configurations called *triangles*. Triangles are the building blocks of all systems, including families, work systems, and peer groups. Any emotional system is made up of a series of interlocking triangles.

For example, in Figure 4.1 the student is involved in three different but overlapping triangles that existed when he was reprimanded for stealing lunch money from a peer. The peer reported the stealing to their teacher, who relayed the information to the student's mother. That evening, the student's mother and father considered the problem and decided about consequences for their son. In Figure 4.1, triangle 1 involves the student, his teacher, and the peer. Triangle 2 includes both parents and the student. The third triangle consists of the student, the teacher, and the mother.

The process called *triangulation* is the pattern of emotional reactions that go on within a particular triangle. Triangulation is fueled by emotional reactivity within the system. The process of triangulation can stabilize anxiety and conflict between two people by the following forces:

> The twosome works to preserve the togetherness, lest one become uncomfortable and form a better togetherness elsewhere. The outsider seeks to form a togetherness with one of the twosome.... The emotional forces within the triangle are constantly in motion from moment to moment. (Bowen, 1976, p. 76)

In dysfunctional families, when emotional forces become highly anxiety-producing, patterns of relationships begin to repeat themselves and people eventually have fixed roles in relation to one another.

Parent and Child

In the case of a child or adolescent, the typical triangulation process occurs between two parents and one child. Satir (Satir & Baldwin, 1983) called this relationship the *primary triad*. She believed that this triad is the primary determinant of the child's identity, self-esteem, and relational patterns. When there is marital discord in a family, the parent who is feeling most alienated may turn to the child for a feeling of emotional closeness. This child may be favored for involvement with parents in a triangle based on the processes of family emotional transmission. For example, the child's place in a particular sibling position may be emotionally important, or his or her personality may remind the parents of themselves or one of their siblings, triggering identification issues (Arnstein, 1979; Smith, 1978). It is difficult to differentiate a self and develop a fluid sense of self when engaged in a triangled relationship across generational boundaries. Under periods of anxiety or family stress, the lack of differentiation is typically expressed by the appearance of behavioral or psychiatric symptoms in the most vulnerable member of the triangle, the child. The child who is triangulated is at risk for physical, emotional, or academic problems.

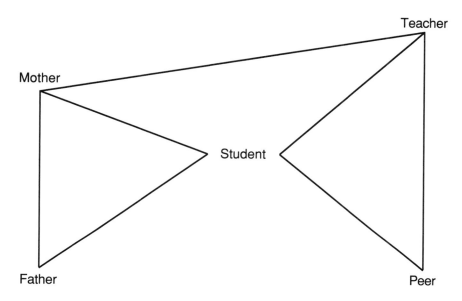

Figure 4.1
RELATIONSHIPS DEFINED BY THREE OVERLAPPING TRIANGLES

Remarriage

Another example of one type of triangulation is found in second marriages where the couple initially connects by comparing the break-ups of their former marriages and the abusiveness of their ex-spouses. The ability to focus on their former relationships may be the third leg of the triangle that keeps an optimum level of distance in the marital relationship. Chapter 6, on special populations, addresses the issues of stepfamilies in depth.

Families and Agencies

What may occur in times of family distress is that the family system triangulates with an outside force such as the school, social agencies, court system, or mental health system. If the emotional tension can then be blamed on that outside agency, the family may unite together to remain calm.

An example of this process often occurs when school personnel are faced with evidence of family abuse. Unless steps are taken to avoid triangulation, as soon as the school confronts the family about the abuse or as soon as social services is contacted, the school professional or social worker may become the "bad guy" who is attempting to destroy an otherwise ostensibly happy family. The family then bonds together and the outside agency serves the role of the third, distant leg of the triangle. To avoid being cast in this position, school professionals need to maintain their neutrality with these families and focus on keeping open communication among all parties involved in the allegations.

In addition, triangles may overlap, causing problems in one system, such as the family, to create problems in another system, such as the school (Friedman, 1986). When dealing with a highly distressed family, if the school personnel suddenly find themselves arguing among the team or feeling high levels of anxiety, overlapping triangles may be in operation.

In the example of the student caught for stealing (see Figure 4.1), three triangles were operating. If communication between parties is clear, if levels of differentiation are adequate, and if there are no unresolved or underlying issues between members of the triangles, the resolution of this problem may go smoothly. However, if the stealing issue becomes overshadowed by unresolved anxieties between people involved in the triangles, the forces of triangulation are operating and the stealing may be exacerbated rather than handled effectively. For example, if the mother believes that the teacher does not adequately manage her classroom, she may not discipline her son for his behavior. If the father believes that his son is a "mamma's boy" and is angry at his wife for giving in to their son, he may explode at the boy or at his wife and reenact his wife's relationship with her abusive father rather than negotiating appropriate discipline. In each of these scenarios, the process of triangulation is in operation.

Detriangulation

The next question becomes how to avoid triangulation. The first step to disentangling oneself from a triangle is to know that the triangle exists. Second, it is important to stay out of the position of taking sides in a conflicting situation. Third, the educator should not talk to a person about a third person and should not listen when someone tries to discuss a third person. For example, if a student comes to you to complain about a teacher, a response that promotes detriangulation is, "I'm sorry you feel that way, but I think things will have a chance to get better only if you talk to that teacher. I'd be glad to help you set up a meeting with him."

Triangulation can also occur between colleagues in a system. If you notice that a co-worker tends to talk to you about other people, the easiest way out of the triangle is to ask that person something about him- or herself or to volunteer something about yourself or your values. These statements are geared toward increasing the connection between you and the colleague, thus decreasing the need for triangulation to manage the anxiety between the two of you. For further discussion of how the school professional can stay out of triangles, see chapter 10 of this text.

Triangles or triadic relationships are not dysfunctional in themselves. In fact, they are the basic building blocks of any system. When the intensity between two people becomes uncomfortable, bringing in a third person will diffuse the tension and allow the system to operate with less anxiety. It is only when the anxiety level within a two-person system cannot be managed that the process of triangulation comes into operation. In this process, relationships are indirect and issues are not resolved openly. The forces of constantly changing alliances keep the tension in the system alive.

GENOGRAMS

A technique used for mapping family history on a chart something like a family tree is called a *family genogram.* The genogram can help the professional and the family view symptoms within a much larger context. A social history typically involves many pages of written material without any standardized format. To use the information presented in a social history, school professionals must read the material, organize it in their minds, and assimilate it into their experience of the family. In contrast, the genogram organizes up to three generations of family data in a one-page visual representation. It can help school professionals identify multigenerational patterns, family roles, sibling position, important triangles, or the time line of significant family events in a brief scan.

In diagramming a family, certain symbols are used. Squares represent males and circles represent females. As much as possible, fathers are drawn on the left side and mothers on the right. Siblings are drawn oldest to youngest from left to right. Marriages and generations are connected by a series of horizontal and vertical lines. For example, the genogram for a two-parent family with two children, a son age 15 and a daughter age 11, appears in Figure 4.2. Other commonly used symbols are shown in Figure 4.3.

The genogram shown in Figure 4.4 was drawn in 1989. It portrays this information: John, age 45, and Elizabeth, age 42, were married for fifteen years and had two children, John, Jr., age 13, and Marsha, age 10. In 1987, the couple was separated and subsequently divorced. John remarried immediately and is now expecting a child with his second wife, Selina, age 30. This is Selina's first marriage.

John's parents are both deceased. They died within two years of one another, during the period from 1984 to 1986. John's father died of a heart attack and his mother died of "loneliness." They were ages 75 and 70, respectively, when they died. John is the youngest of three children and the only boy. His two older sisters are 48 and 50 years old. They are both married and have children. Elizabeth's parents are both still living. Her father is 64 years old and her mother is 62 years old. Elizabeth has a younger sister, age 40, who has been divorced since 1982 but has been involved in a relationship for the past five years. She has no children.

As indicated in this example, much information can be communicated quickly by using genograms. For the school professional, a good way to begin practicing this technique

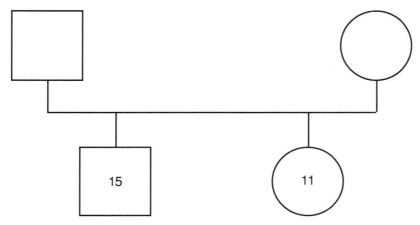

Figure 4.2
A GENOGRAM FOR A NUCLEAR FAMILY

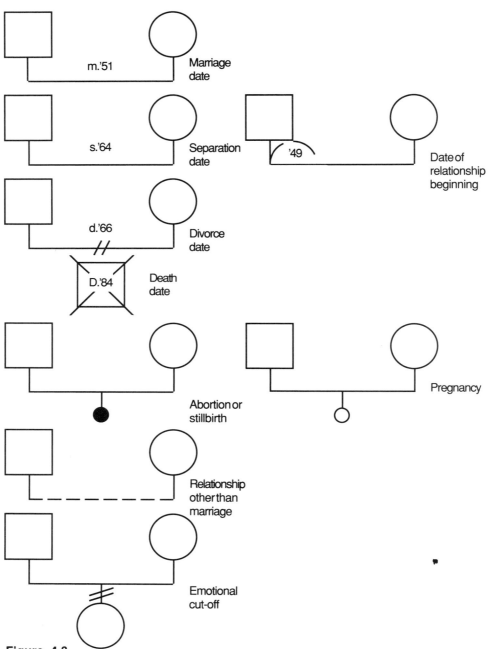

Figure 4.3
COMMONLY USED SYMBOLS IN GENOGRAMS

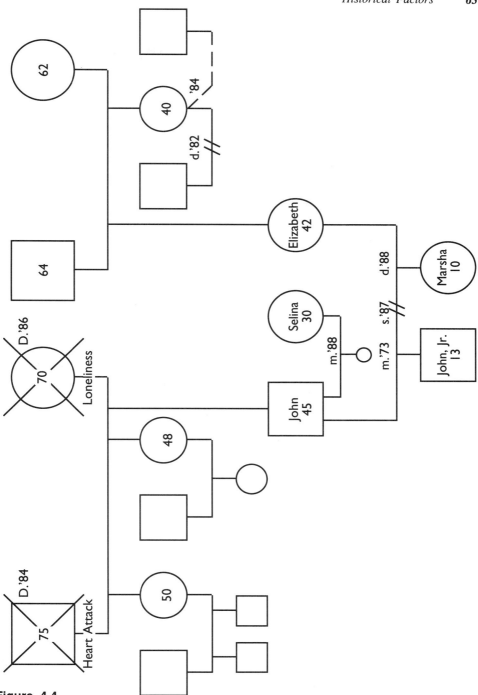

Figure 4.4
GENOGRAM FOR JOHN AND ELIZABETH AND THEIR FAMILIES

is to draw your own family genogram. As the logistics of establishing the basic family history become easier, the genogram can then be used to indicate major triangles, family roles, areas of significant conflict, emotional cut-offs, multigenerational patterns, and family nodal events. For the reader who is interested in a more in-depth study of the use of genograms see Bradt (1980) or McGoldrick and Gerson (1985).

SUMMARY

This chapter provided information from the Bowen (1978) theory concerning how historical factors may affect family and organizational dynamics. The assessment of levels of differentiation was discussed so that school professionals can look at their own interactions as well as individual levels of differentiation within the families of their students. The personality effects of sibling position and the powerful family role definitions that are assigned as a result of this factor were delineated. Finally, the forces of triangulation within the family system, within the school system, and across systems were addressed.

The following case example uses a complex genogram that covers three generations. It identifies some of the historical patterns that have been discussed in this chapter.

CASE EXAMPLE

Megan, a 17-year-old high school senior, comes from a family consisting of her parents, who are both 34 years old, and her two younger brothers, Allen, 12 years old, and Mark, 10 years old. Her parents have been married for seventeen years. Her father is employed as a salesman, and her mother is a secretary.

Although Megan had always been an adequate student, in her senior year her grades began to drop and she had frequent absences. When the school counselor met with Megan to discuss these problems, Megan burst into tears and could not return to her classes for the remainder of the day. On more than one occasion, Megan had begun to cry during classes and asked to see her counselor. Most recently, Megan revealed that she and Chuck, her boyfriend of four years, were considering breaking up. She reported that Chuck had been spending more and more time with his friends and had told her that he needed his "space." Megan felt that she couldn't stand this rejection and needed to end the relationship with Chuck. Megan also reported feeling that her parents were putting excessive pressure on her about applying to colleges. She was too upset about her problems with Chuck to fill out her applications. With questioning, Megan admitted that she was fearful about rejection from college. She was not sure that her high school record was adequate in spite of her good grades.

In trying to establish a historical framework for Megan's attitudes, the counselor asked her about her parents' adolescence. The following information was revealed.

Megan's mother, Anne, is the youngest of two girls, with a sister two years older. When Anne was 4 years old, her parents were divorced and her father married a much younger woman. He subsequently had three more children and did not keep in contact with Anne, her sister, or his ex-wife. Megan's grandmother was remarried five years later to an alcoholic. When Anne was 17 years old, she became pregnant with Megan. When she talked to her parents about her pregnancy, they told her to leave the house and never return. She then moved in with her boyfriend's (Megan's father's) family and got married.

Megan's father, Albert Jr., is the oldest of four children, all boys. His younger brothers are three, five, and seven years younger than he. Albert's father is an attorney and his mother is a housewife. They have been married to one another for forty years. Albert was always an A student and a football star. His family had planned for him to attend college and become an attorney like his father, his namesake. When his high-school girlfriend became pregnant, his parents demanded that Albert "do the right thing" and marry her. They let him know that they were disappointed by him. Albert was forced to go to work after graduation and never returned to pursue his college degree.

Questions and Comments

1. *How would you draw the genogram of this family? Assume that it is 1990. (The reader might want to draw the genogram before looking at Figure 4.5.)*

2. *Using factors from the family history and genogram, how can Megan's behaviors be explained in an historical context?*

    Megan's dependence upon her boyfriend is the result of low levels of differentiation and emotional transmission of the shame related to her mother's pregnancy out of wedlock. Megan is at risk for becoming pregnant herself as part of the family "script" concerning achievement and failure.

    There is a primary triangle between Megan and her parents in which Megan's future is scripted to atone for her parents' failures. Megan has triangulated in Chuck to defuse the anxiety between her and her parents. By focusing on her relationship with Chuck, she avoids dealing with the anxiety about college and possible failure.

3. *What interventions might be used in this case to help detriangulate Megan?*

    The counselor helped Megan identify the process of triangulation in her family. She gave Megan information about colleges that were appropriate for her achievement level and assured Megan that her record was adequate for acceptance.

    During a meeting between Megan, her counselor, and her parents to discuss Megan's crying spells, Megan was helped to bring up the issue of her parents' pressure on her. The family history of Megan's birth and the emotional cut-offs in her parents' families of origin were discussed. Megan was then liberated from the forces of unresolved loss in her parents' history and could be helped to develop her own level of differentiation and self-esteem.

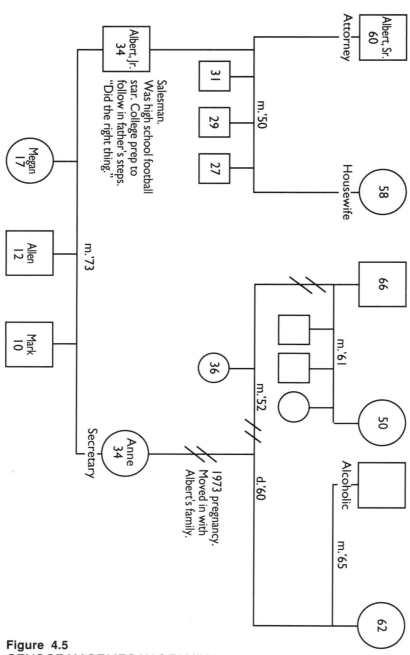

Figure 4.5
GENOGRAM OF MEGAN'S FAMILY

ENVIRONMENTAL FACTORS 5

This chapter initially describes the impact of socioeconomic and cultural factors on the family. It then examines how these factors may influence students' behavior within the classroom. Third, we suggest some ways in which school professionals can take environmental factors and children at risk into account when planning intervention strategies for dealing with students' problems. Finally, the chapter concludes with a case example illustrating the integration of environmental factors into an approach used with a student of Hispanic and Native American backgrounds.

INTRODUCTION

By discussing differing cultural influences we hope to enhance professionals' sensitivity to each family as opposed to perpetuating stereotypes about families in a particular cultural category. Regardless of cultural background, families have more similarities than differences. They struggle with similar issues and demands throughout the life cycle and strive toward the same ends.

Cultural history influences how families cope, express themselves, and interact with external systems. It is helpful if school professionals can ask themselves, "Within this person's experience, is this behavior adaptive, normal, or pathological?" For example, an African-American, Hispanic, or Asian-American child who is being disciplined is expected to indicate acceptance by lowering the eyes. Making eye contact may be interpreted by a parent from these backgrounds as defiance. In contrast, children from white Anglo-Saxon backgrounds are expected to maintain eye contact to indicate attentiveness when being disciplined. The Anglo child who lowers the eyes may be thought of as passively resistant.

A case example told by one of our colleagues may better illustrate this point:

In the 1960s, a consultant was called into a Southern public school to help with the process of integrating a predominantly white and a predominantly black school into one building. He was informed by the teachers that the black students were "unmotivated and slow." He observed students in the school for a few days and found the primary complaint of the teachers to be that the black students "hung out" in the halls between classes and did not respond to the bell signaling the beginning of the next class. The teachers felt forced to walk out into the halls and "round up" the black students. Upon further study, the consultant found that, in the predominantly black school, the time between classes had been ten minutes. In the predominantly white school, the time had been five minutes. In the new integrated school, the bell between classes rang after five minutes. When the consultant shared this information with the faculty, they were able to see the problem as one of scheduling rather than one of racial characteristics. (Personal communication, C. Mohring, 1991)

From this example, it should be clear that a meeting of the minds between family members and school professionals about the definitions of problematic behavior is essential. This type of understanding can often be facilitated when educators have knowledge of the family's history and socioeconomic and cultural patterns. The purpose of this chapter is to help school professionals understand and respond appropriately to these influences.

SOCIOECONOMIC DIFFERENCES

The most powerful cultural determinant of how families interact with society in general is socioeconomic status. This is particularly true in comparing middle-income families to those coping with poverty. Many of the most common ethnic stereotypes actually derive more from the environmental influences of socioeconomic status than from ethnic background. For example, a middle-class black family has a lifestyle more similar to that of a middle-class white family than to a poor black family, regardless of the African heritage in common. As Wilson (1982), a sociologist, argued, "Class has...become more important than race in determining black life chances in the modern industrial period" (p. 389).

Family Systems Factors

One of the first issues met by professionals working with low-income families is facing the realities of how a poor environment affects the normal workings of family life. Aponte (1976a), who worked with poor families from inner-city Philadelphia, found that the structure (see chapter 3) of these families was loose and undefined. He used the term *chaotic* to describe the lack of clear leadership, poorly defined boundaries, and unstable structure that he found when trying to help poor inner-city families. He wrote of his perceptions of the relationship between professional and family, "The socioeconomic difference creates a communication gap that complicates the task of mutual understanding" (p. 432).

As Aponte (1976a) stated, socioeconomic factors affect the most basic development of the family and its communication with the world. To be socioeconomically disadvantaged represents an extreme stressor on the integrity of the family system. The adjustment of students to the school environment is tied to the well-being of the family and when family stability is threatened by poverty, as with other stressors, students will suffer. These children are obviously at risk, and, if a child with special needs is included in the family, the stress is even further multiplied.

Parent Factors

The stresses of financial instability influence parents' self-esteem and mood as well as how they feel about themselves as providers for and protectors of their children. How much stress the parents feel will influence their involvement with and availability to their children, their disciplining style, and the value system that they teach their children.

Numerous studies have shown that low-income mothers have the highest rate of depression of any demographic group (Eheart & Ciccone, 1982). Also, in low-income families, there is often no consistent, positive father figure but rather a male "floater" (Fischgrund, Cohen, & Clarkson, 1987) or a father living in the home who is chronically out of work. If there is an unemployed father at home, he is often tyrannical in his authority and discipline. As Montalvo and Guitierrez (1983) wrote, "The more the man fails against competitive barriers of the American society, the more uncompromising and absolute his power must be at home" (p. 29).

A child growing up in a home with an extremely depressed parent or a parent who is experiencing role loss due to joblessness will bring the effects of these concerns with him or her to the classroom. A case example of a child who was at risk illustrates this process.

> A seven-year-old who had been doing well in his first year of school suddenly began to be distracted in the classroom. He was not listening to the teacher's directions and had received numerous negative consequences over a three-week period. After three weeks, when the teacher called home, she discovered that the father had been laid off from his job one month before. When asked, the boy volunteered that his father's job loss was a principal source of anxiety for him. He stated that he worried all the time about his family and money problems. The teacher began to make her school contacts directly with the father, who was now at home. She told the father of his son's concerns and asked that he provide some reassurance for the boy. She met with the father to devise a plan for getting his son's behavior back on track and for reinforcing the boy when he began to pay attention again.

With this plan, the teacher was able to give the father a new identity as a powerful figure for his son, regardless of his temporary joblessness. As demonstrated by this example, the influence of parental roles in the home will often influence what interventions will work with a particular student in the classroom and in the home environment.

It is also important that the school professional take into account parental needs and demands when planning family contacts. In looking at parental needs, Eheart and Ciccone (1982) studied 36 low-income mothers whose children were diagnosed with developmental delays. The authors found that the biggest problem reported by these mothers was the stress of meeting basic needs of their children such as feeding, cleanliness, and safety. What the mothers' wanted most in terms of services was a support group where they could talk to other mothers with children having similar problems.

If we look at Maslow's (1970) hierarchy of needs, he proposed that love and belonging as well as self-care needs cannot be addressed before basic physiological and safety needs are met. Within this context, talking to an impoverished mother about unconditional positive regard of her child or even about a home behavioral program may be useless when she is trying to make sure she has electricity in the home. The mother may feel that someone who will listen to her feelings and struggles is more useful than someone who will try to tell her how to handle her child differently. It is only after the mother feels heard and supported that she will respect suggestions about her disciplining.

One of our colleagues told us about a situation he addressed while directing a special education program.

A 14-year-old boy was placed in a special education program because of his diagnosis as a slow learner and his aggressive, out-of-control behavior. He had been in the new setting for two months and had failed to respond to various attempts to engage him in classroom tasks and social and recreational activities. His academic skills had not improved and he was rejected by his peers. After some observation, the director discovered that one of the basic problems with this adolescent was his lack of physical cleanliness. He often came to school in dirty clothes and smelling badly, which led to taunting by peers and aggressiveness or withdrawal on his part. Once he had withdrawn into himself, no amount of teacher intervention could seem to engage him in the classroom. If pushed too far, he would explode and become verbally or physically abusive. The director talked to the boy and found that he was aware of his body odor. He had no running water at home and was able to take a bath only about once a week. Now that he had reached adolescence, weekly bathing was grossly inadequate. At an age when he was increasingly sensitive to peer group social interactions, especially with the opposite sex, his awareness of his lack of academic achievement and his inadequacies in basic hygiene left him with a profound sense of alienation. The initial intervention with this young man was for the director to ask the parents' permission to arrange for the boy to have access to the gym showers before school each day. He began bathing every morning and the teasing diminished. The boy obviously felt better about himself and began to become involved in the classroom and make substantial progress toward correcting his academic problems. (Personal communication, C. Mohring, 1991)

In this case, the school professional was able to intervene at the level of basic needs, understanding this boy's poverty and the dilemma of cleanliness that it created for him.

Student Factors

Another important area of awareness for school professionals is the world view and self-image of economically disadvantaged students. Most children growing up in a poor environment experience prejudice on a daily basis. Poverty has an impact upon where the family will live because fewer and fewer living options are open when income is low or the family is dependent upon social welfare. All of these factors influence the growth and development of children within the family and how they approach the demands of growing up, including the demands of the educational system.

Socioeconomically disadvantaged children have so many unmet needs from early years that they see little hope of ever changing their lives or fulfilling their dreams. They become frustrated over the lack of opportunities available to them and susceptible to aggression, violence, apathy, and depression (Smith, 1978). In addition, they are at risk for school failure.

Minuchin et al. (1967) studied twelve low-income families of boys between the ages of 8 and 12 who were living in a residential treatment center. These authors compared their observations of the delinquent boys and their families to those of ten matched families with no delinquent children. Minuchin and his colleagues found that the children who became delinquent shared a view of their home environment as impermanent and unpredictable and they had learned to react to the moment rather than to what might be in the future.

Minuchin et al. (1967) also observed that parental responses in the families with delinquent boys were random and unpredictable, so these children could never learn to internalize rules and set limits for themselves. The emphasis in the delinquent families was on control of behavior rather than on guidance. Because the boys had no expectation of predictable rewards for their performance, their motivation was reduced and they did not learn to be proud of themselves for competence or achievements. Instead, these boys learned that gang involvement and hustling were the subsistence and survival strategies that meant competence in their culture (Coates, 1990).

By the time children of poverty reach adolescence, able to think abstractly, they realize that the things they see in the media are not available to them and will not be theirs without years of hard work and lots of luck. The disillusionment that sets in is a source of stress in itself, and quick sources of gratification become even more appealing. Thus, many of these boys were caught stealing or selling drugs as a way of quickly obtaining the money and status that they desired.

Abi-Nader (1991) wrote of her observations of a program entitled PLAN (Program: Learning According to Needs), working with disadvantaged Hispanic students. The PLAN approach is specifically geared to address the feelings of powerlessness that face many of these at-risk youth. The approach includes a mentor program in which Hispanic college students talk to high-school students about their experiences. The program also seeks to provide successful Hispanic role models. Finally, the curriculum includes frequent references to the future in positive terms; for instance, "when you go to college" rather than "if you go to college." The outcome of this program is that 60 to 65% of the PLAN students ultimately attend college.

Conclusions

Systemic factors, parent factors, and student factors all must be considered by the educator when dealing with socioeconomically disadvantaged families. The process of developing a conceptual style, a world view, and a motivational style begins long before these children ever enter the school system. By the time school professionals encounter families who are economically disadvantaged, the factors of frustration, apathy, and depression must be included in any realistic picture of the overall family system. In fact, these factors typically have immediate impact on the nature of the interactions within educational systems, and they do so with the potency of generations of importance. Many school professionals have experienced the suspicion, mistrust, and reticence that seem to be common in the reactions of many poor families to contact with school personnel. Rather than reacting to these attitudes as if they were directed at a particular person, it is important to remember the historical and socioeconomic context that breeds this type of negativity. Parents may be convinced that the common goal is the adjustment of their child or adolescent if the professional maintains personal boundaries (as described in chapter 4) and understands the parents' initial response to school contact.

ETHNIC DIFFERENCES

This section focuses on the complex issue of ethnic differences and attempts to sensitize the reader to the diversity of cultural traditions in our nation. What follows are examples of how different cultural realities apply to working with families in educational contexts. However, reading about cultural issues is inadequate to the task of understanding the richness that tradition brings to a family. Readers must develop personal sensitivities to and methods of exploring these issues with the families they encounter. Only through interaction and exchange with the families themselves can we be educated about our differences and similarities.

Life Strategies

Cultural background affects every person's value system, style of responding to stress, ways of defining self, and approach to life. As an example, we will look at how different cultures respond to emotional problems in their members, based on the overall life strategy of that culture.

Middle-class Americans, particularly those from a British cultural background, tend to be independence-oriented and to develop a concept of self based on one's potential future. When emotional problems are encountered, they want to know how the person can be helped to function as an adult member of society. Much inner turmoil may precede any external expression of discomfort in British/Irish families, where emotional experience is taught to be contained within the individual (McGill & Pearce, 1982).

Japanese-American culture assigns shame to the emotionally distraught individual. Internal conflict is viewed as the lack of centeredness of the individual with society. This view stems from traditional Asian cultures, in which the general emotional strategy is one of role conformity, centeredness, and balancing of life forces within familial and societal roles (Kuo, 1984). Asian-Americans tend to keep mentally disordered members in the home, unless they are acting out, and to underutilize mental health resources (Lin, Inui, Kleinman, & Womack, 1982).

In contrast, the Jewish-American culture tends to attribute emotional problems to external influences. This approach stems from an Eastern European and Middle Eastern life strategy that teaches the sharing of life. In this culture, life is with and from people and problems are solved by sharing them. Individual expression is secondary to family and community.

Coming from this same cultural root, Iranians and Italian-Americans tend to project emotional problems onto outside events or forces such as loss and social or religious prejudice rather than on internal process. For the most part, however, in these two cultures, outsiders are not involved in family business. The family solves its own problems—family loyalty and solidarity are the first priority (Jalali, 1982; Rotunno & McGoldrick, 1982).

In all three of these Eastern European cultures, disgrace to the family is the worst crime. Because of this credo, psychological problems are often ignored, disguised as physical complaints, or contained within the family for long periods of time before any outside intervention is sought. By the time help is pursued, many difficulties have become real physical problems such as ulcers, anorexia, or bulimia.

A final example of differing ethnic approaches to psychological problems comes from the Native American culture. Native Americans acknowledge culture specific syndromes that are born out of a belief in spiritualism, harmony with nature, and reincarnation rather than traditional forms of mental illness. Some of these syndromes include spirit intrusion, in which ghosts of past ancestors return to affect a person's behavior; soul loss, resulting from behavior that is against tribal law; and windigo psychosis, which is an extreme form of psychotic behavior that is connected with the seasons (Kelso & Attneave, 1981). The school professional who deals with Native American families will need to understand these cultural definitions of illness to be able to join with the family in defining a problem.

Cultural Values

At present, minority students are overrepresented in special education programs. Particularly at risk are Hispanic Americans, black Americans, and Asian-Americans, who compose 21% of the overall population but are most noticeably represented among the special education population (Peschley, 1988). Because of language and color barriers, these three groups are the least well-assimilated in our present culture. By virtue of their minority status alone, many families may feel isolated from educational institutions. This sense of isolation puts students at risk for educational and behavioral problems. What follows is a discussion of the general, traditional values of each of these three cultural groups. This discussion is not intended as an exhaustive picture of specific family and community values within these cultures, but rather a broad overview of old-world values that are a part of the legacy of each culture.

Hispanic Americans

This ethnic group includes many different specific cultural groups, such as Cuban-Americans, Mexican-Americans, Salvadoran-Americans, mainland Puerto Ricans, and Latin Americans. We will consider the commonalities of cultural values across groups rather than the specifics of any one Hispanic subgroup.

In general, traditional Hispanic values include components of dependence, the theory of sacrifice, respect, machismo, and virginity (Garcia-Preto, 1982). Family members are viewed as interdependent, and no sacrifice is seen as too great for the family. It is a parent's job to sacrifice and give oneself up for the children. Children, in turn, are to show gratitude by submitting to the family rules. Although mothers conduct the everyday running of the family, including discipline, they are seen as more passive; their job is to teach respect for the father, who is the ultimate decision maker. Boys are to be aggressive and macho in the outside world but, in contrast, are to mind their mothers at home. Girls are viewed, traditionally, as helpless and needing protection (Adkins & Young, 1976).

There are several ways in which these cultural values may be evidenced in the classroom. For one, the Mexican-American population has the highest school dropout rate of any ethnic group in this country (Bennett, 1990). Teachers may see adolescent Hispanic girls who are overprotected and denied privileges that are appropriate in the Anglo culture. In contrast, often when the teacher believes a Hispanic male child needs discipline, the parents may see the behavior as natural and driven by the male's inherent nature to be macho and somewhat out of control from the Anglo point of view. In these instances, an unspoken conflict arises between cultural value systems.

In a study of Puerto Rican families, Montalvo and Guitierrez (1983) found a large number of children entering preschool and experiencing elective mutism. These authors characterized the identified children as coming from families where there was limited interaction with the outside world. Parents spoke Spanish at home and were often shy and fearful of the English-speaking culture. They communicated to the children that the outside world was a frightening place. Often these children entered preschool and early on witnessed some type of teasing, perceived intimidation by an adult, or saw their parents acting intimidated by the school personnel. From that point on, the children, who could speak English, did not speak at school but continued to speak at home. In response, the teachers left the children alone about their mutism. They backed off and gave the children more time to integrate into the English-speaking environment. Montalvo and Guitierrez found it to be more helpful for parents to be empowered to ask the school to make more demands upon their child rather than fewer. When these parents were able to be more assertive with the school, their confidence in other areas increased and positive changes for the child followed.

Special needs. Nazzaro (1981) presented a paradigm for general characteristics of children with disabilities from various ethnic groups. According to this classification, the primary problems encountered with Hispanic children with special needs are the pervasive difficulties in diagnosis posed by bilingualism.

Adkins and Young (1976) wrote of their experiences in an early intervention program for Hispanic children in El Paso, Texas. They found many factors that interfered with these families being able to obtain appropriate help for their children with disabilities. Within this culture they found a mistrust of medical institutions and a fear of medical procedures and testing that kept many children from obtaining adequate diagnosis of their difficulties. Even when the diagnosis was completed, families often turned to religion, folklore, or superstition rather than doctors or educators for advice on how to intervene with their child. Second, there was cultural pressure to take care of one's own family problems, including children who were not functioning normally, and a fear of losing face if a family member were found to have a disability. Finally, there is a cultural tendency toward overindulgence for children who are found to have a disability. These children tend to be treated as dependent and incapable and to have everything done for them. When a professional from outside the culture begins to recommend that families try to teach their child independence or self-help skills, they may face the force of this cultural stereotype.

Black Americans

Like Hispanic cultures, black Americans include a diverse group of people including Caribbean and African cultures and American southern or urban groups. Our description, again, should be taken as global rather than specific to a particular heritage.

By way of understanding the black experience in America, the following statistics may be helpful.

> Only 4 out of every 10 black children live in two-parent families (in contrast to 8 out of 10 white children). Black children are $3\frac{1}{2}$ times more likely to live in female-headed households than white children. Almost 10% of black children are in households supervised by a welfare agency—four times that of white children. Black families earn 60% less overall than white families. Almost half of all black children are poor, compared to 1 out of 6 white children. (Fischgrund et al., 1987, p. 61)

The African principles of human connectedness and interdependence can be seen in present-day black American cultures (Hale-Benson, 1982). Most black families are embedded in a complex kinship and social network. This network may include blood relatives or close friends. The concept of an augmented family, one in which extended family or friends are allowed into the home for various periods of time, is an integral part of the black culture. The humanistic values of cooperation and "we-ness" that are inherent in the augmented family arrangement are extensions of an African cultural base (Delaney, 1979; Hines & Boyd-Franklin, 1982).

Another characteristic of the black culture is role flexibility or adaptability (Hale-Benson, 1982; Mack, 1981). Various people within the family may interchange roles and functions without engendering a sense of instability in the family system. Whoever is at hand is responsible for carrying out the task, so that older children, grandparents, or neighbors may provide child care, discipline, or household tasks at various times. For the school professional, the definition of who is "family" or who is responsible for helping the student with problems may need to be expanded in this cultural context.

A final consideration in the black culture is the importance of childbearing and child rearing as validation. In the history of the black culture in America, family ties were not encouraged. Black men and women were not allowed to legalize their marriages. Procreation was encouraged to increase the labor supply and fertility in a black female was considered an asset. The identity of women was tied to their role as mothers. What resulted was a matriarchal society with multiple nurturing figures (Pinkney, 1975). Child rearing became authoritarian to develop self-sufficiency and toughness in children as they could be taken away from their biological mothers at any time that they became useful. Black women were seen as all-sacrificing and frequently turned to religion to help them deal with the grief of constantly losing their children. It is upon this basis of physical disconnection that the present black American experience was formed. School professionals need to increase their awareness of these multigenerational forces when trying to intervene in the relationships among parents and children in this culture.

An example of how African-American cultural values extend to the school experience may be seen by many school professionals at the high-school level. Counselors and teachers that we have spoken with expressed frustration at the large number of girls they work with who become pregnant early in adolescence and drop out of school in favor of taking on a parenting role. For many of these girls, the self-esteem that they feel in being a mother outweighs the motivation to continue their studies and work to achieve a career identity (Hale-Benson, 1982). Unfortunately, many of our social welfare programs have functioned to reinforce this dynamic. Even when their own mothers are working at professional jobs and are career-oriented, the peer culture often perpetuates the sense that motherhood is the only identity of value. With an understanding of the multigenerational patterns that contribute to a primary maternal identity, schools may be able to help young people develop alternative role models and begin building self-esteem around competency early in the educational process.

Special needs. Two primary issues are identified by Nazzaro (1981) as affecting the diagnosis and treatment of black students with disabilities. First is the tendency of an Anglicized culture to diagnose black youth as conduct-disordered or juvenile delinquents when they have behavioral problems. Nazzaro argued that perceived antisocial behavior, which may be used in a disadvantaged black culture to achieve status, may go unnoticed when working within "the system." Second, black students with learning disabilities are often misdiagnosed as mentally retarded because of test biases and dialectic use of language.

Asian (Pacific)-Americans

This general cultural category includes Chinese, Filipino, Korean, Vietnamese, and Japanese family backgrounds. As reported by Momeni (1984), Asian-Americans have the lowest proportion of households headed by a woman, the lowest rate of divorce, and the lowest childbirth rate of all ethnic groups in the United States.

Major socialization goals for children still reflect traditional values: a sense of collectivity and identification with the family, dependence on the family, obedience, and a sense of responsibility and obligation to the family (Serafica, 1990). These strong ties mean that often at least one grandparent is living in the family home.

Traditional Asian roles identify fathers as educators and disciplinarians while mothers are seen as protective and nurturing. A wife is expected to have complete obedience to her husband. Loyalty and respect for one's parents and elders is of primary importance. Behaving well is valued more highly than self-expression (delCarmen, 1990).

The most stressful period of development in the Asian-American community is adolescence, when these traditional Eastern values are in direct contradiction to Western American values of independence and self-sufficiency. Where creative ideas and questioning of values are encouraged in our educational system, this encouragement may put the adolescent in conflict with the principles of loyalty and obedience from his culture. Where self-expression and self-disclosure are considered open and desirable in American society, expression in the Asian culture is implicit, nonverbal, and intuitive.

There is increasing evidence that more egalitarian views of male and female roles are being accepted in the Asian-American community. However, such a dramatic change in values may cause some role strain and marital strain in early generations of Asian immigrants. School professionals may see the effects of parental disagreement about sex roles being enacted in role confusion and anxiety in students, particularly adolescents who are struggling with their identity. It may be important for the school professional to be aware of this conflict and to avoid triangulation into the primary struggle between the parents.

Special needs. One of the most frequently cited areas of concern regarding Asian-Americans is general underutilization of mental health services (Tashima, 1981). Although foreign-born Asians and Asian women married to American military men are at very high risk for adjustment problems, their reliance on mental health services tends to be limited. When Asian-Americans do receive mental health services, studies have shown that they tend to be diagnosed as schizoid, schizophrenic, or retarded due to the language barrier and their style of low emotional expressiveness. Frequently this diagnosis is inappropriate. Therefore, children of these two populations may grow up in a household with a severely depressed or dysfunctional parent who is not receiving treatment or who is receiving inappropriate treatment. The children may show signs of moodiness, physical and cognitive lethargy, or withdrawal that come from their experience of modeling the behavior of a parent.

Nazzaro (1981) again speaks to the impact of bilingualism on the diagnosis of Asian-American children, particularly in the areas of hearing, language arts, and learning disabilities. This classification also highlights the effects of the passive learning style and the self-controlled emotional style that are a part of the Asian cultural influence. Both of these qualities may lead educational professionals to view Asian-American children as cognitively slow, disinterested, or nonmotivated.

Cognitive Styles

A final area in which culture affects students is the area of cognitive styles. For the past twenty years, studies have been conducted that attempt to discern the differences between the thinking of mainstream American cultural groups, such as Anglo-Americans, and minority groups such as Hispanic, African, and Native Americans (Anderson, 1988; Cohen, 1969; Hale-Benson, 1982).

In general, the research supports the presence of two very different cognitive styles in mainstream and minority cultural groups. These styles have been referred to as field-independent versus field-dependent (Anderson, 1988), analytic-cognitive versus relational (Cohen, 1969), and linear versus circular (Hale, 1981). Euro-Western or Anglo thought is characterized as field-independent, analytic-cognitive, and linear, whereas Hispanic, African, and Native American thought tends to be field-dependent, relational, and circular in nature.

Historically, American public schools have tended to reward cognitive styles that are typically Euro-Western. Characteristics of this type of thought are:

- o Task-oriented
- o Standardized
- o Objective
- o Meaning is absolute
- o Mechanistic

- o Logical
- o Scheduled
- o Factual
- o Individual mastery
- o Deductive

In contrast, characteristics of minority thought include:

- o Process-oriented
- o Creative
- o Subjective
- o Meaning is contextual
- o Humanistic

- o Affective
- o Flexible
- o Group cooperation
- o Inductive

Given these wide cultural differences in cognitive style, school professionals must begin to adapt their teaching methods and curriculum to address these contrasting forms of thought (Reed, 1992).

For school professionals who wish to study the issue of cultural diversity in more depth, the seminal work on ethnic issues in families is an edited volume by McGoldrick, Pearce, and Giordano (1982). This volume includes discussion of nineteen different ethnic backgrounds and how knowledge of ethnicity can be useful to the professional in understanding family functioning. Life-cycle stressors or situational stressors (such as the diagnosis of a child with a disability) may put families into greater contact with the roots of their traditions and belief systems and challenge their identity.

INTERVENTION

For the school professional, working to achieve a greater understanding of cultural and socioeconomic issues can occur on two levels. First, we recommend interventions aimed at increasing personal awareness and sensitivity to differing backgrounds and families. Second, we discuss specific programs that have been used on the school and community level to increase intercultural awareness and connection.

Personal Awareness

McGoldrick et al. (1982) proposed that "the most important part of ethnicity training involves ... coming to understand (your)... own ethnic identity in a differentiated way" (p. 25). Only by becoming aware of our prejudices and values can we learn to open our minds to the values of other cultures. As a beginning of this understanding, you may want to ask yourself the following questions (McGoldrick et al., 1982, p. 27):

1. How would you describe yourself ethnically and socioeconomically? Is your present socioeconomic position the same or different from that of your parents and grandparents?
2. Who in your family influenced your sense of ethnic identity? How did they teach you these values?
3. Which ethnic groups other than your own do you think you understand best and least?
4. Which characteristics of your own ethnic group do you like most and least?
5. Imagine that your socioeconomic level decreased drastically over the next year. What would change about your life?

By asking yourself questions such as these and discussing your answers with friends and colleagues, you may increase your awareness of your own values, prejudices, and fears.

To increase personal awareness, the school professional will benefit from developing an attitude of problem solving in alliance with the family. When beginning contact with a family of differing cultural or socioeconomic background, a stance of respectful curiosity and openness to learn is helpful. Some techniques suggested to do this are:

1. Self-disclosure and joining. Introduce yourself as "Ms./Mr./Dr. _____. I'm your son's _____." Don't use the parents' first names unless they give you permission to do so. Tell the family an interesting story about your cultural background. "I grew up with a house full of kids and my husband is an only child. What a difference that makes."
2. Family self-identification. How do they see themselves? "Your last name is pretty unusual. Is it German or Swedish? Do you know anything about that background?"
3. Clarification about questions. Tell the family why you need to know this information; how it will be used. "Could you tell me something about the Mormon religion? I'm really not that familiar with it. I wonder how Mark might share some of your traditions with our class."
4. Cultural heritage. Ask questions about family rituals. "The holidays are coming up. How does your family celebrate?"

By expressing an interest in the family's beliefs and values, the professional begins the relationship with the family in a spirit of openness and acceptance. This beginning will then provide the foundation for developing a problem-solving alliance with the parents in order to help their children adapt to the school environment.

Institutional Awareness

As described in this chapter, one of the difficulties with educating minorities in American public schools is the fact that our educational institutions have been formed from a base of Euro-Western thought and values. Hale-Benson (1982) argued that, in order to optimally address the needs of minority children, schools must make changes in their ideology, method, and content (p. 152). Ideologically, she stated that education must teach minorities to struggle and survive. Methods need to include cognitive strategies that are more relational and creative rather than cognitive and structured. Content needs to be ethnocentric in nature, that is, teaching the history, crafts, music, historical and political figures, and important events of various ethnic groups. An excellent example of ethnocentric curriculum can be found in a guide developed by Wendell and Leoni (1986) for the Virginia Department of Education. The guide includes general information about the cultural values of nineteen different ethnic groups. In addition, suggestions for ethnocentric lessons and activities are given for each cultural group. Your local education department may have developed similar guides. For further ideas regarding references for culturally diverse curriculum, see Appendix B.

In order to respond to the needs of various minorities, Cummins (1989) recommended an intercultural school orientation based on the values of inclusion, collaboration, interaction, and experiential learning rather than trying to force minorities to conform to an Anglo orientation by transmission of Anglo values. Some of the ways in which he proposes that schools can create a climate that is welcoming to minority parents and reinforcing to students' identity are:

1. Reflect the various cultural groups in the school district by providing signs in the main office that welcome people in the different languages of the community.
2. Recruit parents or people from the community who can tutor students in different languages or provide liaison between the school system and other parents. In some instances, these parents could be paid with money for teacher's aide positions or grant money allocated for this purpose.
3. Incorporate greetings and information in the various languages in newsletters, parent handouts, and other official school communications. Make materials about school services available in the appropriate languages at local churches, community centers, markets, and other businesses frequented by families.
4. Display pictures and objects of the various cultures and religious groups represented at the school.
5. Encourage students to write contributions in their native language or about their family culture for school newspapers and magazines.
6. Provide opportunities for students to study their culture in elective subjects and in extracurricular clubs. It is often eye-opening for students to become aware that, for example, Africa and China had extremely advanced cultures while the British

(whom we typically study in history classes) were still living in dirty flea-infested castles.

7. Encourage parents to help in the classroom, library, playground, and clubs so that all students will be offered the opportunity to interact with people of different cultures.
8. Invite people from ethnic minority communities to act as resources and to speak to students in both formal and informal settings. These individuals could also be asked to provide inservice education to school personnel to sensitize the school staff to the values and beliefs of the families whom they serve (Cummins, 1989; Lynch & Stein, 1987).

Frequently, school professionals report that, even when services are offered for parent involvement, they are underutilized. In an effort to discover the barriers to parent involvement in a socioeconomically disadvantaged neighborhood, Lynch and Stein (1987) conducted three studies, interviewing a total of 434 families receiving special education services. The sample consisted of Hispanic, black and Anglo families from a metropolitan school district in southern California. According to family reports, the main barriers to parent participation in school meetings were work, time conflicts, transportation problems, and child-care needs. When asked what could be changed to help parents get to the school, the parents who were interviewed suggested that the schools hold bilingual meetings, select times convenient for parents, provide transportation, provide advance notice of meetings, provide child care, provide subjects that pertain to their children, and send personal notes or calls about the meetings.

This study points out the importance of sensitivity to the needs of the parent community. Types of services offered by the school and times of school meetings and parent meetings may all need to be geared differently to different communities.

There are also strategies that individual teachers and counselors can use at the classroom or group level to increase crosscultural awareness in their students. Schniedewind and Davidson (1983) in their book, *Open Minds to Equality*, include different types of activities for grades three through eight that teachers can use to foster an understanding of cultural and racial differences. Examples of chapter titles are "Others' Shoes: Others' Views," "The 'Isms,'" and "Look at your Community." This book also includes resources and curriculum materials for teachers. We highly recommend that at least one copy be available in every school.

SUMMARY

It should be clear that the most important factor in dealing with families of different ethnic and socioeconomic backgrounds is an openness and willingness on the part of the school professional to learn about family values and beliefs. The specific activities and strategies that are used to accomplish this goal will differ from community to community, from school to school, and from professional to professional.

The following case example illustrates the creative use of ethnic issues to help an adolescent boy deal with behavior problems.

CASE EXAMPLE

Jose is a 14-year-old boy diagnosed with attention deficit disorder (ADD). His mother is an Hispanic American; his father, who died in an accident when Jose was 5 years old, was of Cherokee Indian descent. Jose's ADD was diagnosed in the second grade when he was having difficulty learning to read and paying attention in class. At that point, Jose's mother took parenting classes to learn strategies for dealing with a child having attentional problems. Jose had been enrolled in resource instruction for his reading problems. In addition, his teachers had been asked to seat Jose in the front of the room for increased structure and to provide positive reinforcement to him as often as possible to keep his motivation at a maximum. Jose had been prescribed Ritalin by a local psychiatrist and had received counseling for six months to help with the grieving process following his father's death. Jose took the medication until the sixth grade when school personnel, his mother, and the psychiatrist all agreed that it should be discontinued. Jose's reading skills improved, and he was functioning at grade level without the medication up until the eighth grade.

During his eighth-grade year, Jose had become increasingly distractible. His teachers had tried sending notes home to his mother, keeping a weekly assignment sheet that was sent home on Fridays, and after-school study hall. In spite of these efforts, Jose repeatedly failed to turn in assignments. During the first semester, he failed two classes because of zeros from homework. Most recently, if teachers tried to intervene he became verbally belligerent and threatening.

After an episode involving a physical fight with another student, Jose's mother was asked to the school for a meeting with Jose's teachers and school counselor. Jose's mother revealed that she also was having difficulties with Jose at home. He had begun to refuse to do basic chores, even though he had willingly helped in the past. He had frequent temper outbursts where he hit walls or threw books around in his room. She expressed concern about the crowd of friends with whom Jose was spending time. She considered them to be a "rough" group of primarily Hispanic boys who had a reputation for trouble making and "machismo."

Jose's mother stated that she felt badly for Jose because of the lack of a father figure in his life. At 14, Jose was beginning to identify with the macho image and to believe that self-control and doing the right thing were not necessary. He had no appropriate male role models, as the mother had not remarried and none of her family lived close by. And, although Jose attended the Catholic church with his mother, he did not seem to relate to any of the men in the church.

Questions and Comments

1. *What intervention strategies could be used with this family? How could cultural issues be included in the interventions?*

    The team developed a strategy for dealing with Jose's problems that included positive and negative consequences for his behavior at school and at home as well as holding weekly meetings with the school counselor and his mother. It was agreed that the natural consequence for Jose's failure to turn in assignments was having to attend summer school or repeat the eighth grade. The team, including as many male staff members as could attend (to impress upon Jose the power of the message in his own macho culture), met with Jose to tell him of the program and remind him of the consequences. He, of course, resisted but began meeting with the counselor.

The counselor began by asking Jose questions about his family. He refused to answer them and said he didn't want to talk about his family. Because the mother was present, the counselor asked her if she could give some family background. She was specifically asked questions about her Hispanic culture and her husband's Cherokee Indian heritage. While Jose listened, his mother described his father's beliefs about spiritualism and harmony with nature. She described his father as a very strong man but one who practiced emotional restraint and noncompetitiveness. Jose's mother admitted that she knew very little about his father's religious beliefs. She said that he had talked about "healers" and spiritual healing, but she did not know details.

Following this meeting, the counselor went to the library and checked out books on Native American culture and beliefs. In future meetings, he read to Jose and his mother from these books. The mother asked questions about what was being read while Jose sat sullenly by, seeming not to listen.

2. *How might things change for Jose following the interventions? What are the potential results?*

The first hint that the program was working came when Jose chose as his topic for an assigned paper for history class "The Plight of the American Indian." In his paper, he identified how the Indian culture had endured numerous hardships and still kept their pride and a sense of community. He wrote about the cultural values of silence, nonreactivity, and balance with nature. The teacher was so impressed with the paper that she arranged a field trip for the class to see the movie *Dances with Wolves*, which depicts the strength, creativity, and harmony of the Indian culture.

After this point, changes began to be evident in Jose's behavior. He became more self-controlled. He began to talk with his counselor about cognitive strategies for relaxing and remaining nonreactive when he was angry or upset. He allowed his counselor to help him establish a study structure for himself at home, in the service of becoming "balanced" as the Indian culture proposes. Jose began to dress with more of an Indian or Southwestern style and was heard talking to peers about himself as a Cherokee Indian.

As this example illustrates, the openness and creativity of the school professionals in dealing with Jose allowed him to be able to "save face" in his community by forming a new identity of strength born out of control and passive resistance. In this example, the power of Jose's ethnic background was used by the school to help him adapt to the demands of the classroom.

SPECIAL POPULATIONS 6

Historically, the primary model for the definition of family has been two parents and their biological children. However, this definition no longer represents the norm. In our country, at present, 50% of all marriages end in divorce (Beal & Hochman, 1991). There are estimates that nearly fifteen million children under the age of 18 are living in stepfamilies (Furstenberg, 1988). Samuels (1990) has estimated that there are about nine million adopted children in the United States.

In addition to structural changes in the American family, we have also witnessed a dramatic increase in family dysfunction. Approximately two million children are physically and sexually abused each year (Courtois, 1988), and there are at least twenty-eight million children of alcoholics in our society (Ackerman, 1983). With these numbers on the rise, there is increased pressure on our schools to help children with adjustment problems and those at risk for future problems. Parents who are dealing with their own concerns may be less able or less likely to devote themselves to their children's adjustment.

This chapter discusses issues faced by children, parents, and educators in dealing with nontraditional family situations and parental dysfunctions. We begin with the impact of divorce, single parenting, and remarriage on children and their families. We then address issues related to adoption in families. Finally, we highlight concerns faced by educators in dealing with students who have abusive or addicted parents. In each section we provide suggestions for interventions that can be made within the context of the school system as well as outside referral options. We conclude with a case example that illustrates the effects of parental divorce on a fourth-grade girl's school adjustment.

INTRODUCTION

In order to better understand the ongoing experience of their student population, it is important for school professionals to understand the psychological and systemic effects of different family configurations on the child. Table 6.1 highlights the major differences between various family patterns that the school professional may encounter.

Table 6.1
COMPARISON OF MAJOR CHARACTERISTICS IN FAMILY PATTERNS

Stepfamilies	Single-Parent Families	Adoptive Families	Nuclear Families
Biological parent elsewhere.	Biological parent elsewhere.	Biological parent elsewhere.	-------
Virtually all members have recently sustained a primary relationship loss.	All members have recently sustained a primary relationship loss.	The children have sustained a primary relationship loss.	-------
An adult couple in the household.	-------	Usually an adult couple in the household.	An adult couple in the household.
Relationship between one adult (parent) and child predates the marriage.	-------	Relationship between one adult (parent) and one child predates the marriage where stepchildren are adopted.	-------
Children are members in more than one household.	Children may be members in more than one household.	-------	-------
One adult (stepparent) not legally related to a child (stepchild).	-------	-------	-------

Source: Adapted from *Step-families: A Guide to Working with Stepparents and Stepchildren* (p. 16) by E.B. Visher and J.S. Visher, 1979, New York: Brunner/Mazel.

As this table indicates, stepfamilies, single-parent families, foster families, and adoptive families have many common characteristics. However, all of these family configurations differ appreciably from the traditional nuclear family. In the following section, we discuss the implications of these differences for the adjustment of students and families.

DIVORCE AND REMARRIAGE

Children of Divorce

Divorce causes a period of disequilibrium in the lives of the children and parents in the separating family. For the child, this adjustment period lasts at least two to three years (Wallerstein & Kelly, 1980) and may last up to ten years (Wallerstein & Blakeslee, 1990). During this adjustment period, children are at risk for developing emotional and behavioral problems that will be displayed in school. How long and what form the adjustment process takes depends upon a number of factors described here.

Gender Factors

Overall, boys tend to have a more difficult and prolonged adjustment period to divorce than girls (Kalter, Riemer, Brichman & Woo Chen, 1985). Mothers are, most often, assigned as custodial parent (Guidubaldi & Cleminshaw, 1985). The boy's primary male role model, then, becomes a part-time parent. This change was eloquently described by a noncustodial father in his article, entitled "Uncle Dad":

> My father is a pipe-smoking Presbyterian who speaks in witty one-liners; he taught me to stand when ladies enter a room and how to handle hammers, and once, when I was twelve, I saw him rescue a drowning man...from a river and walk away without giving anyone his name. A Hero.... Walking out of my own house twenty-seven years later, I knew I had forfeited the right to be so admired by my own...son. (Smith, 1985, p. 74)

Age Factors

Younger children tend to experience divorce as cause for grief and sadness. The loss may be prolonged because they know that the departed parent is not dead. Their lives may be controlled by longing for the absent parent and conflicting feelings about what they perceive as abandonment. Adolescents whose parents divorce are more likely to act out feelings of anger and embarrassment or to become embroiled in their own relationship conflicts with peers (Guidubaldi, Cleminshaw, Perry, & McLoughlin, 1973). Dating relationships may take on more importance due to feelings of emotional neediness. At extremes, sexual acting out may occur.

Parent Factors

Children's adjustment to divorce is hindered by their parents' need to lean on them for emotional support and to involve them in battles with the divorced spouse. A study of forty adolescents conducted at the University of Georgia found that a high level of parental conflict had a detrimental effect on the academic and behavioral performance of adolescents, whether or not their parents were divorced. According to this study, if parents keep battling after a divorce, the effects on their adolescent children are worse than those of staying in a high-conflict marriage (Rich, 1986).

Wallerstein and her colleagues (Wallerstein & Kelly, 1980; Wallerstein & Blakeslee, 1990) conducted a ten-year longitudinal study of 131 children from 60 divorcing families. After ten years, they found that only one-third of the children defined themselves as functioning well. Another one-third were clinically depressed and still had fantasies of reconciliation between their parents, even if one or both parents had remarried. Most of the depressed children and adolescents were still experiencing intense bitterness between their parents. The final third saw themselves as continuing to struggle with the implications of their parents' divorce in their relationships with siblings, peers, and parents.

These authors argued that the functioning of the custodial parent and the level of conflict between ex-spouses during the entire postseparation period are the primary determinants of the child's well-being. As Wallerstein and Blakeslee (1990) stated, the purpose of divorce is to get away from a bad situation and to start a new life. How people build this new life is of primary importance.

> Getting one's external life back on track, however, does not begin to resolve the profound internal changes that people experience in the wake of divorce. Children's fundamental attitudes about society and about themselves can be forever changed by divorce and by events experienced in the years afterward. (p. xii)

In order to meet the needs of children of divorce who are at risk for various types of symptomatic behavior, school professionals must become aware of the struggles faced by these families.

Psychological Tasks

Wallerstein (1983) outlined six psychological tasks for children in the process of adjusting to divorce. These are:

1. Acknowledging that the marital separation is real.
2. Staying out of parental conflict and distress and resuming age-appropriate involvements.
3. Resolving feelings of loss.
4. Resolving feelings of anger and self-blame.
5. Accepting the permanence of the divorce and giving up reconciliation fantasies.
6. Achieving realistic hopes regarding their own future relationships.

Intervention

Changes in the emotional life of children and the structure of families following divorce may lead to a confusing family picture for educators. When dealing with divorce, school professionals can benefit by holding to several basic principles:

1. Be aware of the potential impact of divorce upon your students; remember that disequilibrium for two to three years following divorce is typical.
2. Take into account the individual child and his or her coping mechanisms when trying to help children move through the psychological tasks necessary to adjustment.
3. Always attempt to reinforce parental hierarchy and keep both parents involved

with their children as much as possible. Maintaining the parental subsystem even though the marital subsystem is dissolved is of primary importance in children's adjustment.

4. Have on file a list of referral sources, including therapists who specialize in divorce issues, support groups for separating and divorcing parents, and local chapters of Parents Without Partners.

Pedro-Carroll and Alpert-Gillis (Youngstrom, 1990) have used a school-based model of intervention for children of divorce for the past eight years. Their model consists of support groups for children grades K through 6 and periodic meetings and support groups for parents. These authors found that about 80% of the students in their project were not told when their parents were planning to divorce. The children had many misconceptions about divorce and tended to feel that they could not ask their parents any questions concerning the divorce. The school-based support groups were designed to clarify misconceptions about divorce and to teach these children how to express their feelings, develop self-esteem and internal coping skills, and get support from their friends and relatives. The goals of the parent groups were to teach parents about their children's heightened needs following divorce, to help them keep their children out of triangles with their ex-spouse, and to provide guidelines for maintaining stability and consistent limits with their children. School professionals may want to adapt this model to their own setting to provide services for students whose parents are divorcing.

Single-Parent Families

It has been estimated, that on the average, women with custody of minor children experience a 73% decline in standard of living during the first year after a divorce (Wallerstein & Blakeslee, 1990). The children, who are recipients of this decline in socioeconomic status, see themselves as survivors of a tragedy. How they handle the change will depend mostly upon the adjustment of their custodial parent and the level of other stressors in their lives.

Disorganization

Guidubaldi and Cleminshaw (1985) studied single-parent families and found that the biggest difference between married and divorced families was a general level of disorganization in single-parent situations. According to their study, even routine tasks and basic scheduling of meals, bedtimes, and so forth were more disorganized because of the role overload experienced by the single parent.

Feiring and Lewis (1985) concurred with these findings. Their study involved single-parent households headed by mothers. They concluded that the primary impact of divorce upon children is due to the mother's lack of economic and emotional support. The mother's sense of well-being influences her parenting ability and thus her children. Her level of responsiveness to her children changes when she is trying to work and provide for the family's functional needs such as cooking, shopping, laundry, and cleaning by herself. There is also a conflict between fulfilling one's own needs for support and friendship and the demands of parenting. If keeping up with household tasks is overwhelming, where is the energy for dating or socializing? The single parent who has a child with a disability will feel an even greater sense of stress and role overload (Somers, 1987).

Hierarchy Dysfunction

One of the most common problems found in single-parent families is a hierarchy imbalance. For many parents, dissolution of the marital subsystem implies dissolution of the parental subsystem as well. In these situations, the oldest or highest functioning child is often cast in the role of a parent (Schulman, 1984). The *parentified* child may operate as the parent's confidant and be given inappropriate information about the divorce. He or she may also be assigned overwhelming responsibility for household tasks or for taking care of other children in the family. When the pressure of these responsibilities becomes too great, the parentified child will often begin to exhibit academic or behavioral problems. The single parent, who is usually unaware of the source of the problems, then tries to exert influence as a disciplinarian. The parent is often surprised when the child responds with oppositional or disrespectful behavior, although this behavior is born out of the parent's inappropriate dependency upon the child (Miner, 1981).

There may also be some positive aspects to single-parent households. If the single parent can relish the independence and freedom in making decisions without having to confer with a partner, he or she can pass this attitude on to the children. Single-parent families tend to work most effectively when there is a sense of interdependence between parent and children without blurring the functioning of the executive subsystem (see chapter 3). Flexibility and adaptability on the part of the parent are critical in this adjustment process. It is also important that parents not begin dating too soon after their divorce. Both the parent and the children need time to adjust to the divorce and to establish a new family life together. The presence of a new partner or multiple partners only heightens feelings of loss and anger and prolongs the adjustment process.

The most effective buffers to the long-term emotional stresses of divorce are adequate social supports for both children and single parents. Berman and Turk (1981) interviewed members of Parents Without Partners about their adjustment to divorce. Participants in their study reported that the most important determinant of their overall positive mood up to 15 years after divorce was the presence of a social support system.

Guidubaldi and Cleminshaw (1985) also stressed the importance of support variables for the adjustment of the single parent. The availability of helpful relatives, including in-laws; the availability of friends and paid child-care assistance; and a positive relationship with their ex-spouse were the three most important factors in single-parent well-being.

Intervention

An inservice education program to sensitize educators to the risks for children of single-parent households is highly recommended as an educational strategy. In single-parent situations, school professionals can serve an important function in attempting to preserve the parental subsystem. To hold to the belief that parents need to work together for their children, in spite of the differences in their marriage, will project an attitude of acceptance toward separating or divorced parents. Record keeping that identifies children from divorced homes and asks for addresses and telephone numbers of both parents is a beginning in maintaining the parental system. In cases of joint custody, schools need to insure that both parents receive copies of important communications from the school, including invitations to parent/teacher conferences and school activities. If one parent has been assigned sole custody, his or her written permission is needed in order to include the noncustodial parent in these events. The educator needs to be prepared to ask the custodial parent for permission to contact the other parent and to give him or her reasons why the inclusion is important to the child's sense of well-being. The idea for the awareness of school professionals is, whenever possible, not to support the dissolution of the parental subsystem by favoring one parent over the other.

For most single parents, access to a support network is the most important factor in their adjustment (see chapter 11). The school may contribute to the formation of a network by purposely including single parents in homeroom, PTA, or other school activities with other parents who have been through similar circumstances. The school may also provide adult education programs and a resource library for single parents regarding adjustment to divorce. Scheduling school activities that recognize the logistical problems of employed single parents by providing baby-sitting services and an evening timetable of events will help to project an attitude of inclusion and acceptance toward single-parent families.

Blended Families

In the United States, approximately 75% of divorced or widowed adults remarry within five years of the dissolution of their marriages (Wald, 1981). However, 40% of remarriages do not survive after the first four years (Friedman, 1981), and this figure increases when children from previous marriages are involved. Even if remarriages do endure, there is general consensus among researchers dealing with remarried, step, or blended families that the process of consolidation and emotional connection in these families takes from three to five years (Larson et al., 1984; Visher & Visher, 1979; Whiteside, 1983). For couples who meet and remarry with the hope that everyone will live "happily ever after," these figures may be staggering. In working with blended families, there are particular problem areas that tend to occur at different stages in the remarriage process.

Premarriage

The first arena for problems occurs before the remarriage actually occurs. How this stage proceeds depends partially upon the age of the children at the time of the remarriage. Younger children may still be mourning the loss of their biological parent or may continue to have fantasies about the reconciliation of their natural parents (Friedman, 1981). For the child who has served a parentified role in the single-parent household, the remarriage may represent on the one hand a relief from responsibility, and on the other hand a threat to his or her position in the family (Schulman, 1984).

Adolescent children may have a particularly difficult time accepting the remarriage because of their own normal identity and sexuality concerns. For adolescents, who may have just begun dating, watching their parent being "in love" and going through the rituals of courting may be embarrassing and threatening. Adolescents may also be particularly aware of the reactions of the other biological parent to the remarriage (Framo, 1981b). If the ex-spouse has not resolved his or her relationship with the parent who is planning to remarry, the ex-spouse may experience again the sense of rejection and depression from the initial divorce. Adolescents, who are themselves struggling with the dynamics of heterosexual relationships, may become embroiled in a loyalty struggle (Visher & Visher, 1979).

Another potential area for problems in the premarriage stage comes from how the children learn about the impending remarriage. Ideally, the children will have had positive involvement with the new spouse (and his or her children) prior to the decision to remarry. The couple should initially tell the children about their engagement together. They should acknowledge the difficulty in their decision and the impact that the remarriage will make upon the children. Children should be informed that, just because the couple love one another, there is no expectation of "instant love" between the children and the new spouse (Visher & Visher, 1979). From this point, the parent will need to make him- or herself available to answer questions and listen to the feelings of the children.

Within the boundaries of the family hierarchy and the personal tastes of the couple, children should be given a role in planning and participating in the wedding ceremony and the new living arrangements. Here is an example of how one couple gave their children a feeling of being included in their remarriage:

> A couple were married after three years of dating, following each of their divorces. The woman had three children from her previous marriage and the man had two children. Their wedding ceremony consisted not only of the traditional wedding vows for the couple, but also of vows to join the two families in a commitment. Each parent initially recited part of the vows with his or her own children. At the end of the ceremony, all of the children and both parents recited a phrase together. For this couple, the symbolism of coming together was expressed through these rituals.

Initial Struggles

Once the remarriage has occurred, the families must then begin the process of "blending." Difficulties during this stage may occur at the individual, subsystem, or family levels.

Individual. At the individual level are the concerns of each person in the blended family about bonding with other family members. Step relationships are new and untested. It is not a given that all members of the family will accept one another as in an intact family (Visher & Visher, 1979). In addition, each individual has personal issues carried from the dissolution of the former marriage and family. Insecurity, poor self-esteem, fear, and grief are all possible repercussions of the previous loss.

Subsystem. At the subsystem level are concerns of the marital subsystem, parental subsystem, and sibling subsystem. The new couple must have time to nurture their attachment, which is the reason for the blending process. All of the early marriage concerns discussed in chapter 3 on the life cycle are replayed in this marriage. However, each person now has a history of failure to bring to the relationship (Friedman, 1981). In addition, the life-cycle stages do not evolve in sequential order in the blended family. The couple must work through the early marriage stage at the same time they are dealing with raising children or helping adolescents leave home.

At the level of the parental subsystem are issues of hierarchy and role definition. In blended families, there is a biological parent outside of the stepfamily unit and a same-sex adult in the household. This configuration makes for confusion about who has membership in the executive subsystem. As Barney (1990) stated:

> We discovered that we had too many actors for the traditional parts of mother and father, and we had to create some new roles for them. My husband has found a spot as an older friend and advisor to one of my sons.... After giving up...my accustomed role of nurturer, I have learned to be comfortable playing the part of counselor and house manager to my husband's children, leaving the mothering to their mother. (p. 146)

Quite often in blended families parents complain of hearing the phrase "He/she is not my father/mother" in response to disciplining. In blended families, the parent–child relationships precede the marital bond. Therefore, when a difference in disciplining techniques and household rules arises, history often wins out over the couple's relationship (Perkins & Kahan, 1979). If children feel that they are in charge of making family rules because their desires are more important than those of a spouse, a hierarchy dysfunction develops.

Blended families often involve more than one sibling subsystem. This subsystem may be divided into subgroups such as siblings who live with this family, siblings who live with the other parent, stepsiblings who live with their other parent, stepsiblings who live in this family. Sibling rivalry takes on a new and more complex meaning (Framo, 1981b). The logistical problems that must be resolved early in the blending process, such as who sleeps in which bedroom, who gets the most time with each parent, how money is divided, what are bedtimes, chores, and so forth, frequently get played out between siblings and stepsiblings.

Family. There are initial struggles that occur between the two families that are coming together as well. Members of the blended family come together from what may be two very different historical backgrounds. The rules and rituals of one family may have been very different in the other family. If children visit with their other biological parent, they now spend time in more than one family. Behavior that is allowed at dad's house may not be tolerated at mom's house and vice versa. Schedules, eating habits, religious beliefs, rituals, and bedtimes may all be different from one family to the other. Flexibility and tolerance for differences are important in minimizing struggles across families (Visher & Visher, 1979).

Long-Term Struggles

Once the blended family has survived the first four to five years, the initial cohesion struggles should be temporarily resolved. However, blended families experience unique problems and concerns throughout the life cycle. When children reach adolescence, identity and commitment issues often resurface. Stepparents who felt bonded with and accepted by their stepchildren may suddenly find themselves the "bad guy" once again. When normal adolescent power struggles surface, the parent may threaten the child with return to the other biological parent if the child doesn't "straighten up." Adolescents, in turn, may threaten to run away to their other parent when they aren't happy with the rules of their current family. It is important that any change of custody and living situation be made by parental consensus and not during an emotional battle. If parents decide that it is in their adolescent's best interest to change homes, the parental hierarchy remains intact.

Finally, cohesion issues often resurface if the new married couple has children of their own. Stepchildren who had adequately bonded to their new parent may now feel that their place has been usurped by the baby in the family. As one 13-year-old girl stated:

> My father told me that I would become second best with my mom and stepfather when the baby was born. It turns out that he was right. Why should they care about me when they have this cute little boy that belongs to both of them in the house?

In terms of the classroom, teachers may notice that children who live in blended families go through periods of acceptance and periods of regression. It is important that the long-term nature of the adjustment to divorce and remarriage be taken into account when trying to understand the needs of children of divorce.

Intervention

It is important for teachers to make note of children in their classrooms who live in blended families. Once again, one of the primary roles for teachers is to reinforce the parental subsystem. In the case of blended families, clarifying who is to be identified as part of this subsystem may be a complex task. When handouts are sent home for "parents," teachers may want to include more than one copy of the handout for children in blended families so that students can define "parent" for themselves and distribute the handout as necessary.

Also within the classroom, teachers can use exercises designed to help children become more accepting of people from diverse backgrounds and cultures (see chapter 5). Similar exercises may be adapted to increase tolerance for stepsiblings or stepparents who come from a different family and, thus, have a different historical background. A quick classroom suggestion is to ask students to discuss how their family celebrates certain holidays. For instance, for some families, Thanksgiving isn't Thanksgiving without a turkey and dressing. For others, a certain dessert or vegetable dish represents what it means to have Thanksgiving dinner. If students can be exposed to different symbols from different peer families, they may be able to more easily negotiate the rituals and symbols in their own blending family systems.

Barney (1990) has suggested that educators make an effort to normalize the concepts of stepfamily, adopted family, foster family, and other nontraditional family constellations. This may be accomplished through class discussions, student sharing of experiences in different types of families, or a curriculum that addresses the changing picture of the family.

Larson et al. (1984) have recommended an eight-week workshop for stepparents that can be conducted within the school. For school professionals who want to experiment with this model, some suggestions for workshop topics are:

o How to build a shared history with a new family.
o Negotiating parental roles in a blended family.
o Common pitfalls of remarriage and blended families.
o How to hold a family meeting.
o Increasing communication skills.

Many of the ideas and skills presented in this book will be useful in designing a stepparent workshop.

ADOPTIVE FAMILIES

Children who are living with adoptive parents are becoming increasingly numerous. Estimates indicate that there are as many as nine million adopted children under the age of 18 in the United States (Samuels, 1990). Given these figures, many teachers will be confronted with the unique concerns and adjustment problems of adopted children.

Brodzinsky (1990) has indicated that adopted children are at increased risk for developing psychological and academic problems, although this difference diminishes by the time they reach adolescence. He cited initial stresses in the adoptive family system to account for this increased risk. Adoptive parents have often had to deal with the stress of confronting infertility and that of the adoption process itself (i.e., agency evaluation, waiting periods, cycles of hope and disappointment). Adopted children, on the other hand, are usually born from unwanted pregnancies or family situations in which their presence taxed the family system beyond available emotional and tangible resources. Children who have been offered for adoption may carry a sense of insecurity, anger, guilt, and self-blame. Infants may suffer from problems with primary attachment.

Factors in Dissolution

Barth and Barry (1988) identified several factors that may contribute to the dissolution of adoption efforts. Problems may arise when the adoptive parents are inadequately prepared or when a previously unknown characteristic of the potential adoptive child is discovered (i.e., mental retardation, physical problems). Adoptions may fail because the adoptive parents have ineffective problem-solving strategies and lack strong social network supports. Finally, the absence of or delay in postplacement contacts with the placing agency may be a factor in the failure of many adoptions (Barth & Barry, 1988).

Special Needs Adoptions

Interestingly, adoptions of children with special needs tend to be more successful than average. Samuels (1990) found that cross-race adoptions and adoptions of children with disabilities had higher than average success rates (about 75% successful). Glidden (1989) noted a similar finding in 42 families adopting children with mental retardation. Coyne and Brown (1985) found a failure rate of only 8.7% in families adopting children with developmental delays.

These results may be promoted by several factors. First, adoptive parents in these cases may be better informed and more considered in their decisions than others. Caseworkers who deal with special needs adoptions usually orient their work toward matching the child with a family who can best provide for his or her needs. Second, these parents may hold more realistic expectations of the adoptive child, particularly with regard to potential problems because they are openly informed and educated about the child's special needs prior to the decision to adopt. Finally, for these parents, seeking and using an external support network may be encouraged or legitimized.

Adoption Adjustment

Raynor (1980) identified factors that tended to interfere with successful postadoption family adjustment. Parental prejudice and self-fulfilling prophecies tend to diminish the likelihood of successful adoption adjustment. Parents who hold images of the ideal child and attempt to mold their adopted child to their expectations tend to have greater difficulty. When parents have early doubts that are not adequately addressed, adjustment is more problematic. Finally, first-meeting trauma and legal delays were also identified as negative factors.

Positive adjustment to adoption appears to be a complex process. Brodzinsky (1990) identified several stages in the adjustment process.

Infancy

In infancy, parents must resolve feelings related to infertility and develop appropriate role models for themselves and realistic expectations of the child. They must manage anxieties and issues of social stigma (if present in their community). Finally, they must develop appropriate attachment to the child.

Preschool

Most children are able, by age 7, to understand some of the meaning of being adopted. During the preschool stage, parents should make the child aware of the adoptive status and create a climate where questions can be raised and dealt with in comfort. At this stage, the child's understanding of adoption is limited; most children are primarily aware of being "chosen."

Middle Childhood

In middle childhood the child's increasing cognitive ability leads to the awareness that being "chosen" by one family implies being relinquished by another. This awareness may challenge the child's sense of security and belonging. At this stage, parents must be sensitive to the child's ambivalence and potential sense of rejection with the attendant grief and insecurity. An atmosphere of openness to the child's need to explore the issues of the adoption is extremely important.

Adolescence

In adolescence, the adoptee must be assisted in dealing with biological issues and the usual adolescent concerns regarding identity, which are made more complex by adoptive status. During this stage the adoptive parents may need to assist the youth in learning about the birth parents or, at least, give their permission for this search to take place.

Overall, the best predictor of the adoptee's social adjustment, according to Hoopes (1990), is the child's perception of relationships in the family in terms of belonging and stability. The parents' openness and comfort in discussing issues about adoption was found to be closely related to the older adoptees' sense of identity and self-esteem.

Interventions

When dealing with adoptive families, any action on the part of school professionals that enhances successful adoption is desirable. One of the most helpful activities is helping adoptive parents develop realistic expectations for their children. Often adoptees are only children. Parents may need information about child development and age-appropriate achievement or may be anxious about and reactive to minor concerns. Basic education in child development may help parents with these concerns.

Educators may also help parents by normalizing problems that arise. Adoptive parents might need assistance in guarding against the tendency to make biological or genetic interpretations of their child's behavior or academic achievement. The educator's ability to place observed behavior in an appropriate developmental context may be critical to helping these parents maintain their connection to, and sense of responsibility for, the child. This is an area where skills in reframing (see chapter 12) are useful.

In addition, external network supports are important in encouraging adjustment for adoptive families. The school may provide some social supports through its personnel, programs, and parent groups. Use of these resources should be encouraged in addition to school professionals identifying other available resources external to the school and family. External resources may include community programs, agencies experienced with adoption concerns, or information sources and educational materials (see chapter 11).

In the classroom, teachers need to be aware of the issues related to children who are adopted and adjust classroom activities as needed. For example, if students are given an assignment to draw a family tree, teachers should be aware of the concerns this assignment may cause for adopted children. Questions should be dealt with in a relaxed and open manner with attention to the individual child's needs. Teachers should maintain open communication with parents and may be instrumental in helping parents identify stages, issues, and questions in the child's adjustment.

Finally, educators should be aware that adopted children are predisposed to emotional difficulties, particularly in the areas of trusting relationships, sensitivity to rejection, feelings of belonging and stability, and self-esteem. Many misbehaviors in these children arise from their neediness and identity confusion. Nurturing is often more effective as a management strategy than punishment.

Conclusions

For educators in the 1990s, the definition of normal family characteristics may be complex and confusing. In this section, we have provided some guidelines for understanding the adjustment process of the child and family in divorced, single-parent, remarried, and adopted family situations. We have identified many of the factors that make children in these family situations at risk for emotional or behavioral problems. Just as we have discussed the need for families to remain flexible in their adjustment process, so too must school professionals maintain a sense of flexibility and openness to understanding family dynamics in alternative family situations. As always, curiosity and emotional connection to each family are the most important tools to understanding and working with families in educational contexts.

FAMILIES WITH DYSFUNCTIONAL PARENTS

In this section on families with dysfunctional parents, we discuss child abuse and neglect, incest, and alcoholic systems. Professionals who come into contact with these types of dysfunctional parents will tend to want to assign blame to a particular problem member of the family. The underlying principle of this entire book, and particularly of this section, is to help the educator view parental dysfunction as part of a system, not as a problem within an individual.

Abusive Families

In abusive family systems, it is more functional, in terms of children's long-term adjustment, for school and community professionals to work with an intact family than to try to separate the children from a dysfunctional parent. Resolution of these problems comes from addressing the needs of the system, not dissolution of the family. Focusing on blaming and ostracizing tends to consolidate the defenses of the family rather than changing the cycle of problems.

In cases of abuse, the school professional must take on the roles of both helper and enforcer. By law, any accusation or evidence of child abuse must be reported to child protective services. We recommend that the school professional who is trying to work with family systems take a particular approach to reporting cases of abuse. First, talk with the parents and tell them about the accusation or evidence. Inform them that this information must be reported to child protective services. Many school policies require that parents be informed before a report is made (Council for Exceptional Children, 1979). Give the parents the opportunity to make the call themselves, but tell them that if they do not call, you are legally obligated to do so. If possible, make the initial telephone contact with protective services in the presence of the parents. By using this approach, parents are allowed an opportunity to feel somewhat in control of the process. Families can then feel actively involved in the resolution of problems rather than becoming defensive and isolating themselves from helping professionals (Palazzoli, Boscolo, Cecchin, & Prata, 1980).

Child Abuse and Neglect

Child abuse and neglect are both multigenerational problems (Berger, 1985). In most cases, abusive parents and people who marry abusive parents were themselves abused or neglected as children. Growing up in this type of family system, they may have developed a belief that hitting is a legitimate form of discipline. In addition, many adults who were abused have low self-esteem, unmet dependency needs, highly distorted and unrealistic expectations of themselves and their children, and problems with empathy (Council for Exceptional Children, 1979; Martin, 1980). In trying to understand the dynamics of abuse, it will probably be helpful to draw a genogram of the families of both parents (see chapter 4). Viewing the abuse in a multigenerational context may help the school professional stay clear of blaming and emotional reactivity.

Abusive families tend to have the following characteristics:

o Isolation from social supports.
o High levels of environmental stress, such as financial problems and medical problems.
o High levels of parental conflict.
o Dominant/submissive pattern in the marital relationship.
o Low levels of physical contact of any sort.
o Inconsistent and overly punitive discipline.
o Chaotic family structure.

(Berger, 1985; Burgess & Conger, 1977; Martin, 1980; Otto & Smith, 1980).

A child with special needs may induce feelings of resentment in parents who feel overwhelmed and needy themselves. In this case, the bond between parent and child may be too weak to protect the child from parental anger and frustration. The parent may not be clear about the child's areas of deficit and may perceive poor performance by the child as a power struggle rather than a developmental problem. The parent may then react with increased dominance, anger, and subsequent abuse (Council for Exceptional Children, 1979).

Children who are raised in violent and abusive homes learn to relate along dimensions of aggression and submission but not along lines of equality and negotiation. They learn to focus on the needs and moods of their parents rather than themselves to avoid punishment. Students from abusive families may be aggressive toward their peers but overly fearful in response to a teacher reprimand. Symptoms of bed-wetting, nightmares, and psychosomatic complaints are often seen in young children who have been abused (Thaxton, 1985). These children may also have extreme anxiety about any sort of failure, so they will hold themselves back from attempting new experiences or struggling with challenging academic material.

Interventions

For school professionals, the first step in knowing how to help children from abusive family situations is understanding the problem of abuse. Attending workshops or lectures dealing with the issues of abuse and neglect may be useful. The Council for Exceptional Children (1979) has developed a ten-session curriculum for training educators about the prevention and treatment of child abuse. This excellent training package, consisting of audiotapes, filmstrips, overhead transparencies, and resources, takes the educator through the identification, reporting, and treatment of abuse and neglect. We recommend that each school system obtain a copy of this resource.

Parent training through S.T.E.P. programs or behavioral programs has also been effective in decreasing some cases of physical abuse (Otto & Smith, 1980; Wahler, 1980). These training programs can easily be taught by school professionals. At a minimum, the school building or school funding can be donated for parenting groups that are taught by an outside resource person.

Wodarski (1984) outlined a successful eight-month treatment program for abusive parents that included two months of weekly training sessions in each of the four areas of child management skills, marital enrichment, vocational skills enrichment, and interpersonal enrichment. This program addresses issues of parenting, the marital relationship, and the self-image of the abusive parent.

The isolation of abusive families may be addressed through the school system with parent support groups. Attempts by teachers to involve parents in positive outlets with their child may decrease negativity in the family system. Finally, school professionals who work to build a relationship with these parents may then be in a position to make a referral to a local chapter of Parents Anonymous or to outpatient psychotherapy.

Incestuous Families

Sexual abuse of children occurs across social, economic, racial, and educational categories. It is estimated that in 80 to 90% of the cases, the offender is male (Schaefer, Briesmeister, & Fitton, 1984). Although father–daughter incest is the most common form of sexual abuse, it has recently come to light that sexual abuse of male children is more common than previously thought. Furthermore, sexual abuse can occur with family members other than fathers, including cousins, uncles, grandfathers, and siblings. In about 80% of cases, the perpetrator is a relative or friend of the abused child's family (Schaefer et al., 1984). This accounts for one reason why sexual abuse is underreported. Because the offender is a member of the family or known to the family, the abuse is denied, forgotten, or kept secret.

Systems Issues

Incest, like other forms of child abuse, is a transgenerational process. Parents have often been victimized as children either through rape or sexual, physical, or emotional abuse. These parents tend to have relatively poor models for what it means to be a nurturing parent. A nonoffending spouse who was abused as a child may have unconsciously chosen to marry an offending spouse because of his or her own unresolved issues from the family of origin. It is this pattern that makes the process of incest a systemic, rather than an individual, problem.

Characteristics

The characteristics of families in which incest occurs include:

o Boundaries inside the family are unclear and diffuse. There is a lack of privacy between family members.
o External boundaries are rigid. The family is isolated from outside contacts. Children must remain cut off from the world to preserve the secret (Minuchin & Fishman, 1981).
o The victim is often *parentified*. He or she is used in an adult way to meet the needs of others (Courtois, 1988).
o The relationship between mother and victim is often distant or rejecting in nature (Schaefer et al., 1984).
o The family maintains an illusion of happiness. Conflict is avoided; family loyalty is paramount (Machotka, Pittman, & Flomenhaft, 1967).

Personality Issues

Children who have been raised in this type of family system learn a number of undesirable lessons about life. These lessons include:

o Don't trust yourself or others.
o Be loyal; keep secrets; obey the family.
o Put others' needs before your own.
o Love means being hurt or used.
o Don't ask for help.

o Don't show hurt feelings; stay in control.
o Don't be a child. (Calof, 1988)

Because of the pressure to keep the family secret and remain loyal, children will often exhibit physical, behavioral, or emotional symptoms rather than talk about their concerns. For boys, stomachaches, encopresis, and fire-setting are typical symptoms that may arise from unresolved sexual abuse. For girls, withdrawal, fearfulness, and a tendency to sexualize relationships inappropriately may be symptomatic indicators. Any of these symptom patterns that are evident in the classroom, along with family dynamics of secrecy and isolation, are indicators that further attention may be warranted.

Disclosure

Historically, incest has been handled as a legal issue. Offenders are typically separated from their families, and criminal charges are brought against the individual. Often, even after a child has disclosed the sexual abuse, he or she will deny the initial report. In these cases, the pressure from the family is overwhelming. When the investigation is begun, the child is usually blamed for the shame and the potential break-up of the family. The nonoffending parent will often reject the victim, accusing the child of lying, being seductive, or causing trouble. The motive to preserve the family is so great that even siblings who have themselves been victimized may reject the child who has told the truth. The child then not only suffers from the abuse but also from abandonment and isolation from the remainder of the family system. As discussed in the introduction to this section, these dynamics are important to consider when reporting cases of physical and sexual abuse. The school professional must keep in mind his or her role as a helper to the child and the family as well as an enforcer of state laws.

Interventions

Incest is, for many professionals, one of the most emotionally loaded family dysfunctions. Most of us have a strong tendency to blame the offender and move to protect the victim. While protection is important, the school professional can best adopt a healing attitude toward these families by recognizing that all family members, in these cases, are victims and are involved in a family system that is out of control. It is only through healing and regaining control in the family system that members of the family move beyond the initial stages of identification into a healthy resolution of these problems.

The school professional must, legally, report any knowledge of incest to child protective services, and treatment by appropriate professionals must be initiated. Beyond the legal concerns, when a school professional is aware that a family is in treatment, he or she can be most helpful by dealing openly with the family, accepting the role of all family members in the problem, and providing individual support for the student who has been abused. A small suggestion, gleaned from the mental health field, is to refer to those involved in incest as incest *survivors* rather than incest *victims*. This minor language change provides an atmosphere of healing instead of one of emotional damage.

Finally, particularly for younger students, a school curriculum that deals with appropriate and inappropriate touching, privacy issues, asking for help, expression of feelings, and self-protection may be useful to increase incidents of reporting. The school social worker can help with developing such a curriculum.

Addictive Families

Since the 1960s, our society's awareness of problems with drug and alcohol addiction has increased dramatically. More recently, concerns of adults who were raised in alcoholic homes (Adult Children of Alcoholics) have taken on the status of a social movement. Unfortunately, for all the increased consciousness and attention, addiction continues to be a leading social problem. Large numbers of students currently live in homes where one or both parents are addicted to drugs or alcohol. With estimates as high as fifteen million actively addicted adults in the United States (Valliant, 1983), educators, knowingly or unknowingly, encounter these children regularly.

Characteristics

Characteristics of families in which parents have addiction problems include the following:

- o Denial of the problem. "There's an elephant in the living room" and everyone pretends not to notice.
- o Rigid external boundaries. Family is isolated from social supports.
- o Rigid internal boundaries, poor interpersonal communication, no expression of feelings (Treadway, 1987).
- o Unresolved family history or sudden or traumatic loss of a member (Coleman, Kaplan, & Downing, 1986; Stanton, Todd, & Assoc., 1982).

Parental Concerns

School personnel must be concerned with the impact of addiction on the parental subsystem. For the chemically dependent person, the ability to parent effectively is severely diminished. Emotional availability to spouse and children is limited, and, depending on severity, all aspects of the individual's functioning may be impaired.

The nonaddicted spouse may be viewed as an *enabler* who tolerates aberrant behavior in order to preserve the relationship and family (Wegscheider-Cruse, 1985). In the absence of a functional marital subsystem, the nonaddicted spouse often turns to older children for emotional support and assistance in coping with the demands of managing the family. The hierarchy in the family is disrupted, and the boundaries between the family and external systems are rigidified in order to preserve the family secret. Thus, family members are cut off from external supports as well as from one another.

Child Concerns

For children, the chemically dependent family is characterized by inconsistency, conflict, and emotional stress. Treadway (1987) quoted a child living in an alcoholic home:

> I could always tell what kind of night it was going to be by how my father came in the door. I would listen for how he put the key in the lock. If he fumbled around and didn't get the key in, I would know it was going to be the kind of night that I would just make myself scarce. (p. 18)

As described by this child, these are families in which the addiction organizes the family system. A child in this kind of family feels that the adults upon whom he or she is supposed to trust and depend behave in unpredictable ways. Children learn to survive by becoming self-sufficient, by blocking out feelings, and by learning not to depend upon others. Even when the parent stops drinking, these family patterns and personality styles are still intact (Treadway, 1987).

Wegscheider-Cruse (1985) identified the following patterns or adaptive roles that children take to survive in an addictive family.

1. *Family Hero or Super Kid*—Overachiever, needs to control, can't fail. Hides feelings of hurt, inadequacy, confusion, and guilt. As an adult will probably become a workaholic and marry a dependent person.
2. *Family Scapegoat*—Delinquency, always in trouble. Hides feelings of hurt, abandonment, anger, rejection. No self-worth. As an adult will probably become an alcoholic or addict.
3. *The Lost Child*—Shyness, withdrawal, a loner. Hides feelings of unimportance, abandonment. As an adult will probably be indecisive, nonassertive, depressed, isolated.
4. *Mascot or Family Clown*—Clowning, hyperactivity. Hides feelings of sadness, anxiety. As an adult will probably become a compulsive clown, won't be able to handle stress, will marry a hero, have dependent relationships.

These personality patterns and roles often become so ingrained in the developing child that they are carried long into adulthood. For the teacher, the same behavior patterns are often evident in the classroom context.

Students at Risk

Another area of concern for the educator is the risk that the child of a chemically dependent parent may become addicted. Alcoholism is clearly a genetic and biochemical as well as a psychosocial phenomenon. A landmark study of adoptees in Denmark found that children born to alcoholic parents and adopted into nonalcoholic homes at birth developed alcoholism in adulthood at a rate five times greater than that of children of nonalcoholic parents. A variety of subsequent studies have confirmed this genetic link (Valliant, 1983).

Bennett, Wolin, Reiss, and Teitelbaum (1987) conducted a study in which they interviewed 68 grown couples in which one spouse was a child of an alcoholic. They reported several significant emotional and behavioral factors that mitigated against becoming an alcoholic in adult life, even with a genetic history. These factors were:

1. The alcoholic family maintained family rituals, holidays, and family dinners while the child was growing up, in spite of the behavior of the alcoholic parent.
2. The child related to people and activities outside of the alcoholic home.
3. The young adult selected a spouse from a stable, nonalcoholic family and emotionally attached him- or herself to this alternative family.
4. The couple anchored themselves in a network of nonalcoholic friends, established their own family rituals, and maintained limited involvement with the alcoholic family of origin.

This study indicated that emotional and social supports can work to disentangle the child of an alcoholic from the multigenerational nature of this problem.

Interventions

When working with students who are children of addicted parents, the teacher can provide extensive education that should be useful. Curricula regarding the process of addiction, expression of feelings, and identity formation are all relevant to the support and healing of children who are growing up in addictive households. Information about local chapters of Alateen or local C.O.A. meetings may be helpful.

An excellent handbook for teachers, *Children of Alcoholics; A Guidebook for Educators, Therapists, and Parents*, was written by Ackerman (1983). This book includes information about the dynamics of alcoholism as well as an extensive appendix of resources and referral options. We recommend that each elementary and secondary school have at least one copy of this book available as a reference.

Often the nonaddicted spouse is aware of and uncomfortable with the family situation but feels unable to break out of the family rules to proceed toward change. School professionals can provide support to the nonaddicted spouse to obtain resources and help in order to change the system. Suggestions may include attending local Al-Anon meetings or support groups and reading literature on the family dynamics of addiction. As nonaddicted spouses become healthier, they may provide more support for their children and become more able to engage the addicted spouse in treatment.

If the nonaddicted spouse can elicit help from a network of friends and family, he or she may want to pursue a process known as *intervention* (Forman, 1987). During an intervention, the addict is confronted by his or her family, friends, and employer about the effects of the addiction, and treatment recommendations are made. The intervention process is led by a counselor who specializes in substance abuse treatment. School professionals may want to develop a list of counselors in their area who do interventions.

SUMMARY

The days of the nuclear, intact family as the primary family constellation have faded in the face of a host of pressures and issues encountered by the modern family. Children who are raised in families where they must deal with divorce, stepfamily issues, or dysfunctional parents are more the norm than the exception. For the school professional, awareness of the issues and dynamics of alternative family configurations and parental dysfunction is imperative. If children from alternative family situations, who are at risk for emotional and behavioral problems, are identified early, many future problems may be prevented.

The following case example illustrates the inclusion of family issues in planning an intervention for a 10-year-old girl experiencing symptoms of stress and depression that were affecting her school performance.

CASE EXAMPLE

Hilary, a 10-year-old girl in the fourth grade, had begun to complain of frequent headaches and tiredness. Her complaints had resulted in her having to be excused from class almost daily. In addition, her school absences had increased in the previous two months and her grades, previously average, had deteriorated.

After sending numerous written notices home, the teacher contacted Hilary's mother by telephone and requested a meeting with both parents. During this conversation, the mother informed the teacher that she was not sure whether Hilary's father would attend the meeting. She gave the teacher her husband's office number and suggested that she contact him there to inform him of the meeting.

The teacher contacted Hilary's father at the office, and he agreed to a meeting time. He also informed her that he and his wife had made a decision to divorce three months earlier but were still living in the same home, awaiting a settlement agreement. He tended to work late to avoid being in the same house with his wife for extended periods.

The parents both arrived for the meeting and listened, sullenly, while Hilary's teacher described her concerns. The parents stated that they had not told their children about their plans to divorce. However, they believed the children were aware of the divorce because they had overheard their parents arguing. The teacher then asked how the stress of the present arrangement was affecting each of the parents.

Following the teacher's question, the parents began to blame one another for Hilary's problems. The mother stated that Hilary was upset because her father was never at home. The father felt that Hillary was responding to her mother's lethargy and crying spells.

It became clear to the teacher that the decision to divorce had been initiated by the father. When she inquired as to why the couple were still living in the same home, she was met with another round of accusations. The father claimed that, if he left, his wife would "take me to the cleaners" by filing charges of desertion. The wife felt that her husband was staying in the home to "play a waiting game, hoping I will give up and let him off the hook."

Comments and Questions

1. *What interventions could be tried with these parents?*

Initially, the teacher pointed out that Hilary's difficulties were, most likely, her response to the family confusion and her own stress level. She asked about any signs or symptoms of stress in the other children, ages 16 and 12.

When the teacher was able to elicit the parents' concern about their children, she was then able to give them some information about the effects of parental divorce on children of different ages and the necessity for as much stability and predictability as possible. She suggested that the parents, together, openly discuss the plans for their divorce with the children and give them an explanation of why the living situation remained as it was. She also suggested that the parents each consult their attorneys and get a time frame for resolving the settlement issue so that the children could be given a general plan. She stressed to the parents that the worst possible outcome for the children was to become embroiled in their parents' disputes and loyalty conflicts.

From her knowledge of the possible concerns about divorce in children Hilary's age, the teacher then asked that each parent sit down with Hilary and reassure her that (1) the divorce was not her fault; (2) her parents' separation did not mean they did not love her; (3) she would continue to have contact with both parents, even after the divorce; (4) Hilary did not need to feel responsible for her parents' happiness—her parents would handle their personal feelings about the divorce by getting support from their friends and family, not their children; (5) the parents were each available to Hilary to discuss her feelings about the divorce, and she had permission to talk about it with her friends; and (6) it was important that Hilary attend school, be with her friends, study, and do the things that 10-year-olds do everyday.

Finally, the teacher offered the parents resources for reading about the effects of divorce for themselves and their children. She also provided information about postseparation support groups and a group for children of divorced parents.

DYSFUNCTIONAL FAMILIES 7 OF THE STUDENT WITH SPECIAL NEEDS

C hapters 2 and 3 provided a background on the family life cycle and the structural concepts of hierarchy, boundaries, communication patterns, and subsystem functioning. These concepts form the basis for a deeper and more specific understanding of the families who have children with special needs. This chapter builds upon structural family principles to provide a framework for looking at how some families become rigidified and inflexible in response to the stresses of dealing with a child or adolescent with a disability. We conclude with a case example of a girl with diabetes who is a member of a dysfunctional family system.

INTRODUCTION

This chapter describes the characteristics of dysfunctional families in which there is a child with special needs. The focus here is on helping the school professional understand the structure of these families with the particular challenges posed by four broad groups of disabilities: physical disabilities, including chronic illness; behavior disorders, including social maladjustment; learning disabilities; and mental retardation. Part II of this book provides strategies for responding to these problems as they are observed, through student behaviors, in the school context.

It is helpful for educators to recognize the family patterns that researchers have observed in working with families of a child with recurring behavioral, emotional, or physical symptoms (Berger & Jurkovic, 1984; Minuchin et al., 1978). In recognizing these family patterns, educators can have more realistic expectations of the families with which they come in contact. In addition, this information enables teachers, counselors, and principals to relate more authentically to families. The acceptance and understanding that such authenticity provides forms the basis of relationship building between school and home that leads to trust and mutuality of problem solving. A parent who hears understanding in the voice of school personnel is far more likely to unite with, as opposed to challenge or undermine, what educators are trying to create with his or her child.

Family Changes

When a child is diagnosed with special needs, a series of predictable and important changes occur within the family. First, the parents are required to focus extra energy on the diagnosed child to insure that the child receives help from the available resources. The parents may need to obtain evaluations of the child, medical follow-up, and special tutoring (Buscaglia, 1983).

Second, siblings of the child are made aware of the problem and are asked, either directly or indirectly, to make allowances for the special child (Atkins, 1987). A third change occurs when professionals outside the usual family structure are included in important family decisions and begin to receive information about the workings of the family that previously had been private.

A fourth development is the feeling, within many families, of being stigmatized as a result of the identified child's problem (Goffman, 1963). Families often begin to form a common identity around the presence of a child with special needs. For example, people may refer to them as "the family with the Down syndrome child" or "the family with the handicapped child" rather than "the Jones family" or "the lawyer's family." The more visible and profound the disability, the greater the potential for stigmatizing the family. In addition, because of the special problems often associated with caring for a child with a disability, parents may feel more tied to their homes and thus more isolated and lonely (Kew, 1975; Tavormina, Boll, Dunn, Luscomb, & Taylor, 1981). Finally, parents may feel that they have lost control over their lives and that physicians, diagnosticians, educators, and counselors are in control (Sloman & Konstantareas, 1990).

Family Reorganization

These four basic changes begin a process of reorganization in the daily family life and structure that is far-reaching in its implications. Just as the falling of the first domino will lead to the eventual collapse of an entire chain of dominoes, the diagnosis of one child within a family system will affect all other members of that system. Adapting to a diagnosed child requires flexibility on the part of all family members. Following diagnosis of a child, boundaries that were clearly defined are renegotiated and functional roles of family members change. For example, parents who both work outside of the home and have established patterns for taking care of housework, meals, and errands may face the struggle of adjusting schedules so that one parent can be free to take a child to doctor's appointments or special treatment facilities.

Life Cycle Adjustments

Just as chapter 2 describes the processes required to effectively move through the family life cycle, effective reorganization of the family around a child with special needs requires changes at each developmental stage (Buscaglia, 1983; Haley, 1973). A family with a toddler with a disability will face the struggles of toilet training, limit setting, and nurturing. As the special needs child becomes a teenager, the family will have to meet the demands of biological changes, independence issues, and identity formation.

As in all families, these varied life cycle demands will require flexibility and adaptability. In families with a child having special needs, the life cycle of the family is often interrupted, and sometimes arrested, at the point of diagnosis (Kew, 1975; Wilchesky & Reynolds, 1986). For these families, the diagnosis is such a crisis that the family is unable to adapt and maintain flexibility. Thus, the family structure "freezes" at the life cycle stage it was experiencing at the time of the crisis (Hughes, Berger, & Wright, 1978).

As discussed in chapters 2 and 4, the specific process of how life cycle adjustments are made will depend somewhat upon the family constellation and sibling position of the disabled child. A family with four children ranging in age from infancy to 15 years old, the youngest of which is diagnosed with spina bifida, will automatically have more potential caretakers to share the load than one in which the diagnosed child is an only child. However, in order to insure normal development for the older children in the family, the parents must juggle car-pooling for various functions, entertaining peers, and so forth with taking care of the disabled infant. The parent with an only child will have none of these demands.

In addition, the extent of adjustment will depend upon whether or not there is a parent available in the home on a full-time basis and whether or not the family has adequate social network supports (Gallagher, Beckman, & Cross, 1983). Thus, in looking at family adjustments, it is important for the school professional to know something of the make-up of the family of the identified student. Specifically, important information would include numbers and ages of siblings, sibling position of the student, parents' work status, and involvement with extended family. In knowing these types of family information, the educator can build the relationships that are essential in collaboration between parent and school.

None of the family adjustments previously described is a problem in and of itself. In fact, the adaptations of parents, siblings, and professionals are necessary when a child presents physical, emotional, or intellectual symptoms. However, problems arise in families when these changes become frozen in time. For example, when parents continue to focus the same amount of energy on the special child as they did at the initial diagnostic stage, the child's independence may be compromised. When parents continue to expect nondisabled siblings to treat the diagnosed child as different, the siblings will eventually begin to resent the expectations, and the child with special needs will end up feeling isolated and incompetent. When professionals continue to delve into the daily life of the family, all family members may begin to feel compromised and intruded upon.

Family Characteristics

Teachers, counselors, and other school professionals working with a student with a disability who continues to have difficulties adjusting to classroom demands should look for these predictable family characteristics, which were described in chapter 3:

o Dysfunctional family boundaries.
o Overprotection.
o Lack of conflict resolution.
o Parental asymmetry.
o Marital relationship subordinate to parental roles.

These structural characteristics are symptomatic of chronic family dysfunction that will impact the child's school adjustment.

Not all families experience such problems, but when they do these diagnostic signs are indicators that the family either has not faced and resolved the implications of the child's disability or has not been able to move past the initial adjustments required when the child was first diagnosed. The specifics of how these characteristics manifest themselves differ from family to family. However, within areas of disability we can find some predictable indicators of family distress that fall into the categories listed above. The following subsections are designed to give the school professional a window into observing these families with a different eye; an understanding of the common struggles faced by families with a child having special needs. Such an understanding provides the basis of relationship building that allows for mutual problem solving between parents and schools.

PHYSICAL DISABILITIES—CHRONIC ILLNESS

For purposes of our discussion, this category of symptoms will include illnesses such as diabetes, asthma, chronic allergies, chronic pain, Attention Deficit Hyperactivity Disorder, and mild cases of spina bifida, cerebral palsy, or multiple sclerosis. We have not included in our evaluation the impact of more serious illnesses such as cancer, leukemia, or AIDS. In this section we describe patterns that have been observed in dysfunctional families having a child with chronic illness or physical disability. The mere presence of a chronic illness in a child does not predict whether the family will be dysfunctional (Ferrari, Matthews, & Barabas, 1983).

Dysfunctional Family Boundaries

In dysfunctional families having a child with a physical disability or chronic illness, individual differences of any family member such as likes and dislikes, opinions, and needs related to age are not well-tolerated or are ignored. In addition, personal privacy is at a minimum (Liebman, Minuchin, & Baker, 1974). A good example of this type of family is one in which all children have the same allowance, bedtime, and household rules regardless of age. Typically, there is very little accommodation for developmental differences between the needs of a first grader and a middle-school child in these families. As one 10-year-old child with seizures expressed:

> I went to my girlfriend's house and she got dressed in the bathroom with the door shut. I couldn't believe it. At my house, you're not allowed to close doors. My parents think if you close a door you're trying to hide something, or maybe I'll have a seizure. What if I just want to get dressed without being seen?

Dysfunctional families of children with physical disabilities tend to exhibit clear indicators of enmeshed family boundaries. The child with the physical problem is particularly vulnerable to the intrusiveness of other family members. In many ways, this pattern is a predictable outcome of having a medical problem. How many of us have commented on the lack of privacy in hospitals and other medical settings? When a child is required to undergo physically intrusive procedures on a regular basis, and his or her physical health and well-being depend on these procedures (for example, catheterization), the entire family tends to be aware of the child's physical condition. In addition, older siblings, grandparents, and even close friends may be given permission to intervene in the child's physical routine or management.

As a result, the child may have difficulty developing normal personal boundaries around hygiene and health. Teachers may recognize the manifestations of enmeshment in these children who describe, in detail, the specifics of their physical routine, bowel habits, or eating habits in inappropriate ways that identify them as peculiar within their peer network. In these situations, teachers should make sure that the child's right to privacy is respected and guarded in all possible ways. Any talking about physical symptoms should be done alone with a teacher or counselor, not in the classroom.

Overprotection

Parents in dysfunctional families of a child with physical illness tend to be overprotective and have difficulty with the disabled child's natural attempts to become independent. The fine line between adequate protection and overprotection is a difficult one in families with a chronically ill child. However, results of a study of sixty children and adolescents with diabetes indicated that in families where independence and participation in age-appropriate social/recreational activities was promoted, children perceived themselves as more competent and had better diabetes adjustment than in overprotective families (Hauser, Jacobson, Wertlieb, Brink & Wentworth, 1985).

The parents of a chronically ill child have usually been trained to look for physical signs of distress in their son or daughter and to respond to these signs in particular ways (e.g., monitoring blood sugar, providing medication). When the child is initially diagnosed, the parents and family are required to focus almost exclusively on that child's physical needs to the exclusion of themselves and other children (Beckman-Bell, 1981; Shapiro, 1983). Often when the boy or girl matures and begins to want to take over personal physical management, the parent who has been in charge feels rejected or displaced. What is this parent to do with extra time now that he or she is no longer needed in this way? Parents may need help at this point to develop a more normal, meaningful relationship with their child (Hall & Taylor, 1971).

Parents of a child with a chronic illness or physical disability often call teachers to make special requests on their child's behalf. It is very common for overinvolved parents to ask that their child be excused from physical education classes or certain classroom activities. Frequently, this is their response to their child's normal complaint about gym suits, heat, dirt, or any of the uncomfortable aspects of the classroom. Of course, any physical disability should be integrated into the physical education and classroom plan for an individual child through adapted exercises. The important role for educators in these situations is to recognize overprotection, withhold judgment of parents, empathetically help parents see what is happening by normalizing their child's complaints, and remain firm on using only medical opinions to excuse students from any classroom activities.

Lack of Conflict Resolution

Another common reaction of families having a child with a chronic illness is the avoidance of conflict and prohibition toward displaying anger (Koch, 1985). Family members typically have difficulty expressing wants, needs, or feelings other than physical discomfort. Again, because individual differences are ignored, how can an individual have a want or need that is different from that of the whole? Quite often, family members other than the disabled child will have numerous physical complaints such as headaches, stomachaches, or backaches. It seems that the physical dimension is the only one in which family members can express differences. School personnel should simply observe such occurrences and see if they eventually become part of a pattern that might suggest the need for counseling or outside referral for a student and his or her family.

Anger is an emotion that tends to be avoided in families with a child who has chronic illness or physical disability. Typically, an expression of anger is reinterpreted by the family as an expression of physical discomfort.

A child with diabetes explains:

> Whenever I get upset, everyone starts to check my blood sugar. I must be low or high, I can't just be mad.

When conflicts do surface, they are typically ignored, with little opportunity for resolution. As a result, it is common to find long-held resentments in these families that have never been adequately discussed or understood. The problem of dealing with anger often leaves family members feeling isolated from one another and from members of their social network. Children from these types of families will not typically pose a behavior problem in the classroom. Rather, they will frequently complain of physical symptoms that may be traced to a difficult interaction with a peer or teacher that was not settled. It would be useful for educators to attempt to help the child to see those connections in the classroom setting.

Parental Asymmetry and Marital Subsystem

Finally, there is often an imbalance of parental roles vis-a-vis the child with a disability. One parent, typically the mother, has taken over primary management of the child and the other parent is underinvolved. The parent who is in charge of "nurse duty" usually feels overwhelmed and misunderstood, while the other parent feels excluded. These dynamics understandably make for poor communication between the parents and emotional distance in the couple. Often this asymmetry is unknowingly reinforced by school personnel who contact the mother to discuss issues regarding the child rather than including both parents. When dealing with these families, educators need to include both parents in meetings and phone contacts.

The marital subsystem in a family with a child having a chronic illness is usually subordinate to all other subsystems. As a result, studies such as one by Tew, Lawrence, Payne, and Rawnsley (1977) report a divorce rate in families with a child having a physical disability that is twice that of matched control families. Parents in these families often feel compelled to put the disabled child's needs first, any other sibling's needs second, and their own needs last on the list of priorities. As discussed, this dynamic may be adaptive in the initial stages of the child's diagnosis and adjustment but becomes dysfunctional when it continues even after the child has become more capable and mature. The teacher may find these parents willing to offer any amount of time to attend special activities with their child or provide homework supervision. However, they may not have had time alone with their spouse for a vacation or even an evening for years. In these instances, teachers may make suggestions such as parents going out to dinner or lunch together before or after a school conference. Simple, probing questions and reinforcement of time together for parents may help these families become aware of a new possibility in their relationship.

Not all families having a child with chronic illness will demonstrate all of these structural characteristics. In many situations the family dysfunction will be seen in only one area or will be more obvious in one area than another, such as overprotection. The discussion of these characteristics is intended to give the educator a framework from which to observe and understand the family of a child with chronic illness or physical disability.

BEHAVIOR DISORDERS AND SOCIAL MALADJUSTMENT

The wide variety of symptoms that fall within this category precludes identifying many specific family characteristics. However, there are some broad areas of concern that tend to identify dysfunctional families with a child presenting behavior problems.

Dysfunctional Family Boundaries

Boundaries in these families tend to be either enmeshed or disengaged. Typically within the enmeshed category are families in which a child is chronically depressed, in a repetitive conflict with a parent, or involved in the marital conflict of the parents (Safer, 1966). Enmeshed boundaries are indicated when, metaphorically, the child gets cut and the mother bleeds. When children are asked how they feel about something, a parent may answer for them. Language contains frequent references to "we" instead of "I." Parents in these families tend to be overprotective in the same way as parents of the chronically ill, involving themselves in the child's homework, style of dress, and choice of friends. Indicators of normal differentiation or independence in children are viewed as rebellious behaviors by the parents.

As an example, in one family seen for family therapy, the 8-year-old girl had crying spells. She would frequently cry at night, complaining about how difficult school was for her and how alone she felt. Her mother's response was to sit up talking with her daughter until the child finally fell asleep. Then the mother, who was also depressed, would stay awake all night worrying about her daughter's unhappiness. The next day, when the child was too tired to go to school, the mother would become angry at her.

Another presentation of enmeshed boundaries may be seen in single-parent families where the identified child has taken over the role as emotional supporter and confidant for the custodial parent. Due to the responsible nature of the *parentified* child, school personnel may not actually view him or her as needing intervention. In reality, the child needs as much assistance as the acting-out or aggressive student. Family counseling may be necessary in order to restore the appropriate parental hierarchy.

Families with disengaged boundaries are at the opposite extreme. Parents provide few limits and are underreactive to their children's behavior (Fox & Savelle, 1987). An example of this type of family is one in which a child who steals is described as "having this little problem with borrowing things." Teachers may feel that parents in this type of family are distant and uninvolved with their child. With children who externalize anxiety by acting out, parents tend to ignore signs of difficulty until a crisis occurs or the problem is pointed out to them by someone outside the family. School personnel generally recognize the possibility that there is a problem in these situations. The challenge is to help the families of these students see, with new eyes, the reality of the situation before it requires referral for special education.

Overprotection

Paradoxically, there is often a quality of overprotection in these families. When the child has acted out and is identified by the school or court authorities, the parents often feel compelled to protect their child from these outside influences (Johnston & Zemitzsch, 1988). In this way, the child has the parents' covert endorsement and avoids facing the consequences for the behavior. This type of overprotection operates externally to the family, with outside agencies or the school, but does not operate internally or around personal boundaries as in the families of the child with a chronic illness. As we described in chapter 4, this process involves triangulation between the student, the parents, and an outside authority. These triangles limit the emotional functioning of the student with a behavior disorder.

An example of how this type of overprotection might play out would be a student stealing another student's watch. The parents might actually know the truth but staunchly protect their child by suggesting that the other student forgot to retrieve the watch he had asked their child to hold. Some variation of excuse would be provided. Generally, the parents are angry with school personnel in these instances.

In families with enmeshed boundaries, the overprotection tends to work in a different way. Instead of the angry lying, parents would react as if they themselves had been accused of stealing. They would deny the possibility of their child stealing and the thought of investigating that possibility would not likely cross their minds. These parents would tend to react defensively to contact by school personnel by withdrawing and becoming unavailable for discussion or mutual problem solving. Prior awareness of dysfunctional family boundaries may help the school professional plan contacts that take into account the family climate of overprotection or disengagement.

Lack of Conflict Resolution

In dysfunctional families in which there is a child or adolescent with emotional or behavioral symptoms, the expression of anger and conflict tends to take one of two inappropriate forms. One of these tendencies is exhibited in families where there is a high level of internal chaos and parents tend to feel overwhelmed with the tasks of providing for and structuring family life. In these families, parents are highly reactive to any expression of anger or potential conflict in their children. Discipline may be punitive or abusive in nature, and parents may be physically or verbally abusive of one another as well (Minuchin et al., 1967). Educators may notice that these parents call their children names when trying to set limits on their behavior or when confronted with the slightest difficulty on the child's part. This type of family dynamic is usually multigenerational in nature and may benefit from referral for outside counseling (Anderson & Goolishian, 1986).

A second type of difficulty with conflict resolution is seen in families where anger is an emotion to be avoided at all costs. In these families, children are taught, either covertly or overtly, that to be angry is to be bad. In contrast, feelings such as sadness, depression, or hurt are seen as acceptable and deserving of parental attention and intervention. In this manner, any conflict or anger between family members is denied and not directly expressed. However, unresolved long-term resentments may result in acting-out or chronic depressive symptoms that professionals will then witness in school.

Parental Asymmetry and Marital Subsystem

In many families where a child has an emotional/behavioral problem, there is considerable discord between the parents about the definition and handling of the problem. For example, the mother may identify her son as "depressed" while the father may view the son as "lazy." This type of long-term disagreement and emotional distance between the couple may be a symptom of more extensive marital difficulties. The school personnel dealing with differing parental views must avoid taking sides in this dispute. Eliciting input from both parents is important in families with this dynamic. The parents may be willing to learn to work together for the benefit of their child while they would not be motivated to settle their differences solely for their own happiness. Again, the marital subsystem takes a back seat to the functions of the parental subsystem.

In this section dealing with behavior disorders, we have referred to a wide variety of problems and symptoms in children and adolescents that may be observed in the school. Given the range of possible behavioral/emotional problems, the structural characteristics that we described should make you familiar with some examples of how these problems manifest themselves in dysfunctional families. However, these descriptions are not intended as exhaustive examples of all the possible ways family dysfunction may be exhibited.

LEARNING DISABILITIES

The category "learning disabilities" includes many different types of learning problems and consequent behaviors. Children with learning disabilities range from those with severe disabilities who cannot function in a normal classroom to those who are mild underachievers and get C's and D's when they are capable of making A's (Smith, 1981).

The specifics of the structural dynamics in these families depend upon when and how the diagnosis of learning disability was made and how extensive the disability was. Unique to this category of special needs is the elusive quality of the disability. In contrast to, for example, diabetes or mental retardation, children with learning disabilities may have experienced difficulties that have gone undiagnosed for years (Abrams & Kaslow, 1977). Often these children have undergone a series of failures that have led them to feel insecure, poorly motivated, and ignorant. Parents and teachers may have been involved in various attempts to correct the child's school failures through interventions, including homework monitoring, behavioral checklists, punishment, or coaxing (Sloman & Konstantareas, 1990). The longer the child has had school problems with an undiagnosed learning disability, the more likely that the child, parents, and school professionals are frustrated and angry with one another about the struggles around the child's problems.

Not Visible - hard to deal with. Function as disabled in some areas but not others be able to discern

Dysfunctional Family Boundaries

More than with any other disability area, the possibility for poor communication between families and the school system is inherent in the subtlety of this diagnosis ("Our Son Has Had Trouble...," 1986). Frequently, parents have seen more than one outside professional about their child's problems and may have requested various evaluations of the child that resulted in little or no progress. Without an understanding of the child's disability, parents may blame teachers for poor instruction and classroom management, and teachers may blame parents for inconsistency or lack of support in an effort to explain a child's school failure.

A letter from a mother of a child with a learning disability illustrates this cycle of blame:

> His nursery school teacher said I babied him because he couldn't button or zip.... His kindergarten teacher said I should discipline him more because he was too lazy to learn his letters and numbers. His first-grade teacher called one parent conference after another. I tried to help Henry sit still and learn his letters.... [My husband] says I spoil him.... His folks say, "A few good spankings will set him straight." Mother says I just need patience. Dad says, "...He's all boy." ...The pediatrician says...he's a late bloomer.... I'm trying everything I know how to do. I'm exhausted from trying. (Smith, 1981, p. 150)

In these families, boundary problems may arise not so much within the family as between the family and external resources. From their history of involvement with the school system and other professionals, parents and the child with special needs may have developed a "we/them" mentality. The family's external boundaries may be rigid and inflexible, which may lead to a sense of isolation for all family members. Observing this situation should provide incentive for school professionals to remain patient and continue to strive for alliances with these types of families.

Overprotection

Some parents with a child with a learning disability are overprotective and show enmeshed boundaries (Amerikaner & Omizo, 1984). These family dynamics frequently appear in situations where the diagnosis of the child was delayed and there has been confusion or conflict between the parents and the school system. Many times, but not always, these students have overall levels of intelligence in the average or low-average range and may have been identified as "slow learners" or "mentally retarded." The parent, who feels that his or her child is not retarded and may have seen evidence of the child's intellectual abilities in the home, may feel compelled to protect the child from teasing, labeling, and incorrect school placement.

Another example of overprotection can be seen with the most serious, severe, and all-encompassing disabilities such as dyslexia (Perosa & Perosa, 1981). A child who has a high score on an intelligence test but who cannot read will usually be diagnosed early in the schools. Due to the student's high intelligence, it may be difficult for parents to reconcile themselves to the fact that their child cannot read normally. They may overprotect their child by lashing out at the schools for poor instruction or programming (Silver, 1984). It is important for teachers to remain patient with these parents until they learn enough about their child's disabilities to understand the symptoms.

As discussed previously, parental protection and advocacy may be important and adaptive in these situations. However, when the parent continues to be overprotective long after diagnosis and placement issues have been resolved, dysfunctional family dynamics will result.

Parental Asymmetry and Marital Relationship

In these families, as in all systems, the added stress of identifying and dealing with a child having learning disabilities tends to intensify any parental disagreements or lack of cohesion. Frequently, one parent is well-versed in the nuances of the child's diagnosis while the other parent has only a vague idea of how the child's learning disability affects educational performance. Because of this difference, the parent with the most knowledge tends to be the primary person who intervenes by helping the child with remediation or organization. With this potential dysfunctional system in mind, school professionals should work to insure that both parents receive copies of diagnostic reports, attend planning meetings, and have an opportunity to ask questions about their child's disability.

Because of the link between learning disabilities and motivational problems, many parents will have had problems with discipline issues. One parent may feel that the child is trying his or her hardest and should be reinforced for trying, while the other parent may focus on grades and assume a lack of motivation. Behavioral systems may have been tried and failed so that both parents are left feeling as if they, themselves, are failures. This type of conflict may lead to increased distance between the couple and less and less focus on the positive aspects of the marital subsystem ("He Pits Jane and Me...," 1988).

School professionals working with families of students with learning disabilities need to observe, probe, and use their experience with each family to get a clear picture of the underlying dynamics of acceptance and integration of the student. Educators should not assume that what families present on the surface is the complete picture of their struggle or dynamics in relation to the student.

MENTAL RETARDATION

Within this population there are at least two broad subgroups to consider when discussing family dynamics and dysfunction. These groups are Educable Mental Retardation, (EMR) or milder retardation, and Trainable Mental Retardation (TMR) or more serious retardation. Since Dunn's (1968) "Swan Song" was published, there has been a gradually increasing momentum for mainstreaming children and youth with mild retardation. General educators in the 1990s will be more accustomed to contact with and exposure to these students and their families. With the Regular Education Initiative (Skrtic, 1991), general educators can anticipate more interaction with families who have children with trainable mental retardation. Therefore, with an eye to this change, we are providing information concerning family dynamics of both groups.

Dysfunctional Family Boundaries

All parents with a child who has been labeled "retarded" must go through a process of dealing with the realities of their child's limitations and altering their hopes, dreams, and expectations for a "normal" child (Kew, 1975; Strom, Rees, Slaughter, & Wurster, 1981). With EMR children, parents may notice some differences in their child or some delay in developmental milestones, but they may continue to deny the reality of their perceptions until the child reaches school age and is identified by an outside professional. With TMR children, it is more likely that the diagnosis was made early after the child's birth and that intervention was begun in infancy. The family situation with a child diagnosed with retardation is ripe for enmeshment and identification of the child with a disability as the central important characteristic of the family, which leads to the loss of personal identity.

Within families where boundaries are extensively enmeshed, there is often an understanding that the child with retardation will never leave home and be on his or her own. Family members may be apprised of their future responsibility for the child, and family plans are made with the retarded person as a permanent member of the nuclear family. Older siblings may be told early on that it is their responsibility to support this child and take him or her into their households when the parents can no longer provide the necessary support ("I'm Not Going to Be...," 1987).

The dynamics of enmeshment are particularly evident when working with teenagers with retardation whose parents deny the implications of peer relationships, sexual development, and vocational issues for their child. For example, many parents do not assume the responsibility for providing guidance regarding interest in members of the opposite sex, sexual protection, or basic family life education that they would normally provide to their nondisabled children (Beavers, Hampson, Hulgus, & Beavers, 1986).

Overprotection

Family members are reminded daily that the child with retardation is not "normal" and that adjustments must be made to accommodate his or her disabilities. However, the extent to which the retardation will interfere with the child's life depends, in large part, on how far the family will be able to go in helping the child be treated as normally as possible (Mink, Meyers & Nihira, 1984). Parents often believe it is cruel to push a child with retardation to reach for achievements that may be outside of his or her capabilities. So the parents set in their own minds the limits of the child's functioning, which may underestimate the child's potential and work to keep the child within those limits. Parents may believe that their child will be made fun of or used by society if they are not there to protect him or her. If the overprotective parent communicates fear of the world to the child, then he or she is disabled not only intellectually but also socially.

Dudley (1983) conducted an interesting sociological study of twenty-seven adults labeled *retarded*. He lived with his subjects for a period of time so that he could experience their lifestyle firsthand. Dudley found that those of his subjects who had been allowed to openly discuss the realities of their retardation, the realities of societal fear and stigma about retardation, and the demands of adulthood were more likely to be able to adjust than those who had been overprotected.

Again, in the case of overprotective parents, school personnel should observe without judgment and help the parents to free their child gradually from their own fears. Providing an arena for open discussion of such questions as, "What does retarded mean? Will I always be retarded? How can people tell that I'm retarded?" may improve communication between students and their parents.

Lack of Conflict Resolution

In an extensive longitudinal study of 104 TMR children and their families, Nihira, Mink, and Meyers (1981) found that the single most important factor in the school adjustment of these children was the harmony and quality of parenting. With this information in mind, it is clear that conflict resolution is an important skill for parents of a student with retardation.

School professionals may find two types of family dysfunction in conflict resolution in families of students with retardation. One type of dysfunction involves parents who have few or no skills in advocating for their children with retardation. Some of these families have multiple problems, including cultural deprivation, poverty, and intellectual slowness on the part of the parents. Professionals may find that these parents act very compliant and agreeable about their children but then fail to follow through with school requests or training programs.

These parents tend to have few assertiveness skills and may feel that attempts to disagree with school personnel or even to ask questions are of no use in changing their situation. Often these parents are used to heavy questioning and complying with agency rules in order to obtain food for their children, shelter, and medical help. They may have developed a style of nonassertiveness in response to these other experiences. In these situations, school professionals should help the parents formulate and express questions and disagreements, communicate their unique perceptions of the child, and develop a mutual working relationship with the school system over time. School personnel may provide much of the help needed to network these parents. For suggestions about networking, see chapter 11 and Appendix C.

The other dysfunctional pattern that is common in these families is a heightened level of conflict with agencies, schools, and any professionals who are involved with the student with retardation. Typically, the conflict with schools centers around placement issues and labeling during the student's school career. Within these families, there is often a high level of general anger that may be directed at people outside or within the home. As a result, the families tend to be isolated and have little social network involvement in order to help with the retarded child. It is our experience that, quite often, the intense anger is a mask for overwhelming sadness and guilt that the parents feel toward their child. As emotional expressiveness in families with a retarded child is often limited (Margalit & Raviv, 1983), the parents may have no one with whom they can express these feelings and may have, over many years, projected blame onto outside sources in an effort to avoid looking at their own feelings of blame and doubt.

Parental Asymmetry and Marital Subsystem

Families in which there is a child with retardation tend to develop the classic situation where the mother accepts primary responsibility for the child's management. As Berger (l984b) stated:

Because the task of arranging for the youngster's treatment falls mostly on mothers, a predictable structure for families...is one in which there is a very close mother/child dyad. The closeness of this dyad is reinforced by the fact that when agencies that serve handicapped children seek "parent involvement," they tend to mean mother involvement. (p. 144)

This intense closeness is particularly evident in families with a child with retardation because many of the functional living skills and personal hygiene skills that are a long-term part of the training for retarded people, classically fall into the mother's domain. Thus, the close-mother/distant-father dynamic that we have discussed as troublesome in all families of students with special needs easily evolves in families having a child with retardation.

Corrales, Kostoryz, Ro-Trock, and Smith (1983) interviewed and observed 24 families with children having intellectual and developmental delays. They reported significant marital distress in 16 of the 24 couples. In addition, almost all of the families with high marital distress were rated by the observers as families in which one parent had formed a coalition with the disabled child. School professionals can be most useful by helping parents become aware of this dynamic over time and developing strategies to intervene on their own behalf.

A second process that often occurs between couples with a child having retardation is mutual blaming, guilt, and grieving (Turner, 1980). The question, "Why do we have a retarded child?" is often answered by one or both parents by looking to genetic history or prenatal care and focusing blame on the other parent. Of course, some of this questioning and wrestling with themselves and with God is a natural part of the process of accepting a child with disabilities. It is when this dynamic continues over a prolonged period that marital distance and dysfunction are inevitable.

Couples need to be helped to understand that the process of grieving for the lost "normal" child and feeling angry about the reality of having a child with retardation are predictable stages for parents of children with disabilities. Rather than turning on each other, the couple needs to be helped to turn to each other for support and resolution of the grieving process. Support groups are invaluable in helping parents with acceptance and grieving. The schools should provide parents with information about the availability of these groups in their community. (See chapter 11 and Appendix C for further information on referring parents to external resources.)

It might be beneficial for general educators to network with special education professionals who are more familiar with these family dynamics to develop a better understanding of families having children with retardation. Mainstreaming of these students provides an opportunity for consultation and cohesion between various educational disciplines that may result in learning on all fronts.

SUMMARY

This chapter has provided a framework for assessing dysfunctional family patterns in families having a child with special needs. Four broad categories of students with special needs were discussed: physical disabilities and chronic illness, behavior disorders, learning disabilities, and mental retardation.

The purpose of the following case example is to pull together the content of this chapter by threading one example through the five structural concepts that we have highlighted. This example is not designed to indicate how the school system should specifically intervene with a family presenting these symptoms. It is intended to give you experience in integrating information and observations to make hypotheses about the dynamics of a particular family. More specific applications and interventions for use in the school will be covered in Part II.

CASE EXAMPLE

This family became the concern of the middle-school personnel where the 10-year-old daughter attended the sixth grade. The daughter, the youngest of two children, had been diagnosed with insulin-dependent diabetes at the age of 8. Her older brother, a senior in high school, was described as a model child. He played on the school football team, was an A student, and participated in student government. His plans for the future included attending college, and he had already received early acceptance notices from two colleges. In contrast, the 10-year-old was viewed as a very difficult child. Her grades were in the low C range with occasional D's and F's, in spite of testing that indicated an above-average IQ. She had few friends and was somewhat overweight.

During the past school year, this child had been absent from school an average of once per week. In addition, she frequently asked to leave the classroom to go to the school clinic due to what she described as "low blood sugars." At these times, the school nurse would give her orange juice or a protein snack, if necessary. The nurse would also call the child's mother, a former nurse, to receive instructions. At the time that the principal called a meeting of her teachers, this child was going to the clinic on the average of three times per day. Needless to say, this time out of the classroom was contributing to her poor grades. When the girl's mother had been contacted by one of the child's teachers about her missed work, the mother became indignant because the teacher would not agree to require less work of the student due to her frequent absences. The mother had then called the school principal about the "unfair treatment" her daughter was receiving.

Questions and Comments

1. *What are the dysfunctional structural characteristics of this girl's family? What information is used to diagnose these structural components?*

Based on information received over the year by the student's five teachers, the team made the following observations about the family structure.

Dysfunctional Family Boundaries

This family displayed enmeshed boundaries between the mother and this child and disengaged boundaries between the father and child. The father, who owned his own business, worked long hours and was essentially unavailable for family time. He appeared to have a better relationship with his son than his daughter. He regularly attended his son's football games but was not involved in his son's other activities or in providing significant emotional support to him. The mother had always been the backbone of this family's life. Prior to her daughter's diagnosis with diabetes, she had been very involved in both her children's achievements and had worked part-time as a tutor. She had been president of the booster club at her son's high school and had led her daughter's Girl Scout troop.

After the diagnosis, the daughter had become this mother's mission in life. The daughter no longer attended Girl Scouts because she felt that the other girls made fun of her because of her diabetes. The mother began to cook specific meals at the daughter's request on a daily basis in an attempt to keep her blood sugar in check. The mother quit her job because she felt she had to be available for intervening in her daughter's blood-sugar monitoring. The daughter had begun to have tantrums at home when she did not get her way. The mother identified these outbursts as "high-blood-sugar attacks" and would try to calm the daughter by giving her what she wanted. As the mother became more involved with this child, the father became more and more distant. He felt that the mother's approach to his daughter was "spoiling" her and making her "weak." The mother felt that her husband did not understand the medical implications of diabetes and thus could not provide sound judgments about managing his daughter's behavior.

Overprotection

This mother was extremely overprotective of her daughter following her diagnosis with diabetes. Previous to the diagnosis, the girl had played on a soccer team and had attended Girl Scouts. Following her diagnosis, she quit both of these activities and began to spend more and more time at home. Her mother often allowed her to stay home from school because of the slightest physical complaint. Over the past two years, this child had become less and less functional with peers and more and more dependent on her mother in all areas of her life. The mother's request to be called by the school nurse each time her blood sugar was monitored was another example of the overprotection. The school nurse was highly trained in diabetes management, and the girl's trips to the clinic often found normal blood sugar in spite of the child's complaints. The mother's attention to these "spells" only served to reinforce the child's dependence.

Lack of Conflict Resolution

This family showed indications of problems with conflict resolution both within the family and in dealings with the outside world. Within the family, it appeared that the parents had avoided dealing with their basic differences about management of this child. Rather than openly arguing about or discussing their differing opinions, the mother had become more and more involved with protecting the child and the father had become more involved with his business and with ignoring his daughter's complaints. Although the son may have resented the changes in his family due to their handling of his sister's illness, he had not expressed his feelings to either parent. He had also adapted by becoming more and more involved in his own activities and life outside of the home.

Problems with conflict resolution in the outside world were also evident. When the girl reported being "made fun of" by peers in her Girl Scout troop, her mother's answer was to quit going to scouts rather than trying to reach some resolution in her daughter's relationships. The mother was very reactive to any perceived mistreatment of her daughter by peers, teachers, bus drivers, or extended family members. Her way of managing her anger was to keep her daughter out of school as often as possible, drive her daughter to school so she would not have to deal with the driver or students on the bus, instruct her daughter to avoid peer interactions, and withdraw from extended family relationships. All of these choices meant that the conflict was avoided rather than reaching some resolution.

Parental Asymmetry

It was clear that the balance of power between this couple was very one-sided. The mother had taken over sole management of this child's life while the father had withdrawn from interaction. The mother made all significant decisions regarding physical and emotional functioning of the family. No one within the school system had ever spoken with or met the father. Although he was a respected businessman in the community, he had little power to influence the day-to-day workings of his own family.

Marital Relationship Subordinate to Parental Roles

Although the school personnel had little information about this couple's relationship, they could hypothesize that the marital relationship was not going well. The mother would not allow this child to stay alone because of the possibility of a blood-sugar crisis. The girl felt she was too old for baby-sitters and would have an "outburst" any time the possibility of a sitter was mentioned. Thus the parents had not been out of the home together in the two years since the girl's diagnosis. It was also probable that the father's anger toward his wife because of her unavailability to anyone other than her daughter, and the wife's anger toward her husband because of his withdrawal from family life, contributed to significant tension and distance between the couple.

2. *What intervention strategies could be used by the school to help change this family's dysfunctional structure?*

The team of teachers and principal decided to request a meeting between both of the girl's parents and all school personnel involved with the identified student. At this meeting, they asked that the mother, because of her nursing experience, provide inservice education to all of them regarding diabetes, its management and complications. Teachers agreed to ask specific questions about symptoms of low and high blood sugar so that they could feel comfortable dealing with this child in the classroom.

In addition, the teachers and school nurse presented the parents with an intervention plan for their daughter's frequent trips to the school clinic. Each time the girl went to the clinic, her finger was to be pricked and blood sugar monitored and written on a log to be sent home at the end of each day. The girl was to carry the log with her at all times so that, if she asked to leave a classroom, the teacher would check the log for the most recent blood-sugar monitoring and the intervention. The parents agreed that monitoring blood sugar more often than once every two hours was not necessary unless the child was exhibiting severe physical symptoms (which were described by the mother). If the student asked to leave the classroom and she had been checked within the last two hours, her request was to be refused. If she insisted that she was experiencing a "low," she was to be given a container of orange juice that each teacher would keep in the classroom. In addition, each time that the girl did visit the clinic *both* parents were to be called with a report on her blood-sugar monitoring. The father agreed to carry a beeper so that he could be reached at his office or while on outside calls. The parents agreed that each night before their daughter went to bed they would both look over her blood-sugar log with her and discuss any questions.

Finally, the teachers consented to send home a weekly progress report for the student in each subject. If she had a weekly average of B or above in any class, she would receive reinforcement from the teacher of that particular class and from her parents. This agreement was made in an attempt to replace the negative attention that the student had been receiving with more positive time with her teachers and parents.

PART II

APPLICATIONS OF
FAMILY SYSTEMS

Part II initially focuses on team functioning as it relates to students with special needs. The needs of many at-risk students will be considered by educational teams, and by legal stipulation, the needs of all students with disabilities must be considered by a team. Because it covers team functioning, chapter 8 does not specifically relate to family systems concepts. The next four chapters, 9 through 12, integrate family systems concepts with concrete and useful applications for school professionals. These chapters include information about meeting with families on a less formal basis than team meetings, serving as a family liaison for students who are at risk or have special needs, and finally working with groups and in the classroom. The final chapter in Part II provides insights about barriers to working with families and important strategies for avoiding or dealing with those barriers.

TEAM FUNCTIONING AND FAMILY INVOLVEMENT 8

This chapter is designed to help you understand effective team functioning, with families being a focus of, as well as cooperating in, that process. We first describe three different educational team approaches. Then we provide information about the people who serve on teams. Next is an introduction to the stages teams pass through as they develop and change. Planning and implementing a team process follows. Information on avoiding problems and facing challenges precedes a brief overview of the problem-solving process. The chapter concludes with information on the interaction between the school and families and provides specific suggestions.

TEAM APPROACHES IN EDUCATION

There are three different team approaches to working with students with special needs commonly referred to in the literature: multidisciplinary, interdisciplinary, and transdisciplinary teams. Because most school programs for students with special needs use one of these three models (or a variation of one), it is helpful to have a broad view of all three. The models are briefly described so that you can identify which type is used in your system and be familiar with its strengths and weaknesses. If you work with more than one system, this information is also helpful. In addition, this overview can help professionals who move to a new system.

Multidisciplinary Team Approach

In the multidisciplinary model professionals from various disciplines, such as education, psychology, occupational therapy, and art therapy, each work individually with the student or family. That is, the professionals work in isolation from one another as they evaluate students and provide services. The multidisciplinary model was originally developed to serve patients with medical problems that can be relegated to one particular discipline. In this approach the different professionals working with one patient might not even regard themselves as part of a team.

Coordinating services to an individual student can be very difficult using the multidisciplinary approach. A major disadvantage of the multidisciplinary model is the potential for failure to consider the whole child. It is even possible that two or more professionals could make recommendations that conflict with one another. When professionals from different disciplines meet, their recommendations can be complex and conflicting. For example, a therapist may be encouraging parents who are overly involved in their child's education to back off. At the same time, the school counselor might independently be working to involve parents in a home-school behavior management program. In some schools multidisciplinary team members provide their different recommendations and then leave the teacher to sort through their ideas and implement suggestions.

Interdisciplinary Team Approach

The interdisciplinary team approach (Orelove & Sobsey, 1991) is considered more sophisticated than the multidisciplinary model. The interdisciplinary model provides a formal structure allowing interaction and communication among team members. In this approach, each professional does his or her own assessment and implementation; however, programming decisions are made by the group. As Fordyce (1982) said, "Interdisciplinary differs from multidisciplinary in that the end product of the effort—the outcome—can only be accomplished by a truly interactive effort and contributions from the disciplines involved" (p. 51).

This model is an improvement over the isolated functioning of the multidisciplinary team, but is subject to the same disadvantages. Decisions are affected by the orientations of each professional and may, therefore, result in disjointed outcomes for students. The difficulties inherent in group interaction can also cause problems.

In an article on physicians' involvement in interdisciplinary teams, Bennett (1982) looked at a variety of problems inherent in interdisciplinary teamwork. He stated: "Parents may become confused, rather than enlightened, by the interdisciplinary process if sufficient care is not taken to coordinate and synthesize the numerous professional evaluations" (p. 313). He also suggested several other problems, such as turf issues and differences in assessment approaches and management strategies, as well as discouragement of strong, effective leadership if one discipline views leadership attempts as arrogant.

Transdisciplinary Team Approach

The transdisciplinary model has three characteristics (Lyon & Lyon, 1980). First, it uses a joint team approach that assumes the team must perform services together. Second, it takes a staff development approach in which the expertise of each team member is valued and used to train others on the team. Finally, the roles and responsibilities of team members are shared by more than one person on the team.

As you might expect, this model presents few difficulties in coordinating services. However, some professionals have trouble with the notion of training other team members to implement procedures that they consider to be their area of expertise. This notion, called role release, presents interpersonal difficulties for some professionals. For example, if a counselor is required to train a parent to implement a program, the counselor might feel demeaned when the parent is seen as capable of implementing a program that the counselor needed a master's degree to learn.

The integrated therapy model is a feature of the transdisciplinary model wherein therapy services become integrated within education. Therapy goals are integrated within educational goals on IEPs. This feature is based on the assumption that therapists and teachers work together in program assessment, planning, and delivery. (For more information on the integrated therapy model see Rainforth, York, & MacDonald, 1992.)

EDUCATIONAL TEAMS

A variety of people contribute to the team process. Working together for the benefit of a student with special needs, they share their theories, philosophies, beliefs, experiences, and skills. Differences of opinion are expected and are most beneficial when viewed as contributing to a whole picture, as opposed to being seen as competing with other members' perspectives.

This section deals with the various people who serve on the educational team. An understanding of each person's beliefs, knowledge, and skills helps each team member to respect the others as well as to collaborate with one another.

Family Members

In this book family members come first, when many books either fail to include them as part of the team or place them last. It should not surprise you that we believe family members (usually parents) are critical to the team process. Parents and other family members are not usually in the schools on a regular basis. Nevertheless, beyond parents' legal rights to participate in assessment and planning, schools should invite their participation and view them as competent to provide information and suggestions. Parents will vary in the degree to which they would like, or be able, to participate. Recognizing and responding to the different preferences is showing respect for them as parents.

Teacher

The teacher has the primary responsibility for the education of the student with special needs. The regular classroom teachers in elementary and secondary schools can provide much insight into the needs of the student. Their observations of the student within and outside the classroom provide concrete descriptions on which the team can build a realistic picture and therefore make more effective recommendations. Suggestions provided by team members are filtered through the regular classroom teacher's lens for practicality.

Special Educator

The responsibility of the special education teacher is to teach students with special needs who have been found eligible for special education or related services. The special educator also serves as a liaison between the family of the student and the school system. Serving as a member or coordinator of a team of professionals working with the student, the special educator plays a unique role in the education of students with special needs. The special educator is an advocate for the student and provides the expertise of advanced training in a specialized field (or fields) of education.

Paraprofessional

The paraprofessional, or teacher's aide, often plays an important role in the education of the student with special needs. The paraprofessional can provide valuable information about the student's functioning as well as suggestions about practicality of interventions. Too often professionals do not recognize the value of the paraprofessional's wisdom.

Psychologist

The psychologist in most of the schools across America functions as an evaluator of students' intellectual and emotional abilities. Moran (1978) referred to this as the cognitive and affective functioning level of the assessment process.

In addition to that responsibility, psychologists may also be called upon to assess the student's learning style or problem-solving approaches. This information is particularly helpful when evaluating process-level data. Moran (1978) presented a strong warning about referral for this kind of testing. She recommended that such testing "should be considered only if the teacher cannot program for the student without it, and only if the teacher can specify a presenting problem which must be answered in order to instruct the pupil" (p. 83).

Many psychologists have assumed the role of helping develop behavioral strategies to be employed in the school or home. Some psychologists are also trained to work with families regarding issues of grief and loss. It is becoming more common for psychologists to have training in family systems models and therefore to be able to assist in interventions that consider the whole family system as opposed to the individual student as the sole focus of the intervention.

Counselor

Counselors will provide some of the same services as psychologists, depending upon their training and the needs of the school system. Some schools have counselors in every elementary building and more than one counselor in each secondary school.

Counselors on teams can provide diagnostic information as well as input on family matters. Increasing numbers of counselors are being trained in family systems concepts and are able to provide an intervention focus that reflects the family unit. They may also provide input on current group process opportunities in the school. For example, the counselor may lead a group for students who need follow-through after in-patient substance abuse treatment or a group for students whose parents are divorcing.

Educational Diagnostician

Most school systems employ educational diagnosticians. Educational diagnosticians are experienced special educators who have received additional training. They assess students' academic abilities and achievements and provide essential information on which team members rely. The diagnostician administers both formal, standardized measures as well as informal tests of academic functioning. They often engage in trial teaching to determine by which method the student learns best.

Social Worker

The school social worker will be the person on the team most familiar with family matters. He or she serves as a family advocate with extensive training in the realm of family functioning. The social worker is also most familiar with community resources from which the student with special needs and his or her family might benefit.

The social worker might even be the person the team appoints to coordinate services among the community, school, and home. However, not all social workers are familiar with the concepts of the specialized field of family systems. They may be well trained in aspects of family concerns and not have been exposed to the concepts of family systems approaches presented in Part I of this book.

Administrator

The administrator is responsible for policy and decision making as well as implementation of matters of placement, transportation, related services, equipment, and scheduling. Administrators are also required to ensure compliance with regulations. In many school systems administrators head prereferral and eligibility teams.

Administrators who sit on teams include principals, program directors or specialists, and special education coordinators, as well as people with other position titles or roles. Administrators can free up material, time, personnel, and financial resources, thereby facilitating the implementation of programs and related services for students with special needs. To facilitate effective family interventions, it is important that they have some training about family systems concepts.

Nurse

The school nurse is frequently the person with the most realistic information on the physical health of students with special needs. Among other areas, nurses are trained to deal with first aid, seizures, and medication, as well as to provide information on hygiene and diet.

Other Specialists

A variety of other specialists may be included on teams for particular students with special needs. Physicians can help the team by providing input on health and medication. Although few physicians actually attend team meetings, they can provide valuable input through phone or letter. Physicians vary widely in their ability to deal with, as well as their interest in, school-related problems (Levine, 1982). Bennett (1982) underscored the increasing involvement of physicians on interdisciplinary teams.

At times occupational or physical therapists will be included on a team for a student with special needs. The occupational therapist works with fine-motor skill development, including such skills as buttoning, zipping, writing, and typing. They also frequently work on daily living skills, such as eating, with students with severe physical impairments. The physical therapist, on the other hand, works with gross-motor skill development, including skills such as walking, balancing, skipping, playing ball, relaxing, and general coordination. They assist students with more severe physical disabilities.

Student

The student may also be a member of the team. Generally, elementary school students will not attend team meetings, although elementary students have been consulted about their preferences for pull-out, in-class, or integrated service delivery models (Jenkins & Heinen, 1989). That study indicated that professionals should ask students for their preferences.

Secondary-level students may be able to provide input about their educational programs. They can also provide realistic and accurate information about family considerations. In a heartrending commentary, Greer (1989) described his mistake of not including a secondary student as a team member or asking for her input about the service delivery model used. His former student told him years later that he had ruined her life because he had not left her in a special education classroom.

Even though federal and state laws clearly state that students may attend meetings, many school systems overlook the student as a potential contributor to the team. With the current emphasis on personal involvement in growth processes, students will likely become more frequent members of teams.

TEAM FUNCTIONING BY STAGES

The process of meeting the educational needs of at-risk and special needs learners involves several stages, though some students will not need to go through all of the stages. This section includes information on screening, prereferral, referral and evaluation, eligibility, and individualized educational programs.

Screening

Screening is a process of selecting students who may be at risk for school difficulties. It is the domain of the regular classroom teacher. When a student has a problem in school, the teacher should be concerned, whether the problem is academic, organizational, or behavioral. Clearly, different problems require different solutions! However, what may not be so obvious is the fact that the best solution requires an understanding of the cause of the problem. Understanding the cause requires careful and systematic exploration of the student's performance, behavior, prior school experiences, developmental age, disability, and family life.

Because the classroom teacher has responsibility for the student's education, he or she is the most appropriate person to begin exploring most problems. Classroom teachers also have the most knowledge of, and experience with, the students in their classroom. The teacher has the opportunity to observe the student in a variety of situations and does not make decisions based upon a short observation under nonclassroom conditions. The teacher also has the opportunity to observe the child across the whole day and week. Such opportunities are particularly pertinent to tracking and understanding any underlying family problems. For example, the teacher might observe that Mondays are particularly stressful for a student and wonder about what occurs on the weekend at home. Under these circumstances, the screening process is more reliable.

The teacher is responsible for creating positive change by using information gathered during the screening process. The teacher analyzes problems and attempts interventions based on those analyses. He or she carefully documents these interventions for future use if the need arises. When the changes or interventions that the teacher attempts do not produce results, or if the teacher runs out of solutions, then it is time to ask for assistance from a team of other professionals.

Prereferral

Most school systems have committees or teams that operate more or less formally to help teachers who need assistance with at-risk or special needs students. In a larger view, this process is referred to as teacher consultation (Friend, 1984; Idol-Maestas, 1983; Idol, Paolucci-Whitcomb & Nevin, 1986). A variety of names are used to refer to teams that sidestep the special education process—Teacher Assistance Teams (Chalfant, Pysh, & Moultrie, 1979); Mainstream Assistance Teams (Fuchs, Fuchs, & Bahr, 1990); and our choice, the prereferral team.

This step is not the beginning of the special education process. The purpose of the prereferral team is to help the teacher solve the specific problems that led to the request for assistance. This team tries to assist the teacher by analyzing information and suggesting possible solutions that sometimes include involving families. The next chapter includes more extensive information about prereferral teams and family involvement.

At one time professionals viewed all problems as deficits within the student. Over time our views have evolved; most professionals now recognize the importance of context. The student is influenced by classroom variables such as teaching style and organizational arrangement. It is difficult for teachers to judge the effects of these variables on the achievement and behavior of a particular student. Also, different students respond differently to the same teaching techniques and behavior management strategies. Adaptations in instruction, differing management strategies, or fresh strategies in the home may reduce academic troubles or inappropriate student behaviors. Members of the prereferral team are viewed as consultants whose aim is to help the classroom teacher devise strategies to overcome learning or behavior problems.

It is important for educators to join with parents during the prereferral stage. Professionals should share concerns and interventions with parents during prereferral team meetings, regularly scheduled parent–teacher conferences, or specially arranged conferences. Effective communication skills are critical in all of these processes. Professionals will not take parents by surprise when they have kept them continually informed or involved as team members. In addition, parents are a valuable source of information about their child. When a student's performance varies tremendously between different contexts such as home and school, the teacher should examine potential causes of that discrepancy. Also parents have been known to suggest the very intervention that the teacher successfully adopted, thus precluding the need to refer a student for an evaluation.

Unfortunately, there are times when the prereferral intervention does not succeed. The next stage in the process of attempting to meet the student's needs is referral and evaluation.

Referral and Evaluation

Referral and evaluation is the process by which students and their families enter special education. The chance that a family will have a positive experience is increased if all professionals handle this process sensitively and efficiently.

The teacher develops the referral for evaluation. He or she communicates the student's status, reports prior interventions used, specifies the referral question, and prepares the student for referral. The referral question states what the teacher would like to determine from the assessment that will follow. An example of a referral question is "Would Tom benefit from remedial instruction in reading?"

Once the referral is made, the building administrator ensures that parents are informed of their rights and that they consent, in writing, to an evaluation. The administrator must also ensure that appropriate evaluations are conducted by qualified personnel and that an eligibility determination is made within a predetermined number of working days. Evaluations must be free from cultural bias.

School districts should have written information for parents regarding their legal rights, called "procedural safeguards." It is helpful to review that information to ensure that it is clear enough for the parents in your particular community to understand. All parents must receive such information before giving consent for evaluation. If you do not know about this information, be sure to find copies and become familiar with it. Professionals should also know who has the responsibility for providing this information to parents. Different school systems rely on different people to provide the information.

Parents must also be provided a description of any action, rationale for that action, and alternatives proposed by the school. At this stage, the proposed action is evaluation of a child to determine whether a disability exists and what types of individual programming would be most appropriate.

Next, parents must be informed about assessment procedures, data, and other information that will be employed to decide whether to pursue evaluation. Names and purposes of tests that will most likely be used are helpful for parents.

Last, parents must be provided information that the committee used in making a decision about a referral. This usually includes information on academic functioning, peer relationships, and health status.

Eligibility

After the formal assessment of the student is completed and the reports that interpret the assessment results are written, a new team meets to evaluate the results. Again, this team is referred to by many different terms; we will refer to it as the eligibility team. (See Lambert, 1988; Ysseldyke, 1979; Ysseldyke & Algozzine, 1983; Ysseldyke, Algozzine, & Allen, 1982; Ysseldyke, Algozzine, & Epps, 1983; Ysseldyke, Algozzine, Richey, & Graden, 1982.) This section includes information about who serves on this team, the procedures employed during eligibility team meetings, and record-keeping procedures.

Membership

The members of the eligibility committee include someone capable of interpreting the tests administered, the special education administrator (or someone with expertise in the field of special education designated to take that person's place), one person who has observed the student or been directly involved in the actual assessment process, the teacher, and other professional(s), as necessary. There should be a broad base for decision making to ensure that the decisions that are made represent the best thinking from a variety of perspectives.

Some school systems also include the parents on this team. We are in favor of parents having the opportunity to be involved in the eligibility meeting. Although it may take longer to include parents, it is worthwhile to include interested parents. Not all school systems agree; however, by law all must include parents in the next stage, developing the Individualized Educational Program.

Determination of Eligibility

In examining the results and interpretations of the various professionals who have evaluated the student, the eligibility team must make two important determinations. They must first determine whether the student qualifies as exceptional according to federal and state guidelines. Just as important, they must determine whether the student needs special education services to profit from the educational experience.

Both conditions must exist before the student is eligible for special education. It is possible that a particular student might meet either, but not both, standards and thus not qualify for special education. For example, it might be determined that a student is indeed performing poorly in school and the services of a special education teacher in a resource setting might be beneficial but the student does not meet the definition of any of the disabilities. In this case, it is illegal to use special education to label the student "disabled" just so that he or she can receive special education.

However, when the team decides that the student has a disability that requires special education or related services, the committee must identify the disability and recommend what, if any, related services are required. These recommendations relate to the educational and other related services that the student needs if he or she is to receive an education appropriate to his or her learning needs and abilities.

Records

The eligibility team keeps a written record of its meeting that must be signed by each member. Any member who does not agree with the consensus of the group has the right to refuse to sign the minutes. That individual then submits a written report explaining reasons for the disagreement with the determination of the team. Once signed, the minutes of the meeting are placed in the student's confidential folder.

If the eligibility team determines that the student is eligible for special education services, then a summary of this report is prepared. This summary is used by the next committee, which is the Individualized Education Program team.

Individualized Education Program

The Individualized Education Program (IEP) is supposed to be the cornerstone of educational programming for students with disabilities. It is the vehicle used to develop programs that provide free and appropriate educational experiences for each of these students.

The IEP must be developed by a team before the student is placed in any special education program. The student's parent(s) must also agree to the program before it may be implemented. These conditions are designed to ensure that the program the child receives meets his or her unique learning needs, not that the individual student meets the requirements of a given program. In other words, a program is designed to fit the individual student; the student is not made to fit a program. This stipulation is intended to avoid previous practices that placed a student in a program according to a label such as "learning disabilities" and expected all students so labeled to profit from identical educational experiences. IEPs are part of what makes special education "special."

The IEP team members include a person who is qualified either to supervise or provide special education, the student's teacher, the parent or guardian, the child (if appropriate), and other individual(s) chosen by the school or parent. The meeting must be scheduled at a time that is convenient to both the school personnel and the parent(s).

An IEP is similar to a contract. It delineates the educational program and related services, if any, the school system is obligated to provide for each student with a disability. The school system and teacher are not, however, legally responsible if the goals of the educational program are not met. The law recognizes that education is a complex endeavor; though educational personnel can be held responsible for providing the opportunities for success, they cannot be held responsible for ensuring that each student will be successful. The next chapter includes much more information on IEPs and involving parents in that process.

As this section on the stages of team functioning shows, a professional could belong to a whole host of teams. Beyond that, imagine the parents trying to keep up with all of these teams and also to provide meaningful input for their child. Clearly, providing the best educational opportunities for the child requires careful planning and implementation of the team process. Without such consideration these teams would not be able to function effectively.

PLANNING AND IMPLEMENTING TEAM PROCESS

There are at least four aspects that are important to effective planning as well as implementation of team process. First, clarity of purpose is critical to productive team functioning. Second, smoothly functioning teams employ effective *task* (e.g., giving information, summarizing) and *maintenance* (e.g., encouraging, harmonizing) behaviors. Third, leadership is best when it is shared, and chairpeople are most effective when they assume a democratic style. Finally, all members are not automatically involved in team meetings; increasing involvement must be a concern of all team members.

Purpose

Groups that work effectively together perform as a collection of individuals with clarity of purpose and goals. According to Losen and Losen (1985), team meetings, dealing with learners with special needs are for the purpose of planning or reviewing.

Six possible activities for planning meetings are (a) meeting before a referral to review information and provide suggestions; (b) reviewing referrals for special education services; (c) deciding whether a student is eligible for special education; (d) determining placement options in the least restrictive environment; (e) considering related services; and (f) developing an IEP. Awareness of these six activities allows team members to know their purpose from the beginning.

Review is required for monitoring the IEP as well as modifying the student's educational program, related services, or placement. The review process must be completed at least once a year. Having a clarity of purpose about assigned activities is one way to improve team functioning.

Task and Maintenance Behaviors

Any particular behavior of a team member can be classified according to its basic function. Team members speak either with intent to get the group task accomplished (task behavior) or to improve relationships among members (maintenance behavior) (Benne & Sheats, 1948). Table 8.1 lists the types of behavior that relate to task functions. Examples of each task function relate to teams in schools. Of course, not all of team process is about task functions. Maintenance functions are critical for the team to smoothly function within a supportive climate that maximizes the use of each team member. Group maintenance functions are described in Table 8.2.

Together task and maintenance behaviors allow team members to get their jobs done smoothly and efficiently. All of these behaviors are the responsibility of each team member. It is helpful to observe these behaviors in others as well as to note what shows up missing in meetings. You may choose to set a goal of increasing your repertoire or calling to the attention of other team members what typically occurs in your team meetings.

Leadership

Leadership is the responsibility of all members of the team and should be shared by all. The chairperson of the team cannot be responsible for all of the task and maintenance behaviors, nor would that be desirable. Shared responsibility makes for more effective team functioning.

Beyond each team member's responsibility for assuming a role in leadership, the role of the chair of the team is important. Pfeiffer (1980) examined studies on the effects of leadership styles on the special education team. He found that when chairpeople are too directive in resolving problems, their ideas are seen as unacceptable; the other team members may become hostile. Being given a voice in decision making and in sharing ideas and suggestions was deemed important by team members.

Pfeiffer (1980) also found that team members do not want problems handed to one discipline or individual to solve. He maintained that at least two team members from different disciplines should be involved in all aspects of the problem-solving process.

Losen and Losen (1985) stated that sharing responsibility for team process does not simply happen, it evolves. Effective sharing of responsibility must be nurtured and reinforced by the chairperson as well as other team members. Losen and Losen (1985) provided suggestions for leadership conducive to team functioning. They recommended the chairpeople *not* provide direct orders, interrupt proceedings with their own suggestions, ignore team member's suggestions, withhold praise or encouragement, make general critical or nonobjective comments, or demand respect or allegiance. The authors recommended that chairpeople *should* offer guiding suggestions, provide information timed to be of value, stimulate self-direction, appreciate others' values and views, and respect

Table 8.1
TASK FUNCTIONS

1. *Initiating.* For effective team functioning, someone must take the initiative. Proposing tasks, actions, goals, suggesting a procedure, and defining group problems are examples of initiating. Someone might say, "Let's build an agenda" or "Let's write the suggestions on the board so we don't forget them."
2. *Seeking or giving information or openness.* For a task to be accomplished, it is imperative that there is a clear and efficient flow of information, facts, and opinions. An example of information giving is, "I have some research data that might help in making our decision." This ensures that any decisions are based on as much information as possible. Information seeking helps the entire group, not just the one asking questions. An example of this is, "How did Carlie perform during resource activities?"
3. *Clarifying and elaborating.* This involves interpreting ideas or suggestions as well as clarifying issues before the team. Such statements communicate a collaborative stance. For example, "Let me elaborate and build upon that idea" or "I think what Mr. Jones means is that he doesn't know whether his son has the self-confidence to make himself comfortable enough to return to the regular classroom full-time. I agree and...."
4. *Summarizing.* This involves pulling together related ideas and suggestions or offering a decision or conclusion for team consideration. Summarizing allows the entire group a chance to reflect on where they have been, where they are, and where they must go. Summarizing statements are interjected at various times during a team meeting and not just in concluding the meeting. An example might be, "It seems as though so far we have made these points...."
5. *Consensus testing.* Although not all decisions can or should be made by consensus, much teamwork is a result of consensus decisions. These are statements that check with team members to determine the amount of agreement that has been achieved. For example, "Have we made a decision about this speech therapy?" Such a statement reminds team members that they must sooner or later commit to a decision, thus adding a bit of positive work tension to the team process.

---

differences in opinions.

Orelove and Sobsey (1991) indicated steps that administrators can take to facilitate a transdisciplinary approach for individuals with severe disabilities. The following ideas are adaptations of leadership activities, especially on the part of the principal, that encourage team process.

1. Encourage individual team members to see themselves as responsible to the team.
2. Encourage the team to see itself as responsible to the student and family and to see the learner from a family systems perspective.
3. Encourage family members to become involved at the level they choose.

Table 8.2
MAINTENANCE FUNCTIONS

[handwritten annotations: "Documentor organizational keeps on task/time"]

1. *Gatekeeping.* Without gatekeeping, information will be lost, multiple conversations will develop, and quieter team members will be cut off and withdraw. These types of statements attempt to keep the channels of communication open, facilitate participation by team members, and focus on sharing. "Mary never had the opportunity to explain her suggestion" or "If we would all speak one at a time, we could hear everyone's ideas" are examples of gatekeeping.

2. *Encouraging.* This allows relevant information to be shared, heard, and considered. It involves being respectful, warm, and friendly toward others. For example, "Mrs. Guissepe, is there something you would like to add before we move on?"

3. *Harmonizing and compromising.* The aims of harmonizing are to reconcile disagreement, reduce tensions, and allow team members to explore differences. An example is, "It would be beneficial if both of you would specify your objections to the other, rather than name call." An example of compromising would be, "It looks like Dan and I both have viable suggestions. Also, the team looks evenly divided about these two suggestions. In order to move forward in the meeting, I would like to focus on Dan's suggestion and retract mine." It is important not to overuse these types of statements. In addition, it is easy to use them inappropriately and thereby reduce the effectiveness of the team. You do not want to harmonize or compromise if it results in masking important issues or discounting creative solutions.

4. *Standard setting and testing.* This focuses on the effectiveness of the task and maintenance behaviors of the team members. It is a matter of watching to see how the group operates and then sharing those perceptions with team members. For example, "Are we off task?" or "I can't keep up. Could someone summarize this discussion for me?"

---

4. Arrange school schedules to allow for regular team meetings, with coverage of classrooms when necessary.

5. Demonstrate effective communication skills during team meetings.

6. Encourage teachers and related services personnel to work together with family members to assess students and to develop goals and objectives.

7. During meetings, encourage the use of clear, simple language that parents and other professionals can understand.

8. Do not prevent conflict; help to resolve it when it occurs.

Involvement

Encouraging involvement means involvement of all members of the team, including parents. Studies (Pfeiffer, 1980; Ysseldyke, Algozzine, & Allen, 1982) have shown that parents and regular classroom teachers tend not to be involved in team process. Yoshida, Fenton, Maxwell, and Kaufman (1978) found that level of satisfaction increased with higher levels of participation on the team. Thus, involving all team members is critical to effective team functioning.

Pfeiffer (1980) recommended that a "floating substitute" be secured to substitute for any teacher attending a team meeting. He also recommended that a general education teacher serve as a constant team member to represent general education, which should enhance the status as well as involvement of that teacher. A standing team member would be more likely to help the occasional member feel more comfortable and be more involved in team process.

The findings of Yoshida, Fenton, Maxwell and Kaufman (1978), concerning the lack of involvement by regular classroom teachers in team meetings, was built upon by Trailor (1982). She investigated the effects of role clarification on the participation level of classroom teachers on teams. Regular classroom teachers in an experimental group helped develop seventeen role statements for classroom teachers as participating team members. She found that those teachers who helped define their roles as team members (i.e., clarified their roles) contributed significantly more than the other teachers during team meetings. Thus, greater role clarification positively affects participation during team meetings. This has implications for training team members.

Fisher (1980) identified three factors that influence team effectiveness: *intrapersonal*, *interpersonal*, and *group identity*. Each of these factors has implications for involvement of team members.

Intrapersonal Factors

Each team member should be open-minded about potential outcomes and sensitive to the feelings and beliefs of other team members. Each person must be committed to the team and its process and be willing to commit time and energy for that purpose.

Each team member actively shares responsibility for the team's decisions. They also share their feelings and ideas, even knowing that they may be off-track. Team members are honest about their feelings and thoughts. Team members express their views even when they may be criticized. They also find ways to constructively criticize others, especially during team meetings.

Interpersonal Factors

For group decision making to be effective, all team members must participate. It is incumbent upon team members to encourage participation by all members.

Teams with members skilled in communication are more effective. Team members should consider it their responsibility to learn effective communication skills. Supportive and accepting communication that is not defensive is most effective.

Members should evaluate problems and issues, not other members. A climate of mutual trust evolves from such communication. Team members clarify communications that are unclear. They check others' reactions and describe ideas in detail. If they disagree with an idea, they should describe their reservations rather than reacting judgmentally.

Group Identity Factors

Team members who are sensitive to group process will know *when* to communicate a particular idea. Team members who do not contribute should be encouraged to resign. A member who is not committed to the team will negatively affect the group process.

Patience with group process is necessary, especially during the early stages when the team is being established. It is important to provide ample opportunity to think through ideas, allowing for greater creativity and more effective decisions. The team should avoid unrealistic, "formula answers" to difficult problems.

AVOIDING PROBLEMS AND FACING CHALLENGES

Understanding the characteristics of teamwork helps team members avoid problems. Lowe and Herranen (1981) have provided insight into specific characteristics of teams, including teamwork as an evolutionary process. Bailey (1984) contributed another view of the team process. An understanding of his triaxial model can also help to prevent problems in team functioning. This section concludes with a discussion of potential challenges that team members face. Together these three topics better prepare the professional to avoid or deal with challenges.

Stages of Team Development

Six stages in the development of a team were described by Lowe and Herranen (1981). Patterns of interactions, common emotions, and individual team productivity were described for each of the six stages. Although their stages related to teamwork in hospital settings, the same stages can be seen in other settings.

Stage I: Becoming Acquainted

People bring different perspectives to the team. Some enter because it is mandated; others by choice and recognition of its value. While team members are becoming acquainted, the leadership style might be autocratic, democratic, or absent. Generally, there is a hierarchical structure with the professional at the top of the pecking order being anointed as leader. Interaction patterns are polite and impersonal; group norms have a social focus. There is no group consensus regarding the student goals; each professional on the team sees his or her goals as most important. Emotions are held in check, and there are few conflicts. Stage I is characterized by high individual productivity and low team productivity.

Stage II: Trial and Error

Once professionals recognize the need to collaborate on common goals, this stage begins. Pairing with an ally is the typical interaction pattern that emerges. Such pairs increase individual productivity rather than group productivity. Role conflict, role ambiguity, and role overload stem from team members testing the waters. The nature of the team is similar to that in Stage I; members are concerned about turf issues.

Stage III: Collective Indecision

In this stage members are attempting to avoid conflict and achieve equilibrium. Boundaries begin to develop. Team members are aware of the appeal of groups as well as their disadvantages. Little is accomplished because there is no emphasis on accountability. There is a lack of leadership; conformity is expected. Role conflict is not dealt with, and there is low morale and covert anger. As you might expect, both team and individual productivity suffer. No one feels heard by other team members.

Stage IV: Crisis

As a result of a crisis stemming from collective indecision, roles and responsibilities are defined and boundaries are drawn. An informal and formal leader develop, and aspects of group process become a focus of attention. Negative emotions emerge because they can be handled. Team members begin to value one another for particular expertise and potential assistance for the student. Team productivity continues to be low.

Stage V: Resolution

Teamwork has finally begun when the team members commit to working as a unit. Open communication leads to sharing leadership, decision making, and responsibility. Accountability is important for the individual and team. Team productivity is high. This stage is fragile; the team needs to move to maintenance.

Stage VI: Team Maintenance

Sharing by team members allows the focus to be on the student's needs. All team members see the student from a holistic view and value other members' expertise. Effectiveness depends upon internal group processes and how conflicts are handled. Expectations are continuously clarified, norms evolve, team members respect self and others, accountability is important, and a common language develops. According to Lowe and Herranen (1981), this is the critical stage in team development.

As with any developmental model, each team will not necessarily experience every stage described. Some teams will not go through the stages in this fixed sequence. All teams have growing pains. It is important to recognize those as normal and part of the evolution of a well-functioning team.

The Triaxial Model

Bailey (1984) has proposed a triaxial model (see Table 8.3) for understanding processes within teams working for individuals who are at risk or have special needs. Bailey's model shows the complex and difficult task of organizing effective teams. His breakdown provides insight into avoiding, recognizing, and ameliorating problems experienced by team members.

Bailey's model is based on the work of Tseng and McDermott (1979). Three premises, called "axes," form the basis for Bailey's (1984) model:

1. Team growth is a developmental process. Some problems in team functioning can be attributed to the stage of development at which the team in functioning.
2. Teams are composed of individuals. Thus some problems may result from interpersonal problems or subsystems within the team.
3. The team is a functioning unit. Some problems can, therefore, be expected to stem from whole-team dysfunction.

Table 8.3 presents more information about Bailey's model. An understanding of these problems can help team members pinpoint the focus of analysis and intervention.

Challenges

There are a variety of other challenges to team functioning not already covered in this

Table 8.3
THE TRIAXIAL MODEL

Axis I. Team growth is a developmental process. Team dysfunction can occur in the developmental sequence within a given team meeting. There are six typical steps in IEP meetings: review assessments, discuss present status, develop a long-range plan, make placement decision, determine instructional objectives, and design an implementation plan. Team members should analyze their sequence within meetings to determine whether a pattern of dysfunction emerges. One particular step might show up as problematic. In other cases, the actual sequencing of steps might need to be changed.

Axis II. Teams are composed of individuals. The ideal team will have a leader present who performed as a member of the team. Each member possesses equal power and influence. On the ideal team conflicts and disagreements are based not on personality conflicts, but substantive issues. There are seven potential problems relating to individuals.

The Dominant Leader may be resented by others, cut down on discussion, or foster dependency. The purpose of the team is collaboration, so even if domination is not resented, it is inappropriate.

Dominant Team Member(s) stem from personalities, hierarchies, or perceived power. Dominant behavior is counterproductive when that person will not listen to others' opinions. Not all domination is obvious. It may be very subtle, such as professional domination by a psychiatrist.

The Inferior Team Member could be any person. Often, teachers and parents are inferior members. Their opinions may be viewed by others or themselves as less worthy than other members' opinions. People who are viewed as inferior eventually quit making contributions. That withdrawal reinforces the others' view of them as inferior. It is important for team functioning to equally value all contributions.

Specific Conflict Between Two Members results in team dysfunction. Conflict is a natural and expected part of team functioning; however, when it pervades all meetings and interferes with planning, it is dysfunctional. An example of such a conflict is when two members always take diametrically opposed positions, regardless of usual opinions.

One Member Conflicting with All Others is highly disruptive of team functioning. This is even more dysfunctional when the person is highly vocal. Eventually such a person is rejected, regardless of the quality of the input.

Factions within the Team occur when subsystems compete with one another. Winning should not take precedence over the task of the team, meeting the student's needs.

One Member Isolated from the Group refers to a member who does not appear to belong to the team socially. A feeling of being in the "out crowd" is not conducive to healthy team functioning.

Axis III. The whole team is a functioning unit. In Axis III the structure or organization of the whole team is the subject of scrutiny. Ideal teams are well organized, possess clarity of roles, and are structured yet flexible. There are four types of whole team dysfunction.

The Underperforming Team occurs when team members are unskilled or not invested in the team process. The task is not completed due to whole team dysfunction. Team tasks are perfunctory. Often the underperforming team has an ineffective leader; members are unable or unwilling to take responsibility for seeing that the team accomplishes it goals.

The Overstructured Team occurs when members' roles are rigidly defined. The meeting is also usually inflexible, with substance taking a back seat to structure and the agenda. Rigidity in roles and routines restrict interactions and prevent social and emotional content.

The Team with Ambiguous Roles occurs when members are unclear about who does what. Planning is not integrated due to territoriality or confusion and withdrawal. Basically, no one takes responsibility for team process, and the result is inadequate planning for the student.

The Disorganized Team lacks leadership, direction, and structure. Meetings may even appear chaotic. This stems either from poor leadership or confusion about roles and purpose. Members sometimes become overly involved in their social lives. At other times, different members are flowing in and out of the meeting due to late arrivals, early departures, and telephone calls.

This three-dimensional model allows the determination of the level of dysfunction—team development, team subsystems, or whole team functioning. This breakdown allows for a considered diagnosis of team dysfunction and improves the likelihood of teams being functional in the school context.

Source: Drawn from "A Triaxial Model of the Interdisciplinary Team and Group Process" by D. Bailey, 1984, *Exceptional Children, 51* (1), pp. 17–25.

section. It is important to frame challenges as potentially resolvable and not as impossible situations. Our purpose in focusing on challenges is not that they be viewed as stumbling blocks, but to help you recognize and avoid as well as resolve these very human situations. These challenges are divided into four categories: philosophical and theoretical differences, isolation of family members, interpersonal challenges, and resistance to change.

Differences in Philosophical and Theoretical Orientations

Team members often confront differences between their training as well as theoretical and philosophical orientations (Courtnage & Smith-Davis, 1987). Therapists are typically trained in a medical model that emphasizes determining the underlying cause of the behavior and then focuses therapy on that "cause." Family systems therapists are, however, trained in theoretical models that do not reduce challenging situations to such simplistic, linear explanations. The emphasis on individual versus systemic thinking may be cause for misunderstanding between team members. Further, it is likely to result in fundamental differences in approaches to students as well as family members.

This difficulty is intensified by the isolated preparation of professionals such as teachers, counselors, therapists, nurses, and occupational therapists. Professionals frequently use their own jargon or shorthand when meeting in teams. Others, especially parents, may not understand the terminology and may become frustrated when trying to provide input or simply to follow the team discussion.

Another aspect of the philosophical and theoretical challenge to team functioning is the actual team model employed. A multidisciplinary approach has a greater likelihood of facing philosophical and theoretical problems. The nature of the approach lends itself to such misunderstandings. It is most difficult to understand, coordinate, and value the orientations of other team members when their approaches are not integrated, which follows from the multidisciplinary team approach. The interdisciplinary team model has a higher likelihood of team collaboration with fewer theoretical and philosophical challenges. This is because interdisciplinary teams are more interactive.

Isolation of Parents or Other Family Member

Another challenge to effective team functioning is the isolation of family members. Parents may be apprised of their rights; however, the question of whether or not they understand those rights has been raised (Roit & Pfohl, 1984). Parents may also be confused by the educational processes used in the schools. If parents are involved only at the stage of developing the IEP, their isolation is exacerbated even further. It is important to afford family members opportunities to be involved throughout the process from prereferral to planning the educational program. Long-term involvement will reduce the sense of isolation on the part of any family members who choose to be involved to a greater degree in the educational life of the student with special needs.

Interpersonal Challenges

Professionals steeped in a medical model may find themselves feeling threatened by the egalitarian nature of teams that include parents and paraprofessionals. Trusting others to provide helpful information is imperative in this type of team functioning. Rising to that challenge is difficult for some professionals. However, in time, most of those who were originally threatened will find that their risk taking is worth the effort.

Another aspect of interpersonal struggles is a lack of clarity regarding team members' responsibilities. Each person's role must, therefore, be continually clarified. Role conflict will ensue if team members are unsure of their current functions.

Resistance to Change

People resist change for a variety of reasons. While resistance should be viewed as a normal and expected aspect of any change process, leaving it unchecked can be destructive. Therefore, it is important to recognize reasons for resisting change.

Team members may resist change because they (a) feel inadequate, (b) fear the unknown, (c) lack trust, or (d) are unable to see the larger picture. Generally speaking, when team members become more familiar with team functioning, they overcome their lack of self-confidence and sense of inadequacy.

The fear of the unknown, in this case working collaboratively on an egalitarian team, can be reduced through effective communication. Training that responds to questions and concerns effectively lowers the level of fear about new team functioning.

There is a lack of trust when the people involved do not have faith in those initiating change. As changes are being planned, representatives should be involved in planning and decision making. This allows those involved in change to consult trusted colleagues about their concerns.

Inability to see the larger picture occurs when team members are not part of the change process from the beginning. It is difficult for them to understand the goals and need for change. Once they understand the benefits to the total team functioning, it is likely that they will be more supportive.

Again, focusing on challenges is intended to be positive. The purpose is to recognize and avoid or resolve problems. Chapter 13 further elaborates upon resistance to change.

PROBLEM SOLVING

The problem-solving process will be briefly described in this section. Problem solving is a multistep process that leads to conflict resolution. These five steps are critical to group problem solving. The steps are time-honored; most problem-solving models are only slightly different variations of the one described. Teams will be involved in continual problem solving, dealing with team process issues as well as content concerns.

Step 1: Define the Problem

No one can effectively solve a problem that is not well defined. Most team members would expect that this would be an easy step in the process of problem solving. In reality, it is a challenging step.

It is important that all team members focus on the real cause of the problem and not the symptoms. People often become wrapped up in symptoms and fail to see the forest for the trees. A good example of this is a content-oriented issue of a student having behavioral problems in school. In trying to solve the problem, many professionals will spend too much time on the surface manifestations of the problem. For example, consider a child who has trouble concentrating and staying in his seat in school. Some would focus on the student's in-school behavioral excesses. But by examining the problem, the team might find that no parent is available to supervise the student in the mornings before school. Lacking supervision, the student might be getting hyped up by eating junk food and watching overstimulating videos before going to school. Thus the problem is redefined as one that originates at home rather than in the classroom.

Step 2: Collect Facts and Opinions

Once the problem is understood, team members gather the facts and opinions needed to further understand the situation. It may not be possible to get all the facts, but it is important to move forward and not allow the situation to become a crisis. It is critical to find out what the situation is, what happened, who is involved, and what policies and procedures are involved. All of those answers help team members design realistic solutions.

Step 3: Generate Solutions

This step involves brainstorming for possible solutions. No idea should be criticized at this point. When team members begin criticizing or evaluating ideas at this stage, they effectively shut off the production of creative solutions. This step should be freewheeling and fast-moving with everyone on the team providing potential solutions.

Step 4: Select the Solution

There are two aspects to the fourth step. First, the team must be very clear on the results they expect from the solution. The goals or end results must be specified. Then each of the solutions generated in the previous step can be evaluated in light of the agreed-upon goals of the team. The best few solutions should be selected and put to the test of potential feasibility as well as maximization of resources.

Step 5: Implement the Solution

Timetables for the solution should be established by team members. Further, the team should specify the evaluation techniques to be used and make plans for follow-through.

INTERACTION BETWEEN FAMILIES AND SCHOOLS

This section focuses on five aspects of working with families. The need, desire, and availability of family members to be involved in the education of the learner with special needs are considered first. Second, a family systems perspective on team issues is addressed. Reasons for nonparticipation as well as how to overcome unwanted nonparticipation are covered in the next two sections. The final section describes means of involving families who want to be involved.

Need

It is imperative that team members consider the desires of family members for involvement on the team (Foster et al., 1981; Turnbull & Turnbull, 1982; Winton & Turnbull, 1981). Thus first and foremost should be consideration of the degree to which each family member would like to be involved in contributing as a team member. Some parents might want to be more involved than their schedule and responsibilities allow. Other parents might not be interested in involvement, regardless of other responsibilities, and their choice should be respected by educational professionals. In 1981 Lusthaus, Lusthaus, and Gibbs found that parents wanted to be involved in schools by giving and receiving information. Parents were also interested in being involved with decisions about the "kinds of information kept on their children; medical services for their children; and transfer of their children to other schools" (p. 257). It would be interesting to see how parents would respond now, a decade later.

Professionals currently maintain that school personnel should encourage family involvement while also recognizing that there are a variety of reasons for limited participation or nonparticipation. Those reasons are elaborated upon later in this section. After researching family involvement, Winton and Turnbull (1981) stated that, "The information for this study supported a model of parent involvement in which services are matched with the individual needs of families. A distinction is made between involvement with a child and involvement with the program" (p. 18). They further indicated that it is important to recognize that it may be a tremendous contribution to the program for the parent to be uninvolved. Professionals all too often assume that they are acting in the best interests of the student by encouraging parental involvement in their program.

Turnbull and Turnbull (1982) have indicated that there should be involvement options for parents. Some parents might not be involved with the school program, by choice. Another option would be to allow parents the opportunity to be informed about goals and objectives. A third option would be full and equal decision-making opportunities for parents who choose to participate at that level.

Yanok and Derubertis (1989) have compared parental participation in regular and special education programs. "The results of this study suggest that, even though 13 years have elapsed since the passage of P.L. 94-142, the Act has not significantly altered the levels of school participation of parents of exceptional children" (p. 198). The positive conclusion that they reached from this study was that parents of exceptional children and parents of regular education students appear to view the schools as addressing the needs of their children equally.

Family Systems Perspective

Foster et al. (1981) stated that, "To think well about their work with families, professionals need to adopt a more comprehensive theory of family functioning. Family systems theory offers a sophisticated approach for understanding the complex set of interrelationships that families present" (pp. 63–64). They further indicated that a systems framework provides a means of anticipating both direct and indirect effects of interventions made on a family basis. This is a useful direction for understanding individual child development and family functioning and development.

In 1983 Pfeiffer and Tittler described the benefits of teams adopting a family systems orientation while determining eligibility. This approach recognizes that families and schools are intimately interrelated and linked through the student. By shifting to a family focus, the referred student is no longer viewed in isolation but within the context of his or her family. By observing the family, team members can better understand and predict the student's behavior in school as well as social functioning in the family. Also, if other family members can be helped to redirect some stress from the student, the student's dysfunction should lessen, with an increase in the possibility of remediation in school.

In another study (Tittler, Friedman, Blotcky, & Stedrak, 1982), children's progress appeared to be significantly related to the family's willingness to become involved with the schools and cooperate within the educational setting. However, this does not negate the original warning in this section that families who do not want to be involved should not be forced into further school interactions and responsibility.

Reasons for Nonparticipation

McMillan and Turnbull (1983) have indicated that while it is important for professionals to respect the right of parents to choose not to participate in their child's educational program, it is also important to determine whether or not those parents were not participating based upon an informed choice. These authors also suggested that lack of parental participation might be related to specific child and family characteristics.

Suelzle and Keenan (1981) corroborated that point of view. Their findings indicated that families with lower incomes, older children, and children with more severe disabilities were less likely to be involved in their child's education.

Weber and Stoneman (1986) investigated the differences between parents who did and did not attend IEP meetings. They looked at family characteristics, maternal knowledge about the IEP process, and the mother's knowledge about the IEP itself. They found that poor families, with limited parental education, who were nonwhite, and who were headed by single parents were overrepresented in the group of parents who did not attend the meetings. Mothers who viewed teachers and other professionals as responsible for their child's education were often nonparticipants. These authors considered it important to reach out to families, providing programs responsive to their particular needs that are sensitive to the demands faced by the parents, empower the parents, and provide a sense of control. They indicated that parents are able to make an informed choice about participation in their child's education when they fully understand both the rights and the opportunities that are available from the schools. They concluded that many parents lack basic information that is needed to make that choice.

Parental anxiety contributes to lack of participation in their child's education (Losen & Losen, 1985). Parents may be anxious for a variety of reasons. The primary source of anxiety is concern about what was happening to the child. Parents tend to depend upon team members to identify the child's difficulties and provide remedial services. Thus they may feel somewhat at the mercy of the expertise of the professionals, especially if they are not themselves knowledgeable about their child's problem. Also, parents are most likely anxious not to appear stupid, confused, or indecisive. Thus they may restrict their input and be passive during the team meetings that they do attend.

An additional source of anxiety identified by Losen and Losen (1985) was the parents' feeling of having failed their child. Such a sense of guilt is common among parents of children with special needs. Parents may be concerned that their parenting skills are being judged or evaluated negatively by professionals and that they have made mistakes that resulted in their child's special needs. These thoughts would naturally lead to passivity on the part of parents. They might think that the professionals involved would have better solutions.

A third source of concern identified was mistrust of school staff (Losen & Losen, 1985). They could either believe that professionals had misdiagnosed their child or that the professionals might not be competent to deal with the special needs of their child. Some parents resign themselves to professional input at that point, where others, feeling a sense of helplessness, resist any efforts to reassure them. Concern and doubt about competence of professionals could also reflect their own personal doubts about how to deal with the special needs of their child.

A fourth parental concern is that involvement in special education would actually cause their child to be seen negatively by other teachers as well as peers (Losen & Losen, 1985). Some parents may find it difficult to accept their child's level of need and thus remain doubtful about the differences between their child and other classmates. Thus they may allow the schools to plan programs for their child yet not be supportive of those programs in the home.

Losen and Losen (1985) found guilt feelings, beyond inadequacy, to relate to feelings that the parents had failed others in the process. Parents may fear that friends and relatives will learn about their perceived poor parenting skills unless they comply with the recommendations of the schools. This is particularly true of parents of children who are belligerent and "act-out." When school personnel indicate that acting-out behavior that is not reduced could lead to more restrictive placements, the parents may not challenge the recommendation. The parents' input would be missed if they fear reprisal toward their child.

An additional reason for parental passivity and lack of involvement with their child's educational program stems from prior negative experiences with schools. For example, a prior teacher, principal, or other professional may have led the parents to conclude that to obtain the best for their child they should remain silent. Parents may also fear that their child will be mistreated or a more restrictive environment will be recommended if they contribute their own personal opinions to the process. Even though these negative expectations may be unrealistic, it is important to get them out on the table. For example, a parent may have heard through the grapevine that a particular principal is a strict disciplinarian, or that a social worker might be more negative while interacting alone with parents than during a team meeting.

Overcoming Nonparticipation

As early as 1979 Gilliam suggested that information be presented to participants, including parents, prior to team meetings. More time can be devoted to discussion during those meetings when all participants have prior information. This is a means of increasing team members' contributions about the student's program and placement.

Losen and Losen (1985) indicated that a preteam meeting between the parents and one professional could alleviate sources of nonparticipation and anxiety. They suggested that a professional with good communication skills meet with the parents to discuss procedures used and test results. All questions the parents might have would be answered, and the professional would maintain an egalitarian attitude.

Results of testing could be presented in this preteam meeting. This meeting allows parents to raise issues and questions about the process or results without wasting other team members' time while one professional explains results in lay terms. In addition, parents should be aware of the purposes for the upcoming meeting with the entire team. They may want to suggest alternative procedures prior to that meeting, such as observing their child in different settings.

The preteam meeting can help ensure that the parents understand procedures used, which should help decrease their passivity, defensiveness, or resistance in the team meeting. The preteam meeting also provides an opportunity to deal with parental doubts, guilt, and sense of inadequacy. It is far easier to deal with these issues in an intimate conference than a full team meeting.

Another critical event to avoid in the full team meeting is the parents' first learning about significant results of the assessment. No humane professional would expect parents to be able to respond to learning that their child is for example, dyslexic, and also help plan their child's education during the same meeting.

To involve parents meaningfully, it may also be necessary to provide services that allow them to contribute to the team process. Such services include babysitters and transportation that assure the possibility of their attending meetings. Pfeiffer (1980) has indicated that such strategies were highly successful in increasing parental involvement.

Involving Families

Involving families in reviewing test data and options for service delivery models as well as decision making and goal setting is important to the team process. As discussed above, it is critical to involve parents in a preteam meeting to explain the procedures involved and the test results. This allows for a smoother and more effective team meeting.

Reviewing Test Data

During the team meeting it is valuable to refer to the parents' reactions to the test data that were shared at the preteam meeting. Such a statement might be, "Mrs. Smith probably remembers that, during the preteam meeting, I suggested her daughter Kristie could be experiencing greater anxiety than we originally anticipated. When we reviewed the results of the tests, I was able to demonstrate the level on which Kristie is functioning as compared with other students in Kindergarten. As a result, I think Mrs. Smith understands why Kristie needs special help. It is meaningful in particular as Kristie regains her self-esteem and confidence in her ability to function successfully at school tasks. Mrs. Smith, do you have anything further to explain about your reactions?"

Again, it is important that the team meeting not be the first time that the parents actually receive test results that have important implications for their child. This is particularly important when it involves categorization or labeling. It is easy to imagine having your own child be labeled as "retarded" at a meeting and being unable to participate further in providing input or suggestions, or to be involved in decision making.

Information provided during team meetings should be summaries of test results. Going point-by-point through test data takes too much time. Having already viewed test data and having an opportunity to react, parents will not mind summaries as long as their particular reactions to those results are included with the summaries.

Charts, outlines, or descriptions of tests may be helpful when providing summaries. Family members will find this easier to follow than test protocol results alone. It may even be helpful to include brief written descriptions of each of the subtests used. Such descriptions can be used with many different families. It is critical to write those descriptions in lay terms and at the level of the reader. This practice also indicates to the family members that you are interested in helping them understand what kind of tests have been administered and what information was found about the student.

Family members should feel comfortable asking questions about summaries, charts, or descriptions. If professionals' language is not at their level, they may not even be able to formulate their questions. Professionals might need to help them clarify what they question or fail to understand.

Family members should also be informed about the psychometric properties of the tests. Reliability and validity may need to be discussed if some test data are not as valuable as other test data. This is often the case when independent evaluations include results from tests with questionable reliability or validity.

Service Delivery Model

Parents should be involved in the consideration of service delivery options for their child, particularly if the child might be placed in a special classroom. It is important that they are familiar with a variety of alternative service delivery models. If possible, the parents should learn about the options at an early stage so they are more likely to understand the reasons for recommendation of one type of placement over another. This practice could result in fewer due process hearings initiated by the parents. It is also a good check and balance for team members so that they do not too quickly recommend a particular delivery model for a student. When parents are involved in listening to those deliberations, professionals are more likely to be deliberative.

In considering placement of a student, parents benefit from reviewing advantages and disadvantages of different delivery models. These advantages can help parents contribute to decision making, as well as understand that there are ways that disadvantages can be overcome or minimized.

When the number of mainstream activities in which a given student might engage is being considered, team members should indicate how every hour spent out of the regular program benefits the student more than mainstream involvement would (Losen & Losen, 1985). Any special help should be presented during study periods or nonacademic times, such as art or music, unless that activity is considered an important motivator for the student. According to Losen and Losen, students should be removed from academic instruction only when the special program offers something more beneficial than the regular academic instruction.

When the student is removed from the regular classroom, the regular classroom teacher can provide homework to cover content missed by the student. Family members may be able to help the student cover the content so that he or she does not fall behind.

Decision Making

Once test results and service delivery model options have been reviewed, a decision must be made about the student's placement and program. If parents are involved in the steps prior to this point, it is more likely that they will support any decisions made.

In actuality, recommendations or suggestions for a particular placement may be considered by parent or professional prior to the meeting when the decision will be made. It is important to have all information that is needed available at the meeting so that the decision regarding placement will not be delayed.

When team members do not agree about the program, Losen and Losen (1985) recommended deferring the decision. It may be necessary that certain points of contention be researched prior to the final team meeting.

Once the alternatives have been reviewed, frequently the decision simply needs to be confirmed. The review process often makes the best decision obvious. However, when there is no consensus on a decision, it may be necessary to vote. When team members do not agree on the program, it is important to discuss the reasons for their disagreement and try to resolve them. Reaching consensus is preferable to a vote that results in a decision made on the basis of one vote tipping the balance for a particular placement.

Goal Setting

After a recommendation for placement is made, related services and the student's IEP must be considered. Parents should also be deeply involved in these determinations. All objectives should be written in simple, clear language that the parents can understand.

In addition, parents should be informed about the length of time it takes to achieve a particular goal or objective. The parents also benefit from knowing that the IEP is not a binding contract, but a working agreement with stated goals for their child and related services on which they can count.

In the process of involving family members in team meetings, professionals must make them feel comfortable and wanted as well as view them as capable of contributing meaningful input. Parents should never be pressured into accepting a delivery model or program if they feel there is another, more appropriate option. Weber and Stoneman (1986) have indicated that schools should let parents know that their participation is desired and that they have an important contribution to make to the planning process.

PLANNING AND FAMILY 9
INVOLVEMENT

T his chapter builds upon the information about teamwork presented in chapter 8 as well as upon Part I of this book. Its focus is upon two processes: planning with families both for family-focused interventions and for Individualized Education Programs (IEPs). The premise of any intervention is that something in the student's school life is not functioning as well as could be hoped. All school professionals are familiar with academic, social, and emotional interventions with students, but most interventions are on an individual basis. Family intervention is unusual. In this chapter family systems concepts are interwoven throughout the descriptions of these two planning processes, with school-related examples provided.

FAMILY-FOCUSED INTERVENTION

The field of early intervention has led the way in special education in extensive family involvement. In fact, as a result of PL 99-457, all children enrolled in early intervention programs must have an Individual Family Service Plan (IFSP). Recognizing that child and family cannot truly be separated, IEPs are not the focus of intervention; instead IFSPs are paramount. We can take a lesson from this branch of special education. For more information, see Krauss (1990), a description of conceptual and procedural mandates of the IFSP; and Turnbull and Turnbull (1990), an apt description of the differences between the IEP and the IFSP.

The underlying belief of those proposing family-focused interventions is that we must individualize services for families with children with special needs (Bailey et al., 1986) This is also true for at-risk students. Intervention services must be tailored to important characteristics that differentiate families. These characteristics relate to differences in family structure, family interactional patterns, and family life cycles, as well as other family characteristics discussed in Part I.

The family-focused intervention model consists of a sequence of specific activities related to planning, implementing, and evaluating family services. This section of the chapter covers underlying features of family-focused interventions, processes of intervening, and types of interventions implemented.

Underlying Features

The three underlying features that provide a basis for effective family-focused interventions are family uniqueness, goodness of fit, and networking.

Uniqueness

As stated earlier, families differ on a number of important dimensions, including stage of family life cycle and family interaction patterns or structure (boundaries, hierarchy, and power). Also relevant to family uniqueness are cultural and socioeconomic background, historical factors within the family such as triangulation and sibling position, and family configuration (e.g., blended families), as well as the type and severity of special needs of the child and its impact upon the family. Each at-risk student, as well as those with special needs, has a unique mixture of skills, feelings, behaviors, and potentials. Thus, it is necessary to individualize all educational programs to meet personal needs. Likewise, in the effort to relate to families in supportive ways, the professional must respond to the intricate design that each family presents. Like snowflakes, families surface in infinite varieties.

To elaborate further upon this theme we will describe two different families. Table 9.1 presents information on Bobby and his family. After reading this information, jot down some notes, using the outline given under the case information. Your notes will concern family life cycle, needs, cultural and socioeconomic factors, any historical information noted, family configuration, as well as structure including subsystems, boundaries, and hierarchy. Then return to reading the next paragraph. It might be helpful to discuss your notes on Bobby with others who have read the text. Comparing your notes with others can be helpful in clarifying your knowledge.

Next, read the information regarding Christian in Table 9.2. After you have read the case study, write notes on the information listed under "Notes." Again, this can be discussed in class sessions. The purpose of describing these two different families is to make the meaning of "family uniqueness" more obvious.

Goodness of Fit

The second underlying feature of which professionals should be aware is "goodness of fit." Bailey and his associates have outlined a specific methodology for family-focused interventions (Bailey et al., 1988). In that description they referred to goodness of fit, a comfortable, beneficial meshing of the unique family needs with professionals that must be present if we are to help both the student with special needs and the family. This is also true for at-risk students.

Goodness of fit is a concept that is useful in thinking about helping Bobby's and Christian's families (Tables 9.1 and 9.2). You may want to discuss your ideas with someone else who has read the same information, remembering that there must be a fit between your suggestions and the needs of the family.

Networking

It is important that professionals maintain role perspective when making family-

Table   9.1
CASE STUDY: BOBBY

Bobby is an 8-year-old who has been in a self-contained classroom for emotionally disturbed children since kindergarten. He is now being mainstreamed for most of the school day. Bobby is the first child and has a sister four years younger than he. His sister is not really aware that her brother has had a problem. His parents are involved with locating resources that tell them more about his problem. They have made attempts to adjust to having an only son who has emotional problems. Bobby is a very shy, withdrawn child who did not speak to anyone but the teacher for the first year of school. His parents are overprotective and continually hover around him. They pick him up from school daily, even though his school is not in their neighborhood (he is bused across the county). His parents are happily married and appear to support one another, though they do spend an inordinate amount of time with Bobby. It is hard to tell if he is Mommy's or Daddy's little boy.

The mother is originally from Puerto Rico and makes most decisions regarding the child rearing. The parents do, however, make the rules in the house. This is a deeply spiritual family. They talk as though they have a sense that all is well with the world. The parents often speak of a "grand design." They have many friends and relatives with whom they interact and from whom they regularly seek assistance. They have, however, seen few professionals over the years regarding Bobby. They have said that Bobby will "grow out of" his shyness. The father even mentioned that he, too, is painfully shy. The father described an uncle of Bobby's who was much like Bobby when he was young. The parents seem resolved in many ways about their only son having serious emotional problems.

NOTES

Demographics: 8 years old; part-time regular classroom

Family life cycle:

Structure:
   Subsystems
   Boundaries
   Hierarchy

Historical factors:

Cultural and socioeconomic factors:

Bobby's special needs:

Family configuration:

Table 9.2
CASE STUDY: CHRISTIAN

Christian is a 12-year-old student who has been in a classroom for emotionally disturbed children for three-and-a-half years. He is currently being mainstreamed for a portion of the school day. He has an older half-brother, Leroy, who is 16 years old. They have a very close relationship with each other. Leroy really protects Christian in the neighborhood and, in fact, probably fights too many of Christian's battles for him. On occasion Leroy feels embarrassed by Christian, especially when Leroy's adolescent friends are visiting and Christian gets rambunctious. Christian is still a "motor driven" hyperactive youth who talks to anyone who will listen. His mouth and feet are in constant motion. Christian's mother is a single parent. She and Christian's father, who is a carpenter, are divorced. Christian has been very upset about that loss and follows many of the males around in the school building. He is good friends with a custodian and speaks with the assistant principal regularly; both of them are males. Further, he has made a special friend of the floating substitute, who is also a male. Christian's mother seems to realize that she is in a lifelong struggle with him. She has few social supports in friends or family; however, being a social worker, she knows many professionals in the predominately black neighborhood where she works. The mother's main feelings appear to be frustration and isolation. She seems to feel alone shouldering the responsibilities of the family and has little time to herself.

NOTES

Demographics: 12 years old; part-time in regular classes

Family life cycle:

Structure:
    Subsystems
    Boundaries
    Hierarchy

Cultural and socioeconomic factors:

Christian's special needs:

Family configuration:

---

focused interventions. This means viewing themselves as responsible, first and foremost, for their particular role. Teachers are in a distinctive position in relation to parents of at-risk and special needs students. They share the mutual responsibility for educating the student. Teachers have the opportunity to establish a close working relationship with families. They frequently become confidants to parents and function as trusted professionals on whom the family can rely. The counselor, school social worker, consulting teacher, or psychologist might also play the role of confidant.

The teacher, however, functions best not as an isolated intervener, but as a "hub" through which a network of resources can positively affect families. The teacher cannot realistically maintain both the parent–teacher relationship and the primary role of teaching while trying to satisfy the diverse needs of these families. The teacher should see it as his or her responsibility to serve as a facilitator in allowing parents to access a variety of resources that are available in the educational system and larger community.

Before moving on to the processes of intervening, look at Table 9.3 as a final check on your assimilation of the three underlying features in this section. It allows you to look for violations of the three underlying features of effective family-focused interventions.

Processes of Intervening

There are four processes of intervening using family-focused interventions: assessment, planning, implementation, and evaluation. As with so many activities in life, organization is a key factor in effective family intervention. Interventions should be based on the best available data, carefully planned, implemented responsibly, and evaluated critically.

Assessment

Sound assessment is the foundation on which effective intervention is established. Can you imagine taking a drug prescribed by a physician before he or she diagnosed what was wrong? Or, worse yet, imagine being operated on before the need for it had been established!

There are two complementary parts to assessment for family-focused interventions. The first is determining the status of the family on such dimensions as family life cycle, interaction patterns, historical factors such as sibling position and triangulation, cultural or socioeconomic factors, the needs of the child or youth, and family configuration.

The other component of assessment in family-focused interventions is eliciting the family's needs and establishing resources. A relationship involving trust and mutual commitment allows family members to feel free to provide information to professionals about those needs. The professional can then use that information to draw conclusions about the family's life cycle, interactions patterns, and so forth.

The professional then reflects that information back to the family. An example of this would be the professional saying, "Mr. and Mrs. Estevas, to me it sounds as though Miguel's older sister, Maria, is really feeling the pinch of spending so much time helping Miguel with his homework. It also seems as though the two of you are overloaded with two-year-old twins." Of course, much more could be reflected over time. Once a professional reflects and confirms the information, he or she has created a data base that is held jointly with the parents.

The data and conclusion should be explicit. For example, consider a family with an

Table 9.3
CASE STUDY ANALYSIS

Refer to Table 9.2 and the case of Christian. Take each of the following three suggestions and evaluate them for violations of the three underlying features.

Suggestion 1: Christian is referred to the medical center for further evaluation of his hyperactivity.

Suggestion 2: Since Christian's mother is a social worker, she is asked to chair a "parent group" for parents of students in Christian's middle school. The meeting will be held in the mornings. The teacher assumes the responsibility of interviewing and finding a "big brother" for Christian.

Suggestion 3: Leroy, Christian's brother, is to be seen by Christian's teacher weekly for counseling sessions.

Your Analysis of Violations of the Three Underlying Features

Uniqueness:

Goodness of Fit:

Networking:

---

adolescent child and a younger child with a physical disability. The family may be asking the adolescent to help the younger child find friends. The parents may also expect the adolescent to come home after school, wait for the sibling to arrive, take care of the child, take the child around the neighborhood, and be sure that the child is content. Having all this information, the professional might think, "This looks like a family that is enmeshed and is parentifying the older sibling."

No professional would want to say to a family, "Maybe you are expecting too much from your adolescent" without enough information confirming that fact. Neither would one say to the parent, "Your family seems to be enmeshed." Instead the professional would make comments to help the parents realize that adolescents have needs of their own. Providing information about the family life cycle and differing demands at each stage of development would help the parents realistically view the needs of their adolescent.

As conclusions are developed and agreed upon, problems and needs are prioritized in terms of the immediacy and seriousness felt by the family. When assessing needs of family members, the professional might list them as they surface in the conversation. A simple listing is all that is needed. For example, in the Estevas family mentioned above, needs might include time for spouses together, help with Miguel's homework, time for Maria to do her own homework, time for the mother to herself, and the siblings' need for information on genetics and possible impact on their own future families.

Later, the professional and family members can discuss potential solutions and prioritize them. Family members will decide that there are some things that are more serious than others and some things that need immediate attention. This prioritization process reflects both seriousness and immediacy.

There are structured assessment tools that may help, particularly in the area of family needs. Turnbull and Turnbull (1986, pp. 368–373) have provided an excellent Family Information Preference Inventory. This inventory can be reproduced for noncommercial purposes, and we highly recommend its use. Such an instrument is helpful in the assessment step of the family-focused intervention process. Mothers should not be the only ones to complete questionnaires. Concerns shared by more than one family member will likely receive higher priority; individual concerns might be the subject of joint discussions with family members.

When assessing the functioning of the family, it is important to assess relevant child variables. Also important to establish is how the family members view their own needs for support, information, or training. Observations of parent-child interactions are another rich source of assessment data. From the information gleaned and observations made, school professionals develop tentative hypotheses about family needs.

Once the functioning and characteristics of the family, including all the dimensions of family systems as well as family needs from their point of view, are known, it is time to move into the planning process. It is impossible to move into the second step unless professionals have invested considerable time with family members understanding their particular characteristics as well as personal needs and desires.

Planning

Most educators are masters at planning. The focused interview is conducted with parents and at times with other family members. The face-to-face interview allows school professionals to validate needs of the family, reprioritize those needs when indicated, and elicit family members' suggestions about what solutions might fit them. Generally, the interviewer has a list of areas to pursue while talking with the family.

From the data base that is developed and summarized into a prioritized listing of needs and problems, goals can be generated. A goal is essentially a description of what occurs when the problem or need no longer exists. Goals should be outcome-oriented, time-limited, and stated in measurable terms. It is more functional to state goals in relative (as opposed to absolute) terms. For example, reducing temper tantrums to one an evening as opposed to eliminating them entirely is a realistic, functional goal. Another example would be having an adolescent complete homework three out of the four nights that he has it each week, as opposed to completing it four out of four nights of the week.

Once the goals have been established, professionals are ready to join the family in generating plans to achieve these goals. Goals are critical to the planning process. Goals are a must; they serve as a map to reach the destination.

Plans are best established according to the three *W*'s: *What* action is to be taken toward achieving a particular goal? *Who* will be responsible for that action? *When* will the action be completed?

In family-focused interventions, planning must be a process involving both parents and professionals. Examples of some solutions that might be planned together with the Estevas family include having the grandmother tutor Miguel, allowing time alone for the spouses at least every other evening, and having an aunt babysit while the mother has three mornings out a week. These are realistic plans when based upon family input and prioritization of their needs.

The necessity of joint planning involving professionals and parents cannot be emphasized strongly enough. Investment is highest when all parties have had the opportunity to examine alternatives, express concerns, and influence decisions.

Implementation

It has been said that no decision has really been made until action has been taken. Likewise, the best of plans are only good intentions until they are implemented. If any party to the plan is reluctant to proceed to implementation, then a re-examination of the data and planning process may be warranted. A critical question in such a case is, "What has prevented individuals from freely expressing their concerns during the planning part of the process?"

Freedom to express concerns may not be the explanation for lack of implementation. Unforeseen barriers to implementation may be the cause of the reluctance. For example, perhaps the grandparents, upon whom the family was going to lean, had to be hospitalized and thus could no longer help the child with homework. When a barrier develops, the professional should be flexible and insure effective communication about the new circumstances.

Types of interventions typical of family-focused interventions are the subject of the next major section in this chapter. Bailey et al. (1988) have listed three types of direct professional support: informational support, instrumental support (helping families achieve tasks or functions), and socioemotional support (e.g., listening). Indirect support such as facilitating services and case managing was also discussed.

Bailey and his colleagues (1988) warned professionals about attempting to provide services in which they are not skilled. For example, in good faith and with the best intent, a teacher might attempt to provide counseling for parents bereaved by the loss of a child. Unskilled and untrained in counseling, the teacher might actually do more harm than good. This is not to say that the teacher should not talk about the death of a child whom he taught; he simply should not assume the role of counselor in those interactions. A caring and supportive teacher is called for in this example.

Evaluation

Once a plan is implemented, it is time for the final component in the process, evaluation. Good plans contain built-in evaluation in terms of measurable and time-limited goals. Goal attainment is always helpful in evaluation. Evaluation might also include readministration of the initial family inventory.

It is critical to assess other aspects, in addition to the degree to which the desired outcome was achieved, during evaluation of family-focused interventions. Each family member's level of satisfaction with the process should be determined. It helps to ascertain what was ineffective as well as what worked. This evaluation then becomes the basis for an updated assessment to use in the development of a new intervention cycle. It is usually combined with results from the readministration of the family inventory mentioned earlier.

The four steps of assessment, planning, implementation, and evaluation are a dynamic interrelated process for change. This is not a start-and-stop model, but a cyclical process. Each new round builds on the successes of the last, leading to increased impact and effectiveness.

When the parents and professionals evaluate where they are in the process, they realize they have worthwhile assessment information relating to the first step in the process. This allows family-focused interventions to recycle at deeper and deeper levels.

Table 9.4 presents questions to answer about the four processes of intervening. We recommend discussing those questions with others.

Types of Interventions

Having covered underlying features and the four-step process of family-focused intervention, we now turn to a specific consideration of types of interventions conducted by professionals. We will briefly describe seven different types.

Emotional Support

Many families with children with special needs suffer from feelings of grief, isolation, anxiety, or frustration. It is crucial that professionals provide an atmosphere of trust and safety. Having a sense of being understood and cared about is a most basic and powerful family intervention.

The emotional support that school professionals provide is not something that will necessarily be listed by the parents as a need. Professionals can, however, assume that all families benefit from emotional support. This especially includes those who are at risk.

Perhaps the *reflecting* that was mentioned previously is the best way that professionals, who are not trained for in-depth responses, can provide emotional support. It is

Table 9.4
DISCUSSION STARTERS ON THE FOUR PROCESSES OF INTERVENING

1. What are some reasons trust is so important in the assessment process?
2. The assessment step is considered critical to the family-focused intervention process. To what do you attribute that?
3. Goals seem to be time managers' answer to the world. Why so?
4. Provide a well-stated goal for a family-focused intervention and defend its aspects and value.
5. Mutuality in planning appears to be a "sacred cow." Why?
6. How do you see evaluation fitting into the process of family-focused intervention?

supportive simply to listen to someone who is in emotional pain (Lambie, 1987). It is, in fact, often distracting when a professional hurries to suggest solutions rather than being at the feeling level of the person. Professionals' responses all too often relate to solutions rather than reacting to the family member at his or her level of emotional response.

Again, "being understood" is, by itself, a powerful family intervention. Active listening, with its emotional support, often leads to more specific intervention strategies such as the other strategies described here.

Resource Identification

Few family members know of all the useful resources available to them. Resource identification might include making information available, including written materials about the child's special needs, rights and responsibilities, and procedures, as well as due process. Links with specialized personnel within the school and community should be provided frequently.

One of the most valuable resources to parents is parent groups. These come in three basic varieties. First, parent support groups focus on coming together to share emotional support. They also assist one another in learning to cope with the facts of having a child with special needs. Second, parent education groups are oriented toward providing information about particular conditions such as learning disabilities. They may also train parents in management techniques or other topics such as time management. Third, parent advocacy groups center around teaching and encouraging parents to become strong advocates for their children. The Association for Children with Learning Disabilities is one such example.

Resource identification may also involve helping parents locate and gain access to other parents, finding ways of gaining needed experiences such as sitting in on IEP meetings, or visiting alternative programs. Further information concerning parent groups and other sources of resource identification are included in chapter 11 of this text as well as Appendix C.

Technical Assistance

Professionals may directly intervene with families by suggesting at-home management strategies, training techniques, or helpful hints about working with specific behavior problems. This information would, of course, be provided because family members had indicated the need for it. Technical assistance may be an outgrowth of observations made, hypotheses tested, and conclusions drawn by professionals. In some cases professionals would recognize family characteristics, such as enmeshment, and use the family's language to convey areas that need attention.

While the best collaborations between parents and teachers tend to preserve their respective roles—that is, teachers teach and parents parent—much of what works in one setting can be applied to the other. The exchange of what works between parents and professionals frequently enhances the effectiveness of both. Chapter 10 covers parent–professional conferencing in detail; such sharing can also easily be accommodated in that process.

Referral

The fourth type of intervention might include referral to family therapy or medical, counseling, psychological, or financial services. Referrals are made when the specialized needs of families go beyond what the professionals in the schools can reasonably be expected to provide.

In particular, teachers should not become so involved with families that they rob themselves of personal discretionary time. Families with children with special needs are frequently desperate for someone to listen to them, and it is natural to want to help them in any way. Teachers should be particularly cautious about stepping out of their roles. At the same time, teachers play a valuable role in using the trust and mutual commitment they have established with parents to help link families with other needed services.

Family therapy is a prominent alternative for referral when the professional can identify structural or interactional patterns in the family that warrant such an intervention. Part I of this book covered this type of information. Sibling groups are another option for referral either when problems arise among siblings or simply for mutual support. Siblings were mentioned in chapters 2 and 7 of this text. A part of chapter 11 is devoted to the process of referring family members for other services.

Normalization

Professionals have pointed out the difficulty both parents and school professionals face in maintaining perspective and avoiding overemphasizing the deficits of the student with special needs. Professionals can help parents who are overemphasizing deficits by helping them view their child's behavior as normal.

Many parents perceive their child's behavior through the "disability filter." They are in danger of forgetting that most actions of even the most atypical child, are age-appropriate and normal. For instance, "normal" students have a bad day at school every now and then. They also have minor problems at home, but the same behavior in a child with special needs tends to be thought of as symptomatic. Teachers have a marvelous opportunity to help the family develop a normalizing perspective, as do the other professionals in the building.

Reframing

Reframing is another type of intervention that is sometimes used in normalization. Reframing involves offering alternative interpretations of behavior or events that essentially change the meaning of the behavior for the family. Its objective is to alter the pattern of the interaction.

For example, many children with attention deficit disorder have difficulty following complex directions and therefore do not do anything. A father may label his child's lack of compliance as defiance. If the school professional can help the father relabel the behavior as "confused," it would be likely to change the emotional loading and the sequence of interactions. Similarly, a parent who complains of a child's pestering may respond differently if the child's need for attention and reassurance is emphasized.

Appendix A describes Virginia Satir's model. She was a master of the art of reframing. By itself, reframing can be an effective intervention provided by school professionals. Satir (1983a) referred to helping families to see situations with "new eyes." She might have characteristically said, "Yes, that is how you saw your son yesterday. Now you've learned so much about yourself, your parents and their parents. How do you see your son now?" Chapter 12 includes a section on reframing. For more information, see Watzlawick (1976).

Contextualization

Contextualization shares some similarities with normalization and reframing. It is a process of helping parents and family members interpret behavior "in and through" the context in which it occurs.

For example, physical complaints may develop when a child faces demands on his performance that he feels inadequate to meet. Consider a kindergarten child, Emma, who was the only child in her class unable to recognize the letters of the alphabet. She began to complain about headaches and wanted to go to the infirmary every time the teacher taught letter recognition in class. In another example, an adolescent might be withdrawn or rejecting toward siblings after a difficult social encounter with peers at school. In a third example, being afraid could induce a child to become aggressive or threatening in order to increase social differences. An example of this was seen with an adolescent, Shawn, who was afraid of a peer's size and threatening manner. Shawn would tell the peer that he had a black belt in karate and invite him to fight, when in fact he had never even attended a karate class.

Professional intervention assists parents and other family members to respond effectively to a child's behavior by helping them become tuned in to the significant contextual factors. Once they notice and understand the context from which the behavior springs, it is much easier for them to accept and respond to the student. The intervention actually attunes the family members to the context. How the family members respond once they notice and understand the context depends upon the situation. In the example of Emma, the family members could be coached to support her by commenting on the way they would feel being in a class for which they were unprepared. In the second example, the siblings might be coached to lie low and not bother the adolescent until he or she had time to come to terms with the situation at school. This would be especially important for enmeshed families, rather than getting in the middle of the special needs student's own problems. If Shawn's family (in the third example) was disengaged, after attuning the family to the context, professionals might also coach the family to reach out to Shawn by commenting on how threatened they might themselves feel in a similar situation. This could lead to stronger positive alignments between the needs of the adolescent and family members as well as healthier cohesion in the family interaction pattern.

Now that we have examined the family-focused intervention, a relatively informal process, we will focus upon IEPs, a formal process. Family-focused interventions can be used with both at-risk and special needs students, whereas IEPs are required only for students with a disability.

INDIVIDUALIZED EDUCATION PROGRAMS

The Individualized Education Program (IEP) was intended to be the cornerstone of educational programming for a student with a disability. The IEP is the vehicle used to develop programs that provide free and appropriate educational experiences for students who are determined to be eligible for special education.

At-risk students can, at the discretion of the local school system, also have written IEPs. However, any school system providing IEPs for students who are not determined to be eligible for special education does not have to follow federal or state regulations regarding content or process.

This section presents further background information on IEPs for special education students. Next, potential challenges or barriers to the effective inclusion of parents in the IEP process are addressed. Finally, ways to involve families in the IEP process are described and related specifically to family systems concepts.

Background

An Individualized Education Program written for a student must be developed by a committee and include the parent in the process. Furthermore, this process must be completed before the student can be placed in a special education program. The parents must agree to the program before it may be implemented. As stated in chapter 8, these conditions are intended to insure that the program the student receives is designed to meet his or her unique learning needs, rather than having the individual student meet the requirements of a given program.

The IEP outlines the educational program for each student with a disability for the period of one year. The IEP sets learning goals for the student and specifies the related services, such as family counseling or occupational therapy, that will be required to help the student meet those goals.

This introductory section concerning IEPs includes information on components of IEPs, research results relating to family involvement in the IEP process, advantages and disadvantages of IEPs, and barriers to IEP development identified by parents as well as teachers. This book does not tell how to write IEPs; its focus is on family involvement. For further information on developing and implementing IEPs, read Strickland and Turnbull (1990).

Components

The first component of IEPs is a description of the child's current level of educational performance or functioning. This statement should include strengths as well as weaknesses. Just as it is important to include family resources when assessing families, it is valuable to state strengths of the student. This information is gleaned from the assessment process.

Annual goals and short-term objectives to reach those goals follow the statement of the student's level of functioning. Goals and objectives must be tied to the student's strengths and weaknesses. Family involvement in the process of stating goals is critical.

A statement of the specific special education and related services must also be provided, along with the extent to which the student will participate in regular education programs. The IEP specifies the date when services will be initiated and how long these services are expected to last. Parents should be involved in writing these statements.

Criteria for achievement of specific objectives must also be indicated. Dates when objectives will be introduced and when they are expected to be mastered are also specified.

Another important component is evaluation of the Individualized Education Program. The IEP must state when, how, and by whom the program will be evaluated. It is required that all IEPs be reevaluated at least annually. During the annual review the student's program is examined in its entirety. The progress made in accomplishing short-term objectives and long-term goals is determined. In addition, the continued appropriateness of the student's present educational placement must be reviewed.

A complete evaluation of each student receiving special education must be performed every three years. The student must undergo a new comprehensive assessment that includes all of the components present in the original assessment process. Parents or professionals may request a comprehensive assessment sooner if they feel the present educational program is not meeting the needs of the student.

Research Results

As early as 1979 Gilliam noted the importance of increasing participation in the decision-making process. He also specifically mentioned the need for encouraging parents and professionals "to share their knowledge about the child and the placement functions" (pp. 467–468).

Even earlier, Yoshida, Fenton, Kaufman, and Maxwell (1978) had noted "that planning team members' attitudes toward parental participation will be a major factor in determining the actual role parents take during planning team meetings" (p. 531). They found that parents were expected to provide information to the team, but not to be actively involved in making decisions about their own child's educational program.

Another study (Goldstein, Strickland, Turnbull, & Curry, 1980) of 14 actual IEP conferences found that only one was devoted to parents and educators actually writing goals and objectives together. Further, that one case involved a father who was a psychologist and familiar with IEPs. In that case the mother attended and participated in writing both goals and objectives.

In 1990 Smith published a three-phased review of both data-based research and position papers on IEPs published between 1975 and 1989. He described literature as falling into normative, analytic, and technology-reaction phases. The normative literature described norms and procedures for IEPs as well as professional concerns about that process. The analytic phase of literature included studies of data-based research with teacher involvement and perceptions being important as well as parental involvement and the team approach. The technology-reaction phase focused on computer-assisted systems that could manage the IEP process and provide documentation.

Of interest here is the information Smith (1990) related about parental involvement described in the analytic phase. He cited four studies as representative of concerns about professionals' perceptions of the parental roles, the actual roles of parents, parents' perception of their role during the IEP conference, as well as parental satisfaction with their role in the IEP conference. His summary of the studies indicated "little interaction by parents when they attended the IEP meeting, with parents being perceived by school professionals as recipients of information. Despite this passive role, parents have generally been satisfied with the IEP conference and its outcomes" (p. 9). The entire article by Smith (1990) is excellent reading.

Advantages and Disadvantages

There are many advantages to writing IEPs. They form a working guide that allows parents to keep focused on current goals and objectives for their child. This provides parents with the opportunity to reinforce skills at home that are being covered in school. The IEP process also presents the occasion for parents to interact with teachers in a constructive manner as opposed to the first time they hear from school personnel about a problem.

Additionally, the focus in IEP meetings is on possibilities rather than problems. Another advantage is that a written document (IEP) is taken home and parents don't have to rely on their memories. At the high school level the IEP meeting presents the occasion of discussing the type of diploma or certificate toward which the student is working. This prevents parental disappointment and alienation later because it is discussed long before graduation.

There are also disadvantages to IEPs. It takes considerable time to develop these plans as well as coordinate meeting times for all involved. Parents may have their own struggles such as masking their lack of understanding or acceptance of the IEP, transportation problems, or difficulty accepting their child's disability and level of functioning. The parents may have unrealistic expectations of their child or the professionals who implement the IEP. No process or document is perfect; however, like pregnancy and delivery of a child its outcome is worth the trouble.

Think about advantages and disadvantages from the perspective of the family first and then the student. Follow that with the perspective of school personnel, including teachers, principal, and support staff. Reflecting on your thoughts with peers would be valuable. If you are using this book for a course, that might include classroom discussion or merely talking with classmates before or after classes.

Barriers

There are some barriers to involving parents in the IEP process that originate both from the teachers' and parents' points of view. Those will be described before we move to the phases of the IEP conference and how to involve parents in each phase.

Barriers for Parents

Several barriers to parental involvement in IEPs have been described by Turnbull and Turnbull (1986, 1990). Four of these are logistical problems, communication problems, lack of understanding of the school system, and feelings of inferiority.

Logistical problems. Examples of logistical problems are difficulty with transportation, child-care problems, involving fathers, and time. Families will have different resources and interaction patterns that lead to these barriers. Some are disengaged and may not want to be involved. Others may be overwhelmed with few resources available. Still others result from what Aponte (1976b) referred to as "underorganization." This is most frequently observed in schools in areas where families are of low socioeconomic status.

Professionals should find ways to ameliorate these barriers so that parents can participate in the development of IEPs. This includes networking to assist with transportation and babysitting as well as arranging meeting times convenient for parents. More information on networking is provided in chapter 11. In addition, an understanding of family systems concepts and family characteristics is more helpful in responding to barriers stemming from unique family characteristics.

Communication. The identified problem with communication relates to language and cultural barriers. Certainly professionals can find ways to work with minorities. Home visits, translators, written texts, and outreach are viable ways to counteract these barriers. Whoever chairs the IEP conference should be able to relate effectively to the family's cultural and socioeconomic background as well as to overcome language barriers.

Lack of understanding school systems. Parents also need help from professionals to be able to understand schools. It is important to provide information on parental rights and responsibilities. Parents may also need help to understand the ways in which they can call upon those rights as a support for them. Turnbull and Turnbull (1990) cited a study by Thompson involving training parents through lecture, discussion, audiovisual materials, and simulated activities. Mothers receiving the training were twice as likely to contribute to the IEP conference as those not receiving the training.

Feelings of inferiority. Professionals must let parents know that they are valued. The role and value of partnership between home and school must be conveyed. It is easy for parents to feel overwhelmed by large committee meetings. They need to know that professionals value and appreciate their input. Again, the IEP chairperson with a link to the family can be very helpful. For example, a Puerto Rican family would probably find it easier to have an IEP chairperson who speaks Spanish or is of Spanish descent.

Barriers for Teachers

Teachers identified additional barriers to parental participation, including parental apathy, and professional time constraints. Teachers also identified parents' lack of time and the schools' devaluation of parent input.

Parental apathy. Apathy should be taken in stride by the teacher and not personalized. Professionals are not responsible for motivating everyone! It is most helpful to consider what is known about the particular family characteristics and recognize that there are good reasons for parental apathy. They may not have the personal resources at the time to be involved in one more activity. The "straw that would break the camel's back" may be recognized by the family and not by the professionals. Families may be able to gauge what additional involvement will stretch them too far. The important thing is for professionals to recognize situations that will not change and conserve their personal energy. It is important to recognize the difference between things that can be changed and things that cannot and accept those things that cannot be changed.

Professional constraints. Time is a major factor in developing IEPs. Teachers have indicated that they spend approximately six hours on developing new IEPs (Price & Goodman, 1980). It is important that professionals provide sufficient time for conferences, even if they have to lean on others to do some tasks. Dictating reports, using volunteers for scheduling, and receiving inservice training on time management are all helpful possibilities. Time well spent early in the process of developing IEPs will save time over the long term, especially as related to parental involvement.

Time barriers can work against effective and clear communication with parents. It is common for professionals facing time constraints to inform parents about their "rights" and not encourage them to participate in decision making. The results are predictable—adversary versus advocate.

Family Involvement

Family involvement in the IEP process is typically seen as parental involvement. It is hoped that professionals view parental involvement in IEPs as important. The federal government did when it required parental involvement in the development of IEPs.

There are six components of the IEP conference: preconference preparation, initial conference proceedings, review of formal evaluation and current levels of performance, development of goals and objectives, determination of placement and related services, and concluding the conference (Turnbull & Turnbull, 1986). Each of these components will be described and related to involvement of families as well as understanding ways in which dysfunctional families might operate in that phase of the IEP process.

Not all school systems link determination of placement and related services to the eligibility process; they hold those meetings separate from development of the IEP. In those systems, parental involvement would obviously be beneficial during that earlier stage.

Preconference Preparation

From the assessment process, much information concerning the family's unique characteristics and process has already been accumulated. Those on the team who know most about family systems should meet with professionals involved in the IEP conference. It is important to have a view or review of family functioning so that ideas they present are taken into consideration, given the context from which they arise. It is also helpful to know about the family's process so that the professionals provide input that fits the given family. For example, professionals would not want to encourage increased parent/child involvement for field trips if it was already determined that the parents were overly involved with their child. All professionals will want family characteristics to be utmost in their minds as they begin mutual program planning.

The chairperson for the IEP conference should be chosen based upon who might be best able to chair the meetings. When considering particular characteristics of the family, one of the potential chairpeople will most likely stand out as the best for the particular family. Some professionals will work better with enmeshed families; others will be more effective with disengaged families. A member of a minority group might offer to chair the conference of a minority family. A single parent might be the best chair for a single parent of a student with special needs.

The chairperson's responsibilities are to coordinate the preconference proceedings, chair the actual IEP meeting(s), and provide follow-up support. It is easy to see why some type of matching of family to chairperson might be more effective.

Initial Conference Proceedings

The beginning of any conference sets the tone for what is to come. Most have heard about or attended large conferences with a keynote speaker whose skills and sensitivities prompted the audience to look forward to the remainder of the conference. So too in a small conference dealing with one pupil is it important to get off to a good start. Professionals concern themselves with many students. During an IEP conference professionals and the parents are concerned only about that one child.

Critical to effective human interaction is allowing all other concerns or unresolved problems to recede from your mind. The skill of putting all other things from your mind and focusing wholly on the present concern is essential. Counselors and therapists must regularly employ this clear focusing of their energies, so it may be easier for them than those unaccustomed to such specific focusing. Prior to walking into the meeting, professionals would benefit from taking a minute to clear other concerns from their minds and to focus clearly on the situation at hand. Thirty seconds of deep breathing followed by a quick review of the child's records and unique family characteristics will help you focus clearly. In addition, you may want to use an affirmation such as, "This student and family [name and family] are my only concern at this time. I give them my full attention." These suggestions are part of low-stress living and abound in the literature on stress.

It is important that the chairperson speak with the family members, including the student, while everyone is arriving. Most of the professionals will be familiar with one another. Everyone should be introduced before the meeting becomes more formal so that they have a chance to interact informally. On occasion, with contentious parents, informal introductions may not be in order; however, they must always be made, whether informal or formal in nature.

Turnbull and Turnbull (1986) have recommended "greeting parents and their guests, making introductions, reviewing an agenda addressing timelines (time schedules) for participants, and providing information on legal rights" (p. 245). These are all basic to effective initial conference proceedings.

Keeping distinctive family characteristics foremost in your mind is most helpful. If family members respond coolly to a professional's greeting, the professional should review their family patterns. They may be disengaged within the family and only generalizing this functioning outside of the family. Certainly, most people operate in similar ways within and outside of the family. Also, as mentioned in the chapter on cultural factors, cultural background should be considered. Someone from a northern European background might have a more reserved style than a southern European, who might be more extraverted.

Review of Formal Evaluation and Current Levels of Performance

If the homework has been done adequately, the chairperson already will have covered information on test results. Chapter 8 recommended a premeeting conference that presents test results prior to determination of eligibility. This allows families to join the group of professionals in planning the educational program. It will, however, be most helpful to quickly look over test results so that everyone remembers the current level of functioning and strengths and weaknesses. During IEP conferences that are held after the initial conference, the teacher(s) should present information on progress to date for goals and objectives set at earlier IEP conferences.

Development of Goals and Objectives

An earlier section of this chapter covered contents of IEPs. Goals and objectives are important aspects of IEPs. Family members, including the student when possible, can contribute to developing those goals and objectives. They should also feel comfortable responding to their impression of goals and objectives presented by the professionals.

When parents are aware of goals and objectives, it is much easier for them to follow up on them at home. Certainly parents want their child's learning to generalize to other situations. Their involvement can focus the rest of the family on common purposes and tasks. Siblings may be able to participate in reinforcing learning goals.

Again, family considerations are important in this step of the conference. Some families from lower socioeconomic strata might find it difficult to relate to the goals and objectives presented. It is important to invest time in conferences with those parents so that they can become familiar with the educational program and come to value it.

Other parents might be unwilling to let school professionals know that they do not understand something like goals and objectives and simply attend out of a sense of obligation. When this situation occurs, professionals should hypothesize how the parents might be reacting and respond to their situation. In these situations it is important to put the parents at ease by sharing realistic expectations of their understanding. Allowing them to ask questions is helpful. Professionals should empower parents rather than letting them stay in the dark. Clarification of goals and objectives is most helpful; as in all stages of the IEP process, language at family members' levels is imperative.

Beyond those commonsense types of joining, it is beneficial to consider family functioning from a family systems perspective. If the student is presenting his ideas with excessive strength and the parents are acquiescent, it might confirm a professional's hypothesis that there is an inversion of the hierarchy. It may not be possible to completely address this situation in the IEP meeting; however, school professionals should at least note the situation and later convey it to the appropriate professionals. The social worker, counselor, and psychologist might find that information helpful in future meetings with parents. If the family is seeing a therapist, such objective and descriptive information could be valuable. However, educators must not volunteer such information outside the school system without a signed release from the parents.

In the example of the overly assertive adolescent, one way of intervening is to acknowledge the situation and place the parent(s) at the top of the hierarchy with a statement such as "Ken, I notice that you are being really assertive here. I would also like to hear from your father and mother. Mr. and Mrs. Takayima, what are your thoughts and feelings about this goal?" Depending upon the situation, this might be a viable option, though professional discretion is always advised. Support for healthy family interactions is critical. Modeling of effective human interaction by professionals can also be beneficial.

There are endless possibilities in which parents and students will demonstrate their family functioning. This is a choice time for confirming as well as establishing hypotheses regarding unique family characteristics. What is observed might also help professionals plan strategy for future family involvement as well as help refer families for family systems therapy or other counseling.

Determination of Placement and Related Services

As stated earlier, some school systems do not determine placement and related services at the same time that they develop the IEP. Whatever the practice, parents should receive information that allows them to comprehend the different placement options as well as their respective advantages and disadvantages. Information about related services must also be provided. The general practice in schools is to merely recommend a particular delivery model and assume the parents will not object.

Once the necessary information on delivery models and related services has been provided, parents should be encouraged to offer their view. Parents might even benefit from visiting classrooms to further investigate the options. Professionals should not make any recommendation until the parents have expressed their thoughts and opinions. If the parent suggests an option that is obviously not in the child's best interest, professionals should provide information on their views. An example is, "Mrs. Bellissimo, I have heard parents who have said the same thing in the past. In your shoes, I might say the same thing. What I am not sure is evident is the fact that a few months in a self-contained classroom might be less restrictive than two years in the resource model." Effective communicators will validate the parents' thoughts, even when holding another view. Professional thoughts and opinions should then be voiced. With effective human interaction skills, the professionals and family members can reach a decision together on placement and related services.

Again, all of the distinctive family characteristics will come into play. Professionals sometimes, in the interest of time, allow reticent parents to withhold their views. However, when everyone is involved in the decision making, they will be more likely to support the path taken. Without sharing their views they will not feel a part of the process and may subvert the results without even realizing it. Thus, it behooves professionals to solicit family involvement.

Concluding the Conference

A synthesis of the recommendations and plans for following up are developed. The chairperson will have the responsibility of summarizing the conference as well as listing tasks for the future and assigning responsibility for those tasks.

Before concluding the conference a timeline for review should be made explicit by the chairperson. Other means of regular communication between the family and school should also be established. Disengaged families, in particular, would likely benefit from more frequent family-school interactions. Enmeshed families, on the other hand, might benefit from less involvement in the pupil's progress. The main thing for professionals to consider is that any plans for continued follow-up activities should fit the unique family characteristics. A family with three preschool children may not have the time for much involvement with detailed follow-up activities. Recognizing the reality of the family situation helps guide the kinds of plans made.

Concluding remarks are best focused on the value of shared decision making and the expression of appreciation for family and professional collaboration. The end of the conference is the perfect opportunity for professionals to again show their appreciation for and value of family involvement.

One caveat about IEP conferences: Professionals and family members alike should commit themselves to attending full meetings and not just dropping by to provide their input. To provide meaningful input and involvement, parents and professionals must make a commitment that they honor in all ways.

SUMMARY

This chapter described family-focused intervention for both at-risk and special needs students and detailed the IEP process as it relates to involving parents. Interwoven within both processes were insights and methods arising from family systems approaches. Next we move to the prereferral process and conducting family conferences.

PREREFERRAL AND
FAMILY CONFERENCES 10

Family conferences are as old as schools and teachers. You may, therefore, wonder if the better part of wisdom would be to skip this chapter. However, it is well worth reading for its information on family systems concepts and ways in which to approach parent–professional interactions. This chapter, like the two previous ones, builds on the concepts presented in Part I, focusing on family involvement from a family systems perspective.

Prereferral is the best time to begin involving parents. In fact, if the parents are involved in this early stage and if professionals use family systems concepts, the chances increase that referral for special education will not be needed. The prereferral process is used with both at-risk and special needs students who are in the regular classroom. The family conference is aimed at families with students with disabilities who are in special education classrooms; however, students in both situations and personnel will overlap.

Initially this chapter covers three considerations basic to family involvement. Then general principles that relate to family systems ideas are presented. These principles involve many of the concepts described in Appendix A. We follow those principles first with information on prereferral interventions and then with family conferences, weaving family systems examples throughout.

BASIC CONSIDERATIONS

Classroom teachers are in a special position for relating to parents of at-risk and special needs students, as are principals. Parents may not see school counselors, social workers, psychologists, or other helping professionals. Even when parents have had contact with these specialists, it is frequently irregular and in response to problems. The teacher, on the other hand, has an opportunity for more frequent, routine contact with family members.

This contact provides a basis for establishing and maintaining a trusting relationship. Whereas the parent may view the school psychologist as intimidating and judgmental, the teacher is often seen as an understanding and nonthreatening source of valuable information. The different contexts in which teachers and parents relate to the student enriches the information and idea exchange between parents and school.

The basic considerations covered in this section are sensitivity, climate, and locus of control. These considerations are basic to all interactions, called "interviews" here, between school and home.

Sensitivity

Simpson (1982) stated:

One generic aptitude associated with successful interaction with others is an interest in and sensitivity to people. Individuals who expect to serve the needs of parents and families must possess a genuine interest in people and a willingness to invest time and energy in arriving at solutions to their problems. (p. 17)

The success of a parent–professional interview always hinges on the attitudes, values, sensitivity, and understanding of the professional. Professionals can learn many human interaction skills. These skills, however, will lack foundation if the professional is not committed to meeting the needs of these families. Both professionals and parents should assume the responsibility for sound working relations. However, the professional must also have the attitude and motivation necessary for beneficial interactions to occur. Such development is a basic part of professionalism on the part of the school representative.

Climate/Mood

The single most important word to describe the climate of a successful professional–parent interaction is *trust*. Trust emerges if people feel safe enough to take interpersonal risks. The risk taking can then result in successful, productive relationships.

Several interactive elements are essential in the development of trust in the parent-professional relationship. Simpson (1982) described many of these elements, including willingness to invest time and energy, a shared commitment to the student, willingness of both parties to advocate for the student assertively, maintaining sensitivity to each other's needs, willingness to confront and reinforce each other, a positive outlook, and finally honesty.

Many people feel that being honest and direct involves a significant degree of interpersonal risk. It is, however, critical to effective interviews that professionals have these qualities and take the lead in modeling appropriate risk-taking behavior. In his text, "Conferencing Parents of Exceptional Children," Simpson (1982) provided a questionnaire involving twenty risk-taking situations with which professionals are often faced in relation to parents. Table 10.1 lists his questions. You may find it helpful to complete that questionnaire.

After completing (or at least reading) the questionnaire, you might find it instructive to answer the following five questions.

1. What items were you surprised to see on the questionnaire?
2. Are there any items you feel are inappropriate to interviewing?
3. Did you learn anything new about yourself? If so, what? If not, why?
4. Which items are more difficult for you personally?
5. Are there items you would add to the questionnaire?

Table 10.1
RISK-TAKING QUESTIONNAIRE

How comfortable are you in...	Very Comfortable	Somewhat Comfortable	Natural	Somewhat Uncomfortable	Very Uncomfortable
1. Telling parents you don't know	___	___	___	___	___
2. Telling parents that you made a mistake	___	___	___	___	___
3. Suggesting to parents that another professional made an error	___	___	___	___	___
4. Suggesting to parents that they should consider therapy for themselves	___	___	___	___	___
5. Telling parents that there are behaviors displayed by their children that you dislike	___	___	___	___	___
6. Displaying your emotions in a parent–educator conference	___	___	___	___	___
7. Confronting parents with their failure to follow through on agreed-upon plans	___	___	___	___	___
8. Talking about your own problems in a parent–educator conference	___	___	___	___	___
9. Praising parents for things they do well	___	___	___	___	___
10. Having parents take notes during conferences	___	___	___	___	___
11. Allowing parents to observe in your class while you are teaching	___	___	___	___	___
12. Allowing parents to tutor their child at home	___	___	___	___	___
13. Allowing parents to use behavior modification procedures with their child at home	___	___	___	___	___
14. Telling parents their "rights" under PL 94-142	___	___	___	___	___
15. Having parents assume an active role during Individualized Education Program conferences	___	___	___	___	___
16. Having parents ask you to defend your teaching strategies	___	___	___	___	___
17. Having parents bring a friend to Individualized Education Program conferences	___	___	___	___	___
18. Having parents call you at home about a problem their child is having at school	___	___	___	___	___
19. Having parents recommend specific curriculum	___	___	___	___	___
20. Having parents review school records	___	___	___	___	___

Source: From *Conferencing Parents of Exceptional Children* by R. Simpson, 1982, Rockville, MD: Aspen. Reprinted by permission of PRO-ED.

If you know others who have read this book, it would be beneficial to discuss your answers to these five questions. You may find some interesting differences in your answers to those five questions. It would be even more interesting to investigate the reasons for those differences.

It is natural for professionals to feel uncomfortable with some of the items from Simpson's (1982) list. When developing a climate of trust, professionals must manage their discomfort effectively. Realizing that you take risks and recognizing the attendant feelings about risk taking will help you empathize with parents as they take even greater risks.

Locus of Control

Effective interviewing is a mutual, shared activity. Regardless of the specific purpose of the interaction, all interviews are opportunities to exchange information and views, share feelings, and make joint decisions. The preservation of trust and the establishment of a sound working relationship require the maintenance of a shared locus of control, that is, that professionals and parents mutually share in the control.

Parents get anxious, frustrated, and angry when they think that professionals are interfering with their ability to influence decisions affecting their child. Professionals must be sure that parents know they will not only have the opportunity but will be expected to influence decisions. Shared control and joint decisions are generally more difficult to achieve than unilateral decisions. However, sharing the locus of control maximizes the investment in the outcome of the involved parties.

These basic considerations are relevant to all forms of interactions with families, whether within the auspices of prereferral, conferencing, or other school related interaction. These basic considerations are not directly linked to family systems concepts. They are, however, critical to effective human interaction and maximize the use of family systems concepts by school professionals.

GENERAL PRINCIPLES

As mentioned in the introduction to this chapter, many of the ideas in this section relate to family systems concepts. Prior to reading this section of the chapter, you might want to read or review Appendix A with its information on the Satir process model and the Bowen theory. A quick reading will help you focus on the systems concepts presented and allow you to better comprehend and therefore use the following principles.

This section initially focuses on Satir's process for transforming family rules, an aspect vital to change and growth. It then explains and reflects on the "Five Freedoms," the heart of Satir's view of healthy communication. School professionals should be able to help family members use these processes in their relationships. Finally, the Bowen theory is revisited, with attention directed to the process of detriangling, one of the most difficult processes to achieve. Kerr and Bowen (1988) indicated that the process of detriangling takes considerable time and attention. You can learn to detriangle by merely reading about it; however, an understanding of the process will serve you well.

Transformation of Family Rules into Guidelines

Satir believed it was possible to find something useful in any rule. Recognizing that some family rules are outdated, inflexible, or restrictive, Satir focused her energies on helping individuals transform the rules with which they grew up. Such transformation allows rules to *guide* the individual while also providing protection. An example of a rigid rule is, "I should never be angry." This is neither always possible nor healthy. Being angry may be a significant way to lead to positive change in a situation as well as discharge energy that might otherwise be pent up, later exploding in unproductive ways.

Steps

Satir would have helped such a person transform the rigid family rule by going through a series of transformative steps that result in a guideline. The first-order transformation would be "I can always be angry." This possibility would be checked out with the person. Most people would say "No, not always." Then a second order would be produced, "I can sometimes be angry." Most people who have grown up with that rule, faced with a professional aware of what constitutes healthy family rules, would say "Well, maybe." The third-order transformation would be "I can be angry when [and then list three occasions]." Examples would be "when (a) it will make me feel better, (b) there would be a possibility for change, and (c) I might eventually feel closer to the person with whom I am upset." Clearly, this type of transformation allows the individual to use the family rule in a way that it continues to provide guidance for life. This process is elaborated upon below in the sections titled "Implementation" and "Further Exploration."

Questions

Satir and Baldwin (1983) provided a list of questions for family rules (see Table 10.2). When a family member compares the family rules to these questions, other possibilities reveal themselves. The questions can also be consulted when professionals attempt to identify family rules that might be in need of transformation.

The school professional's role is to help family members know more about and transform the rules that interrupt their lives. With that change comes improved communication and self-esteem. These are two of the most important aspects of healthy human functioning.

Implementation

Although it is not always possible to help family members transform obsolete, rigid, or ineffective rules, there are occasions when school professionals can find the time to be of assistance. Telling the following story is one way a professional can introduce the concept of the need to transform rules to families for whom it would be relevant.

> A newlywed couple argued profusely for their first two Thanksgivings about how to cook the turkey. The husband insisted that the legs had to be cut off and placed beside the turkey in the pan. The wife was equally adamant that the legs not be removed. One day, when they were visiting his parents, the wife asked her mother-in-law about how she had always cooked the turkey. The woman replied, "We didn't have a large enough pan in which to cook the turkey so we had to cut off his legs."

Counselors can help transform a family rule. For example, a father and his 16-year-old son argued frequently and on occasion came close to exchanging blows. In the process of counseling, the counselor worked with them on the family rule that "Children never question rules established by a parent." While this rule sounds appropriate for the father's

Table 10.2
SATIR'S QUESTIONS ABOUT FAMILY RULES

The following series of questions can be used by school professionals when determining what family rules need transformation. The first two questions help the professional determine potential rules for transformation into guidelines. The following three questions help the professional probe areas of human interaction that might reveal a rule in need of transformation. Most ineffective family rules stem from aspects of information sharing, differentness, and expression of feelings, thoughts, or opinions within the context of the family.

1. Are the rules humanly possible?

2. Are the rules up to date and relevant to a changing situation?

3. What are the rules governing differentness?

4. What rules surround the sharing of information?

5. What rules govern what family members can say about what they are feeling, seeing, and hearing?

Source: From *Satir, Step by Step* (pp. 202–205) by V. Satir and M. Baldwin, 1983, Palo Alto, CA: Science and Behavior Books.

4-year-old son, it does not fit an adolescent's situation. In fact, it could by its very nature instigate authority problems with any adolescent. In counseling, the father and son were led in a process of transforming that rule. The father was taught that his son had become old enough to think about which of his father's rules did and did not fit for him. In the process of rule transformation, the father began to realize that respect for elders is not automatic but is earned by flexible and supportive rules that fit the age of the children and situation involved.

Here is another example. Recall from chapter 2 that parents need to adapt family rules to the developmental level of each child. The emphasis here is on what the counselor (C) would say to the parent (P).

    C: Mr. Emmerson, I'm glad we have this opportunity to continue discussing the situation with your son Tim. I have thought about the early curfew Tim has on the weekends. Tell me how that came about.

    P: Tim has the same rule as our other son, Ralph. Since it would be too late for Ralph to come home after 9:00, my wife and I decided that Tim would also have to come in at 9:00. We cannot see how we could allow Tim to come in later, when Ralph has to be home by 9:00.

    C: How old is Ralph?

    P: 12.

C: So Tim is four years older than Ralph, and he still has to live by the same rules. Is that the way it was in your house when you grew up?

P: No, my older brother got away with murder. He was always coming in late and waking me up. My parents let him come in whenever he wanted and he got in a lot of trouble. Then, later they cracked down on me and made me come in earlier than he did at my age.

C: I can see how that could affect the kind of rules you have designed for your two children. Mr. Emmerson, could you imagine Tim always having a 2:00 a.m. curfew?

P: No. That's not in the realm of possibility.

C: If not, could you just imagine that on some occasion Tim might be allowed to have a later curfew?

P: I suppose so, like for the junior prom.

C: What might be some other times Tim could have a later curfew?

P: I guess when there's a movie he is seeing that won't be over in time for him to get home.... Also, perhaps when another parent has offered to go bowling with them, he could come in later.

C: Do you think there are big enough differences in a 12-year-old and 16-year-old that they might need different rules?

P: I don't want Ralph to think we're favoring Tim!

C: It might be a good idea to talk with Ralph and tell him why his rule for curfew and Tim's are different. Most kids even look forward to the time when they are old enough for their curfew time to change. I think, when we are most comfortable with our rule differences, our children test us less regarding those inequities. What we are talking about is a recognition, as well as acceptance, of the fact that age makes a difference for all kinds of things.

P: I suppose so. I could even give Ralph the example of Tim being old enough to drive.

C: Right. I think this will make a real difference for Tim. I appreciate your openness to these thoughts. By the way, I have a good article I think you might like to read about age differences in families.

Not all family–professional interactions lend themselves to the transformation of family rules. Sometimes there will not be enough time; other times the issue at hand will have nothing to do with rules. It may not be possible to help people transform family rules because they are not open to that initiative. On other occasions the mix of people may not fit the process of transforming family rules.

One warning about coaching parents regarding family rules: While some families' rules may not fit for you and your family, they may not be ineffective, inflexible, or restrictive. The test of whether a family rule would benefit from being transformed is whether it results in forwarding or restricting the growth of the individual and other family members. The questions in Table 10.2 can be used to assist you in making that decision.

Further Exploration

Before helping family members transform their rules, it is beneficial to practice on yourself first. The exercise in Table 10.3 is designed to provide that opportunity. We have found it beneficial to practice and share with other professionals our own transformed family rules and their resulting impact on our lives. This helps us assist families in transforming their worn-out, inflexible or ineffective rules. It is very difficult to help families do something that you have not yourself accomplished.

You might also like to read more of Satir's work, in particular *The New Peoplemaking* (1988) and *Your Many Faces* (1978). These books are highly readable and can be given to anyone with a fifth-grade reading level. Parents and siblings would also benefit tremendously from them. Satir wrote them for the general public.

Origin of Rules

Most rules have been passed down in families for generations. Cultural influences also affect family rules. McGoldrick et al. (1982) have written an excellent book for family therapists that relates family therapy and ethnicity. In addition, it is helpful to read about the ethnicity of the students in your schools, to better understand and hypothesize about those families and their rules that are culturally governed. Chapter 5 will also be helpful in following up with more information regarding rules and their cultural background.

Five Freedoms

When people are more concerned with conforming to a rule than with the people and situation at hand, a basic freedom promoting healthy functioning has been violated. An example would be if the children of a man with Alzheimer's disease continued operating under the family rule that "You don't stick your nose in another family member's business." In fact, Alzheimer's patients need someone who loves and cares for them to "stick their nose in their business." If all of the children of this man remain frozen in an obsolete family rule that is no longer functional for the person and situation at hand, basic freedoms have been violated. The family members do not, as Satir said, "give themselves permission" to see what is there, to say what they think, or take a risk. Old family rules can be very tenacious as well as destructive. Adults are not usually aware when their behavior stems from not understanding the impact of dysfunctional rules and not giving themselves permission to change their traditional patterns. Even when they are aware, the grip with which they are held can be like a vise.

Satir talked about "Five Freedoms" that are the cornerstone to effective human communication: The freedoms are:

1. To see and hear what is here, instead of what should be, was, or will be.
2. To say what one feels and thinks instead of what one should.
3. To feel what one feels, instead of what one ought.
4. To ask for what one wants, instead of always waiting for permission.
5. To take risks in one's own behalf, instead of choosing to be only "secure" and not rocking the boat. (Satir & Baldwin, 1983, pp. 168–169)

Flexible rules that are based in reality provide these five freedoms. The mother-father-child triad is the source of the most powerful rules for behavior. Parents who set their children free by providing realistic and flexible rules are usually the children of parents who were able to do the same for them. Inflexible rules result in a suppression of these freedoms and unhealthy relationships within and outside the family.

Table 10.3
TRANSFORMING A FAMILY RULE

State a family rule that was not healthy. Usually these are dogmatic statements, "You can never _____ " or "You should/ought to _____ ."

Your family rule _____

_____

_____

Transform your family rule in the following three steps.

I can always _____

I can sometimes _____

I can_____, when:

    a) _____

    b) _____

    c) _____

Complete another family rule transformation if it suits you!

Thus professionals are up against formidable odds when encouraging the five freedoms. Nevertheless, it is their responsibility to help families deal with these five freedoms. Further, schools are another source of rule making in our society. Thus, it behooves us to reflect upon our own rules in schools to see whether students are free in the sense of the five freedoms.

Implementation

School professionals who wish to encourage the five freedoms can, first and foremost, model healthy communication. Second, they can talk about the five freedoms and what they mean. Initially, all school professionals would benefit from training in the five freedoms. Then teachers could talk about the five freedoms in classes, when appropriate. Third, they can make posters of the five freedoms and hang them in the building. Fourth, the school counselor could establish groups for students that feature the five freedoms. Fifth, professionals can encourage families to be *free* by helping them understand and relate to the five freedoms. Parent–teacher organization meetings could be devoted to the five freedoms. One of the mental health professionals on the staff of the school or an outsider could deliver large-group information on the five freedoms. Then follow-up sessions could be implemented, with school professionals leading the small-group interactions.

The most important aspect of working to fulfill the five freedoms is recognizing that knowing what they mean and actually living them are two different things. Some autocratic leaders will not understand how to implement the five freedoms because they cannot allow others to be free to think their own thoughts and feel their own feelings. They see others' freedom as a threat.

As mentioned in Appendix A, reality is subjective. That is, one person in a given situation will react with his or her own eyes and experiences, while another person will react from his or her own filters and background. Thus, it behooves professionals not to encourage others, subtly or obviously, to adopt their view of any situation. That is the beginning point of living Satir's five freedoms.

Of course, sometimes someone's interpretation of a situation is well off the mark. Professionals do not need to allow people to be poor at reality testing. However, each person should have the freedom to see *any reality* as it is for him or her. Consider the case of the person who loves an argument and the one who hates any conflict. You would not be able to convince either that the other's view of reality was legitimate for him or her.

If a student became manipulative, professionals should tell the student how they saw the student manipulating the situation. Thus, the professional has the freedom to see and hear what is here as well as the freedom to say what you feel and think. It is in being true to themselves, with the five freedoms as a guide, that adults can be models for students.

Detriangling

If you have not already done so, this is a perfect time to read or make a quick review of Bowen's understanding of triangles, as presented in Appendix A. Detriangling, like other human interactions, is a complex process. One must be able to identify subtle and obvious means of being triangled as well as triangling others. Words are not the only means of communicating a triangling message. Facial expressions, tone of voice, and other nonverbal cues such as eye contact help communicate a conscious or unconscious intent to triangle.

Kerr (1988) said that detriangling is "probably the most important technique in family systems therapy" (p. 56). When it is used *only* as technique, however, it will most likely be ineffective. Appendix A points out that the Bowen theory is opposed to technique; it focuses on the theory. When an individual understands the systemic situation he or she can relate the cause of the struggle to the emotional process linking people and events, rather than seeing the cause of the struggle as the person or event itself. Just this understanding is beyond most people. Generally people are so emotionally embroiled in the situation that they do not see systems or process. Kerr and Bowen believe that being emotionally neutral fosters detriangling. As Kerr (1988) stated:

> Emotional neutrality does not mean a refusal to approve or disapprove of particular aspects of human behavior, and it does not mean making rules for oneself about not passing judgment on people's actions. A person who adheres to rules usually appears to be more neutral than he actually is. Nor does neutrality mean straddling fences or being wishy-washy. One can have a very clear position with respect to what occurs in a family and in society and still be emotionally neutral. Dogmatic positions, a lack of position, and efforts to change others all betray the absence of emotional neutrality. In essence, neutrality is reflected in the ability to define self without being emotionally invested in one's own viewpoint or in changing the viewpoints of others. (p. 57)

Thus, detachment is of value when detriangling. Being able to remain emotionally neutral when two other people are attempting to triangle you is critical. If you can see both sides of an argument, you will know that you are on the right track. And, if you can keep your thought processes clear and not "put onto" anyone else what you think "should" be, you are even in better shape. Kerr (1988) made it very clear that judging other people's process is intolerant and indicates that you are being triangled.

Kerr (1988) admitted that seeing both sides of a relationship problem can be quite demanding because one person may look like the "cause" of the other person's problem. One appears to be a victim and the other, the victimizer. Worse, one looks sick and the other as though he or she is making the best of a bad situation.

Implementation

To detriangle, the school professional must first accurately see the triangling process. Second, he or she must censor personal emotions and detach from judgments or resentments. Recognizing how feelings affect behavior will allow the school professional to gain control over automatic responses stemming from those feelings. Then, he or she can interact with family members by attempting to make statements indicating that he or she is not embroiled within the triangle and can be neutral. A statement about the observed triangulation will usually not have the desired impact of eliminating or even reducing the process of triangulation because the other person will have a personal view of the situation. That view might not include seeing triangulation. Also, teaching anything in a straightforward manner violates a premise in the Bowen theory and nullifies the process of differentiation of self. That is, direct attempts to influence others are counter to the process of differentiating a self.

It should, therefore, be obvious that differentiating a self is quite important to detriangling. Kerr probably best stated it this way, "Maintaining one's differentiation and detriangling is not an attempt to manipulate or control others but a way of dealing with others' attempts to manipulate and control oneself" (p. 58). Further, when professionals are able to detriangle, it is far more likely that they will be able to improve the relationship of the other two people in the triangle. According to the Bowen theory, when one detached third person sustains a higher level of differentiation than the other two, the other two will raise their functional levels of differentiation.

For further information on detriangling, see Kerr's 1988 article, particularly the interesting case example presented on pages 58 and 59.

Further Exploration

School professionals who are involved with families would learn much from investigating the triangling that occurred in their own families. That is best accomplished with the assistance of a family systems therapist. Not all professionals trained in family work are trained in family systems approaches or emphasize triangulation. A quick way to locate such a person is to find a list of professionals in your area who are members of the American Association of Marriage and Family Therapists. You can then contact one and find out if he or she or someone he or she knows is familiar with Bowen concepts.

Professionals should learn more about all aspects of their own family process. Bowen's training model included lifelong work dealing with one's family of origin. This was, of course, for family therapists who would continually be in situations that lend themselves directly to triangulation. Lifelong investigation of personal family process may not be needed by school professionals, yet a minimum of a year of family investigation would be most beneficial to all. One reason for this is the natural triangle that forms in a school: student-parent-professional. Seeing a therapist weekly is not necessary to pursue family process.

Further, it might be possible to employ a family systems therapist to meet with a small group of professionals interested in investigating family process in the school. That style of learning would be most beneficial because one would learn not only about one's own family process, but also that of others in the group. This would make it easier to understand different family processes and use that in the schools for the benefit of students and families.

PREREFERRAL INTERVENTION

Integrated models, such as that of Affleck, Madge, Adams, and Lowenbraun (1988), allow many special educational students to have their needs met while remaining in regular classrooms. This book focuses on at-risk students and those with special needs. Regular classroom interventions as well as placement in special classrooms are appropriate for these students. While not all students can be educated full-time in regular classrooms, at-risk students and most students with special needs can be. Before referring children for special education assessment, regular classroom teachers should consider multiple educational interventions (Lambert, 1988).

Over the years many researchers and writers (Alexander & Strain, 1978; Bailey & Winton, 1987; Jenkins & Heinen, 1989; Wang & Birch, 1984; Will, 1986) have focused on various aspects of educating students with special needs in regular classrooms, including the Regular Education Initiative (REI). It is not our goal here to debate the merits of the REI. For more on that topic read Skrtic's (1991) text or a *Phi Delta Kappan* article by Raynes, Snell, and Sailor (1991). Their emphasis is on inclusion of students with special needs in the regular classroom.

Prereferral was discussed in chapter 8 as a team process. Only a cursory overview was provided at that point. This section gives further basic information on prereferral interventions. Then the role of the regular classroom teacher and other professionals in involving families in prereferral is addressed. Last, typical problems and how to either avoid or solve those challenges during prereferral are covered. Thus, the discussion of prereferral intervention focuses on families of students who are being educated in regular classrooms.

Introduction

The term "prereferral intervention" was initially used by Graden, Casey, and Christenson in 1985 (Graden, 1989). At-risk students are often considered during prereferral interventions. With bases in collaborative consultation, as espoused by school psychologists (Conoley & Conoley, 1982; Gutkin & Curtis, 1982; Zins, Curtis, Graden, & Ponti, 1988) as well as special educators (Friend, 1984; Idol, Paolucci-Whitcomb, & Nevin, 1986; Idol-Maestas, 1983; Pugach & Johnson, 1988; Reisberg & Wolf, 1986), and in problem-solving teams (Chalfant et al., 1979), such as Teacher Assistance Teams, this early intervention can eliminate the need for referral to special education. West and Idol (1987) presented an excellent interdisciplinary examination of school consultation. The first part of their work focused on theoretical bases and reviewed ten different models of consultation.

Many articles have been written on prereferral intervention and collaborative consultation (Carter & Sugai, 1989; Fuchs, Fuchs, & Bahr, 1990; Fuchs, Fuchs, Bahr, Fernstrom, & Stecker, 1990; Graden et al., 1985; Phillips & McCullough, 1990; Tindal, Shinn, & Rodden-Nord, 1990). Two studies have even been completed on regular classroom teachers' prereferral interventions for students with behavior problems (Sevcik & Ysseldyke, 1986). Fuchs, Fuchs, Bahr, Fernstrom and Stecker (1990) defined prereferral intervention as:

> ...a teacher's modification of instruction or classroom management before referral to better accommodate a difficult-to-teach (DTT) pupil without disabilities.... Implicit in this definition is a preventive intent; that is, (a) eliminating inappropriate referral while increasing the legitimacy of those that are initiated and (b) reducing future student problems by strengthening the teacher's capacity to intervene effectively with a greater diversity of children. (p. 494)

Membership

Members of the prereferral team vary from one school system to another; however, they generally include the principal or the assistant principal, the referring person, consulting teacher, and other specialists such as a counselor, school psychologist, or special educator, as appropriate. Usually, the composition of any one team is based upon the chairperson's selection of relevant members, given the nature of the individual referral.

First Phase

The prereferral process begins with the classroom teacher requesting assistance for a particular student. The teacher describes the academic, social, or motoric behaviors that are of concern. The teacher also shares the information that has been gathered and explains his or her efforts to solve the problems. Different schools have different procedures for these requests. Some are informal; others require a more formal, written request for assistance.

Whether formal or informal, the next step is consultation with the referring teacher. One or more members of the prereferral team and the teacher meet for problem solving. An assessment is made of the discrepancy between the student's current level of performance and the teacher's expected or desired level of performance for the student. Relevant classroom variables are analyzed as they affect this discrepancy between actual and desired performance. Together the referring teacher and member(s) of the prereferral team, which should include a family member, design an intervention. Interventions are implemented and evaluated. If they are successful, then the prereferral process ends. If unsuccessful, the process moves to the next phase.

Second Phase

The next phase of the prereferral process is classroom observations. These observations are designed to collect information on important variables in the classroom setting. Observation also allows the observer to compare the student in question and other members of the class. Classroom observations are not the only type of observation that professionals consider. A social worker, visiting teacher, teacher, other professional, or parent might want to observe the student in the home or in a community setting. Such observations help corroborate functioning as well as point to possible causes.

In the classroom the observer describes curriculum, the tasks and demands of the academic program, and the student's response to these variables. The teacher's, parents', siblings', or other individuals' actions and language in relation to the student in question and the class or situation in general are also described. The observer would specify the way work and space are organized in the classroom, including seating arrangements and grouping patterns as well as interaction patterns. Attempts are made to describe the causes and consequences of behaviors.

Third Phase

Following the observations, the members of the prereferral team meet with the referring teacher to collaboratively design interventions based upon the observations. Interventions might include changes in instruction in the classroom, changes in the way work and space are organized, or the use of behavioral procedures in the home or school. Interventions could also include the use of other resources available in the school such as tutoring, sessions with the guidance counselor, or help from a remedial specialist. A family–school intervention might also be planned. If a parent does not attend this meeting, then a meeting is also scheduled with the student or family to discuss instructional or behavioral changes.

Family Involvement

This section covers training professionals in the prereferral process, the prereferral request, and guidelines for prereferral intervention. It concludes with an example of a prereferral intervention when parents are involved.

Training

All teachers should receive inservice training on the prereferral process. That training should communicate the belief that families are an important part of the prereferral process. Actual examples of cases from the school could be used to highlight the value of families being involved from an early juncture.

Further training might involve an introduction to some of the information from this book that relates to family systems concepts. The social worker or counselor could regularly provide inservice training for incoming teachers. Alternatively, teachers and other new staff could be required to read this book or another that covers the same information.

Prereferral Request

When the prereferral process is formal, the teacher writes a written request for prereferral intervention. An investigation of parental involvement to date should be required on any written prereferral request. Family involvement in the prereferral process should begin as early as possible.

The responses of the family members and their suggestions should be written on the prereferral request. If their suggestions are given any attention in the classroom, or if combined school–home interventions have been attempted, the results should be reported. Reporting results is necessary so that others do not waste time thinking about ideas that have already proven ineffective.

Other helpful information that could be included in the written prereferral request pertains to family process. Any information the teacher has about the family should be presented. This would include information regarding demographics, family life cycle, special family configurations, historical and environmental factors, as well as family interaction patterns, including subsystems, boundaries, hierarchy, and power.

Guidelines

Do not alarm parents unduly before or after making a prereferral request. At the same time, this is the perfect opportunity to apply pressure on the family if that might nip a problem in the bud. For example, families often are reluctant to apply necessary consequences at home. As a result, students arrive at school thinking they can get away with unacceptable behaviors. The teacher might have exhorted the parents to apply appropriate consequences for inappropriate behaviors on the part of their child, with no results. When parents realize that their child is one step from being referred for special educational services, many will be able to do what is necessary to achieve change in their otherwise unruly child.

In other families the parent does not follow through with the kind of help his or her child needs. The teacher may ask the parent to provide a quiet space as well as paper and pencil for the student to complete homework assignments. When the parents realize that their lack of attention to these suggestions has resulted in a prereferral request, that in itself may get the results desired. This type of problem may stem from what Aponte (1976b) referred to as "underorganization," another factor such as "pile up" (McCubbin & Patterson, 1982) mentioned in chapter 2, or a dysfunctional or disabled parent, as referred to in chapter 6. Naturally, other causes can also explain such situations.

The first guideline, therefore, might look like arm-twisting, and in a way it is. However, it is also a very real effort on the part of the teacher to receive assistance from the parents in understanding and solving a problem. The actual guideline is designed to avoid eliciting an overreaction and to apply the right amount of pressure at the right time to parents who have not responded in the past.

Another guideline is to *encourage mutual problem solving* among professionals and family members, including the student when appropriate. Once the prereferral request has been made, it is assumed that the family and teacher were not able to solve the situation together.

When other professionals are involved, parents or the student should be included in the problem-solving process. Imagine clarifying the nature of the problem without the family present only to find out much later, when the child is in special education classes, that the situation was really quite easily resolvable. A home–school intervention program that required freeing up an additional inexpensive resource might have taken care of the problem! Just such an intervention might be made possible by, for example, the school principal, who might be able to recommend and fund a tutor one night a week.

A third guideline is to *prepare family members to contribute* to the prereferral intervention process. They should be familiar with the process through school meetings and information in newsletters. Once the parents are approached about the specific situation with their child and they have assisted the teacher in clarifying the problem, planning ideas, and implementing the plan, the parents need further information on team process. A written description of the purpose, nature, and process of prereferral intervention should be provided to family members. Someone should also be available to answer questions as well as to provide any other assistance necessary.

Case Example
A first-grade student, Raheem, was rambunctious and disturbing other students in the classroom, making it difficult for others to concentrate and complete their seat work. The teacher tried several strategies and finally, feeling discouraged at the lack of progress, called the parents. She explained the situation and discussed the interventions she had attempted. The parents indicated that their older son, too, had been rambunctious in school. They shared Raheem's IQ score of 140 with the teacher. They believed that, like his brother, Raheem might be bored and frustrated with having little to do once the seat work was completed. The teacher had not seen Raheem's test scores because the parents had moved from the Middle East, and school reports did not follow them. She enlisted their support in a home–school intervention. She sent a note home each day reporting on Raheem's disturbing others who were working. If he had a day with no disturbances, the parents provided praise and spent time reading about his favorite subject, outer space. The teacher also provided Raheem with two options after he completed each assignment. Both options were enrichment activities that allowed him to fulfill his intellectual curiosity about outer space. This intervention was effective. Raheem settled down and became a model student.

This prereferral intervention occurred because the teacher knew the prereferral request required her to consult the parents to help solve the problem. Had that not been the requirement, the teacher would have simply made a prereferral request without having consulted the family.

This section has been devoted to the process of prereferral. That process focuses predominantly on the families of students in the regular classroom, those who are at risk. The next section focuses predominantly on the family conferences of students in special education classes.

FAMILY CONFERENCES

Family conferences or parent–professional conferences are an important part of school activities. This section focuses on conferences with families who have children with special needs. Families attend conferences for a variety of reasons. The purposes include, but are not limited to, pupil progress reporting, enlisting support, getting to know one another, and problem solving. This section provides information on planning, implementing, and evaluating conferences with a focus on family systems concepts.

Planning

As with so many other activities, good preparation pays off in comfort, relaxation, and a sense of being on top of things. Prepared professionals are more confident professionals. There are several aspects of planning related to family systems concepts that help professionals set the scene and improve the likelihood of a successful parent–professional conference.

Prepare the Setting in Advance

There are many features to consider in the physical setting that will enhance effective family conferences. There must be adequate and comfortable seating. No adult wants to sit in a chair designed for a 6-year-old for thirty to sixty minutes! Uncomfortable chairs might signal to family members that the school is not able to meet their needs. Family members may not consciously realize that doubts have surfaced about the professional's ability to provide for them, or they might realize it and not know from where that doubt comes.

Another consideration in planning the setting is to allow for privacy. No one wants his or her personal life aired in public. It is the professional's responsibility to ensure privacy, and it signals sensitivity to the families' needs. A closed door, as opposed to open space, signals privacy. In addition, a room appropriate for the number of people at the conference is conducive to a sense of confidentiality. It is uncomfortable for three people to meet in a room than can hold one hundred people. Think about what you would want for yourself or a loved one in terms of privacy.

Freedom from interruptions is another major consideration in preparing the setting. It is intrusive to have phone call interruptions or people walking in and out of the conference space. These are also automatic signals to the family that they are not all that is on the professional's mind. They may draw the conclusion that the professional does not have time for them and their child.

Issues of control and turf come up when meeting family members in the teacher's classroom. When a parent is invited into a classroom, it is the teacher's territory. That automatically puts the family members and teacher on unequal ground. A room designed for conferences is best used when conferences are sensitive. This will not always be an issue; however, it should be considered in any potentially fragile situation.

The last important consideration in the environment is the seating arrangement. The best arrangement is a circle at a round table or in comfortable chairs without a barrier between family members and professionals. The professional should not sit behind the teacher's or principal's desk during the conferences; it puts an automatic barrier between professional and family. It further signals the "Threat and Reward" style of interaction described in Appendix A. Parents might naturally remember times when they were young and on the other side of the principal's desk. The circle or round table is a more egalitarian approach.

If an outsider can tell where the professional(s) will sit when they walk into the conference room, it is probably not an egalitarian situation. It is amazing how subtle the signs of authority can be and how easily that can make family members feel inferior. Alternatively, it can set up a situation where a family member reacts hostilely and angrily due to unresolved authority problems. That person may not even realize why he or she is reacting that way. Even with thorough grounding in Satir's Seed Model (see Appendix A), the professional may not be able to ensure that family members will not react by feeling inferior or being overly authoritative. Attention to detail, however, can help prevent problems and allow the family members to see the professional as a collaborator rather than an adversary.

Know Your Purpose

It is essential that professionals know their purpose in calling for a conference. The purpose is the focal point throughout. It is easy to become sidetracked when interacting with parents, whether or not an issue is involved. A stated purpose, known to both parties (professional and parent), is like a call to the basic mission.

In knowing the purpose the professional is able to focus all his energy to achieve a goal, be it problem solving or getting to know one another. Beyond that clearly framed goal or purpose, other purposes should pervade all conferences. These include, but are not limited to, building rapport and trust as well as gleaning additional family information. The interaction process will allow rapport to grow. Finding out additional information on family considerations must be planned.

Make a Plan

Making a plan sounds logical and simple. In fact, some professionals believe that an evolving process alone will carry them through a conference; they do not bother to plan how they will achieve their purpose. The first plan made should concern the stated purpose, such as reporting pupil progress. The professional can easily plan for that purpose by thinking about how to open the conference, the order for sharing content, and how to close the conference. Each of these is important and should allow the professional to achieve the other two overarching purposes of building rapport and getting to know more about the parents as a family unit.

In selecting or designing an opening to a meeting, the professional will use whatever information is already known about the family. Plan a greeting that matches their style of interaction. If they are formal and proper or disengaged, the greeting should help them feel at ease in the interaction style with which they are most accustomed. People who are distant by nature will not likely warm up to an effusive greeting. This does not mean that the professional should not act naturally. Everyone has the capacity to vary responses as well as actions, depending upon the situation at hand.

Satir was a master at matching clients. She was, in fact, an "object" of research study on her style (Bandler & Grinder, 1979). In that research, the observers found that a critical aspect of Satir's style was that she matched the level of the client. For example, when a client would refer to something using a visual metaphor such as "It really looked good to me," Satir would respond with a visual response, such as "I get the picture." This is a very simplistic example of a complex process, known as Neurolinguistic Programming (NLP), that is quite powerful.

The professional does not need to remain at the same energy level and style as the family throughout the conference. In fact, in NLP training, trainees are taught to initially match the level and speech patterns of the individual and gradually alter their own and let the other follow suit. For example, if a parent asks a question in a very clipped and anxious tone, the professional would deliver the first sentence in the same clipped and anxious style and gradually flow into his or her natural style. This helps lead the person to another energy level with less anxiety attached to the content. As you can imagine, the parent will be able to derive more benefit from a more relaxed and receptive manner. Basically, in such an interaction, the professional subtly validates the parent's view of the situation while even more subtly implying that another frame of the situation can easily be cast.

Deciding the order or sequence for the sharing of pupil progress should be as strategic as planning the opening to the meeting. Most people would like to have any negatives deeply buried in the middle of many positives. It is important, in reporting pupil progress, to begin and end on a positive note. That gives strategy to the report. It is easy for families of students with special needs to expect and focus on weaknesses. The professional can often describe weaknesses in terms of challenges, thus shaping the parents' view of the situation. For example, the professional can refer to Joe's "hard-fought battle with mainstreaming for English class" versus Joe's "failure to adjust in the mainstream."

As mentioned in the last chapter, reframing is an important aspect of working with families. The professional should plan to present positive frames of reference and to have several "reframes" available to present if the need occurs.

Prepare the Family in Advance

Parents must be informed about the purpose of the conference in advance and be given the opportunity to provide input for the agenda for the meeting. Uncertainty about purpose may result in anxiety on the part of the family. For example, if school professionals call parents in to better get to know one another, the parents may assume the child has done something wrong or is having big problems. Prior to the conference parents may be on pins and needles about the meeting.

The professional should also prepare the parents by letting them know whether there are plans to involve anyone besides themselves and the teacher in the conference. They need to know why others will attend. For example, if a psychologist is at a conference a parent may assume that things are worse. Surprises are damaging to trust *and* the working relationship between the teacher and the parent.

Parents should have clear directions concerning where and when the meeting will be held. They should also know in advance what materials to bring or preparations they can make for the conference. Families who are prepared in advance will be better able to see the collaborative and egalitarian aspects to the upcoming conference.

Implementing

Some general guidelines for all family conferences stem from family systems concepts. Traditional recommendations for how to conduct conferences are the subject of many other texts and articles (Kroth, 1972, 1975, 1987; Kroth & Simpson, 1977; Simpson, 1982; Stewart, 1986), and those should be consulted for a refresher on the basics of conducting conferences with parents of students with special needs. The focus here is upon how to implement family systems concepts during family conferences.

Employ Family Systems Principles

Earlier in this chapter several principles stemming from family systems concepts were described. It is important to employ those principles, as appropriate, during family conferences. For example, there may be a perfect opportunity to assist the family in transforming an ineffective family rule into a guideline that works for them. The professional will definitely want to model the Five Freedoms by respecting, encouraging, and validating their opinions and feelings. Remaining objective and noting triangling will also be beneficial, as will detriangling when possible.

Maintain a Self

When meeting with family members, professionals need to stand for what they are as individuals. This is important in all family–professional interactions, but seems to surface more during conferences. People have a tendency to attribute things to other people with no basis. Meeting someone for the first time or interacting with someone you do not know very well, you may have automatic reactions to them that do not fit the reality of that person. Think of a time when you first met someone and automatically disliked her or him. Later, you may have realized that person had reminded you of someone who had treated you poorly in the past and you may have changed your view correspondingly.

Satir used to say to people (usually parents), who appeared to have confused her with someone else, "I think you've put a hat on me." Recognizing this phenomenon, accepting it as human, and being yourself is probably the best approach professionals can assume. It may take a long time for family members to realize that the professional is not the kind of person they thought he or she was. If the professional stands his or her ground and continues being natural, usually the family will come to recognize the professional for who he or she is. In schools it is not unusual for family members to confuse professionals with other professionals with whom they have dealt. If the professional is fortunate, those interactions were positive. If they were not, building trust may be an arduous process.

Billy Joel wrote a song about this process of being who you are regardless of what others see in you that truly does not fit reality. The title of his song is "An Innocent Man." Although he was talking about his relationship with a new woman in his life, it shows a clear understanding of the task anyone has with new relationships. He firmly establishes his understanding of the prior hurt as well as his patience in helping the other overcome that hurt to risk again.

That level of understanding and commitment may be needed in order to reach some family members. It may be a long time before trust is established and the professional may feel as though he or she is taking an undeserved beating at times. That may be the perfect time to say "I think you've put a hat on me" to the family member. Be warned, though, that such words might spur greater agitation. Some people do not like to be caught being wrong.

Another way to communicate the same message is: "I wonder if Todd's former principal did things that way. Here at Crestwood High, the students and teachers mutually write conduct rules at the beginning of the year. My role has been to help enforce rules developed by the students." Clearly, this principal ascribes to the Seed Model view of the world (see Appendix A).

Catalog Family Process

Thorough familiarity with family theory and process is helpful when cataloging family process. Each conference presents the professional with an opportunity to follow up on further developing his or her understanding of family process.

Just as there is an academic file on each student, a family file on family process is most helpful. Sections in such a file would include information on the family life cycle, family interaction patterns, historical factors, environmental factors, family configuration, and the nature of students' special needs. The last part of this book presents a major case study focusing on the family. All of the information presented relates to these areas to be included in the family file. When the professional first meets with family members, he or she begins compiling the file on family process. As more is learned about the family during conferences, additional information can be cataloged.

The objective in cataloging family process is to identify patterns that occur with some regularity. Of particular interest are any dysfunctional patterns that emerge—a family rule that has hampered growth and development over the generations or the negative results of a triangle between grandmother and parents that has been transmitted down through generations.

This cataloging of current life circumstances and dysfunctional patterns is not designed to emphasize or dwell on the negative. The purpose is to help family members change patterns that stunt the growth of the family unit as well as the student with special needs. Of course, educational professionals cannot replace the services of family systems therapists. They catalog family process to better understand a family and, therefore, plan more effective future interventions. Any suggestions made should not be beyond the family's capability to implement. Nor should the professional elicit negative reactions with what the family members perceive as impossible demands and unrealistic expectations. An understanding of family process and circumstance will help the professional avoid those situations.

The important consideration in cataloging observations is recognizing that the professional is always attempting to confirm or disprove any hypotheses. Their place in the family life cycle is factual. The type of family configuration, cultural factors, and socioeconomic status are also facts. The cataloging of these factors is not always done by school professionals, although these facts are important considerations in any recommendations made to the family.

What is not simply fact are observations about interaction patterns and historical factors, such as triangulation or level of differentiation, as well as dysfunctional patterns related to the student with special needs. Thus, it is important to maintain any observations as hypotheses until several professionals confirm the opinions.

Once patterns or facts about the family have been cataloged, it is important to use that information during the conference. For example, if the professional has confirmed a hypothesis that the oldest sibling is a *parentified* child, it is possible to bring up that observation with the family.

Use Mutual Processes, when Appropriate

If there is one underlying theme in Satir's Seed Model, it is working with people as equals. Mutual processes means that the family members and professionals jointly engage in any planning, problem solving, and pupil progress reporting. The professional should be as interested in hearing about the student's progress on the home front as in sharing the progress in school. In other words, reporting pupil progress is a two-way street. When parents realize that professionals are as interested in hearing about their accomplishments and challenges as in telling about progress in school, they will begin to make the shift from bystander to collaborator.

Of course, some parents are not interested in mutual processes. As stated in chapter 9, the needs of the family should be determined on a family-by-family basis. Some family members will not want to share in the problem-solving process. Knowledge of the family life, such as environmental factors and family life-cycle stage may help explain parents' desires and needs. The parents may be overwhelmed or underorganized rather than uninvolved.

This section has provided several guidelines relating to a family systems perspective that can be used during conferences. More could certainly be ferreted out from the literature on family systems, but the four presented here are a worthwhile beginning for school professionals.

Evaluating

The professional should evaluate his or her use of family systems concepts in the process of conducting conferences. Other types of evaluation will be used to complete the cycle of family conferences. Readers should consider the suggestions provided in this section on family conferencing and evaluate their use of them. This will point them in the direction of using more of what works, as well as determining ways to make the ideas that have rough edges more workable.

Evaluate Your Planning

The purpose of evaluating planning efforts is to determine what to change or replicate in the future. Were the family systems concepts brought to bear in such a way that the planning paid off? To answer this question, professionals need to look back on the setting, primary and secondary purposes, planning process and product, as well as on how the family was prepared for the conference. Answering the questions in Table 10.4 can help professionals evaluate their planning efforts.

Question 7 concerns how the family members viewed the conference. Professionals should design a checklist for family members to complete after each conference. It would provide feedback and remove part of the burden of evaluation from the professional's shoulders.

Evaluate Your Implementation

Just as planning was evaluated, so too will implementation be assessed. The professional should ask himself or herself about each of the guidelines presented. For example, "Did I employ family systems principles? If not, why?" Once the professional understands why, he or she can determine a strategy so that the next occasion will not yield the same results. Perhaps there simply was no opportunity to transform a guideline; however, the professional could always model the Five Freedoms. Failure to recognize triangling might help the professional decide to tape record a future conference for later analysis for triangling.

Another good question is whether or not the professional was able to "maintain a self." If not, what factors contributed to the downfall? Is there any behavior pattern, across families, that might suggest when the professional gets pulled into their web and does not maintain a sense of self? Does one type of family resonate with any struggle in the professional's own life and, therefore, contribute to less effective strategies?

Other questions to ask include: "Was I able to find out new information about family process or facts related to family life cycle, environmental concerns, or family configura-

Table 10.4
EVALUATING THE PLANNING

Focus on the following questions. In answering them, consider how you might better plan for family conferences in the future. Any answers with which you are not satisfied should be pursued.

1. Did the setting facilitate open, honest, and confidential communication?
2. Was the seating arrangement comfortable?
3. Did your focal point remain the central theme of the conference?
4. Was your opening effective?
5. Did you close on a mutually supportive note?
6. Did the sequence of the conference facilitate open, helpful communication?
7. Was the family prepared so that they were comfortable participating in the conference? How do you know?
8. Did the family indicate anything else you could consider in the future?

tion? If so, did any of the information help me confirm or deny established hypotheses? How will I use that information in the future? If I met a dead end on cataloging family process, what contributed to the lack of information? How might I get more information in the future? Am I possibly colluding in any way by helping the family deny a reality that is difficult to confront?

"Was I able to use mutual processes that fit the situation? If so, how might I use those strategies again in the future? If not, what could I change in the future to enhance mutual processes? What personal family factors might make it difficult for me to facilitate mutual processes with family conferences?"

This series of questions can help professionals modify their ways of conducting future conferences with families who have students with special needs. Evaluation can be a learning process that will afford insights as well as direction. Furthermore, it will make conducting conferences easier in the future with new and different families.

This section on conferences with families of students with special needs has focused on family systems concepts. It has not presented the full spectrum of information on planning, implementing, and evaluating family conferences. Again, more information is available in texts written with a focus on other aspects of family conferencing with students having special needs (Kroth, 1975; Kroth & Simpson, 1977; Simpson, 1982; Stewart, 1986).

With the information presented in this chapter, it is much easier to focus on the next chapter, with its emphasis on specific tasks in which professionals engage families. It is more realistic to focus on an element of a conference or prereferral interaction when the family systems perspective has been highlighted.

SCHOOL PROFESSIONALS AS FAMILY LIAISONS 11

The school professional sometimes finds that families of at-risk and special needs students would benefit from more assistance than the school has to offer. Many professionals, particularly special education administrators, are concerned about recommending outside resources because the schools might be required to pay for those services. However, schools cannot, and should not, be all things to all people. There are many resources, both free and fee-based, from which families of at-risk and special needs students would profit. Professionals should become familiar with potential resources and serve as family liaisons, linking family members with appropriate resources that meet their needs.

The first section in this chapter, "Sharing Information," is rooted in family systems tenets. It furnishes the basis for the remainder of the chapter. This section provides views that are important to networking, focusing on areas in which school professionals will serve as family liaisons.

Assistance in networking can allow families to take better advantage of their family and social network, as well as a myriad of free or low-cost social services. Networking can also increase the likelihood that families will have more resources with which to assist their child. As mentioned in chapter 2, the presence of a support network is one of the most important factors in family adjustment to life-cycle changes and stresses. The section also covers important aspects of entering support groups, including sibling groups, as well as referral to counseling, focusing on locating as well as linking family members with these groups and services.

Helping family members to not be dependent upon outside resources is certainly good, but being independent does not mean being able to meet all needs alone or within one's own family. The focus here is on sharing information that allows family members to learn more about family life and healthy communication and to know how to obtain beneficial resources.

The underlying belief here was reflected by Gibran (1923) in the section *The Prophet* titled "Teaching."

No man can reveal to you aught but that which already lies half asleep in the dawning of your knowledge....

If he is indeed wise he does not bid you enter the house of his wisdom, but rather leads you to the threshold of your own mind....

For the vision of one man lends not its wings to another man.... (pp. 56–57)

SHARING INFORMATION

Although sharing resources with most families of at-risk and special needs students will present no difficulty, some will resist input from school professionals. Some family members will consider it to be bordering on an invasion of privacy or to indicate perceived failure or inadequacy of the parent. Yet another parent may conjure up a racial, religious, or gender issue. Professionals will seldom know ahead of time when family members may have "put a hat on" them or when family dysfunction will manifest itself in some form that makes it difficult to share information that links them with beneficial resources.

There are many valuable concepts in the family systems approaches that can help professionals more effectively share information with parents of at-risk and special needs students. Information in the next chapter on classroom extension of family intervention will also be helpful when serving as family liaison.

The conceptualization of families as resourceful is an essential view with which to engage family members. When professionals view the family as resourceful, they recognize that the need for additional resources is secondary and temporary. It is also important to recognize that at certain times in the family's life cycle the family may face an overload when meeting demands. An apt analogy was presented by Imber-Black (1986): "The family has not suddenly become bankrupt in terms of its own resources, although its assets may be temporarily frozen or creating no interest" (p. 149).

A resource model of family functioning assumes that families interact with history, culture, ethnicity, social class, politics, interpersonal relationships, individual quirks, and more in a process of continually creating their norms. School professionals can frame their view of the family with this in mind and recognize the impact of context. Seeing context as significant, the professional is better able to make sense of family observations instead of seeing the family as abnormal. This view focuses on the assets of the family and not its deficits.

For example, in one family the suggestion that a son join a little league team may be considered a positive intervention that fits the boy's developmental level and offers him a social outlet. In another family, the same suggestion may be seen as squelching the boy's natural creativity by requiring him to take part in an organized sport rather than allowing him to explore his own physical and social needs. The professional who is aware of the differences between the families might recommend to the second family that they take time to play as a family and explore each individual's creativity through interaction.

The professional's understanding of the concepts of family resources and deficits will affect plans for, as well as interactions with, family members. The family may not be able to interpret the professional's attitude; however, when they deal with professionals who view them as resourceful, trust usually develops. Assuming that each family possesses a wealth of assets that can be tapped is clearly a focus on families as resources. This does not mean that professionals ignore the family's deficits. Both resources and deficits can be acknowledged at the same time. The goal is to view the family's wholeness.

It is essential that professionals deal with and think about their frames of reference, that is, their view of people in general as well as specific individuals. If their expectation for families having a child with special needs is negative they may miss the family resources as well as the possibilities they present for wholeness.

For decades we have focused upon seeing deficits among those with special needs and failed to focus upon the possibilities and resources, so you are not alone if you enter this struggle. Our society has had a jaundiced view toward those with disabilities. We have a history of warehousing our less fortunate and keeping them out of view. Times have changed, yet most school professionals did not grow up with the opportunities to interact with students with special needs that our children now have. Thus, we all have some catching up to do when constructing a frame of reference for students with special needs and their families.

NETWORKING

Not all at-risk families or those who have children with special needs are dysfunctional. But while most of these families will perform functionally, they would benefit from having resources available at times of increased stress. The chapters in this book that focus on family dysfunction are intended to help professionals work with those families that have unusual difficulties. This section focuses on helping any family, functional or dysfunctional, with a child who is at risk or has special needs.

This section is artificially divided into three aspects of networking: the family network, the family social network, and external resources.

Family Networking

The previous chapter discussed "cataloging family process." Doing so allows for a greater use of family resources. It is important that professionals try to note both resources and problems when cataloging a family process. This section on family networking initially defines family resources and then provides information about four family resource areas that can be tapped during interactions with the family members. Both can be cataloged by school personnel for later use.

Definition of Family Resources

Several types of family resources have been identified in the literature (Attneave & Verhulst, 1986; Hansen & Imber-Coopersmith, 1984; Hansen & Falicov, 1983; Karpel, 1986a). Karpel (1986b) defined family resources as "those individual and systemic characteristics among family members that promote coping and survival, limit destructive patterns, and enrich daily life" (p. 176). He was not referring to finances or other material trappings, nor was he including social service resources within the community.

Karpel's (1986b) first element of family resource related to coping and survival techniques. As described in chapter 2, families face a variety of predictable as well as unexpected stressors throughout the family life cycle. Families, particularly those with children having special needs, will vary widely in their resources for promoting coping and survival. Some of these families will cope well with the special needs; others will struggle. It is those who struggle with daily coping that may benefit from family networking.

Another element of family resource identified by Karpel (1986a) is the ability of the family to limit possible destructive patterns. This ability to limit destruction relates to both external stressors as well as internal patterns such as attacking, demeaning, neglecting, or diminishing another. Limiting destructive patterns helps prevent the "pile-up" mentioned in chapter 2 (McCubbin & Patterson, 1982). Some families seem to have *resistance*, which Karpel (1986a) paralleled with immunological resistance to destructive patterns. Examples of such resistance would be of a wife resisting the husband's invitation for a co-alcoholic marriage, parents exercising a clear hierarchy over an acting-out teenager, and a child resisting being triangled into the parents' conflicts.

A third element of family resource relates to enriching daily life (Karpel, 1986a). This element goes beyond dealing with problems and focuses on life's more rewarding aspects. It has to do with quality of life. It has to do with caring and sharing, satisfaction and pleasure.

Karpel (1986a) expanded upon this three-element definition and described personal resources as well as relational resources in families. Examples of personal resources include self-respect, protectiveness, hope, tolerance, and affection. Relational resources include respect, reciprocity, reliability, repair, flexibility, family pride, and loops of interaction.

The personal and relational resources within families are affected by three characteristics: capacity, rules, and active efforts. For example, take the relational resource of *reciprocity*, or give and take, in a family. Reciprocity is how the family balances and holds fair play. Professionals can look to each family member's *capacity* for reciprocity. Then family *rules* regarding reciprocity could be considered. Finally *active efforts* on the parts of family members to initiate and collaborate on reciprocity can be considered. School social workers, psychologists, and counselors would be the professionals most likely to take a closer look at these three factors. Any observations can be added to the catalog of family process.

Areas of Family Resource

Imber-Black (1986) described four family resource areas that focus professionals on the family's strengths as opposed to their deficits. The first area has to do with *religious, cultural,* and *racial identity*. A previous chapter mentioned the work of McGoldrick et al. (1982) on ethnicity and family therapy, which again could be quite useful.

Avoiding stereotypic thinking about people from other backgrounds is certainly beneficial to healthy professional–home interactions. Professionals should also be aware of their own values and any prejudices they may have. Looking for the strengths in the ethnic background of others is quite helpful, and being aware of differences is critical to avoid misinterpreting behavior. For example, Mexican-American families are cooperative rather than competitive. A school professional who tries to use a competitive strategy to motivate a Mexican-American child may get lackluster results and misunderstand them. This child could easily be seen as unmotivated, whereas the truth might be that the child would be easily motivated by a cooperative learning task.

School professionals should observe family interactions with an eye toward recognizing and cataloging any particular identity of the family. Families also identify with religious groups, and these allegiances can be noted as a family resource. Some church groups will have considerable resources that might be tapped in helping families.

The second area (Imber-Black, 1986) relates to the family's *inner language*, which identifies them as a family both to themselves and to others. The professional should look for myths, metaphors, jokes, humor, and words or phrases with special meaning to the family members, note any examples, and use them at appropriate times. For example, a family may refer to themselves as having "dogged determination." When things get rough on the family, the professional could repeat their view of themselves as hanging on with their "dogged determination."

A third area of resource (Imber-Black, 1986) relates to *individual and family commitments, loyalties, or a sense of connections*. It is important to be aware of and publicly recognize commitments and loyalties. An example would be a family that will go to all ends to be sure that their wheelchair-bound child does not miss out on family outings. It is important to point out and validate their convictions about including everyone in the family fun.

The fourth area of family resource (Imber-Black, 1986) relates to the *capacity of the family to interact with the outside world* in such a way that their own integrity as a family is preserved and enhanced. The outside world is everything beyond the family. Rules will exist for dealing with the external world, beyond family, in the same way that rules develop for family relationships. It is important to build upon family resources in dealing positively with those outside the family. School professionals are members of that outside world, and it is valuable to know how the family has interacted in the past with school professionals. Unfortunately, prior experiences with the schools may have been negative. The current school professionals have the responsibility of engaging the family members, which may mean overcoming negative expectations on both sides. Parents may have been seen as recalcitrant by former school professionals. If the professional views the family as having been protective as opposed to antagonistic, he or she will be better able to focus on the family's positive resources and their functional survival skills for making it through an antagonistic situation.

Strategies

All four areas of family resource can be tapped by school professionals. Again, when collaborating with any family it is good to look for resources versus deficits. All those who have contact with the family of a student with special needs can contribute to the cataloging process. It is valuable to have a file on each student to which information on family resources can be added. The file can be divided into the resource areas described here or any other system that meets the needs of the school system. Team meetings can include an agenda item on family resources. There is no reason to leave family members out of the process of recognizing their resources. When family members attend meetings, professionals can observe their use of inner language as well as how they interact with the outside world.

It is important to not only note but also reinforce family resources. When school professionals are in meetings with parents or in one-to-one interactions, they should take every opportunity to validate family resources. An example might be a teacher telling a mother, "I can see your son Timmy takes after the rest of your family when it comes to being gentle. I wish you had seen him with the new student from Iran."

It is also important to validate and encourage healthy family functioning. The healthy functioning of the spousal system is a particular function to be encouraged by school professionals. Too many parents of students with special needs do not invest in the spousal system. When spouses take a vacation together and tell the schools that they will be out of town, the response from the school professionals should be to verbally reinforce their taking care of their marriage and encourage them not to worry about the child at school. "We can handle whatever might come up here."

The sibling subsystem should also be validated as a source of support and a valuable family resource. Too often people feel that the siblings are in a rivalry. It is important to help frame existing or potential sibling relationships positively. Kahn (1986) has an excellent chapter about the sibling system with bonds of intensity, loyalty, and endurance. Knowing whether the family is either disengaged or enmeshed can also be helpful when making comments that might encourage balance and sibling support. When the family is disengaged, the school professional can say something that aligns siblings with one another. For example, "I have noticed that your brother and you act quite differently, but it seems as though the two of you have had a very similar experience in your family."

Another sibling trap is scapegoating or blaming, as described by Satir (1988). If one child in the family seems to be taking the blame more than the others, the school professional can help to point that out. For example, the professional might say, "It looks like Sandy is the 'fall guy' in this family. I wonder if it is really possible that Jane is 'Patty Perfect.' "

It is also important that school professionals not unwittingly reinforce the family *parentifying* an older child. Comments about what a "great little mother" one child makes are inappropriate. Taking care of others often becomes a role of the oldest daughter in families with an excess of stress.

Another resource of potential strength lies in the extended family. Family members may overlook the real possibilities that the extended family has to offer. The school professional can ask whether a grandparent, aunt, uncle, or other relative might be able to help out with different functions. For example, a simple suggestion that an unmarried aunt or uncle babysit once a week so that the spouses could have time together might never have occurred to the family.

The school professional can be creative and energizing when focusing on family as resource. As has been shown, many possibilities exist. It is up to the creative professional to make these possibilities real and focus the schools upon them.

Social Systems Networking

Professionals interested in at-risk families and those having children with special needs have written about social network interventions and the value of social support (Berger, 1984a; Coopersmith, 1983; Dunst, Trivette, & Cross, 1986; Friedrich & Friedrich, 1981; Intagliata & Doyle, 1984; Kazak, 1987; Kazak & Marvin, 1984; Rueveni, 1979). Just as the resources of the immediate and extended family are invaluable, so too are the resources of the family's social network.

Families who face a high level of stress will look to their social network for resources that might enable them to reduce and cope better with that stress. Unfortunately, the social network system may unwittingly add to the stress by providing contradictory and competing suggestions. Parents often turn to family members and friends for advice on how to handle problems. Although they have good intentions and they care, these family members and friends may not realize the parent is searching for advice among many people. One person will suggest a favorite intervention; another might offer diametrically opposing ideas. This can be very confusing for the parent. Thus social network interventions can be invaluable in getting all interested parties to understand and support realistic strategies.

It is also helpful for those within the social network to learn strategies that empower the family in need of help, as opposed to taking away the family member's power and sense of adequacy. In addition, members of the social network system will be able to suggest viable alternatives, as well as become part of the solution by being supportive as well as assisting with interventions.

This section on social systems networking includes introductory information on systems and the influence of external environments on family functioning. Next, social support systems are explained. Finally, findings and strategies, in particular regarding social systems networking with families having a child with special needs, are presented.

Introduction

Systems theorists propose that social networks, with their attendant support, directly and indirectly influence attitudes, expectations, behavior, and knowledge of both family members and other members of the network. Bronfenbrenner (1979) described ecological units or social networks topologically. He saw them as a nesting of concentric structures, one embedded within the other. The child and family are the center. Broader ecological systems move out in concentric circles, including relatives, friends, neighbors, and other acquaintances. Beyond that are larger social units (discussed in the next section on external networking) that include the neighborhood, churches, social organizations, workplace, and school. Social systems theorists contend that these ecological units do not function in isolation but interact within and between levels. Thus, changes in one unit or subsystem will reverberate and impact upon other units or subsystems.

Definition of Social Support Systems

Social support networks are links among individuals and groups. These links relate to size, satisfaction, density, connectedness, and frequency of contacts. As Dunst et al. (1986) indicated:

> Social support is a multidimensional construct that includes physical and instrumental assistance, attitude transmission, resource and information sharing, and emotional and psychological support. There is general consensus among social systems theorists that social support networks function to nurture and sustain linkages among persons that are supportive on both a day-to-day basis and in times of need and crises. (p. 403)

Turner (1981) described social support as an aspect of psychological well-being. Although he did not study at-risk families or those of children with special needs, he did study four diverse populations, one of which was adults with hearing losses. He also traced research about social support and concluded that social support is most important in stressful circumstances. In his study, Turner adopted Cobb's (1976) view of social support that consists of information. Turner related social support as:

> ...information belonging to one or more of three classes: (1) information leading the subject to believe that he or she is cared for and loved; (2) information leading the subject to believe that he or she is esteemed and valued; and (3) information leading the subject to believe that he or she belongs to a network of communication and mutual obligation in which others can be counted on should the need arise. (pp. 358-359)

Findings and Strategies

A variety of findings are presented in the literature on social network systems and at-risk families or those having children with special needs. They indicate the value of considering social systems as valuable assets in reducing stress on family members.

Dunst et al. (1986) examined effects of social support on parents of children with mental retardation and physical impairment as well as developmentally at-risk children. They were concerned with the impact of social support on "personal well-being, parental attitudes toward their child, family integrity, parental perceptions of child functioning, parent–child play opportunities and child behavior and development" (p. 403). Their findings supported the positive impact of social support systems on families with children with disabilities.

Kazak and Marvin (1984) studied stress and characteristics of social support networks of families with and without a child with a disability. They found that mothers are particularly subject to personal stress. Unlike previous research findings, they did not find a significant difference in the marital dyads' stress levels. Interestingly, they suggested that professionals view the differences between families (and their networks) as appropriate accommodations to raising a child with a disability. Specifically, they found both the overinvolvement of the mother and child and the peripheral role of the father in parenting to be appropriate and to be respected by professionals, "unless there is ample evidence that the marital relationship is impaired" (p. 75).

Kazak (1987) examined mothers and fathers of children with disabilities or chronic illnesses and compared them with matched parents of nondisabled children. She looked to personal stress, marital satisfaction, and social network size and density. She found that only the mothers of the children with disabilities experienced higher levels of stress. She again found no differences in marital satisfaction. Finally, Kazak found that mothers of children with disabilities had higher-density social networks than comparison mothers.

Intagliata and Doyle (1984) examined social support for parents of children with developmental disabilities by training them in interpersonal problem-solving skills. From this pilot study they concluded that enhanced problem-solving skills of these parents was relevant and could be a helpful service intervention.

Friedrich and Friedrich (1981) compared parents of children with a disability with a control group of parents of nondisabled children. One of many measures included social support. They concluded that "an appropriate avenue of intervention might increase the availability of social support for these parents to help them cope with this additional stress" (p. 553).

Minuchin and Fishman (1981) described the technique of enactment. Enactments focus on acting out the problem as opposed to simply talking about the problem in the family.

For example, if a student is disobedient to the parents during a social systems networking session, the teacher might ask the parents what they plan to do. This allows the teacher to see the problem as it naturally evolves. It may also present an opportunity for the teacher to intervene while serving as a model for the whole social systems network.

Berger (1984a) recommended the use of enactments in network interventions. He suggested creating a context in which those in attendance act differently toward one another. This is particularly helpful when attempting to look at the family and social network as valuable resources.

> Network interventions, then, are especially powerful contexts for the use of enactments that alter network members' definition of the handicapping condition or of what needs to be done about that condition. (p. 134)

As can be seen, social support has a positive impact upon families with children with special needs as well as those at risk. It is critical that school professionals consider this when relating to families. Psychologists, social workers, and counselors in the schools should be particularly aware of the impact of social systems.

External Resource Networking

External resource networking has to do with helping families form supportive links with resources outside their family or social network. This might include using social service agencies, support groups, counseling services, and a myriad of other possibilities. This section initially suggests means of finding available resources in a local area as well as at state or national levels. It then suggests means of gaining access to support groups and referring families to support groups or counseling.

Finding Resources

There are a host of potentially valuable resources available in every community and state, as well at the national level, that most professionals know about only generally. Every school should have a resource file that all professionals can consult in their efforts to provide resource information to families. As professionals learn about additional resources, they can add to the file. School professionals might even find beneficial resources for themselves or their families. Appendix C includes a variety of suggestions.

Each file should also contain evaluation information, that is, feedback from parents who have used the resources. Parents should be asked to respond to a brief questionnaire covering their impressions and reactions to different resources. There should also be a space for general comments from parents who have used the resource. Should any school professionals have used a resource or know someone who did, they can also add their comments to the evaluation. Neither parents nor professionals should be required to sign the questionnaire; they should not quote or identify by name anyone receiving confidential services. For obvious reasons some people would not like to be identified as having attended, for example, an alcoholics' support group or a group for parents who have abused their children.

It is important to check and purge files regularly, at least once a year. Telephone numbers and contact people change regularly, as do opportunities for group as well as individual support. It is frustrating for parents to hear of a resource that is no longer available.

To generate a file, a group of professionals can get together and divide the workload. A search of resources in the community begins with contacting the local school board for brochures or information on different agencies and services available to families. Then the community mental health center should be contacted for information on their services as well as other resources with which they are familiar. The community parks and recreation association can also be contacted. Local churches are another important source of services. The local phone book is a great help in making recent telephone numbers available.

Beyond the local community, the professionals can contact state agencies such as the Department of Education for information on state-level services and opportunities for networking with families of at-risk and special needs children. The division responsible for special education in the state should definitely be contacted, along with the Department of Mental Health. The division on volunteerism within the state government may also be of service.

National agencies should also be investigated. There are beneficial contacts for a variety of types of disabilities. Many organizations can be found through a national directory. Examples include the Association for Retarded Citizens (ARC), Association for Learning Disabilities (ACLD), and Bereaved Parents. Appendix C contains information on a variety of resources.

Gaining Access to Support Groups and Referrals for Counseling

Support groups and counseling for parents as well as siblings of at-risk and special needs children are invaluable in helping to reduce stress. Whether the school system or a community resource provides the resource, the school professional must make the family member aware of the opportunity. Few parents know on their own about the variety of support groups or counseling services that are available in the community.

The school resource file will allow the professional to select relevant support groups for the family member(s) who need support. When making a referral, it is important to recognize the family member's need for privacy. Some family members will be embarrassed to be considered in need of a support group or counseling, whereas others will not know anything about these opportunities. Do not assume that anyone will understand anything about these possibilities. It is better to repeat information they already have than leave them wondering about your referral.

Who makes the referral is quite important. Someone familiar with the family member who has established a positive rapport with that person is the best professional to make a referral for a support group or counseling. If the familiar professional is not comfortable making a referral, the next most familiar individual can assume that task.

The context or place for making the referral is also important. The family member should come to the school for a meeting or the referral should be made during an already scheduled meeting. A phone call is not an appropriate way to convey a referral for a support group or counseling. When making a referral, time should be invested in building rapport before actually suggesting counseling or a support group. The situation that has led to the recommendation should be retraced so that the parent or sibling understands the reason for the referral.

Then the school professional can talk about an opportunity of which he or she is aware and describe its value. The professional should indicate that the school personnel recommend that such services be considered by the family member(s). The purpose for the recommendation should be very clear, and follow-up information should be provided. If there is a brochure or flyer available with phone numbers, contact persons, and description of services, it should be provided. Cost of services and possibility of insurance coverage should also be discussed.

In some rare cases the school professional might prefer to allow the family member(s) to ask for information about contacting the resource. This is an effective way to handle people who try to make others responsible for them. Waiting for the family member to request further information allows him or her to be more in charge of the personal process and does not leave the whole onus of responsibility on the professional. In such cases the professional might even simply provide contact names and tell the family member where to find phone numbers.

Some family members will appreciate hearing about how other families have benefited from the recommended resource. Some people will be willing to be contacted by phone to discuss their own experiences with a resource such as a support group or counseling. At other times the professional can relate what other family members have told without providing names of those involved.

Family members should always be given time to ask questions regarding the referral. The professional should recommend that they consider the possibility and call later if they have further questions before making contact with the support group leader or counselor.

Again, there is important information on metaphor and reframing in the next chapter that can be used when making recommendations for counseling or support groups. Reframing is helpful when families resist a recommendation. It is invaluable to provide constructive frames when recommending support services.

SUMMARY

This chapter has presented information concerning the school professional as family liaison. Family systems views on the sharing of information with family members were initially described. That set the stage for networking as it relates to the family network, the social systems network, and networking with a variety of resources external to family and friends. The school professional is crucial in helping family members of at-risk children and those with special needs receive the support they need.

CLASSROOM AND GROUP 12
EXTENSION OF FAMILY
SYSTEMS CONCEPTS

The purpose of this chapter is to extend certain family systems concepts into the classroom, as well as into educational, support, and counseling groups held in schools for family members. Family systems concepts and methods can be used to pursue goals in both the cognitive (academic) and affective (social) domains. The chapter begins with information on the extension of family systems perspectives into the academic worlds of curriculum and then instruction. That discussion is followed by information on techniques, including metaphor and reframing, as they relate to family systems concepts. It concludes with a section on socialization, relating to another family systems method, "temperature reading" (Satir, 1983a).

ACADEMIC CURRICULUM

This section initially focuses on Satir's (1972, 1988) five "stances," which are characterizations of human behavior. Four of the five are dysfunctional; the last is a functional, congruent stance. This information could be considered a content area in its own right, and family members might benefit from the information. Further, understanding stances can help school professionals network or make referrals to groups, as well as counsel families. In other words, school professionals should be familiar with the stances and how the knowledge helps them when interacting with at-risk and special needs students and their families. We then move to a different area—concerns of parents about new and controversial curricula that are being considered or have been implemented in the schools.

Communication Stances as Curriculum Area

Understanding the communication stances (Satir, 1972, 1988) can benefit school professionals first individually by allowing them to refine their personal communication style and present a single-level, congruent message. Professionals can then use their knowledge about the stances in schools, first to identify dysfunctional communication and then to intervene and help others recognize incongruent communication and use congruent communication. Satir (1983b) provided many examples of ways trained professionals can help others recognize and change their communication stances so that they are congruent most of the time.

This section first provides a brief background for communication stances and then describes each of the five stances. Next, examples of using the communication stances as a curricular area for students are provided. The next topic covered is preparing to implement that curriculum with applications that include suggestions for exploring personal communication stances and ways to respond to them.

Background Information

In her books *Peoplemaking* (1972) and *The New Peoplemaking* (1988), Satir depicted and described the four dysfunctional communication stances she had found in families across the world: placating, blaming, superreasonable, and irrelevant. Satir and Baldwin (1983) described these stances as "different ways to hide the reality of one's feelings from oneself and from others" (p. 199). Satir also represented the functional stance of being congruent, a healthy way of expressing oneself. Satir's (1983b) text on *Conjoint Family Therapy* provides excellent suggestions for activities a trained social worker, counselor, or psychologist can use to further the learning of family members about their communication patterns.

All four dysfunctional stances begin during infancy in the primary triad of mother-father-child. All four also have potential for renovation through what Satir referred to as a process of transformation and atrophy (Satir & Baldwin, 1983). All stances are systemic in nature, none being able to persist without the support of another. Thus, a family might present a teaming up of two "supportive" or reciprocal stances, for example, the placator and the blamer.

The Stances

This section describes each of Satir's (1988) five stances from the perspective of how these stances look to others, along with their internal states and the underlying reasons for assuming the stances. How the stances appear when they have been renovated or transformed, with strengths growing out of former weaknesses, is also described. Finally Satir (1988) delineated three aspects of communication—self, other, and context that include purpose, time, and place of communication—that would be violated or discounted in dysfunctional communication. For each stance, we detail which of the three aspects are discounted.

Placating. One who assumes a placating stance is trying to conceal personal vulnerability by striving to please others. The placator will go along with something out of need for emotional survival, rather than personal commitment and interest. A placator rejects or discounts self when doing what others expect, thereby not being rejected by others. The placator seems like a "nice" person who avoids conflict and turning others down. Although protective of others, this person is really quite dependent and fragile.

Through a transformative process and letting go of past dysfunction, the placator makes choices that affirm self as opposed to seeing self as worthless unless approved of by others. The placator who has gained a sense of personal worth has the capacity for being tender and compassionate. Transformed, the placator *genuinely* cares for others.

Blamer. The individual who takes a blaming stance is attempting to mask personal vulnerability by trying to control others as well as by indiscriminately disagreeing with them. This stance allows the blamer to feel a greater sense of personal importance in spite of the experience of loneliness and personal sense of failure. This person will complain, bullying others and finding fault with them. One who assumes a blaming stance discounts the other person or people.

Blaming can be transformed into being assertive and taking a stand for oneself. When standing up for oneself, the blamer learns to realistically assert self as opposed to having a knee-jerk reaction to others.

Superreasonable (The Computer). A person assuming the stance of superreasonable seeks to disguise vulnerability with a detached control that focuses on intellectual experience. This allows the person to skirt emotions and thereby anesthetize feelings. This person is cool, aloof, reasonable, and intellectual; his or her clear persuasiveness should not be confused with congruent communication. This type of communication discounts both self and other.

A person who is superreasonable can learn to creatively use his or her intelligence, as opposed to using intelligence to protect self. The professional will sense the connection with emotions in the transformed superreasonable and be aware of his or her wisdom.

Irrelevant (The Distractor). The individual who takes on the irrelevant stance is pretending that the stressor is nonexistent. He or she diverts the focus from the present, feeling-laden situation to something else. To others, that diversion may appear quite off-the-wall. Non sequiturs and scatterbrained comments are frequently observed. This type of communication discounts self, others, and context.

The transformation of irrelevance becomes the ability to be spontaneous and have fun. This person becomes a creative individual capable of congruent interactions, having no need to discount self, others, or context.

Congruent. According to Satir (1988), a congruent person provides leveling responses in which the outward expression, actions, and tone of voice fit the spoken word. Not feeling a need to hide or conceal personal feelings, this person has high self-esteem and loves and values self. Furthermore, others and context do not need to be discounted. This person is balanced or centered in the truth of his or her own feelings and beliefs. Not afraid to challenge the status quo, a congruent individual takes risks to grow and change. He or she also assumes responsibility for personal thoughts, feelings, and actions.

Curricula

At-risk and special needs students can and should go through a curriculum that teaches them about the five communication stances. It might be part of an existing health curriculum or separate from that with its own particular designation. The school might choose to teach students about many of the family systems concepts or simply about the communication stances.

A well-versed teacher could certainly teach this content, as could the school counselor, social worker, or psychologist. The school might choose to teach the designated content to all students, just at-risk students, those with special needs, or another target group. Different circumstances will warrant different decisions.

This content is generally appropriate in middle and high school. By that age students have the maturity and cognitive capacity to comprehend these concepts (Piaget & Inhelder, 1958). This does not mean that aspects of these concepts cannot be taught to elementary-aged students. It simply would not be a formal curricular area to be covered.

Preparing to Implement Curricula on Stances

This section focuses on exploring stances with which professionals are personally familiar and ways to respond to the dysfunctional stances of family members.

Exploring personal stances. The professional who explores his or her own stances and their impact on communication will be better able to recognize and respond congruently to the stances of others. A person who is quite familiar with his or her own typical stances for communicating is more likely to give congruent messages. Because stances that are dysfunctional indicate low self-esteem, it is also important to strive to improve personal feelings of self worth.

Satir made it clear that everyone engages in dysfunctional communication stances. She believed that all of us are capable of assuming all four stances, but that we rely on some more than others. As Satir (1972) stated, "What is so sad is that these four ways have become the most frequently used among people and are viewed by many as the most possible ways of achieving communication" (p. 78). Satir estimated the percentage of each of the four types found in groups of people. She estimated 50% to be placators, 30% to be blamers, 15% to be superreasonable computers, and 0.5% to be irrelevant distractors. She further estimated that only 4.5% are congruent (Satir, 1972).

Satir was *not* saying that people use dysfunctional communication almost 96% of the time, but that 96% of the people use dysfunctional communication some of the time that they are interacting with others. She believed that people fall back on those incongruent stances learned as children when they are in stressful situations. Thus, some students and family members relate in a congruent fashion most of the time and slip into incongruent stances when stressed.

It is helpful for professionals to invest time considering the communication stances with which they are most familiar, both from the perspective of taking the stances as well as being on the other side of a stance. To better understand oneself and the family in which one was raised, it helps to recall some significant interactions from early, middle, and later childhood. Seeing them through the lens of knowledge about the five communication stances has the potential of producing growth. Considering the stances one favored will be helpful, and recognizing the favored stances of each member of your family leads to even further understanding. It is particularly helpful to note family members in reciprocal stances, such as placating father and blaming mother.

After examining the stances from youth, considering one's current life at home and work or school will lead to deeper knowledge. Examining communication stances in a variety of recent interactions will reveal the degree to which one has continued to follow patterns established in childhood. Determining the people with whom one assumes different stances may help show how relating to different people in current life resonates with past circumstances. Are there any parallels between childhood patterns and current life? When is it easy to be congruent? What types of situations call forth the different stances?

After reminiscing about childhood and comparing patterns established in younger years with the present, it is helpful to select a recent situation in which one felt threatened and relied upon one of the four dysfunctional communication stances. It is beneficial to go back over that to clearly recall the sequence of events and determine the dysfunctional stances assumed by each principal character. The next step is to recreate the scene in the mind and rehearse by imagining oneself assuming a congruent stance as opposed to a dysfunctional stance. This makes it easier to be more congruent in the future. While creating a new scene in the imagination, it is valuable to wait for a different response from the other person. Try to imagine how that person would react given a new and congruent response, and then respond with another congruent message. Following that through to a new conclusion and using congruent responses throughout the interactions provides a mental rehearsal for new situations.

So far, this exploration and opportunity for rehearsal occurs in the mind of the individual person. This is a powerful means of changing patterns in current life circumstances. The last technique, requiring the individual to conceive a new possibility, is called "covert rehearsal." Many mental health professionals believe that to the degree one can visualize or imagine a new behavior, one can execute that behavior. Thus, employing this technique can lead to positive change in the use of functional, leveling, congruent messages.

Another challenge is to look for a new situation in which to employ a congruent stance when one might normally employ one of the dysfunctional stances. Later analysis of any communication as well as that of the other person allows a determination of usage of the five stances. If one was not congruent, one could use covert rehearsal and imagine it being different.

Another helpful technique is to observe the use of congruent communication by other people or by characters on television or in movies, videos, or plays. Such observations can further one's own expression of congruent messages.

Dysfunctional stances stem from low self-worth, and mimicking others is not the answer to higher self-esteem. People who have not dealt with many others who are congruent will find it useful to have models that help them expand and grow. If only 4.5% of the population is congruent in their communication all of the time, then it is valuable to search for functional communicators and use their interactions as models from which to expand.

Responding to stances. As might be imagined, an individual who understands personal stances will be better able to be congruent when interacting with others. This is especially important when relating to family members of at-risk students and those with special needs and will also come into play when interacting with other school professionals. Remembering that Satir (1972) estimated that only 4.5% of the population communicates congruently all of the time should help professionals be patient with themselves, their students, and their families. It is not realistic to expect that peers will communicate congruently. Professionals should assume major personal responsibility for communicating congruently and realize that others will at least have congruent communication as a model.

Responding to dysfunctional communication is a challenge. The school professional first identifies the stance assumed by the other person. Next, the professional remembers the root causes of the stance, for example, low self-worth. Then the professional recalls any information about the family background of the person speaking. These steps help the professional remain centered and not move off balance in the direction of a dysfunctional stance.

The professional must then communicate with single-level, congruent messages. It is important not to placate, blame, distract, or become superreasonable in the face of any of those types of communication. The professional's sole responsibility is to communicate congruently.

For example, a principal might be communicating with a parent who is in a blaming stance, saying, "Why don't the teachers ever listen to us? I can't believe Jon is that much of a problem in school. Everything is fine at home." Faced with that statement, the principal might be inclined to either counterblame or placate. Some would become superreasonable and provide facts and quote experts. However, the best option is to be congruent with a statement such as, "Mrs. Wickham, I realize it is frustrating to keep getting reports about aggression by Jonathan. The fact remains that Jon has slugged his teacher twice in the last week, leaving bruise marks. So far the teacher has elected not to call in the police. If this occurs again, she has said that she will call the police. She has already filed a report regarding the last assault. As before, we recommend family counseling...."

In another example, the parent has just said, "I know I have done a terrible job of raising Henry. I'm just a miserable mess of a parent." The school professional, recognizing the placating stance assumed by this mother, might choose to point out the placating stance or simply remain congruent. Some professionals tend to back off from people when they placate. They may be afraid to kick a person who is already down. It is better to remain congruent with a comment such as, "Mrs. Lathrop, all of us struggle in raising our children. I have also had many learning experiences. I agree that there are practices you can change to better respond to your son's needs. To that end, we are recommending a parent effectiveness training group that begins...." In this example the professional seeks to share information regarding the problem *and* has also responded to the discounting of self by the mother by normalizing child-rearing struggles.

In the case of a person who is superreasonable, both self and others are discounted. Any response should focus on both self and others as important. In the following example, a parent is interacting with the school counselor about home issues between two of his children that spill over into school. The father is explaining, "I have read several child psychology books in my undergraduate years. I read that when you ignore behavior of the child you do not feed the situation by giving the child attention for inappropriate behavior. Dr. Benjamin Spock said not to be hard on your children. Additionally, Dr....." To an onslaught like this the school counselor, well aware of the superreasonable nature of the communication, might say "Mr. Mafigliano, when I am in the halls and see your two sons changing classes and getting into it with one another, I have a hunch about what I see. I get the feeling that they are not really looking for attention from adults. My intuitive hunch is that Joe is a bit embarrassed by Rich's antics and tries to disown him. The sense I have of it is that Rich feels abandoned and hurt by Joe's embarrassment. I really wonder about a sibling support group for Joe that is offered at the mental health center in the county. There is no fee and...." In this situation, the counselor indicates by example that simply responding to what one sees may be more important than any textbook offering. Furthermore, the counselor also validated self by relying on personal intuition.

The most difficult dysfunctional communication to respond to is irrelevant. This type of communication discounts self, other, and context. It is critical that school professionals recognize the nature of the communication and not judge the person as not caring about the situation. That is easy to do when the comments sound unrelated to the topic at hand. For example, consider this teacher speaking to a parent about her daughter's inappropriate dress at school. "Mrs. Jones, I'm sure Shironda doesn't leave home looking like she does in school. She turns over the waistband in her skirts so they are much shorter. She has served in-school suspension for breaking the dress code five times this month and I am concerned about her grades and what she has learned this grading period." To which Mrs. Jones replied, "Did I tell you my husband has a case of the flu? Seems like everybody in our neighborhood is having that old flu these days." (Imagine how one might respond to this situation.) The teacher says, "I realize that it is hard to connect with low grades, in-school suspension, and a daughter who is defying school rules. These are critical matters and I am sure you feel the struggle of dealing with this. I also have been concerned that our procedures of serving in-school suspension have not worked. I'd like to meet with you and Shironda about this situation. Before we do that I'd like to map out a strategy about how we can approach her regarding her blatant violation of the school dress code...." The teacher initially refocused on the very real situation or context, then focused on the parental concern, tying it to personal concern for Shironda. Further, the teacher offered to form a joint plan for dealing with the situation, thus focusing again on self and other.

This section has presented several examples of dysfunctional communication by a parent with a functional, congruent response by a school professional. With practice professionals become more fluent while interacting with family members and at-risk and special needs students who engage in incongruent communication.

Parental Concern

Academic curricula may also come into play with parents when new and controversial ideas are contemplated by school professionals. Family systems concepts, including all or the concepts presented in Part I, are beneficial when considering new curricula. Those concepts will help school professionals plan strategies for considering new curricula that affect concerned parents. That understanding also provides a grounding for meeting parents who are unhappy with a curricular change process.

One topic that has received a lot of recent attention in many states has been family life curriculum. The legislatures of many states have joined in the controversy by requiring that schools provide a family life curriculum (sometimes including sex education). It is to be expected that parents, who had the major responsibility in the past for providing this part of their children's education, are concerned about school professionals crossing that traditional boundary.

It is important to recognize that the boundary issue is a major concern of some families. Some families will simply have a legitimate concern that can be easily handled with basic information. Other families may be enmeshed and overinvolved, becoming quite agitated about what their children may be learning. School professionals will probably see more of these families directly raising their concerns and issues. Children from disengaged families will often act out the concerns of the parents, yet professionals will not be told the nature of the parents' concern. By recognizing the boundary issues and having a firm grounding in the principles of family systems, it is easier to face parental concerns with less personal reaction and a greater sense of confidence.

Those who have cataloged family systems processes with families of at-risk and special needs students will find it easier to predict family concerns of those students. They will also know how to approach them to prevent problems from developing. Further, they will be able to use their knowledge while interacting with families of at-risk and special needs students, which is a benefit in dealing with all families. As said many times throughout this text, not all families of students with special needs are dysfunctional. The same is true of the general population. However, if a professional is aware that a particular family has boundary problems or a hierarchy dysfunction, he or she can use this information as a basic framework in any interaction with the family.

ACADEMIC INSTRUCTION

Families may have concerns about academic instruction that can be divided into two areas: curricular topics other than the family systems curriculum and the family systems curriculum.

Non-Family Systems Curricula

There are at least three areas of potential struggle that concern instructional practice and families. First, parents may have concerns about instructional approaches used in the schools. Second, teachers may have concerns about a parent's knowledge of an instructional practice and the need for the practice to remain consistent at school and home. And third, homework links home and school with instruction. Each of these is elaborated upon.

Instructional Practice Concern

Parental concerns regarding unusual approaches are not uncommon. Teachers use more unique instructional approaches with students with special needs than with most other students. Thus, it is more likely that parental concerns will surface. To prevent such concerns, parents should be informed about the nature of any unusual instruction and its estimated duration.

It may help to provide a demonstration or videotape of the instructional practice. Some practices, such as the Neurological Impress Method (NIM), may be particularly time consuming and confusing to parents. This method of teaching reading is highly intensive, with a trained professional working one-on-one with a student. Professionals often prefer that students not read on their own or to their parents while receiving instruction in this method. Once the parents see the intensity of the method, they frequently understand why the teacher is requiring another approach at home, for the time being.

However, it is not always possible to keep parents from being concerned about instructional practices, so professionals should try to lower their anxiety. For example, a mother may be concerned that her daughter is learning "Touch Math," not realizing that the title refers to the child touching points on paper as opposed to humans interacting through touch. In this case, the teacher could easily provide a demonstration or information. If, however, the mother's concern is that "Touch Math" might make her child dependent upon an external crutch, the situation is entirely different. All of the family systems concepts and techniques will be helpful when working with parents who have this type of concern. The professional should look back to the catalog of family process to be clear about their typical family process. Then the professional will be better prepared to join them in resolving their concerns.

Coordinating Home School Instruction

In the second area of concern, the teacher struggles to coordinate instructional practices between home and school. Again, simply providing information regarding the instructional practice is the best prevention. For example, a student with special needs might learn to spell best by practicing with a tactile instructional technique. It is good prevention to talk with the parents about this method and explain how it was chosen (e.g., results of trial teaching), providing information on the instructional practice. It would even be helpful for some parents to be trained to help their child practice spelling words according to the tactile method. However, the professional should be familiar with the family characteristics, life cycle, and process. Some families will not have the time for the added responsibility; others will only make things worse for a child who already needs some distance from an overly involved parent. Chronicling family process, characteristics, and other relevant information will be most helpful in making decisions about how to approach parents.

Informing the parents about special approaches can also prevent school–home conflict. To extend the example above, if the parents do not know about the instructional practice and are trying to get their child to practice spelling with a "look and say" method that served them well, the child might become confused. Further, the child's spelling test scores might even be lower because of that confusion. Wanting to please both the parents and the teacher, the child might not mention any such differences in practice techniques. If, however, the parents see the child using a tactile practice method at home and ask the teacher about it, the teacher has the chance to provide the necessary information and work to improve the parents' trust level. Again, knowledge of the family's process, life-cycle, and characteristics will be valuable when meeting with parents under such circumstances.

Homework and Families

The third and last possible problem area relates to homework. Several types of struggles regarding homework occur in homes. Some parents may be overly involved in the child's homework. Other parents may not provide the needed supplies or study space. Yet other parents may be unable to help their child due to unavailability, lack of knowledge, or lack of concern.

Looking to the family characteristics, life-cycle, interaction patterns, and environmental factors are of the greatest assistance in determining how to handle homework challenges. Considering those dimensions of the family will suggest the course of action, though it is helpful to discuss these situations with others who know the family or during team meetings. There is no one best way to approach an overly involved parent. The objective will be to decrease the involvement. How to do that will be best dictated by considering families on a case-by-case basis. The same is true in dealing with parents who do not supply needed supplies or study space or who are unable to help their child.

Family Systems Curricula

The earlier section on curricula provided basic information on communication stances as curricular content. A well-versed teacher would be able to provide the curricular content to students. School counselors, social workers, and psychologists are excellent resources to provide that information to parents and siblings.

The actual instruction or teaching techniques to be used are not that different from any other type of instruction. The instructor would prepare an overall unit plan with daily lessons detailing objectives, methodology, materials, and evaluation. Satir's (1972, 1988) characterizations of the people assuming each of the four stances are a valuable media prop. Satir's book *The New Peoplemaking* (1988) is excellent for use as a required text.

The most important aspect of instruction is the enactment of the communication stances. After describing the four stances, Satir had people pose in the stances. She then had people work in groups and practice employing each stance by going round robin and alternating the stances employed. A group of four or five reenacts the basic family structure. Individuals who participate recognize familiar and unfamiliar stances from their own experience.

Participants benefit from demonstrations of the four stances and feedback on their interpretation of those stances. For example, with the superreasonable/computer stance, a participant may need feedback on how to stand straighter and stiffer. It is important that the body is aware of and registers the deleterious impact of assuming such a role. This realization helps the participants relate to others and recognize the impact of incongruent communication upon themselves and others. Satir (1983b, 1988) provided many suggestions for activities that allow individuals to explore the communication stances. Those suggestions should be employed when providing basic instruction regarding the communication stances.

TECHNIQUES

Marshall McLuhan (1967) is credited with saying "the medium is the message," and this is true about the manner in which a school professional delivers a message. This section focuses on two techniques used in family systems approaches in which the medium is indeed the message. These are the techniques of using metaphor and reframing. It is particularly valuable to use positive metaphors and to reframe any negative views about disabilities when helping others gain access to resources or engage in counseling.

Metaphor

A metaphor is a figure of speech that uses a term or phrase in connection with something to which it cannot be literally applied in order to suggest a characteristic of one to the other. When one invokes any image or association from one arena to highlight the similarities, differences, or ambiguities in another arena, one is using metaphor. This medium allows people to develop a new awareness by connecting or linking two characteristics, events, ideas, or meanings. In using metaphor, one describes experience and creates new patterns of consciousness, thereby extending the boundaries of subjective experience. Thus, this technique or medium would be quite helpful in teaching, counseling, and therapy. Metaphors allow people to access information in a nonthreatening way; they can reinforce learning as well.

Mills and Crowley (1986) wrote an excellent book, *Therapeutic Metaphors for Children and the Child Within*, that speaks to the use of metaphor in general and specifically its use with children. In their introduction to the first chapter they stated:

> Metaphor is a form of symbolic language that has been used for centuries as a method of teaching in many fields. The parables of the Old and New Testaments, the holy writing of the Kabbalah, the koans of Zen Buddhism, the allegories of literature, the images of poetry, and the fairy tales of storytellers—all make use of metaphor to convey an idea in an indirect yet paradoxically more meaningful way. Recognition of this special power of the metaphor has also been grasped by every parent and grandparent who, observing the forlorn features of the young child, seeks to bring consolation and nurturance by relating an experience to which the child can intuitively relate. (p. 7)

Metaphor can be used effectively with child and parent alike. This technique, or medium, is not one that can be easily taught because it is as much artistic as it is technical. To prepare for the use of metaphor, professionals may want to read the text by Mills and Crowley (1986). An example of a metaphor that might be used when a student is taking on too much is, "It seems like Joey might be too big for his britches." Another metaphor could be, "Is it possible that Rufus is tied to his mother's apron strings?"

Reframing

In chapter 9 reframing was briefly described. This technique is used widely in family systems approaches (Bandler & Grinder, 1979, 1982; Bowman & Goldberg, 1983; Karpel, 1986b; Minuchin & Fishman, 1981; Satir & Baldwin, 1983; Watzlawick, Weakland, & Fisch, 1974) and also by professionals who use other approaches to counseling and psychotherapy.

Underlying all reframing is the desire to help others bring a larger and different perspective to a life situation. It is not an attempt to whitewash or minimize suffering on the part of others. It is a legitimate effort to improve the situation by altering one's view to encompass a new way of "seeing."

Background Information

The following story from the Taoist tradition serves as a good introduction to this section on reframing.

> There once was a farmer who had a wonderful horse that the farmer's family depended upon for their livelihood. His horse ran away one day and all his neighbors said how awful was his fate. To this the farmer replied, "Maybe." A couple of days later the horse returned with a herd of wild horses. The neighbors told him how lucky he was. The farmer said, "Maybe." Soon the farmer's oldest son tried to break in one of the wild horses and was thrown and broke his leg. Again the neighbors said how awful and the farmer said, "Maybe." The next day the people in charge of drafting soldiers rejected his oldest son because of his injury. The neighbors thought he again was very fortunate and he thought, "Maybe." (J. Daniel, personal communication)

Reframing is about transforming the frame a person holds of events so that a different meaning can be attached. With the change in meaning come changes in responses and behaviors. As Watzlawick et al. (1974) said:

> To reframe, then, means to change the conceptual and/or emotional setting or viewpoint in relation to which a situation is experienced and to place it in another frame which fits the "facts" of the same concrete situation equally well or even better, and thereby changes its entire meaning. (p. 95)

Reframing can be used with children and youth as well as adults. In the field of family systems the professional is usually redefining the treatment unit to be the whole family as opposed to the symptom bearer (child with special needs) that is so often seen in schools. Reframing is intended to affect the interrelated cognitive, emotional, and behavioral spheres. Reframing generally results in a change in how people think, feel, and act.

Types of Reframing

There are many uses of reframing. Karpel (1986b) stated:

> Reframing may be used to accomplish different ends. Like psychoanalytic interpretation, which it resembles, it may be intended to foster insight. In other cases it may be used to make alternative patterns of interaction easier to enact or to make it much more difficult to persist in problematic patterns. From a resource perspective, it is probably most often used to identify resources that are *inherent* in the presenting problem itself, as in the use of statements that throw light on patterns of loyalty, concern, and protectiveness in what would otherwise look like destructive or self-destructive behavior. (p. 200)

Reframing can be used to maintain or increase a person's self-worth. Satir and Baldwin (1983) reported the value of helping people to focus on observing what occurred in an incident instead of blaming another person for the situation. Satir referred to this as an "observing ego" in the other person that allowed a reduction of blame and increase in trust to occur. In the example provided, she changed the blaming words "grabbed a hold of my hair" to the observing words "her hands went on your hair. How do you suppose that happened?" (pp. 43–44).

Reframing can be used to diffuse negative feelings such as blaming. An example would be when one family member is angry and his temper is flaring and others are upset because he has broken the family rule that one should not express angry feelings. The school professional might reframe the temper to be seen as a "way of bringing out his thoughts." Further, blame might be reframed into searching for information in a different example of negative feelings.

Reframing may be used to clarify what has been said by one family member. An example provided in *Satir, Step by Step* (Satir & Baldwin, 1983) is that of a father who struggled with making compliments and would beat around the bush with them. A reframe could be to state that the father had complimented or admired someone.

This technique may be used to reframe liabilities and perceived weaknesses as strengths. In so doing the professional may be able to transform the significance level. For example, a single mother taking her adolescent for therapy could be framed as "caring enough about her daughter to find the resources she needed."

Reframing with Children and Youth

When using reframing with children, it is important to consider their cognitive level.

For example, children who are 7 years old or younger overgeneralize how they see their strengths and weaknesses (Piaget & Inhelder, 1969). It may therefore not be possible for the adult to speak about only one aspect of what the child does as a problem. They may not have the cognitive capacity to understand that difference and therefore a reframing will not be possible. For example, a teacher trying to reframe the fighting of two 5-year-olds as a sign of liking one another may find the attempt falls on deaf ears.

At the same time that young children may not be able to cognitively follow a reframe, they may be able to follow a shift related to emotions. For example, a child sensitive to nonverbal changes in the emotional climate, such as making a joke and laughing about the child's irritability, will be able to benefit from this nonverbal reframing. This type of reframing is an experiential level as opposed to a cognitive one.

Once children reach approximately age 7, they will be able to understand reframing that relates to concrete as opposed to abstract thinking. At approximately age 12, the child is able to respond to higher order thinking when a reframe is presented. A reframing statement that "you do not argue with those you do not care about" could be understood by children at this cognitive level.

Also important in reframing with children and youth is the view on the part of professionals that reframing also applies to them. When the professional can see a child's distracting behavior both positively and negatively, then he or she will be more able to reframe the situation for the student. For example, there are times when bullying may be desirable. Satir was famous for asking people to look at any weakness and discover times that such a weakness could be a strength. She used that type of reframing consistently in her *Part's Parties* (Satir & Baldwin, 1983).

Timing

The timing of reframing cannot be externally guided but must be felt or intuited to be appropriate by the professional, given the readiness of the family member or student. Used at a poorly chosen time, or at too abstract a level, reframing can cause a sense of misconnection as well as anger for having misperceived the situation.

One timing guideline is to wait until the individuals have diffused highly intense feelings of grief or anger. For example, when a family has recently learned that their child has Down syndrome, it is not the time to share an example of a parent who is in acceptance. In time the professional may sense that the family is moving out of shock, denial, or anger. The timing is then appropriate for the use of reframing.

Use Language of the Family

Professionals should use language that speaks to the family. For example, a Bible story might be used to reframe something for a Christian family. For an artistic family, a reframe regarding drawing or other visual imagery might speak to them. Likewise, a musical family would appreciate a reframe that they will hear and that is auditory in nature.

Case Example

A 7-year-old boy whose father had recently committed suicide had begun to act out by talking back to his mother and resisting directions. The mother tended to interpret the behavior as "oppositional/defiant" and to react by intensifying her disciplining efforts. When the mother mentioned this problem to the boy's teacher, he commented that the behavior appeared to be designed to keep the mother intensely involved with the boy and could be interpreted as the equivalent of "anxious, clingy" behavior. In the context of recent loss, the mother found the idea that her son would be "anxious and clingy" to be much more acceptable than her previous interpretation of defiance and anger. Her response, then, became more nurturing, resulting in a reduction of the boy's anxiety and acting-out behavior. The teacher's ability to reframe the child's behavior resulted in a positive shift in the family system. This shift allowed the mother and son to help one another through their mutual grief and avoided prolonging a painful symptom.

SOCIALIZATION

Shifting now from *academics* and the cognitive domain, this section takes up *socialization* and the affective domain, covering only one strategy with a family systems base. It is adapted from Satir (1983a). This discussion elaborates upon and expands a method that was only briefly mentioned and demonstrated in Satir's training.

Satir (1983a) developed a method of "clearing the air" in group interactions that can easily be used in classrooms as well as regularly scheduled meetings of ongoing groups. Called "temperature readings," it can also be used in families once parents learn the procedure. If the parents do not attend meetings where this technique is used, they would need training in the method to carry it forward in the home.

Background

Temperature reading is one of Satir's (1983a) lesser known communication processes. Its two basic purposes are for group members to share feelings and to help detoxify negativity on the part of group members. It could be used in a class session or homeroom as well as during educational, support, or counseling groups.

Features

Satir (1983a) included five expressions in a temperature reading: appreciations, complaints, puzzles, new information, and hopes and wishes. During a temperature reading not all five features have to be included, but it must be possible to include them.

Appreciations

Appreciations would be shared with the person being appreciated. In the classroom a teacher might say, "Tim, you are doing an excellent job of assisting Helen in making the transition to a whole new set of instructional materials. I appreciate your help in this matter." In another example, a teacher might tell a parent, "Mr. Juval, I am so glad you told me about the support group you have attended. Now I can tell other parents about your findings. Thanks."

There is no need to fabricate an appreciation. If there is one, the temperature reading is the perfect time to share this communication. It also helps focus on the positive and provides examples of directly sharing an appreciation. Eye contact and tone of voice are important aspects of sharing an appreciation.

Complaints

Complaints are a major reason for conducting temperature readings. Voicing complaints can provide opportunity to detoxify negativity as well as a structure that allows an individual to voice a complaint.

Satir (1983a) recommended that any complaint be accompanied with a recommendation for change. Others should not breed dependency by allowing the one with a complaint not to provide a recommendation. The recommendation for solving the problem does not have to be carried out. It is just a positive strategy for looking toward solutions, as opposed to merely voicing a complaint. Of course, just the registering of a complaint and being heard is very important.

A classroom example of a complaint during temperature reading is one provided by a student who says, "I am having a hard time catching up with all the new algebra since I was in the hospital for a week. I hate slowing the class down and wonder if someone might have the time to help me during study hall in the afternoons." Another example of a complaint is this one lodged by a father to a counselor during a support group meeting: "I have a problem with the time of these meetings. I cannot get from work to home and feed my son before coming here at 6:00. I find group beneficial and would like to have the time moved to no earlier than 7:00."

Puzzles

The third feature of temperature reading is presenting a puzzle. It is used where the one presenting the puzzle has heard something and does not fully understand what was heard. It allows response to rumors to be affirmed or denied. The rumor itself might be something to which others could look forward or something that the individual feared or worried about. Either way, the puzzle has not been adequately addressed.

An example of a puzzle during temperature reading in the classroom is, "I was wondering if it is true that anyone who earns two thousand points will be able to attend a showing of the newest *Star Trek* movie next Friday afternoon?" Another example of a puzzle is a parent querying a social worker, "I overheard a parent at the basketball game telling someone else that there was a support group called Compassionate Friends. I am wondering if you know how I can get in touch with them in this county? My wife and I are still grieving over the loss of our daughter."

New Information

New information simply allows individuals to let others know about an upcoming event, activity, or other opportunity. It is like forecasting a new possibility so that others might avail themselves of the occasion. It also is likely to prevent rumors from spreading as well as to prevent anyone from being left out or being the last to find out about something with which others are familiar.

A classroom example of a teacher providing new information is, "We have a great speaker who will be at our assembly during third period on Tuesday. Her name is Carol Scearce. She is the president of Enlightening Enterprises in Tega Cay, South Carolina. She is the best speaker I have heard. She will be teaching you to make mind maps. That is a special and creative form of taking notes developed by Tony Buzan, from England. She has agreed to provide a special two-hour presentation to the students in our program on Tuesday afternoon. I hope no one misses school on Tuesday."

Another example of new information is when a school psychologist is speaking with a parent group. "I have an announcement about something I know all of you will be interested in hearing. We now have an easier referral process to the county mental health center. Some of you will remember that their waiting list for family counseling was several months long. They have hired two new family systems therapists and the waiting period is nonexistent. Be sure to thank Dr. Wallace when you see her. She was responsible for finding the funds for these new additions."

Hopes and Wishes

Hopes and wishes are quite simply a statement about something that is desired. If the desire remains unarticulated, it has little chance of being fulfilled. Satir (1983a) was concerned that each member of a family or group be able to give voice to their hopes and wishes. This may sound quite simple; however, many people will reserve their wishes when they do not have a structure for voicing them.

A classroom example of a hope or wish is, "Mrs. Anthony, I was wondering if we could have a popcorn party this Friday afternoon. My brother will be home from the service and he wanted to come and visit my school. He will be here this Friday afternoon and I hoped everyone could meet him and visit with him." Another example of a hope or wish is the following comment made by one parent before a parent effectiveness training session began. "I wish somebody would develop a list of child-care opportunities for our younger children so that it would be easier to attend these parent training workshops."

Guidelines

Satir (1983a) recommended that a temperature reading be conducted in families, in groups, and as part of any quality circles at work. These guidelines for temperature readings focus on frequency, leadership, and structure, as well as training of professionals and parents.

Frequency

Satir (1983a) provided one guideline about the frequency of conducting this process. She recommended they be conducted daily whenever a new group formed. Once the group stabilized, the frequency of temperature readings could be gradually lowered, although she indicated they would be more beneficial if held at least weekly. The more struggles there are within the group or family, the more frequently the temperature reading would be conducted. Groups that meet less than weekly would always conduct temperature readings before beginning the meeting.

In a newly formed classroom, temperature readings would be conducted daily for the first week and then gradually reduced to meet the needs of the class, but never less than weekly. Homeroom is a good time to conduct temperature readings in secondary schools. If a teacher has a totally different group of students each period, it is not likely that the time could be invested in temperature reading at the expense of academic time. In the elementary school, time for temperature readings could be made before beginning the academic day and when all students are in the classroom.

When family members are part of a temperature reading process in the school, it is easier for them to implement a similar process at home. Thus, the temperature reading conducted at school activities serves as a model for the parents. The tougher the situation to which they see professionals respond, the better their opportunity to learn from experience.

Leadership

In large groups that met regularly, Satir (1983a) would have the person making a contribution stand next to her. She would often hold the contributor's hand while he or she was speaking, lending support by her presence. Not many professionals would have the presence of Satir in holding a contributor's hand during a temperature reading; thus, the leader should do so only if he or she is comfortable with that style and has the personal savvy to carry that off.

It is quite effective when one school professional is in charge of conducting temperature readings. In the classroom that one person is the teacher. This is not a situation to turn over to shared leadership on a rotating basis. It is best that a professional comfortable in providing congruent messages, as well as helping others to do the same, lead the temperature reading in nonclassroom groups.

Structure

While introducing the temperature reading, the professional initially provides the purposes and then describes the five features. Next, the leader shares personal experiences with temperature readings. Following that, a brief role play of a temperature reading is conducted. Concluding with a question-and-answer session helps eliminate concerns about the process and content.

Temperature readings are valuable for all ongoing groups that operate in schools. Teams that meet regularly would benefit from conducting temperature readings each meeting, as would all ongoing parent groups, be they PTO/PTA, support groups, parenting training sessions, or less structured yet regular meetings. The temperature reading does not take much time, though those that include complaints and puzzles will likely be longer. Temperature readings should be conducted at the beginning of meetings. This allows the air to be cleared prior to engaging new business, thereby increasing the effectiveness of the actual meeting.

Satir (1983a) would help the individual share the offering, assisting with any statements made so that the person provided congruent messages. She would also reframe any complaints so that the person would be open to other possibilities when viewing the situation.

So that parents understand its possibilities, the leader should connect the value of temperature readings with family life situations. The leader can recommend that the parents conduct this process at home and share personal and others' experiences with temperature reading in family situations. The leader can also recommend that families wait to conduct temperature readings at home until they are more familiar with how they work in the school group that is using the process.

Training/Preparation

For school professionals, conducting temperature readings regularly in their own work groups may be the most effective training. This emphasizes "learning by doing," recognizing that there is seldom a better teacher than experience. In conducting real (not practice) temperature readings, professionals will face many touchy or confusing situations. Such real-life opportunities allow professionals to plan better how they will respond to sensitive or difficult situations. These situations quite naturally occur in a spontaneous and open sharing of feelings and thoughts in a group context. Difficult situations should be expected and not take a professional by surprise.

Preparing parents to be involved in temperature readings is also important. Parents may never have experienced such an open exchange of thoughts and feelings. Furthermore, they might not quite believe that their thoughts and feelings are really valued by professionals. It may take a few sessions to establish trust in the process. Therefore, professionals should not be surprised if the first several temperature readings focus largely upon appreciations, hopes and wishes, and new information. When a student or parent shares the first complaint or puzzle, it is important to validate their concerns before moving on with the elaboration.

SUMMARY

This chapter has focused on the extension of family systems concepts into the classroom and education, support, or counseling groups. New possibilities for school professionals abound in the literature; professionals should be creative in the design and implementation of family systems concepts. Communication stances, reframing, metaphor, and temperature readings can be used with both classroom and group instruction.

OVERCOMING BARRIERS 13
TO WORKING
WITH FAMILIES

The focus of this chapter is on potential barriers to following the recommendations presented in this book. The barriers may be based in parents, professionals, or the school context. The intention is to help school professionals prevent barriers from forming. And because it is not always possible to prevent them, the chapter also offers ways to reduce those barriers that do arise.

The chapter opens with information on communication skills, followed by psychological issues that can be manifested as barriers to implementing family systems ideas in the school context. Potential limitations related to training, school norms, and school procedures follow those issues. Next are described concrete barriers presented by reality constraints. Attitudes, resistance, and the process of change form the final focus of this chapter.

COMMUNICATION SKILLS

Parents' communication skills vary widely. Some are quite articulate; others will struggle to make a point. Some will not even try to communicate because they are afraid to sound foolish or inadequate. Beyond parents' communications skills lie the communication skills of everyone involved in interactions. Satir (1983a) understood the many different levels on which people communicate, referring to them as "ingredients of an interaction." That information is also covered in this section.

Parental Communication

For some school professionals, the idea of training parents to be involved in their child's education is novel. For them, there are programs (Edgar, Singer, Ritchie, & Heggelund, 1981; McLoughlin, 1981) that train parents to become involved in their child's education. It is important to help parents learn the communication skills needed to articulate their views and not feel overwhelmed by their team experiences. It is even possible for parents to help one another by sharing their experiences. However, Edgar et al. (1981) did not find that it was a good idea to use parents as trainers of communication skills.

Inadequate Processing of Information

Communication problems can arise because parents are unfamiliar with the procedures employed on teams or because they have not mastered effective communication
skills. These problems are relatively easily remedied. Beyond these problems is the parent
who may be inarticulate due to a disability. Some parents may be mentally retarded and have
trouble processing information given them by the schools. Losen and Losen (1985) have
suggested that someone might accompany them and interpret what is happening. If a case
worker is assigned to the family, that person is a logical possibility because he or she has
already formed a trusting relationship with the parents. Some parents who do not understand
the process or what is being said may become disruptive and be unwilling to admit their lack
of understanding. When these parents refuse to sign off on a placement recommendation,
the school system can request a due process hearing. Seldom would one want to use that
alternative, but it is a possibility.

Parent Training

Much has been written (Courtnage & Healy, 1984; Courtnage & Smith-Davis, 1987;
Crisler, 1979; Fuqua, Hegland, & Karas, 1985) about parental involvement with special
needs children and youth, but none of these studies proposed training of parents. They
focused on parental involvement and teamwork. Further, several articles (Bluhm, Egan &
Perry, 1981; Buktenica, 1981; Golin & Ducanis, 1981; Helge, 1981; Rucker & Vautour,
1981) were published in one issue of *Teacher Education and Special Education* on teams
in special education and the training of members. None of these articles focuses on training
parents for their involvement in the team process. Rather, mentioning including them in the
team process and soliciting their input was the extent of the emphasis on parents. It is only
fair to say that the purpose of this particular journal did not go beyond teacher education
and students with special needs. However, it is logical to extend interest to training as it
relates to all areas of special education, including communication skills of parents.

McLoughlin (1981) described a parent/teacher education model for the joint training
of teachers and parents of children with disabilities. His competency-based efforts were
skills-oriented and focused on "training together to work together," with the outcome being
enhanced cooperation and interaction. His project demonstrated that such an effort can be
effective. Chapters 2, 6, and 7 provide more information about parent training. These
chapters focus on different aspects of training parents, whereas McLoughlin's (1981) work
focused on parents of children with disabilities.

Ingredients of an Interaction

The ingredients of an interaction are everything that goes into making communication.
Satir (1983a) has compared communication with using a recipe with many different
ingredients. A person's interactions with others can be seen as enjoyable and as complex
as making that new recipe for the evening meal. The purpose of being familiar with those
ingredients is to consider all aspects when interacting with others. It is easy to misread
communication if you are not aware of all the ingredients. Just like leaving out the baking
powder in a recipe can result in flattened cookies, so too can failure to understand, recognize,

or respond to an ingredient of an interaction result in flattened communication.

Ingredients

Satir (1983a) spoke of seven ingredients in communication. Figure 13.1 depicts a two-person interaction. Points 1 and 8 depict spoken communication: Point 1 is the initiating point, and point 8 is the responding point of the communication.

Person A, named Adam, initiates a message to Person B, Betty. The other six parts of the interaction (points 2–7) are part of Betty's internal process before she responds at point 8.

Point 2 represents Betty's internal process of figuring out what she sees and hears. She uses her eyes, ears, skin, and so forth to determine what she sees and hears. If she cannot see because she is on the phone or she is blind, she will not have all those avenues of determination open to her. Betty will take in Adam's facial expression, body position, muscle tone, skin color, scent, smell, breathing, voice tone and pace, as well as movement. These factors are called *paralinguistic*; they provide well over half of the meaning of the message. Adam's words are only part of the message. How Adam delivers the words will convey much meaning. Betty will select what she hears and sees from all the possibilities.

Next, point 3 is Betty's connecting with past experiences and learning in order to determine what meaning she makes of what she sees and hears. Betty might well ask herself, while forming the meaning of the message, how aware of the past and present she is as they relate to self, other, and context. (Those three dimensions were described in the last chapter under the five communication stances.) She could also ask herself whether she was aware of any past experiences that could contaminate the meaning she makes of the message from Adam.

Point 4 in the diagram represents the feelings triggered about the meaning Betty made of the message conveyed by Adam. Betty has answered the question, "What feelings do I have about the meaning I have made of the communication?" Note that Satir (1983a), like many people in the field of mental health, believed that feeling stems from the meaning or belief the person holds about an event, situation, or communication.

In turn, the feelings activate point 5, which is related to feelings about the feeling. Satir (1983a) asked the question, "What are my feelings about the feelings about the meaning?" At first this may seem roundabout. However, consider that Betty may feel angry and feel

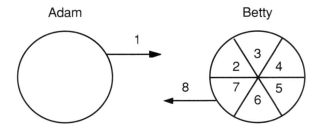

Figure 13.1
TWO-PERSON INTERACTION (ADAM INITIATES; BETTY PROCESSES)

guilty about feeling angry. The feeling associated with the feeling about the meaning needs to be sorted out. It is one situation if Betty feels that her feeling of anger is fine and another if she feels guilty about feeling angry. Again the stances and the rules (in chapter 10) relate to the feeling about the feeling. The feelings about the feeling activate survival rules. Thus, coping stances will come into play if the person discounts self, other, context, or two or three of these. The person is easily caught in an old web of feelings.

Point 6 stems from point 5 and relates to defenses Betty uses. These include such defense mechanisms as denying, projecting, and distorting. If she is using defenses, Betty could look to see whether she would cope by blaming, placating, being superreasonable, or being irrelevant. If, however, Betty owns and accepts her feelings, she does not have to defend herself and can decide how she chooses to respond.

Point 7 represents rules for commenting. The five freedoms, described in chapter 10, form those rules for commenting. Must Betty see what she "should," say what is expected, feel what she "ought," and wait for permission, choosing to be only secure and not rock the boat? Or can Betty exercise the five freedoms? In owning and accepting her feelings, she creates internal safety and does not have to defend herself. She is free to take risks and has choices for what and how she would like to respond to Adam.

At point 8 Betty responds with a message. Betty can make a meaning that matches the meaning intended by Adam. By accepting and owning her feelings, acknowledging and valuing Adam's feelings, as well as considering the context, Betty can take responsibility for her response and express herself in a congruent mode.

The communication is not, however, over yet. Now Adam must go through the same process that Betty just did. Figure 13.2 represents points 9 through 15, as Adam goes through the same steps in the process that Betty went through in points 2 through 8. Communication is more complex than is immediately obvious. There are many places where problems or snags might be found. Understanding one's own process is necessary before understanding that of others.

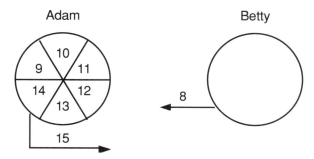

Figure 13.2
TWO-PERSON INTERACTION (BETTY RESPONDS; ADAM PROCESSES)

Variations on a Theme

Although this is a complex process, it can be even more complex when one or both people are not communicating congruently. There are several variations possible. Both partners could communicate congruently, or both could communicate incongruently. Person A might be congruent and person B, incongruent. Person B might be congruent and person A incongruent. With four variations of only two people, imagine the possibilities within a family.

Each person must also consider the internal process of the other. There are many possible ways of misinterpreting others, and miscommunication is more than occasional. That is understandable in light of the number of possible variations. Being aware of the four possibilities is essential when communicating with others. To be unaware of the possibility that one's partner might be incongruent or congruent, as you might also be either one, would lead to even greater problems when communicating. Recognizing that it is easy to miscommunicate can help one realize the need to clarify any communication that seems unclear or that one is unable to read accurately.

When trying to clarify what another person means by a message, one can look to the ingredients of the interaction for potential assistance. One will want to know how the person made meaning from the first message, how he or she felt about that meaning and about the feeling about the meaning. One must try to decipher defenses employed or stances assumed as well as determine freedoms violated by rules for commenting. Before trying to understand another person's process, it helps to have examined one's own.

Examining Personal Process

Understanding one's own process is the first step in being able to use knowledge about the ingredients of an interaction. Beginning with a current interaction is laudable; however, it might be easier to recollect a recent, simple, meaningful interaction with someone else. It would be valuable to recall, as well as memory allows, each of the components. One should think back to the first comment made by someone and then go through to determine the meaning attached as well as the feeling had about the meaning. One should then determine his or her feelings about the feelings even if he or she was not aware of that level at the time. Look to what defenses were used as well as what rules operated to determine whether there was a violation of the five freedoms (see chapter 10). That type of analysis can probably help one better understand his or her response. There is no way to know the internal process of another without engaging in what is called "mind rape." One might, however, try to infer each of the components that form the internal process of the other person. This is merely inference and good practice.

After analyzing a past interaction, one can benefit from analyzing several past interactions to see if any patterns emerge. Are there certain types of meaning made from a particular type of message? Are there feelings attached to meanings that provide a better picture of oneself? Can one determine defenses or rules operating under different feelings about feelings? What one does by answering these questions is analyze a personal communication style. This analysis will serve professionals well when they attempt to transform family rules that would perform better as guidelines, as described in chapter 10.

The next task would be to analyze the ingredients while an interaction is occurring. For one day, while interactions are occurring, the professional should analyze interactions that present a low level of threat. Once that task is successfully finished, he or she can keep the observing part of himself or herself actively analyzing the ingredients of an interaction that is potentially emotionally laden. The professional must not make too large a leap or it may be too hard to follow. The amazing thing about communication is that everyone unconsciously and continually goes through this internal process throughout each day, giving little thought to the internal process.

Application Process

It is actually not possible to apply the ingredients of an interaction. However, an awareness of these ingredients is helpful when overcoming barriers to working with families as well as gaining access to support groups, networking, and referring to counseling.

Miscommunication often occurs when the professional refers to the parents' need for additional assistance. Parents frequently mistake that comment as a judgment about their adequacy as a family or as individuals. Clearly they are uncomfortable when others perceive their needs and judge them to be inadequate. Knowing that they might interpret any recommendation as a judgment of inadequacy can help professionals prepare their communication so that it is more likely to be understood as intended.

Any recommendation should begin with statements about realities within the family, followed by comments about the positive effects of the intervention on other families or individuals. It is important to use a positive frame to present any recommendations; for example, "All of us could use external assistance at times of stress and transition. This is not a sign of inadequacy or even dysfunction, but a normal reaction to stress." Then the specific issues can be linked to the need for additional assistance. When the professional is aligned with the family, they are less likely to see the professional as having judged them as inadequate.

PSYCHOLOGICAL ISSUES

School professionals do not often have the luxury of working with parents who recognize that they may be contributing to their child's problems. That is usually the purview of mental health centers and child guidance clinics. What is often found in schools is that parents are unaware that they themselves have somehow played into their child's school difficulties. Losen and Losen (1985) recommended that no matter how experienced the team members are in family dynamics, "Parents may not be willing to accept even the hint of a suggestion during a team meeting that they are in any way responsible for their child's problems" (p. 113).

Such parents should not be confronted in team meetings (Losen & Losen, 1985). It is important to ensure parental cooperation before including them in team meetings during which decisions about their child will be made. Although infrequent, problems involving parents who are defensive or belligerent frequently stem from alcoholism, divorce, and psychiatric difficulties (Losen & Losen, 1985). This section covers these types of problems and suggests means of dealing with them.

Demanding Parents

Most legalistic and demanding parents have been through prior incidents that led them to mistrust authority. They may easily misread the school's efforts to provide procedural due process as trying to "pull a fast one on them." It may be helpful to allow a trusted friend or professional to be a go between with the school. At all times, it is important to keep the focus on the best interest of the student. Eventually, parents will hear the call to what is in their child's best interest. An outside evaluation, with an impartial evaluator, may help some parents feel better. If they consider such an option, any recommended evaluators should be independent and not vanguards of the system. A case example exemplifies why this approach would be valuable.

> The parents of a student with a chronic physical illness had a history of demanding special treatment for their son. Frequently, if their demands were not met, they would call the superintendent of schools and threaten a lawsuit. School personnel became so numb to parental complaints that they failed to take note when the boy continued to make poor grades through the fifth grade. It was only after independent evaluations were suggested and completed that the boy's severe learning disability in reading was discovered. In this case, parental symptomatic behavior had obscured the focus on the best interest of the student.

There are some rules of thumb (Losen & Losen, 1985) that will help school professionals when dealing with demanding and legalistic parents. As suggested earlier, parents should not be confronted during team meetings. If a conflict erupts unexpectedly during a team meeting, it is best to table any decisions until the conflict has been resolved. Any hostility or mistrust should be validated, and obviously strong feelings should not be denied or ignored. The team should discuss the parents concerns by talking about the origin of their concerns as well as their underlying fears.

The team should also let the parents know when they are on target with a fully intelligible and defensible point of view. A good comment is, "If I were in your place I would probably be feeling the same way," or "Although I do not see it the same way, I do understand your belief and thus the feelings you have about this situation."

When parents become flexible, the professional must be sure not to remain rigid in response. It is better to have a good beginning toward what is best for the student than a due process hearing that may make things worse.

Psychiatric Difficulties

Parents with emotional problems may be unsupportive and unresponsive, needy and seeking continual input and reassurance, or emotionally unstable and disruptive as well as irresponsible. Going into the situation of working with such parents may leave any school professional feeling in a "one down" position.

Regardless of the disruption, it is important that the professional reassure the parents of his or her commitment to their child with special needs. Clarifying and explaining rationale and procedures may be necessary. It is important to have the team work together prior to meetings with irrational parents. Parents can meet individually with the professional with whom they share the best rapport. Some parents would benefit from referral for family systems therapy; the social worker could make this recommendation while meeting with them. It is more likely that the parent will provide more meaningful and honest input with one open and supportive professional.

An alcoholic parent should not be called out to a private conference. Alcoholics' behavior may be unpredictable and they may be difficult people. If they insist on attending and are obviously under the influence of alcohol or other drugs, the meeting should be immediately terminated. However, professionals must be careful that the parents do not feel put down and should help them in any way possible to reclaim self-esteem. Following the meeting, sharing information with the nonalcoholic parent about local Alcoholics Anonymous or Al-Anon chapters might be helpful (see Appendix C).

Losen and Losen (1985) suggested many effective strategies for working with unstable parents. They recommended that the professional attempt to clarify the parents' understanding of their child's problem. Providing more reassurance than is usually needed is also helpful. A strong relationship should be established between one team member and the parents during individual conferences as a precursor to team meetings. Comments should be directed to the most stable or rational parent. Refraining from exchanging angry words is a must. Professionals should not refrain from calling upon external resources such as police, friends, or minister. Chapter 6 elaborates upon families with a dysfunctional parent and provides recommendations for school professionals about working with them.

Angry Parents

Margolis and Brannigan (1986) published a useful article titled "Relating to Angry Parents." That is part of a professional's job in the schools. Maintaining composure under direct attack and confrontation is not an easily developed skill. Even more difficult is empathizing with parental fears and frustrations. Sane, rational parents may become angry and let their anger show. It is very important to recognize that parents may have valid complaints or that a mistake may have been made. Working with the parents to vent feelings and share their understanding of the problem is most important. It is definitely not advisable to give in to aggressive parents when the option is not in the child's best interest.

There are, again, several rules of thumb on dealing with angry parents. Professionals should always make eye contact and be courteous. They should not try to interject their own opinions. Instead, they should listen to the parents. If the professional does not understand the underlying concern because of the level of anger being expressed, a clarification should be requested. The professional should listen actively, reflecting the parents' beliefs and feelings. Summarization of the parents' points may also be helpful. If any mention of their anger is disowned, the professional should steer clear of further comments and relate to the parents' beliefs. The point here is not trying to solve the situation; rather it is to build trust by demonstrating caring and concern.

The professional should try to distinguish the true issues from the pseudo concerns, asking questions that assist in this process. Any questions should be open ended, such as "How is it that this came about?" Questions that begin with "why" should be avoided because they may lead to defensiveness in the parents. Once everything is out in the open, the professional should summarize the points of agreement as well as disagreement. The professional should then determine if the parents have anything to add that would further clarify everyone's understanding.

All of these steps provide for exploration and understanding of the problem from the parent's point of view. The emphasis is on connecting and building trust. The next step is problem solving, which was covered in chapter 8.

LIMITATIONS

This section covers the limitations on using family systems concepts and approaches in schools. Many limitations stem from lack of training, current norms in the schools, and traditional school procedures.

Training

Traditional university training in general education and special education does not require a course in communication between home and school. Often the principal is the only professional required to take a course in "School and Community Relations," with parents being one of many topics covered. Realizing that universities generally require no separate course on working with families, one can see that the family systems approach is infrequently considered in teacher-training institutions.

Further, many counselor-education programs do not require a course on working with families; none requires a course in family systems. School social workers have always been trained to work with families. In fact, that is their major responsibility in most schools. However, not all schools of social work train students in family systems approaches. Few school psychologists have training in family systems, though that does appear to be changing as experts recognize that schools have students for only 9% of their lives.

Although special educators will obviously be required to interact with parents on an ongoing basis, they are not usually required to take a separate course in working with families. This is a vast subject, and family systems concepts may not be included in elective courses.

Thus, there is a very large deficit to overcome before people are able to prepare university professors or call upon schools of social work or psychology to teach content such as that found in this book. Preservice training is very limited, and the in-service needs of all of the professionals already working in schools compound the problem. As requirements for teacher recertification are relaxed, it is even less likely that teachers will take courses that would prepare them in family systems concepts.

University systems are slow to change program requirements. Although higher education has been in the process of restructuring, it is unlikely that, without pressure, institutions of higher education will spontaneously provide courses on family systems. Thus, it behooves those who recognize the value of family systems to assume responsibility for generating interest in such a course. Typically, they will be greeted with a response such as, "We already have an elective course on working with parents" or "We can incorporate that into another existing course." Neither response is appropriate. As can be seen from this text, family systems is a complex field and would need undivided study if one is to learn enough to use the attitudes imparted, information gained, and skills learned.

Other potential sources of encouragement for preservice family systems training would be legislative mandate or school system recommendation. Many states require, by legislative mandate, a separate course in special education. Other states require that it be covered within the education program, thus allowing colleges and universities to cover the field of special education for general educators within a portion of another existing course. Informed superintendents might advise schools of education to provide preservice course work in family systems. Most institutions of higher education respond to input from superintendents.

In-service training is another matter. Although changing dramatically in recent years, staff development activities seldom focus upon family systems training for school professionals. The Commonwealth of Virginia did develop a training module on family systems (Lambie, 1987). This module was used by teams of trainers that Lambie helped train. Teams of three or four from different school divisions were trained using a multiplier model in a statewide trainer-of-trainers program. The school professionals deeply appreciated the content from both a personal and a professional perspective. A trainer-of-trainers model and the use of a team to provide training are highly recommended. It is helpful if one member of the team is knowledgeable about the content and can field questions. The school social worker would be an excellent professional for that perspective.

So far this section has dealt with training of professionals. Another training limitation is the lack of programs that actually respond to training needs of parents of at-risk and special needs students. Few schools provide more than written literature concerning the child study or eligibility process. Parents need more than that. At the very least, parents should be coached in effective communication skills. After all, more effective communicators are also more effective team members.

Norms

A major school norm is not getting too involved with family matters. With the exception of Project Head Start, schools have generally considered family matters to be the responsibility of agencies external to the schools. Referral to mental health centers is not a common approach taken by school professionals. Due to concern about the cost of related services to the school system, school professionals are even less likely to suggest services for students with special needs.

Another norm in schools and elsewhere is to consider the symptom bearer to be the unit of intervention. With students with special needs this norm should shift to viewing the whole family as the unit of intervention. This norm would likely shift as training in family systems concepts begins to make an impression on school professionals.

Shifts in norms are slow and would most likely follow training. It seems that a grass-roots or top-down authoritative pronouncement would be the only ways in which a shift in norms could initially be generated in the school system. Since a grass roots approach is unlikely, someone in the school system would presumably have to assume responsibility for generating interest in family systems. School professionals would need to be given permission not only to know about the family systems concepts but also to use what they have learned without feeling they have crossed a professional boundary. The notion of role release described in chapter 8 is important to this possibility becoming a reality.

School Procedures

Many school procedures make it difficult to benefit from knowledge about family systems. Social workers who are familiar with family systems concepts may have such a large case load that they do not have the time to help other school professionals learn about family systems approaches. With budgetary problems and shrinking dollars, it is even less likely that school procedures will change in the near future.

The current emphasis on elementary school counselors in each school building is a hopeful sign that use of family systems approaches could increase and develop. It augurs well for investment of energies and money in family systems concepts. However, school counselors may be unfamiliar with family systems concepts or may not have the time to implement knowledge and skills learned about family systems. Many elementary school counselors work with children rather than families. School counselors often work quickly with a group of children for a short period and then move on to another group so that more may be served.

Secondary school counselors are almost always in charge of scheduling and have little if any time for counseling students, let alone families. Secondary schools are oriented toward noninterference with families. Students are viewed as old enough to be responsible for themselves and accept natural consequences of behavior. Trying to elicit family support is often seen by professionals and families as enabling students to remain immature and dependent.

These procedures inhibit effective implementation of family systems concepts. A second concern is that teams do not necessarily function in a way that would allow collaboration with family systems. The team may not meet regularly and may communicate via written report; they may have only enough time for the barest of information sharing during team meetings. Once a student is determined to be eligible for special education, the collaboration of team members often decelerates. The teachers are often on their own until the IEP is redone a year later.

REALITY CONSTRAINTS

There are certainly more than the three reality constraints of time, money, and availability of trained personnel. However, these are the ones seen most frequently.

Time

The constraint of not enough time is a concern of all school professionals. However, once the staff has been trained and is competent in implementing family systems concepts, they will save time. One way time is saved over the long term is simply that less time is expended mired in an individual perspective that could be more easily resolved with a family systems perspective.

Money

Not enough money may be another reality constraint. Finding money for staff development and release of personnel to attend training sessions is a real concern. With shrinking dollars, staff development funds may be among the first to be decreased. Again, however, full implementation over the long term may save dollars. Consider the example of students with emotional and behavioral disorders. If the whole family were seen as the unit of treatment, these students would be far fewer in number and would remain in classes for the seriously emotionally disturbed for less time. It is also likely that fewer due process hearings, which are very expensive, would be needed.

Training

The lack of trained personnel is another reality constraint. As mentioned above, changes in the institutions of higher education are slow to develop. With the emphasis on restructuring in the past several years, little energy is left for new endeavors and changing programs of study. Arends (1990) pointed to the slowness of universities to respond to criticism. He also suggested that, "Teacher preparation of the future could be under the auspices of inspired and well-funded district-based human resource development units or state-based special academies for teachers" (p. 141).

Thus, expenditure of initial funds for staff development in school systems would be invaluable. Again a trainer-of-trainers model that allows more people to be reached with fewer funds is useful. Information on a three-year multiplier model of inservice education in mainstreaming is available in a final report on a federal grant (Lambie, 1983). Further, schools of social work and psychology at universities and colleges are excellent resources for those who might design modules as well as train trainers. Virginia has a module on family systems written for a trainer-of-trainers model of inservice training (Lambie, 1987). Lambie and Scearce (1982) have written about the multiplier model, as instituted in two school systems in Virginia. Lambie (1986) has also written about potential pitfalls during training.

ATTITUDES, RESISTANCE, AND CHANGE

Attitudes are an interesting phenomenon. They are defined as strong beliefs or feelings toward people and situations. Attitudes, both favorable and unfavorable, are acquired throughout our lives, and as Martin, a professional in the field of substance abuse/addiction, said on a videotape, "Attitudes have us, we don't have them...and they will change about an hour after we die." A sobering thought indeed. Attitudes involve a "for" or "against" quality that makes them obviously an attitude as opposed to an opinion. A poster often seen in schools, "Attitudes are contagious—are yours worth catching?" is a great way to think about attitudes. It becomes obvious that those with a positive attitude toward change will bring about positive results.

M. Scott Peck (1978), the author of *The Road Less Traveled* and other wonderful books, has an excellent quote that fits here.

> It is only through a vast amount of experience and a lengthy and successful maturation that we gain the capacity to see the world and our place in it realistically, and thus are enabled to realistically assess our responsibility for ourselves and the world. (p. 37)

Several negative attitudes impact on the family systems concept being incorporated into the school system. Resistance to change also affects implementation of change processes and must be understood to make way for effective change. A model for change is helpful in understanding, expecting, and validating concerns of employees about the change process. This will be our focus in dealing with negative attitudes as well as resistance to change.

Negative Attitudes

The most prevalent attitude that would make it difficult to employ family systems concepts is: "It is someone else's responsibility to work with those families. I do not have enough time. What do they expect from us anyway? It is not in our job description. Our local education association or federation will support us on that."

Another negative attitude toward such changes stems from fear of failure and the repercussions such failure might bring. Teachers and principals, in particular, might be concerned about employing strategies usually reserved for counselors, social workers, and psychologists. A natural concern relates to how their using the strategies might result in a setback, as opposed to growth and development of the family. Without extensive training and well-understood boundaries regarding who employs these strategies, these fears would be well-grounded. Obviously, this is a fear for which it behooves anyone implementing such change to address adequately.

Negative contagion, a third negative attitude problem, may occur in some school buildings. In these cases the teachers have bonded together to keep out anything new and different. They denounce new endeavors as "old wine in new bottles." Together they form a prodigious force that is hard to convert.

Resistance

People resist change for a variety of reasons. Some feel inadequate, others feel their security is threatened, still others may not trust those in charge of the change process, and then there are people who do not see the larger picture (Reece & Brandt, 1987). We will briefly elaborate upon each of these reasons.

Feelings of Inadequacy

When people learn new skills they accept additional responsibility, which may stretch their abilities and make them feel a lack of self-confidence. For example, using computers is a fairly recent development in schools. Most school professionals feel uncomfortable with computers until they finally crack the code and become computer literate. It is very important to support professionals who are learning new skills. All should feel that they can and will make mistakes as they learn. Permission to learn from mistakes is important; sharing stories with others and exchanging ideas for problem solving can be very helpful. Those who are newly implementing family systems concepts and strategies will quickly learn that they are not the only ones who lack confidence and feel inadequate. Groups are great for mirroring and learning more about oneself.

Issues of Security

As Maslow (1970) made clear, personal security, both physical and psychological, is one of everyone's basic needs. When the expectations for school professionals change and they must make major changes in their work, some may worry that if they are unable to keep abreast of the changes they may be phased out or seen as less worthy. It is therefore important to make certain that school professionals know the onus is on those in charge to adequately prepare them for implementing family systems strategies. Any lack of understanding or failure of implementation should be met with a careful check on the preparation of the employee and the necessary coaching provided to reach an appropriate mastery level.

Issues of Trust

Lack of trust is another reason people resist change. In this case mistrust is aimed at those responsible for directing and implementing change. There may be large differences among schools within one system, depending upon how much the principal is trusted. When school professionals are only let in on upcoming changes after all of the decisions and planning are complete, they are less likely to trust and therefore may resist even the most appealing change. It behooves the change makers to include all levels and variety of school professionals as representatives whose opinions are heard. Further, those chosen as representatives should be professionals who are trusted by their peers. Anyone perceived as a company person will not engender automatic trust.

Narrow Focus

Many school professionals will be unable to see the larger picture and understand that the learning will pay off in the long run, both in terms of time and money. They may not see the most important benefit, which is that the needs of at-risk and special needs students will be met in a more satisfactory manner. If school professionals are to lower their level of resistance, it is imperative to explain the overall picture and reasons for the change that includes family systems concepts and strategies.

Change

The process of making lasting and meaningful change is complex and challenging. The literature on change (Baldridge & Deal, 1983; Corbett, Firestone, & Rossman, 1987; Fullan, 1982; Guskey, 1986; Hall & Hord, 1987; Huberman & Miles, 1984; Sarason, 1982; Showers, Joyce, & Bennett, 1987) is replete with advice about initiating change within educational institutions. This section presents information regarding the Concerns-Based Adoption Model (CBAM) because of its attention to the concerns of school professionals, thus affecting attitude toward change.

Aspects of Change

As can be seen from the different stages in the Concerns-Based Adoption Model (CBAM), this change model has to do with personal aspects of change. Change is seen as a process and not an event (Hall & Hord, 1987). Further, it is critical to understand the point of view of participants who are involved in the change process.

The CBAM model has three dimensions: stages of concern, levels of use, and innovation configurations. This discussion covers only the stages of concern. Hall and Hord (1987) includes more complete information on CBAM.

Stages of Concern

Hall, Wallace, and Dossett (1973) and later Hall and Hord (1987) have conceptualized stages of concern about educational innovation. They delineated seven levels of concern about change that relate to how professionals perceive innovations and how they feel about an innovation.

The lowest stage of concern, *Awareness*, to which the developers (Hall et al., 1973) of this model attribute a zero, involves little concern about or interest in the innovation. This is the level of concern one has toward anything about which he or she knows little to nothing.

The next stage of concern, *Informational*, pertains to a general awareness of the innovation. The professional will have an interest in learning more about the innovation or change. At this stage professionals are not concerned about how the change will affect them. They are generally concerned about aspects of the innovation such as characteristics, requirements for use, and effects of the change. A level of 1 is assigned to the informational stage of concern.

Personal concern, assigned a level of 2, occurs when the professional is uncertain about the professional demands of the innovation as well as personal adequacy in meeting demands. The professional might analyze his or her role in relation to rewards in the organization as well as decision-making processes and find these to be of personal concern at this time. Potential conflicts with current commitments could also be of concern. Financial and status implications are another potential personal concern.

At the next level of concern, *Management*, assigned a value of 3, professionals focus their attention upon the processes and tasks of using the innovation as well as the best use of information and resources. Of prime concern are issues that relate to organizing, managing, and scheduling the innovation, as well as efficiency and time considerations.

A value of 4 is assigned to the stage referred to as *Consequence*. In this stage, professionals focus their concerns on the impact of the innovation on their particular students. Relevance to the lives of their students as well as outcomes and changes needed to increase outcomes of students are of concern.

The *Collaboration* stage, with a value of 5, has to do with concerns about coordinating with others. Professionals will want to know about cooperating with peers in using the innovation.

The final stage, *Refocusing*, is concerned with how the innovation might benefit others. Some professionals might be concerned about replacement alternatives. It is certain that professionals will have definite ideas and opinions about proposed or existing forms of the innovation.

Following the logic of this model, "it is possible to anticipate much that will occur during a change process" (Hall et al., 1973, pp. 8-9). A basic premise of the model is that everyone can be a change facilitator.

Implications

Note the word *facilitator*. This is a key concept because anyone might expedite the change process and facilitate, rather than manipulate, change. The facilitator would know about individual concerns and respond to those so that others would be more effective in applying innovations.

Understanding the CBAM model would help the professional in any change effort he or she might initiate; the effort to use family systems concepts/approaches with at-risk and special needs students would have a better chance for survival. Before a professional attempts to introduce an innovation in the schools, it is critical to become more aware of the aspects of change.

SUMMARY

We believe in possibilities. We know that challenges can be met, and barriers can be broken. We wish you the best in your endeavors to implement change and apply family systems concepts in your schools. We are available to help you find family systems professionals within your state who could provide consultation or training in this field. Family systems approaches can make a significant contribution to your at-risk and special needs students and, further, all of your students would benefit from such growth and development by the professional staff.

PART III

FAMILY SYSTEMS CASE STUDY

T his case study is intended to consolidate the reader's understanding of the principles discussed in this book. This example illustrates how family of origin issues (chapter 4) can affect a nuclear family many generations in the future. The concepts of family structure (chapter 3) and the family life cycle (chapter 2) are clear in this family's issues, dealing with lack of parental cohesion and the relocation of the family. The effects of socioeconomic and cultural concerns (chapter 5) upon the type of intervention planned for this family are also portrayed. The contribution of the mother's depression (chapter 6) and the family's rigidity (chapter 7) to this boy's symptoms are examined as well. Finally, the case illustrates the role of the school professional in networking and family referral (chapter 11) as well as collaboration with the family and outside professionals.

SCHOOL INTERVENTIONS

This case involves a 13-year-old boy, Mike, who was referred for therapy by his school counselor. The presenting problem was Mike's refusal to go to school; it had lasted six months. Before referring Mike for outpatient psychotherapy, school professionals had attempted the following interventions:

1. Phone contacts to the mother, Mrs. Wright, from Mike's teachers and school principal, asking about his health and offering assistance.
2. Letters to the family from the school principal and county superintendent of schools, requesting that the parents contact school officials about their son's repeated absences.
3. Referral to a child study team who had enlisted Mike, after three months of absence, in homebound instruction. The referral for psychotherapy was made after six month's absence, requesting the therapist's opinion about whether or not homebound instruction should be continued.
4. Referral to a probation officer for school truancy.

This intervention resulted in a home visit by the probation officer and threats of a jail term for the mother if Mike did not begin attending school. However, there had been no follow through on these threats.

HISTORICAL INFORMATION

The outpatient therapist initially met with Mrs. Wright to gather information about Mike's problem. Although the appointment had been scheduled for both parents, Mrs. Wright stated that her husband refused to attend therapy. The therapist then made contact with Mike's school counselor and his probation officer. After these three conversations, the therapist had the following information about Mike and his family:

Mike was the youngest of three sons of Mr. and Mrs. Wright. His parents had been high-school sweethearts and had married immediately following their graduation from high school. They had been married for 22 years and lived in the same home in a small town in rural Georgia for that time. Both sets of grandparents also lived in this town and maintained close ties with Mike's nuclear family. The family genogram is depicted in Figure 14.1.

Mr. Wright was the older of two boys; Mrs. Wright was the youngest of three girls. She was extremely close to her family, the Thomases. She reported having at least one telephone conversation with each sister and her mother every day since her marriage. The Thomas family attended the same church as the Wrights and shared in socializing and entertainment. In addition, when the boys were growing up, Mrs. Wright shared babysitting with her sisters and mother. As she was the only sister who was not employed outside of the home, Mrs. Wright kept her sister's children during the week and allowed her children to spend time with her parents and sisters on the weekends. Mrs. Wright described her father as a "stable, devoted" man who supported the family and "spoiled" her. He owned a store in the community and was well respected.

Mr. Wright's family was involved with Mike's family through more "male" activities. The uncle and Mr. Wright took the boys fishing or hunting and attended sporting events together. Mr. Wright was close to his mother, who had worked two jobs all her life to support him and his brothers. Mr. Wright had served the function of "man of the house" since his father, who was an alcoholic, disappeared when Mr. Wright was six years old and left the family penniless. Mr. Wright had worked after school and become a manager in a local grocery store. If he had not met his wife and decided to get married, he had planned to go to college on a business scholarship provided by the store. As it was, he was a married man and a father within a year of graduation. He had stayed with the grocery store for 22 years and remained a manager.

According to Mrs. Wright, she had never learned to drive because she had always depended upon her husband or family for transportation. She had never worked outside of the home, although her sisters had paid her for babysitting their children while they were working. In addition, her father gave her money whenever she asked. Mrs. Wright used her creative energies to sew, cook, garden, and make crafts. She stated that she had always kept busy with these activities because her husband had worked sixty to seventy hours a week for most of their married life.

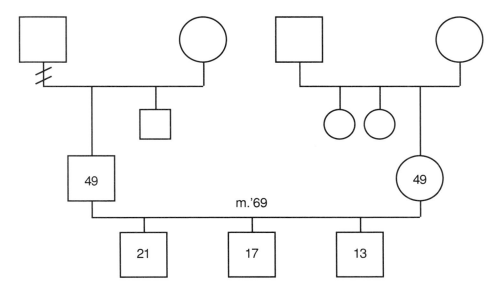

Figure 14.1
GENOGRAM FOR WRIGHT FAMILY

HISTORY OF PRESENTING PROBLEM

By 1988 Mike's father had saved enough money to buy his own store. This had been a dream of his for a long time. When he finally had enough money in savings, he began a search for a good investment opportunity. Although he looked, there were no such opportunities available in the small town in which he and his family lived. After a year of searching, he found a gas station for sale in the suburbs of Atlanta, about eighty miles from his hometown. Against his wife's wishes, he bought the business six months later. In May, he and his oldest son left for Atlanta to work in the gas station. May through August of that year, Mr. Wright and the eldest son lived in an apartment in Atlanta, while Mrs. Wright and the 17- and 13-year-old sons remained in their home.

The business took almost all of Mr. Wright's time, and he was unable to travel home during these four months. Mrs. Wright and one of her sisters came to Atlanta for a weekend and Mrs. Wright decided that she "hated the city." However, when she confided in her mother and sisters that she missed her husband, they urged her to move to Atlanta and support his decision. In September, the eldest son moved back into the family home and began attending a local junior college, the 17-year-old son moved in with his maternal grandparents so that he could complete his senior year of high school in the same school, and Mrs. Wright and Mike moved to Atlanta.

Mike was enrolled in the eighth grade in a large suburban high school. His mother took him to school on the first day to make sure that he arrived safely. He attended that one day of school and refused to return to the high school for the next six months. At first, Mike had complained of being ill. His aunt came to Atlanta to get him and took him back to their hometown to see the family doctor. He was pronounced healthy and urged to return to school.

After a month's absence, Mike's father began urging him to return to school. According to the mother, he threatened Mike with grounding, removal of allowance, and finally physical punishment. Mrs. Wright, who described her husband as "hot tempered," forbid her husband to spank Mike. In addition, although he was grounded by his father, it was Mrs. Wright who was left to enforce the grounding while her husband worked in the store. Because Mrs. Wright felt sorry for Mike, she was never able to stick to her guns about grounding him.

When Mr. Wright discovered that Mike and his mother had been returning to their hometown on weekends and Mike was allowed to spend time with his friends, he became angry and confronted his wife. She accused him of being gone all the time and being unwilling to give her emotional support. She stated that she was not able to deny Mike time with his friends because she thought he was refusing to go to school because he was depressed about moving. She hoped that, if he spent time enjoying himself, he would become less depressed and more accepting of the move. In her eyes, he would then return to school voluntarily.

Mr. Wright, who felt that Mike's refusal to attend school was rebellious in nature, then withdrew even more from the family. According to his wife, he had become angry and sullen when he was home and often drank too many beers. He began working longer and longer hours; the mother and Mike spent more and more time together watching soap operas and playing cards. Neither one of them had made friends in their new neighborhood, and neither one of them were able to drive. Mrs. Wright and Mike continued to return to their hometown every weekend, without Mr. Wright.

DIAGNOSIS

Mrs. Wright, who was very dependent and lonely, was overinvolved with Mike. She depended upon him for her daily entertainment and company. Mike's symptom served the function of keeping her busy and helping her avoid confronting her own loneliness and the distance in her marriage. Mrs. Wright and Mike were aligned in the sibling subsystem in a coalition against the father. Mr. Wright, the functioning parent, was undermined by this alliance. He became ineffective and withdrew from interaction with both his wife and Mike. In addition, Mrs. Wright's family of origin was involved in undermining Mr. Wright by continuing to provide transportation and money to her and Mike.

INTERVENTION

The therapist asked Mrs. Wright's permission to contact her husband at work and request his presence at a meeting concerning his son. Contrary to his wife's characterization of him, Mr. Wright was more than willing to attend the meeting. He talked to the therapist at length about his frustration regarding his son and said that he would be willing to do anything that would solve the problem. The therapist then scheduled a meeting, at the high school, to include the child study team, the homebound teacher, the parents, the probation officer, and Mike.

During the first part of the meeting, Mike was asked to wait outside. The therapist made this request purposefully to indicate to Mike that he was not part of the executive subsystem and that the adults would make the decision as to how to proceed with his problem. In addition, excluding him from this part of the meeting broke up the alliance between Mike and his mother.

The meeting began with ventilation of feelings of frustration on the part of the parents, teachers, and probation officer. The therapist then asked questions about Mike's intelligence and physical and emotional development. As the meeting progressed, it became clear to everyone that Mike was capable of attending high school. However, the homebound instructor said that Mike was not motivated and that, even with the one-to-one attention, he was not keeping up with his school assignments. The therapist began to reframe Mike's problem as a developmental lag. The therapist used evidence that had been presented by those present to convince the parents that Mike needed to be given nurturing, support, and structure to begin to grow up and face the challenges of being a high school student. The explanation was centered on Mike's need, like younger children, for structure and help in becoming motivated to complete homework, chores, and other skills of growing up.

With this reframe in mind, the therapist advised that Mike had not been receiving enough structure and reinforcement. The parents were asked if they would be willing to work together to provide for these needs. In step one of the intervention, the mother was assigned as Mike's homebound instructor. She agreed to structure a mock classroom for teaching Mike about attending school and growing up. For six hours per day, she was to instruct Mike in his various high-school subjects. The probation officer agreed that, if the mother were tutoring her son, threats and charges against her regarding the truancy would stop. Mike's teachers agreed to provide weekly lesson plans for her to follow, and the homebound tutor agreed to come to her home once a week to help her plan assignments and clarify any information about which she was unclear. In addition, teachers offered to be available by telephone if Mrs. Wright had any questions about assignments. The purpose of this intervention was to intensify Mike's and his mother's dependency upon one another so that they would, eventually, become unhappy with this arrangement.

Step two was to elicit the father's help. He agreed to be in charge of waking Mike up each morning and helping him get showered, dressed, and fed in preparation for his day at "school." Because the father needed to be at his store by 7:00 each morning, Mike's school day was scheduled to begin by 7:30 and end at 2:30, with an hour break for lunch. This intervention was designed to decrease the distance between Mike and his father and to give Mrs. Wright the message that she was supported by her husband.

Step three was to define Mike's visit to his hometown each weekend as "confusing" to a child with his "delayed developmental level." If he was to be helped to adapt to his new home and to the structure of school, he needed to have the stability that living in one place provided. In this regard, the mother agreed that they would only visit their hometown every other weekend and then only for the day. Mike, because of his "delays," needed to sleep in the same house consistently. Mr. Wright agreed to take Sundays off and spend time with his wife and Mike. He also agreed to begin exploring options for a local church with his family.

This intervention served many purposes. First, Mike was identified as "delayed" and the only way to convince the adults otherwise was to return to school. As long as he was "delayed," he was "incapable" of spending every weekend in his hometown. Thus, he was, essentially, put on the same grounding schedule that his father had threatened, but ostensibly for very different reasons. It was hypothesized that, if Mrs. Wright and Mike were no longer able to get their social needs met on weekends in the hometown, they might begin to search for connections with other people in Atlanta. Finally, Mr. Wright agreed to become more involved with and supportive of his wife so that her loneliness would decrease and her need for Mike as her support system would diminish.

As the final step in the intervention, Mike was asked to join the meeting. His position as the baby of his family was emphasized, and he was told the reframe that his school refusal indicated his "delay in growing up." His parents then advised him of the plan that had been designed by the adults and pledged their mutual support of his efforts to "catch up" in development. Clearly, Mike was less than happy about these proceedings.

OUTCOME

After two weeks of school at home, Mike returned to high school. His mother offered to attend his first day with him, but he declined, saying that would be "babyish." His teachers introduced him as a new student who had recently moved to Atlanta so that he did not have to face the stigma of being absent for so long. In addition, Mike received supportive services from his school counselor to help him cope with joining this new social arena. With coaxing, he tried out for baseball in the spring and made the team.

Mike and his parents continued in periodic family therapy. With help, Mr. and Mrs. Wright were able to set up a reinforcement schedule for Mike in which he could earn visits to his hometown or trips to movies, sports events, and other events in Atlanta by his behavior during the week. Any absence from school, unless accompanied by high fever or vomiting, resulted in no privileges for the weekend. At first, Mike almost exclusively chose visits back "home" as his reinforcement. As time went by and he began to develop friends on his baseball team and at school, his request for visits became less frequent.

Through therapy, Mrs. Wright was helped to look at her own loneliness and isolation. She obtained a bus schedule and, with support, began shopping and sightseeing in Atlanta by herself. She asked one of her sisters to begin teaching her how to drive and got a promise from her husband that, as soon as she got her license, they would buy her a car. She began helping her husband in the store on a part-time basis. Eventually, she was able to use her skills at crafts to help him make buying and display decisions for the store. Mr. Wright continued to take Sundays off and spend them with his wife, even when Mike no longer needed the support.

This case study represents successful collaboration between the school professionals, an outpatient psychotherapist, a probation officer, and parents. Without this collaboration, the interventions would not have been possible.

APPENDICES

THEORETICAL UNDERPINNINGS OF FAMILY SYSTEMS APPROACHES A

This appendix initially describes the Satir Communication Process theory. That information is followed by a delineation of three family systems theories: the Bowen theory, structural family therapy, and strategic family therapy. The concepts presented can assist you in understanding families. The explanation of each approach includes a brief historical account of the development of the theory, as well as specific theoretical concepts and principles from each perspective. This information can enrich your understanding of family systems concepts.

SATIR'S PROCESS MODEL

This section provides an overview of the Satir Process Model. A brief historical account of its development is followed by a description of Satir's philosophical view of humanity, systems orientation, and homeostasis. Six critical concepts form the next section. Satir's model contrasts with the theoretical concepts of Murray Bowen's approach. Satir did not spend time propounding theory. Her approach was more conceptually and methodologically based than theoretically grounded.

Historical Information

Virginia Satir, like Murray Bowen, was one of the earliest pioneers in the field of family systems. She popularized the family therapy movement with her engaging presence as well as exciting and practical methods.

Satir was a teacher from 1936 to 1941. She became interested in families while teaching children and making home visits. She later received a master's degree in social work from the University of Chicago. From 1955 to 1958 she was an instructor in the Family Dynamics Residency Program at the Illinois State Psychiatric Institute in Chicago. In 1959 Satir moved to California and joined the staff at the Mental Research Institute in Palo Alto. She developed a formal training program in family systems therapy while there. She left Palo Alto to join the staff at Esalen Institute, Big Sur, California. She was director of residential training at the Esalen Institute from 1963 to 1965.

In 1964 Satir published the first of many books, *Conjoint Family Therapy*, which is currently in its third edition (1983b). In 1972 she published *Peoplemaking*, which was intended for the general public and written at a fifth-grade level so children could also benefit from the book. Satir continued to write a variety of professional and popular books, updating her concepts and methodology. *Peoplemaking* came out again in 1988 as *The New Peoplemaking*, a greatly expanded version of the popular book.

Satir founded the AVANTA Network, devoted to promoting her process model throughout the world, and the network continues her work today. Satir held month-long training seminars for professionals in the summers from 1981 through 1987 in Crested Butte, Colorado. The AVANTA Network continues to offer that training; it is one of many different training opportunities in the Process/Communication Model. Satir presented a variety of other training seminars and speaking engagements around the world until she became ill in the summer of 1988. Virginia Satir died in October 1988. The January/February 1989 issue of the *Networker*, a professional journal devoted to family systems approaches, contained a tribute to Satir entitled "The Legacy of Virginia Satir." It is excellent reading for those who would like more of a flavor of her life and being.

Satir received many awards for her work, including a notable one from Germany. In 1982 Germany selected ten living people to receive awards for making a positive difference in the world. Satir was one of the ten people selected. She had a positive impact on people and is remembered for her charisma, emphasis on positive intentions, solution-oriented focus on the present and future, accent on equality, and action orientation.

Background Information

Satir was assured of and convincing about the potential for goodness and wholeness of people and the world. She believed in human potential and the individual's ability to transform his or her own life.

A description of Satir's "ways of viewing the world" is helpful as a basis for understanding her work. According to Satir, there are two ways of viewing the world. One, which is hierarchical in nature, is known as the threat and reward model and is familiar to Americans. The other she referred to by several different terms, including "organic and seed" model. These ways of viewing the world were described by Satir and Baldwin (1983) in the book *Satir Step by Step*.

The threat and reward model regards people as inherently bad and weak by nature. Thus, a hierarchy is necessary to determine and maintain standards of behavior. People at the top of the hierarchy believe that they are acting for the good of all. They use rewards and punishments to enforce the standards. From this practice evolves dominance and submission. People are viewed in terms of their degree of conformity to the standards. Those at the top of the hierarchy do not take kindly to difference. In turn, they do not see themselves as individuals. Instead they get their identity from prescribed roles. For those at the lower end of the hierarchy, the consequences of these ways of defining people and their relationships include stagnation, fear, despair, hopelessness, and rebellion. Those at the top may appear happier with their jobs.

In the threat and reward model, events are seen as linear. Any lack of conformity is interpreted as the hierarchy failing to maintain conformity. This cause-and-effect view of the world results in blame and fault finding. Change is not welcome because it is a threat to the status quo.

One can only imagine how this model would impact upon family functioning. Parents would be dictatorial and accept little input from the children. Family members would frequently blame others; there would be little acceptance of responsibility for personal behavior. Threats would be common, and rules would be enforced with punishments. The parents would set the standards for behavior and hold to those standards even when they no longer fit the situation. For example, a boy might be told men do not cry. Even when the situation would legitimately warrant crying, the parents would reaffirm that inappropriate standard for behavior.

Most school professionals have seen children who come from families that operate with this model. The children may find it confusing when rules and standards are not carved in stone and punishments are few and far between. It then becomes the task of the school professionals to work with expectations and disciplinary procedures that are not consistent between the home and school.

There are also some schools that function from a threat and reward model and professionals within schools who operate from such a position. Satir and Baldwin (1983) provide an example: "The student must follow directions and look at his teacher to prove that he is paying attention, regardless of whether he actually concentrates better by attending in a different way" (p. 162). The schools can expect resentment and hostility under these circumstances.

The seed model contrasts with the threat and reward model. People are seen as having an innate potential for goodness and wholeness. That which is unique within people is cause for celebration and support. People are defined in terms of their uniqueness and encouraged to know and value themselves. Relationships are based on mutual appreciation of the uniqueness of self and others and are egalitarian in nature. Change is a by-product of this way of being in the world. A growth orientation is the outcome.

The seed model is a systemic paradigm, with relationships between all components. Events are viewed as a result of many variables rather than being linear, like the threat and reward model. Events within people's lives are understood as a result of complex, interrelated variables in contrast to a cause-and-effect interpretation or in terms of blame.

School professionals will find children whose families ascribe to the seed view of the world to be vastly different from those who grow up in the threat and reward model. Interestingly, a school system may operate from a threat and reward model and have students who grew up with a seed model family life. Confusion will arise with students who face dramatically different sets of expectations in the two different contexts.

In reality, the stark contrast between these two models may not be so obvious. There are more shades of gray than there are actual extreme opposites. It is possible, however, to determine whether a person, family, or school ascribes to a threat and reward model or seed model.

By observing the model from which the pupil comes and understanding the two models, the professional becomes better able to work with families and pupils in the school. Rather than blaming the child for not complying, the professional can step back and recognize that the family's view has shaped the pupil's behavior. In ways that are constructive, professionals can work together to help the student be successfully educated within a system that may be quite different than the home in which the pupil is raised.

In addition to knowledge about the two views of humanity, it is also helpful to understand Satir's perspective on systems. Satir and Baldwin (1983) stated that in a family, "Every part is related to the other parts in a way such that a change in one brings about a change in all the others. Indeed, in the family, everyone and everything impacts and is impacted by every other person, event, and thing" (p. 191).

They further described two types of systems, *open* and *closed*. Closed systems operate on the rigid application of rules regardless of their appropriateness. The closed system is described as "dominated by power, obedience, deprivation, conformity, and guilt. It cannot allow any changes, for changes will upset the balance" (Satir & Baldwin, 1973, p. 192). The family members are ruled by fear, punishment, guilt, and dominance. Self-worth is quite low in these families. Symptoms develop when someone from such a system has come to the end of his or her coping abilities.

An open system is just that, open to change with changing contexts. These systems accept all expression and feelings, including hope, love, anger, frustration, sadness, joy, and compassion. As you would expect, members from such systems have higher levels of self-worth.

Satir also ascribed to the systems perspective of *homeostasis*. Homeostasis involves the innate tendency to establish a dynamic balance amidst changing conditions and relationships. Within families one will find complementary behavior of the family members and predictable patterns of communication. Family members operate to maintain the survival of the family and achieve balance within the family system. Satir believed that families attempt to preserve homeostasis by finding different means of adapting and adjusting to change. In particular, they establish rules for behavior as well as communication styles. From the efforts to preserve homeostasis stem behaviors that, rather than restoring homeostasis in times of transition, may actually result in symptoms. A frequent example of a symptom given by Satir was delinquency on the part of a youth. She saw such symptoms as indicating imbalance in the family system.

Finally, Satir continually emphasized *process* versus *content* of human interactions. The way in which family members dealt with a problem rather than the content of the problem was her focus for intervention. She was famous for saying, "The problem is not the problem; the problem is the process." She also contended that once a new process for resolving one situation was learned, then other situations could be resolved with the newly learned process.

Conceptual Understandings

Satir's two models of the world provide a background from which her family systems concepts can be appreciated. As stated earlier, Satir was pragmatically oriented rather than theoretically governed. This section provides a framework that allows the professional to better understand family systems and thus profit from information contained in the remainder of this textbook.

Six of Satir's concepts will be briefly described. These are: triangles and the development of self-identity and personhood, the aspects of the self, learning and change, self-worth, rules, and four communication patterns used as coping mechanisms.

Triangles and the Development of Self-Identify and Personhood

Most children have parents who provide the basics for human survival. Those parents also provide the initial schooling about the world. The senses allow the child to perceive the world. Anything not understood is fabricated. Thus, memories from the early childhood years are a combination of truth and fabrication. The child unwittingly misinterprets information while trying to make sense of what occurs in the family. The more dysfunctional the family, the more this operates. Frequently this misinterpretation follows the child in later life and affects coping abilities.

Thus, the family has the initial impact upon coping with difficulties later in life. Satir saw the:

> experience of the primary triad (father, mother, and child) as the essential source of identity of the "self." On the basis of his learning experience in the primary triad, the child determines how he fits into the world and how much trust he can put in his relationships with other people. (Satir & Baldwin, 1983, p. 170)

The patterns of responding to stress used later in life develop when the child is very young, according to Satir.

The child also learns about contradictions in communication or inconsistencies between what is seen and what is said, or between what he or she feels and hears. An example of such an incongruent message would be a little boy noticing that his mother looked angry and wondering what was wrong. The nonverbal aspects of the communication affect the child, who attends to voice tone, touch, and looks. The mother, whose parents had taught her that family members must never be angry, would respond by denying feeling angry and indicate that everything was fine. The child then has to decipher that discrepancy. Further, the child probably will consider himself to be a possible cause of the anger. Such mixed messages damage the child.

In the mother-father-child triad, it is usual for one individual to feel excluded at times. If the child interprets communications between the parents as being a rejection, the child will develop a low sense of self-worth. The child learns about being included and excluded from the primary triad. These experiences help shape the personality of the child.

Also developing from the primary triad is the child's sense of personal power. There are many possible points children can learn about personal power. They might learn that they have the power to generate negative feelings between the parents. Another possibility is learning that the child has no power. A third is that the child can have a positive impact on the parents.

As was typical of Satir, she saw the possibilities of the triad as being supportive, powerful, and resourceful. She emphasized that functional families with high levels of self-worth are cooperative and suggested cooperation as a possible goal for all interested in transformation.

The Aspects of the Self

Satir utilized the concept of the mandala to illustrate the eight aspects of the self. The mandala is a symbol with concentric circles that represent parts of the whole that, when taken together, create more than the sum of the parts. This holistic view of the individual stems from the Eastern concept of the mandala.

Figure A.1 depicts Satir's conceptualization of the eight aspects: physical, intellectual, emotional, sensual, interactional, nutritional, contextual, and spiritual. The eight aspects interact with one another and influence the individual's health. At the center of the mandala is the core of the human being that Satir referred to as the "I Am." Together the eight aspects of the self create a system.

Learning and Change

Becoming more fully human was Satir's theme. She had banners with this theme hanging in her training rooms and devoted her life to enabling people to become more fully human by learning and changing.

Some people change because they are in pain; others because they want to mature and grow. Satir's process of change was similar for both types of people. In order to change, individuals would benefit from feeling their *life force* as well as being willing to take risks. Ability and willingness to learn at both the cognitive and emotional levels are essential.

According to Satir, we have all *learned* how to be human and we can all *learn* to be more fully human. As ingrained as some experiences from a stressful childhood might be, we have the capacity to replace our old *learnings* with new and more beneficial *learnings*. Satir focused on learning as opposed to unlearning. She believed that old, no longer needed or wanted learnings will atrophy or fade away when they are replaced with new and more beneficial learnings.

Satir also focused on the importance of being supported when taking risks to change, although she did not negate the need for helpers using tough love when needed. This type of learning is a natural evolution from the seed model.

Satir recommended that helpers enable individuals to find their own answers as opposed to having ready-made answers and static rules for communication. Further, she believed that we all have within us answers that can be rediscovered. This leads the helper to assume a role of a guide, helping the individual find personal answers.

Self-Worth

Central to Satir's work and teaching was the concept of self-worth. The value an individual assigns to himself or herself, the self-love and respect that are distinct from anyone else's view of the individual, constitute the person's self-worth.

Satir viewed the first five years of a child's life as critical when considering the level of self-worth. Later in life significant others and a positive environment can improve the level of self-worth.

Individuals with low self-worth are anxious and unsure of themselves. They are hypersensitive to how others see them. They may interpret exclusion from a dyad as rejection and become more anxious. The eight aspects of the self are not well-integrated or developed in individuals with low self-worth. These people oppose change and prefer the safety of conformity.

Parents with low levels of self-worth beget children with low levels of self-worth. Although Bowen uses different constructs to explain this, what he says is similar. These

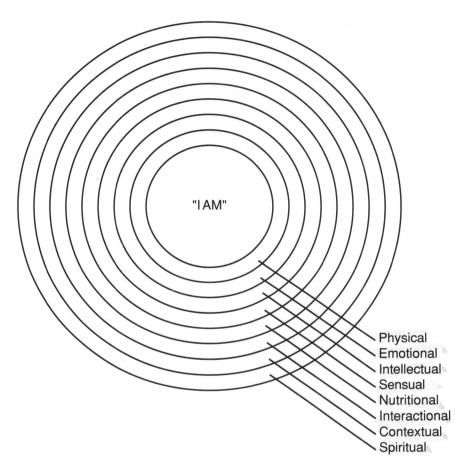

Figure A.1
THE MANDALA

Source: From *AVANTA Process Community III: The Third International Summer Institute* by V. Satir, 1983, Crested Butte, Colorado: AVANTA Process Community.

families ascribe to the threat and reward model. Submission and dominance are prevalent, and incongruent messages are common.

Satir believed that raising the self-worth of individuals was an essential focus for intervention. She also contended that most problems seen in therapy were associated with low self-worth.

Rules

Each family has a set of rules unique in the expectations and standards set. Rules include those that are overt, such as who does what chores, and those that are covert, such as "no complaining allowed." The rules of the system dictate how family members are defined and behave. The rules affect the expectations individuals have of others. People assume that others have the same rules as their family. They expect to observe in the rest of the world the same situations that occurred in their families.

This is not to say that rules are not valuable. They are truly necessary for survival. They establish beneficial norms for behavior. It is when rules are inflexible and rigid that they no longer benefit the individuals in the family. Those who rigidly apply the rules have damaging "shoulds," "oughts," and "musts" in their repertoire.

Satir focused her energies on helping people to transform rules they grew up with in the family. An example of a rigid rule is, "I should never complain." This is not always possible or healthy. Complaining may be a significant way to lead to positive change in a situation.

The helper's role is to assist family members in knowing more about and transforming the rules that interrupt their lives. With that change comes improved communication and self-worth. Part II of this text presents information on how to help families work with ineffective or rigidly held rules.

Communication Patterns

In *Peoplemaking*, Satir (1972, 1988) described four coping styles she found in use around the world. Established out of low self-worth, these patterns are those of placator, blamer, superreasonable, and irrelevant. These patterns are described here as they function in the family; chapter 12 includes information on dealing with these patterns, or stances in the schools.

These coping mechanisms begin in the primary triangle as a means of dealing with family stresses. To better understand the four dysfunctional stances, it is important to know about the dimensions of an interaction. A text by Satir, Stachowiak, and Taschman (1975) delineated three dimensions of all interactions: self, other, and context. The self is the communicator, the other is the person to whom the interaction is being sent, and the context is the situation in which the communication occurs. Healthy communication contains a balance of all three dimensions.

The placator, with feelings of low self-worth, will try to please others at the expense of self. Incongruent communication results when the self is denied. Placating conceals feelings of inferiority.

The blamer, also feeling low self-worth, tries to control others or is disagreeable. This person is seen by others as hostile and tyrannical. Blamers disregard the other in favor of self and context. Underneath, blamers feel vulnerable and like failures.

Superreasonables also feel diminished self-worth. They deny feelings and intellectualize. Those with whom they work might describe them as rigid, intellectual, or manipulative. The context becomes the whole focus of the superreasonable. When self and other are restrained, incongruency occurs. Superreasonable people feel very vulnerable.

The irrelevant individual, too, experiences low self-worth. Self, other, and context are all discounted in communications. This person appears erratic and inappropriate and feels anxious and lonely.

On the other hand, congruent communication does exist. It emanates from people with high self-worth. They do not distort communication and clarify as well as improve interactions. There is a balance of self, other, and context in their communications.

All people have patterns on which they rely most heavily. In times of great stress, normally congruent people usually fall back on one of the four patterns. The patterns are complementary and systemic in nature. The blamer and placator need one another to function. Satir emphasized the capacity of all people to relearn what was originally a learned communication style. She believed that individuals could learn to be congruent in their interactions and cease to rely on the four dysfunctional stances.

Although they are quite briefly described here, Satir's concepts are pertinent to this text. This information is a foundation on which to build further concepts as well as methodology. Other chapters focus on how to use this foundation when working with families of at-risk and special needs children.

THE BOWEN THEORY

This section provides an overview of a transgenerational process, the Bowen theory. A brief historical account of the development of this theory precedes an explanation of two variables important to understanding the Bowen theory. This discussion is followed by a description of Bowen's eight basic theoretical concepts. Understanding Bowen's theoretical concepts is beneficial to education professionals who are working with students who are at risk or have special needs.

Historical Information

Murray Bowen was a pioneer in the field of family systems therapy. Developed between 1957 and 1966, the Bowen theory stemmed from observations Bowen made while examining families with a schizophrenic family member. A physician and psychiatrist, Bowen worked at the Menninger Clinic in Topeka, Kansas, and then moved to the National Institute for Mental Health (NIMH) in Washington, DC. Under Bowen's direction, whole families with schizophrenic members were hospitalized while he was working at NIMH. He was later affiliated with the Medical College of Virginia in Richmond, and finally with the Georgetown Family Center, a part of Georgetown University in Washington, DC. Bowen died in October 1990. The March/April (1991) issue of the *Family Therapy Networker*, a journal devoted to family systems approaches, contains a special feature on Bowen's life and work.

Early in the development of his theory, Bowen decided that a new language, with a systems viewpoint, would be critical to the accurate description of families. He was influenced by systemic concepts of biology that furnished him with a framework to define the basic concepts of his theory. Kerr and Bowen (1988) clearly stated that general systems theory is "not a satisfactory integrative theory. It is a kind of 'umbrella' theory that has been imposed on a variety of natural systems" (p. x). They further wrote that people and families are "driven and guided by processes that are 'written in nature.' In this sense, the human family is a natural system. It is a particular kind of natural system called an *emotional system*" (p. 26).

In the Bowen theory the connection between theory and practice is paramount. Theory and therapy are seen as too intertwined to separate. There is essentially no therapy without theory; theory dictates what will be accomplished in therapy. Between 1959 and 1975 Bowen developed eight concepts that constitute the core of his theory. These were described in a collection of Bowen's works, *Family Therapy in Clinical Practice*, first published in 1978.

Background Information

According to Bowen, biological processes account for a person's affinity for individuality and togetherness. Individuals function differently based upon learning. The more emotionally reactive the person, the more the biological process has the upper hand. The more neutrality and choice the individual demonstrates, the more cognitive and feeling resources are being used.

Individuality or separateness and closeness or togetherness are two counterbalancing processes within human relationships. Rooted in instinctive drives for autonomy and connection, these forces are by nature fluid and variable. When a person experiences too much separateness, then he or she feels desire for togetherness and vice versa. Bowen saw the movement to seek equilibrium between these forces as characteristic of all human relationships.

The opposing functions of intellect and emotion similarly seek a balance. The use of logic and reason to describe the world and behave rationally are characteristic of the intellectual system. The automatic functions of the autonomic nervous system, the instinctive states that derive from basic life processes, and the subjective, feeling states are characteristic of the emotional system. The balancing of these two systems results in a continual interplay between the functions. The balance between the two would ideally be achieved by maintaining their characters as separate processes while interacting with one another. An imbalance results in the loss of distinction, or fusion, of the intellectual and emotional systems. The intellectual function is abandoned, with resulting reliance on the emotional function.

Choice is limited when the person is overreliant on the emotional system. A person capable of achieving a balance between the emotional and intellectual systems is able to make choices about separateness and closeness. Imbalances result in a reactive individual with little separate initiative. Boundaries between self and others are affected, and emotions dominate relationships. These people live in conflict, withdrawal, and dependence. Differentiated people are those who are less responsive to their emotional reactivity. That neutrality allows for choice in how to handle separateness and closeness. It stems from combining both feeling and cognitive resources.

Balancing the force for togetherness with the force for separateness as well as balancing intellectual functioning with emotional functioning are important principles to understand. Balancing or maintaining equilibrium between these two principles determines the degree of integration of a self and thus the health of the individual. Different degrees of balance between togetherness-separateness and emotional-intellectual functioning are required of different relationships. For example, in marriage one expects to see more togetherness than in friendships.

Varying movement along continua of togetherness and separateness as well as intellectual and emotional functioning results from the naturally occurring changing circumstances within relationships. Two main variables, the degree of anxiety and the degree of integration of self, govern the equilibrium between the intellectual and emotional systems as well as the forces toward togetherness and separateness. When anxiety is high, or chronic, the tension results in a fusion of the intellectual and emotional systems, with a concomitant increase in the togetherness force. Physical, emotional, or social symptoms are seen as a result of this fusion.

The integration of self is the ability to differentiate one's self from others. The degree to which one can use intellect to monitor and control emotions, while surrounded by the emotional intensity of family relationships, determines the level of integration or differentiation. Also an indication of integration of self is the ability to remain in relationships with others while maintaining a sense of self apart from others during a time of emotional intensity.

Physical, emotional, or social symptoms occur when the individual does not adapt to tension. Chronic anxiety stresses the person and symptoms develop. Substance abuse, emotional disturbances within children or their parents, and physical symptoms such as asthma and diabetes can have manifestations in school that appear to be related to stress in the home.

Theoretical Concepts

Bowen's observation of the togetherness–separateness forces as well as the intellectual–emotional systems and their relationship to the integration of self, impact of anxiety, and emergence of symptoms all led him to develop eight key concepts of human functioning. The concepts are differentiation of self, triangles, nuclear family emotional system, family projection process, emotional cut-off, sibling position, multigenerational transmission process, and societal regression. The concepts that more directly affect children will be elaborated upon in greater depth.

Differentiation of Self

Pivotal to understanding Bowen's theory is the concept of differentiation of self. This concept describes people in terms of their ability to keep their intellectual and emotional systems from becoming fused. People whose systems are fused are dominated by the emotional system and force for togetherness. People who are able to balance their intellectual and emotional systems are able to make choices about how they will deal with life experiences. At the same time that differentiation describes a capacity to make a choice, Kerr and Bowen (1988) made it clear that capacity does not determine the correct or best choice.

Differentiation of self and chronic anxiety are the two main variables that explain level of functioning. The level of differentiation within one's family of origin affects one's own level of differentiation.

Anxiety also affects one's level of differentiation of self. As Kerr (1988) stated, "Acute anxiety is fed by fear of what is; chronic anxiety is fed by fear of what might be" (p. 47). Higher levels of chronic anxiety place a greater strain on people's adaptive capabilities. Individuals who are better at differentiating between their own intellectual and emotional systems have more functional means for and choices about adapting to anxiety. They will have fewer symptoms in their lives.

In terms of understanding levels of differentiation of self, Bowen (1978) described *solid self* and *pseudo-self*. He viewed the solid self as the part of the person that is resistant to fusion of the intellectual and emotional systems. It is able to maintain a healthy balance between the forces for togetherness-separateness. The solid self embodies the individual's beliefs, principles, attitudes, and opinions that are nonnegotiable under any circumstance.

The *pseudo-self* is quite different. A fusion of the processes of the emotional and intellectual system results from anxiety and stress. Bowen (1978) referred to pseudo-self as the "pretend" self. It has soft beliefs and principles; thus, it takes its beliefs and principles from someone else. The expected return for this action is belonging to the other and a sense of togetherness.

The levels of solid self and pseudo-self are different among individuals and within an individual over time, depending upon life circumstances. When there are few stresses, an individual with a low level of solid self may appear to have a strong solid self. However, when a stressful situation results in anxiety, the actual level of the pseudo-self will emerge. Having a child with a disability is an example of a stress on parents that can bring out their pseudo-selves.

When the intellectual and emotional systems are fused, couples will be at the lower levels of differentiation because the emotional system will have the upper hand. One member of the marital dyad may adapt for a long time and may even lose parts of the solid self he or she once possessed. Chronic physical illness and psychoses are examples of this in its most extreme form.

In the Bowen model, differentiation is not confused with being an individual. Sometimes people reactively function on a pseudo-self level. They claim their individuality and manifest emotional reactivity to the desires of another. Instead of being closer to the other person, they become further apart.

Triangles

Bowen saw the triangle or three-person unit as the smallest stable relationship system. In families and in groups the triangle is the basic building block of relationships; it is part of a human's instinctive nature (Kerr & Bowen, 1988).

Bowen (1978) maintained that when anxiety was low a triangle would consist of a comfortable twosome and a less comfortable outsider. The twosome strives to maintain togetherness. A third person is drawn in by the twosome when the anxiety level increases. This results in a lowering of anxiety within the twosome and creates a triangle. When high levels of anxiety affect the members of the triangle, the outsider position may be more attractive because the outsider can escape the intensity of anxiety.

Kerr (1988) described a typical example of how a triangle operates.

> A husband, on the outside (in fact or fantasy) of the relationship between his wife and his oldest daughter, becomes sullen. The wife predictably reacts to his sullenness by focusing more on him and attempting to cheer him up. The daughter, in reaction to being on the outside in relation to her two parents, becomes overly solicitous toward her father. The mother, reacting to being on the outside in relation to her husband and her daughter, criticizes the daughter's

physical appearance. The daughter responds defensively, and she and her mother have a long discussion to resolve their differences. (p. 53)

The emotional system, with its force toward togetherness, drives triangles. Individuals who have higher levels of differentiation of self are more able to observe and handle the relationships within the triangle. Individuals with lower levels of differentiation of self, who fall back on the emotional system and need for togetherness, are reactive to any tensions within the triangle.

Kerr (1988) pointed to the reality of family triangles spreading to outside systems. Under stress, anxiety may be spread to the schools, the work place, or some other agency. Kerr also explained that:

> Parents never want such an outcome [impaired functioning] for any of their children. For the most part, they dedicate themselves to preventing it. However, their anxiety that things go well may obscure their ability to see that they are acting in ways that foster the very outcome they most want to prevent. (p. 55)

Kerr (1988) perceived triangles in families lasting forever. He viewed the "emotional circuitry" of a triangle as outliving the people who are its members. When one family member in the triangle dies, another person generally replaces that individual. Through the generations the family members may be involved in acting out a conflict that was never resolved between grandparents or great-grandparents. As Kerr (1988) stated, "So a particular triangle was not necessarily created by its present participants; nor do triangles form anew or completely dissolve with the ebb and flow of anxiety" (p. 53).

School professionals would do well to consider Kerr's (1988) statement that, "Intolerance of aspects of the human process is a manifestation of being triangled into it" (p. 57). It is critical for professionals to understand human process and their own vulnerabilities and to detriangle from families. Frustrations and intolerance are signs of a need for professionals to become informed about human processes, in particular systemic processes, as well as to develop new ways of working with families or family members.

Nuclear Family Emotional System

This system includes processes and patterns of emotional functioning within a single generation of a family that replicate those of past generations and will be repeated in future generations. Bowen contended that individuals with similar levels of differentiation marry one another. Spouses with higher levels of differentiation balance their emotional and intellectual systems with little fusion. They generally have few problems in their marriage. Spouses with lower levels of differentiation, with fusion of the emotional and intellectual systems, have more pseudo-self than solid self. Each process or pattern of symptoms is magnified by anxiety.

The patterns or processes comprise three categories of dysfunction within the nuclear family: marital conflict, illness in a spouse, and impairment of one or more children. Symptoms are physical illness, emotional illness, or social illness. All of these are viewed from the family systems lens as being linked to the same basic patterns of emotional functioning within the nuclear family. In other words, the patterns that contribute to the development of an emotional illness are the same as those that contribute to a physical or social illness. Kerr and Bowen (1988) made it clear that, "This does not mean that patterns of emotional functioning in a family *cause* physical, emotional, or social illness; the creation of a specific illness depends on the combination of many factors" (p. 164). More on the impairment of children is found in chapter 4.

Family Projection Process

This process was first described by Bowen in 1966. In later writings (Kerr & Bowen, 1988) this concept has been subsumed under the *nuclear family emotional system* or *differentiation of self.*

The family projection process originally begins with anxiety in the mother regarding some aspect of her child's functioning, which the child responds to with anxiety. The mother might become anxious about something her child said or did, something she feared her child might say or do, or something she imagined her child to have said or done. The child's anxious response is interpreted by the mother as a problem with the child. The mother might become overprotective in response to the child. Her view of the child stems from her own anxiety more than from the child. However, the mother begins to act as though her view of the child were truth. Eventually the child acts like the mother's image, and the mother begins to calm down. With the mother's greater calm comes the child's greater calm. Finally the child internalizes the mother's perception and behaves like the mother's picture of the child.

Bowen contended that the family projection process is part of every family, varying in content and degree. The content within the same family even varies from child to child. Parents may become anxious about a particular trait or behavior in one child and about a different trait or behavior in another child. Kerr and Bowen (1988) stated that, "The mother is not malicious; she is just anxious. She is as much a prisoner of the situation as the child" (p. 201). This realization can help school professionals to be nonjudgmental and more patient while working with parents.

Emotional Cutoff

This theoretical concept, added in the 1970s, describes a way of gaining distance from fusion in the family of origin. The range of cutoffs is from minor to major significance. The person who institutes the cutoff is trying to reduce anxiety. The cutoff may in fact reduce anxiety; however, that is not always the case. Not dealing with a difficult situation is relatively easy for most people. It can also result in losing potentially positive relationships and support as well as opportunities for learning about oneself within the context of the family.

Emotional cutoff describes the manner in which people deal with emotional reactivity between the generations. The greater the emotional reactivity, or fusion, the higher the probability that the two generations will cut off. Cutoffs occur both in the forms of physical distance and emotional withdrawal.

As Kerr (1981) indicated, emotional cutoff reflects a problem of fusion, solves a problem with distance, and also creates another problem. Cutoffs are only temporary solutions; the unresolved emotional attachment to the parent continues in spite of the child's determination to distance from it. In the future the unresolved emotional attachments are carried over into the child's own marriage or parenting. The fusion will continue. When people use cutoff as a means of dealing with the past, they are using emotional distance in the present. The lower the level of differentiation, the more one can be expected to see cutoff used as an attempt to gain distance.

Adolescence is a time of particular vulnerability. Choosing friends of which parents disapprove, getting in trouble with the law, and abusing substances are ways adolescents try to cut off from parents. This declaration of independence from family is not the same as differentiation of self. It in no way resolves the emotional fusion with the parent.

Sibling Position

Bowen based his understanding of sibling position on the work of Walter Toman (1969). Toman delineated ten important categories of sibling position that affect future relationships. Bowen (1978) stated that there was no single piece of information more important to understanding family systems functioning than the sibling position of family members in present and past generations.

The Bowen theory stresses the importance of functional sibling position when diagnosing emotional reactivity. A child might function as an oldest in terms of responsibility or as a youngest in terms of impulsivity, risk-taking, and dependency. Bowen saw shifts in the functional nature of sibling positions as indicating the family projection process within the family of origin. When siblings function as would be expected of their sibling position, it indicates a low incidence of projection and higher level of differentiation within the family.

Also important is the degree to which an individual actually fits the profile that would be expected. If an oldest child acted more like a youngest child, the hypothesis would be that the oldest child was the focus of the family projection process. An exaggeration of the characteristics, such as a youngest child being extremely impulsive, leads to the observation that there was a high level of fusion in the family of origin and present marriage.

Multigenerational Transmission Process

This concept describes the family projection process through multiple generations. Children who are the object of the family projection process will have a lower degree of differentiation than their parents. Then, as adults, they will project emotional reactivity and lower levels of differentiation on their own children, and that will be passed down to the next generation. Bowen believed that as lower and lower levels of differentiation emerge, a schizophrenic child would develop. He indicated that it would take eight to ten generations to produce a schizophrenic individual.

This concept centers on lower levels of differentiation and emotional reactivity, with the fusion of the intellectual and emotional systems being passed through successive generations. Bowen contended that individuals marry other individuals with an equivalent degree of differentiation. Thus, their children would be expected to develop the same or lower level of differentiation as the parents.

For professionals within the schools, it is important to realize that what is observed in the classroom is the result of many generations of transmission process. This perspective makes it easier to be patient with and understand families and their schoolchildren.

Societal Regression

The last of Bowen's eight theoretical concepts, societal regression is based upon the degree of anxiety in society. Bowen hypothesized that the same process of gradual regression to lower functioning that occurs in families is also occurring in society. When there is increasing chronic societal anxiety, society reacts with decisions based on emotion rather than intellect. This is parallel with the fusion of the emotional and intellectual systems that leads to lower levels of differentiation and inability to define a self.

In 1978 Bowen published a text with a chapter titled "Societal Regression as Viewed Through Family Systems Therapy." In this chapter he outlined the reasons for his belief that society is regressing. In particular he pointed to the environmental crisis people have created, increasing crime and use of drugs, as well as the new norms for sexuality. He predicted a series of crises before a major final crisis prior to the middle of the twenty-first century when those who survive will be ones "who can live in better harmony with nature" (p. 281).

This concept may not be relevant to understanding families with children having special needs; however, it does demonstrate the value of understanding systems theory. It is easier to understand any system, such as cultures, institutions, businesses, or schools, when one understands theory from the perspective of the smallest relationship system, the family. The concepts of family systems enable professionals to better understand other systems in which they live and work as well as the people found there, including themselves.

STRUCTURAL FAMILY THERAPY

This section provides an overview of the theoretical basis for structural family therapy. A brief historical account of the development of this model is followed by a description of three general concepts basic to understanding how families can be described in structural terms.

Historical Information

In the 1960s, Dr. Salvadore Minuchin, a pediatrician turned psychiatrist, and his co-workers at the Wiltwyck School for Boys near New York City began developing a model of family therapy designed for dealing with delinquent youngsters from low socioeconomic backgrounds. Their book, *Families of the Slums: An Exploration of their Structure and Treatment* (Minuchin et al., 1967), was the result of three years of research funded by a grant from the National Institute for Mental Health (NIMH). The approach they developed focused on helping chaotic, multiproblem families change those patterns of behavior that had led to the placement of one of their members at the School for Boys. Structural family therapy involves a focus on the present rather than the past, on changing behaviors rather than gaining intellectual insight, and on short-term rather than extensive treatment.

In 1965, Minuchin and Braulio Montalvo, a colleague from the Wiltwyck School, moved to Philadelphia Child Guidance Clinic, where they began to develop a family-oriented treatment team. This inner-city, traditional child guidance clinic was to become transformed into the mecca of structural family therapy. Many clinicians who eventually became well-known as family therapists, including Jay Haley (Haley & Hoffman, 1967), M. Duncan Stanton and Tom Todd (Stanton, Todd et al., 1982), Lynn Hoffman (1981), Harry Aponte (1976b), and Marianne Walters (1972), originally worked with families from a structural perspective at Philadelphia Child Guidance Clinic.

In Minuchin's next book, *Families and Family Therapy* (1974), he delineated a model of effective family functioning that included the qualities of openness, flexibility, and organization. These three basic traits and the language that Minuchin developed to describe them will be discussed in greater detail later in this section. He also introduced the technique of structural mapping of families to help the therapist develop specific goals for treatment. It is in this book that Minuchin began to discuss the need for the therapist to join in the family's process and language in order to effect change. In Minuchin's approach, it is only after listening to the family and joining with them to bring about change that the therapist can begin to restructure patterns in communication and behavior.

In his writing, Minuchin not only introduced his theory to the psychological community, but also included transcripts from actual sessions in which a structural family therapy approach had been used. Minuchin's therapy style was unique in that he was directive with his patients and very active during the sessions, frequently walking around the room and asking family members to change seats. Considered bold and controversial, he was one of the first trainers in the field to videotape family therapy sessions and show the videotapes as examples of principles of structural family therapy. This format later became a strategy of choice in training for all approaches to family systems therapy.

Although Minuchin's original therapy approach was based on the nuclear family as the unit of treatment, in the epilogue to *Families and Family Therapy* (1974) he opened the door for including extended family and other social networks in the concept of "family." He wrote, "To include the entire family as a factor...enlarges the perspective from the traditional concentration on the individual.... Yet even this focus distorts the view...for it ignores the linkages between family and society" (p. 255). In the 1980s, structural family therapy began to include an emphasis upon extended systems that interact with the nuclear family and generational patterns that influence the family.

Although structural family therapy was originally developed from applications with families from lower socioeconomic levels, the approach was generalized in the 1970s and 1980s to include all families. This extension came about as a result of ten years of research at Philadelphia Child Guidance Clinic funded by a grant for work with children with psychosomatic illness. This research involved children who were suffering from diabetes, asthma, and anorexia nervosa. Both the children with diabetes and those with asthma had numerous hospitalizations resulting from episodes of ketoacidosis or breathing difficulties that did not respond to conventional medical treatment.

As part of the research, the identified patients were videotaped with their parents and at least two siblings engaging in a series of interactive family tasks. The videotapes were then coded on dimensions of family structure by blind observers. This interview included phases during which the identified patient witnessed parental conflict from behind a one-way mirror and sat in the room during a conflict between his or her parents.

Comparison of the results of these interactions with interviews conducted with "normal" children and their parents found that the identified patients were much more involved in their parents' conflict than normal children. The patients tended to serve as mediators of parental conflict and to become involved in alliances with one parent against the other. In addition, there was evidence that the children with diabetes had an exaggerated response to parental conflict that resulted in an increase of free fatty acids in the bloodstream.

This research also involved a therapy component in which the principles and techniques of structural family therapy were applied in working with the families. Minuchin (1978) stated, "Our findings clearly indicate that, when significant family interaction patterns are changed, significant changes in the symptoms of psychosomatic illness also occur" (p. 21).

Minuchin continued his work at Philadelphia Child Guidance Clinic until 1982, when he went into private practice. During this time, he and his colleagues expanded the principles of structural family therapy to working with families coming together as a result of a remarriage, families with a schizophrenic child, and families of adolescent drug abusers as well as numerous other types of families who came for treatment at the clinic. Minuchin continues to present workshops both nationally and internationally on the principles and practice of structural family therapy.

Background Information

The theory underlying structural family therapy is descriptive in nature. Based on specific values dealing with how the family should function, the therapy is practical and directive. This section will describe some of the underlying premises and values that resulted in development of the approach known as structural family therapy.

Minuchin (1974) clearly identified the necessary balance between the general systems principles of homeostasis and adaptability when he wrote:

> The continued existence of the family as a system depends on a sufficient range of (transactional) patterns...and the flexibility to mobilize them when necessary. The family must...be able to transform itself in ways that meet new circumstances without losing the continuity that provides a frame of reference for its members. (p. 52)

The concepts of structural family therapy stem from the premise that family members interact with one another in predictable patterns that can be observed and are repeated over time. Therapy is aimed at changing these patterns by changing the organization or structure of the family. Minuchin and his colleagues believed that, as the behavior of family members changed, the basic patterns and structure of the family would change. As the structure was transformed, the experience of the individuals in the family would be different.

Minuchin (1974) wrote that the primary job of the family was to "enhance the psychosocial growth of each member" (p. 51). To accomplish this task, the family must operate with some predictability and stability. For instance, children should be able to forecast that each time they misbehave they will receive a similar response from their parents. A classic example of the effects of lack of predictability comes from families in which there is an alcoholic parent. Children in these families learn early in life that they cannot depend on the alcoholic parent's reaction to their behavior. Only when they become older are they able to understand that the source of the instability is the parent's drinking behavior.

In addition to creating and maintaining stability, the family must also be able to respond to changing circumstances with some degree of flexibility. Stress upon the family such as moving, financial problems, illness or death of an extended family member, or identification of a child with physical or learning problems can overload the general functioning of the family system. If the family is not capable of responding to these demands by changing roles and communication patterns, family conflict and dysfunctional behavior will result.

The role of the therapist is to help families adapt to changing circumstances with changes in the structure of the family. Once the family experiences the changes and the adaptation that goes with the new structure, the homeostatic mechanism of the family should operate to continue the new structural pattern. In families where restructuring changes do not continue or where conflicts are not resolved, what began as a problem of a family in transition may continue as dysfunctional patterns. Eventually, according to Minuchin's theory, these dysfunctional family patterns will result in the identification of a family member (usually a child) with behavioral, emotional, or physical symptoms.

Theoretical Concepts

Minuchin's view of the family as a relational context with predictable structural patterns led to the development of three theoretical constructs regarding family functioning: subsystems, boundaries, and hierarchy.

Subsystems

A two-parent nuclear family is composed of four major subsystems, each with its own interaction patterns and functions. These subsystems include the spousal or marital subsystem, composed of the husband and wife; the parental subsystem, which includes the parents as executives or decision makers for the family; the sibling subsystem; and the extrafamilial subsystem, including extended family, friends, and social supports.

The individuals included in each subsystem will differ from family to family. For example, in single-parent families there is no spousal subsystem. The parental subsystem in these families often includes a grandparent or an older sibling who has parental permission to make decisions regarding younger siblings. The extrafamilial subsystem may include aunts, uncles, and cousins who live nearby or may be composed mostly of family friends or work colleagues.

Each member of a family may belong to several subsystems. For example, a teenage child may be allowed periodic entrance into the parental subsystem in the form of babysitting. This same child will also be a member of the sibling subsystem. In addition, if the teenager is involved in extracurricular school activities, he or she will be an integral member of the extrafamilial subsystem.

Membership in each subsystem will demand different interaction skills and ways of functioning in relationships. When interacting with parents, a teenager must know about respect and authority. When acting in a parental role, such as babysitting, he or she must know about leadership and responsibility. Interacting with siblings or peers, this same child must learn about sharing, cooperation, and empathy.

Each subsystem has particular functions for the family system. The spousal subsystem promotes interdependence of the marital couple, conflict resolution between the pair, and sexual and emotional satisfaction. Although information about this area is not readily available to school professionals, some general observations can give educators a sense of the patterns of interaction between a couple.

The functions of the parental subsystem include the emotional and physical support of children, the establishment of family rules, the dispensing of appropriate discipline, and the socialization of children. School professionals will often find dysfunction in the parental subsystem in the form of abusive, unpredictable, or absent authority. Further discussion of the effects of imbalance in the parental subsystem is contained in chapter 3.

The sibling subsystem provides recreation, companionship, and role modeling for its members. Interaction with siblings provides a social laboratory for learning negotiation, cooperation, and competition with peers of different ages. The child's identity is formed, in large part, from positive and negative experiences within their sibling group (Bank & Kahn, 1975).

Finally, the extrafamilial subsystem provides a social network with whom the family can socialize and compare ways of interacting and family rules. The network offers emotional and instrumental support such as sharing of family celebrations and values and training in general life skills. Often families with a child with special needs become isolated from social supports, resulting in increased tension within the nuclear family.

Boundaries

The boundaries of a subsystem are defined by Minuchin as the rules that govern who functions within that subsystem and how each person carries out his or her function. An example of a rule that defines a boundary would be "The children in the family do not make decisions about how bills are paid." This rule places a boundary between the sibling subsystem and the parental subsystem.

For subsystems to function appropriately, boundaries must be clear enough to allow subsystem members to carry out their functions without interference from those outside the subsystem. For example, young couples quite often have marital difficulties if there is frequent involvement with and input from in-laws into their early marriage negotiations. If the couple purposefully goes to their in-laws for advice on specific issues, such as money management, there need not be a blurring of boundaries.

In healthy family interactions, boundaries are described as clear and permeable. When boundaries are blurred, subsystems have problems functioning. In these families, parents tend to be overprotective and have difficulty with their children's attempts to become appropriately independent. There is little individual privacy. Aponte (Aponte & Van Deusen, 1981) has stated that in these types of families members function as if they were part of one another. Minuchin (1974) coined the term "enmeshed" to describe families with blurred, unclear, or undifferentiated boundaries.

On the other end of the continuum are families in which boundaries are inappropriately rigid and impermeable. Family members have little to do with one another; there is very little emotional support or closeness in these families. Only a severe crisis or a high level of stress can activate parental involvement. These types of families are called "disengaged" by Minuchin and his colleagues.

Hierarchy

Hierarchy is a term used by Minuchin to describe the distribution of power in families.

A member at the top of the hierarchy is one who has the most relational power within the family. Families operate best when there is a clear hierarchy with parents occupying the upper levels, adolescents or older children next, and younger children at the lower levels.

Observers find many different ways in which hierarchy problems occur in families. One type of problem occurs in families with weak or ineffective parents. In these families, children tend not to listen to parents' directions, and there is often much sibling conflict. In many low income or highly stressed families with multiple problems, the weak parental subsystem may be exacerbated by a general disorganization at all levels. Bills are left unpaid, phone calls unanswered, and there is a general sense of a lack of leadership in these families.

A second type of hierarchy problem occurs when a child functions regularly in the parental subsystem. This child assumes an inappropriate level of responsibility for the family and often misses out on age-appropriate experiences and activities. A child in this position is referred to as a *parentified* child (Minuchin & Fishman, 1981). At the extreme, parentification is a process that occurs in families in which there is inappropriate involvement between a parent and child.

Another hierarchy difficulty is found in families where members repeatedly align together across subsystem boundaries against another family member. An inflexible alignment is known as a *coalition*. This type of problem is frequently seen in families where parents avoid dealing with their marital conflict by focusing on problems in a child. For example, an adolescent who complains about mom's nagging is often acting out his father's resistance to what he perceives as his wife's nagging. Rather than the father confronting his wife, the adolescent, in a coalition with his father, acts out the conflict from across generational boundaries.

In summary, Minuchin used these three constructs to describe family dynamics and to identify the forces that lead to the development of problems in the family system. Subsystems with identified functions serve as the structural elements in the family. Boundaries are the mechanisms by which the family accommodates to the need for balance between stability and flexibility. Hierarchy is the organizing principle by which subsystems are arranged. By articulation and extension of these constructs, Minuchin and his collaborators have provided a useful model for applying general systems theory to the problem of family dysfunction.

STRATEGIC FAMILY THERAPY

This section describes the general theoretical principles underlying the practice of strategic therapy. A brief historical account of the development of this model is followed by a discussion of the basic theory of change from a strategic perspective.

Historical Information

The term *strategic* is most often used to describe family therapy approaches that focus on identifying the function served by psychiatric symptoms within the family system. Further, the strategic therapist assumes responsibility for directly intervening into the system to effect change. Finally, the focus of strategic therapy is on here-and-now behaviors, with little or no connection to historical events. This focus contrasts with the Bowen and Satir approaches, which treat the individual within a context of family history.

The two settings historically associated with the strategic approach are the Mental Research Institute (MRI) in Palo Alto, California, and the Family Therapy Institute in Washington, DC. Although each setting is known for the use of particular techniques, this discussion will focus on the commonalities in theory rather than the differences between their approaches. For a more detailed discussion of strategic therapy techniques, see the reference list at the end of the book.

Many of the clinicians who are important in the strategic therapy movement were originally trained and influenced by two men, Gregory Bateson (1972) and Milton Erickson. Bateson was an anthropologist who directed a ten-year grant in the 1950s to investigate communication among both animals and people. Jay Haley, John Weakland, and Don Jackson, all of whom made major contributions to strategic therapy, worked on Bateson's grant.

Milton Erickson was a physician who developed a unique brand of psychotherapy techniques based on hypnosis and paradoxical instruction. As Haley (1985) stated:

> Erickson had one major concern in his professional life—finding ways to influence people.... He seems to have been the first major therapist to expect clinicians to innovate ways to solve...problems and to say that the responsibility for...change lies with the therapist. (p. vii)

Haley, Jackson, and Weakland all studied extensively with Erickson; the influence of his beliefs can be seen in their later work as advocates of the strategic approach.

In 1959, Jackson left Bateson's research project and formed the Mental Research Institute (MRI). Several important contributions to strategic therapy have evolved from the MRI group, including brief therapy techniques designed to effect change in families in ten sessions. In addition, this group maintained that therapeutic change could occur whether or not the entire family was involved in treatment. At MRI, members of the family who were motivated were advised how to change their own behavior so that the dysfunctional family patterns would then change.

Jay Haley moved from Bateson's project in 1967 to the Philadelphia Child Guidance Clinic, where he worked for nine years with Minuchin and his colleagues. Haley then moved to Washington, DC, and began the Family Therapy Institute. Haley has contributed to the field by training therapists in specific interviewing techniques designed to discover behavioral and communicational patterns within the family. He has also developed a model for treating severely disturbed young adults that focuses on the family's failure to allow the person to leave home and become independent.

Although Jackson, Bateson, and Erickson have all died, the ideas that they germinated continue to grow in the field of family therapy. The Mental Research Institute and the Family Therapy Institute continue to provide training and therapy. Both Haley and Weakland, who are prolific writers, provide supervision to therapy trainees and conduct national workshops on strategic therapy approaches.

Theoretical Concepts

Strategic therapy is grounded primarily on the general systems principles of homeostasis and levels of interaction. Probably the best-known concepts arising from the strategic therapy movement are those of family homeostasis and the double bind as a communication pattern in the etiology of schizophrenia. The concept of the double bind was the first theory of paradoxical communication. The double bind is a communication pattern that occurs when an individual appears to offer a choice to another. However, no matter which option is chosen by the respondent, the person ends up in a bind.

For example, a mother buys a red sweater and a blue sweater for her son's birthday and presents them both to him with the question "Which one will you wear to the party?" The boy answers that either sweater will be fine. The mother then insists that the boy choose one of the sweaters. If the boy asks for the red sweater, she responds "You don't like the blue one?" If he chooses the blue one, she asks why he doesn't like the red one. In other words, he is given the illusion of choice but he will lose in this communication no matter which "choice" he makes.

The study of this type of communication pattern within families led strategic therapists to develop general theoretical concepts regarding family homeostasis and the importance of family development and problem definition.

Family Homeostasis and Symptom Development

In 1957 Jackson first discussed the idea of psychiatric symptoms in an individual as systemic responses to family communication. In other words, people within a family govern one another's behavior by their responses to each other. Jackson believed that families have a natural movement toward stability or homeostasis just as other living systems do.

According to strategic therapy (Watzlawick et al., 1974), psychiatric symptoms are the results of attempts by family members to change an existing difficulty. When difficulties arise in daily living, parents or spouses usually attempt to apply a solution to make things better. For example, if someone is depressed, family members try to cheer the individual up. It is a natural tendency that if initial attempts at cheering up do not work, the family members try harder—more cheering up. However, once a symptom is present and a family attempts to treat the symptom, they often only succeed in making it worse. The solution then becomes part of the family behavior dealing with the problem. The symptom is maintained by a particular sequence of behaviors within the family.

In this example, Johnny looks depressed so the family tries to cheer him up. If this does not succeed, they try harder. Johnny sees the family working hard to make him feel better but he still feels depressed. Only now he feels guilty about being depressed and taking so much family energy. In addition, the family is angry that they are trying so hard and Johnny is not responding, so they begin to withdraw from Johnny. Johnny then becomes more depressed. This sequence of behaviors is circular. If the therapist can discover this circular sequence and help change the family's reactions at any point along that circle, strategic therapy proponents maintain that the symptomatic behavior will then change.

Life Cycle

Strategic therapists look at the family's stage of development as important in understanding the etiology or cause of symptoms. Families are seen as prone to developing problems at transitional points, such as the birth of a child or a family relocation. At these times, due to the stress of transition, families are less able to adjust their interactions to accommodate necessary changes. In other words, the forces for homeostasis outweigh the forces for flexibility. Haley (1980) described this phenomenon as akin to a stairway. The family must make adjustments to move from one step to the next. Families with a symptomatic member have become "stuck" on one step and cannot move on to the next step in the life cycle. It is the therapist's job to help the family introduce new behaviors that will help them move on up the stairway.

All families become unbalanced at times and react to stress with nonproductive interpersonal cycles. Many people understand this process as a "button-pushing" phenomenon. Once a particular topic is broached or once a particular action takes place, each family member can then predict how the other family members will react. It is as if everyone is watching a very familiar one-act play but they cannot seem to change their lines to come up with a more productive outcome. In healthy families, there comes a point when someone does "change his or her lines" and the nonproductive cycle is broken. In pathological families, these cycles continue to repeat over and over for months or years at a time. In these families the cycles repeat until a crisis ensues. Still the system does not change because family members develop symptoms to provide a stabilizing force toward resolving family stress.

Just as the old saying goes about people pulling together in times of crisis, the family tends to pull together around the symptomatic member, who is usually a child, and thus avoids making any real changes in the family patterns that caused the initial crisis. This pulling together around the symptom-bearing member might make it look to observers as though the family had changed its dysfunctional patterns and was functioning better. However, the essence of the system has not changed and the dysfunctional process will resurface as the problematic family member begins to function more healthily.

Haley (1980) viewed many severely disturbed young people as being stuck at the leaving-home stage of the family life cycle. With these families, the parents need to have their own lives and identities that are oriented around something other than child rearing. If child rearing is a mother's only purpose in life, then the underlying fear of leaving home is that mom will suffer from no longer having a job. A strategic therapist would identify the young person as suffering from problems in maturity and independence. He or she would then work to have the parents in this situation become more controlling and demanding of their symptomatic child in order to help the child mature. As the parents effectively assert their control, the patient's concern becomes how to get out from under this structure. The patient then begins to work toward gaining independence and leaving home rather than on maintaining the parent's symptom. Once the child has given up the symptom, the family is then unstuck and can begin to introduce more adaptive behaviors. The mother can then give up her focus on the young person and devote her energy to managing her own needs as her role naturally changes.

Problem Definition

According to the theory of strategic therapy, there is no objective reality. How one looks at things determines what one sees. What one sees determines how one behaves. How one behaves determines how others respond.

Families usually seek help from a therapist long after symptoms have developed in a family member. The family has already applied its solution to the problem, and no change has occurred. The family is demoralized by their maladaptive solution but cannot see how to approach the problem differently. The symptom is seen as beyond their control and as resistant to change.

In strategic therapy, it is the therapist's job to help the family define the problem in a way that a solution is possible. How one defines the problem determines what one will do about it. Therefore, much of the skill in strategic therapy lies in asking questions that help the family begin to entertain alternative views of the symptom. The therapeutic process of expanding the family's definition of the problem is known as *reframing*. When family members begin to view the problem differently, the therapist then gives directives concerning how individuals can begin to behave differently. In this model, action or strategy replaces traditional interpretation and insight therapy.

The ways in which reality can be defined can be seen in a classroom example. A first grader has begun to destroy property in the classroom and to hit other students. At first, the teacher views this behavior as angry and aggressive. She responds by setting limits on the child and using time-outs. The teacher later finds out from the school counselor that the child's parents have recently decided to get a divorce. At this point, she views the same behavior as depressed in nature. The next time the child acts out, she takes him aside and asks him about his feelings about the divorce. In each case, the teacher's perspective on reality governed her behavior.

The approach of strategic family therapy was developing on the West Coast at about the same time that structural family therapy was developing on the East Coast. Both approaches differ from Bowen and Satir in that the focus is on behavior and communication of the family in the present. Structural therapists tend to develop goals aimed at changing family roles and behaviors in the here-and-now. Much of strategic therapy is oriented to techniques used by the therapist to induce change in communication patterns in the family system. In fact, this approach is known for being long on technique and short on theory. The three theoretical concepts discussed here—family homeostasis, family transition, and problem definition—are used to help the therapist determine where to direct efforts toward change.

BIBLIOGRAPHY **B** OF READINGS

ABUSE

Ackerman, R.J., & Graham, D. (1990). *Too old to cry: Abused teens in today's America.* Bradenton, FL: Human Services Institute.

Armstrong, L. (1978). *Kiss daddy good-night: A speak out on incest.* New York: Hawthorne Books.

Bass, E., & Davis, L. (1988). *The courage to heal: A guide for women survivors of child sexual abuse.* New York: Harper & Row.

Farmer, S. (1989). *Adult children of abusive parents.* Los Angeles: Lowell House.

Hagans, K.B., & Case, J. (1988). *When your child has been molested: A parent's guide to healing and recovery.* Lexington, MA: Lexington Books.

Mundy, J., & Bell, S. (1991). *Let's talk: Coloring books.* Los Angeles: Western Psychological Services. [Ages 4-9]

O'Connor, D. S. (1987). *I can be me. A helping book for children from troubled families.* Deerfield Beach, FL: Health Communications. [Primary grades]

ADDICTION

Bradshaw, J. (1988). *Healing the shame that binds you.* Deerfield Beach, FL: Health Communications.

Cruise-Jesse, R. (1989). *Children in recovery: Healing the parent-child relationship in alcohol/addictive families.* New York: W. W. Norton.

Moe, J., & Pohlman, D. (1988). *Kid's power. Healing games for children of alcoholics.* Deerfield Beach, FL: Health Communications.

Todd, T. C., & Selekman, M. D. (Eds.). (1991). *Family therapy approaches with adolescent substance abusers.* Boston: Allyn and Bacon. [Professional text]

Treadway, D. C. (1989). *Before it's too late - Working with substance abuse in families.* New York: W. W. Norton. [Professional text]

Whitfield, C. L. (1988). *Healing the child within.* Pompano Beach, FL: Health Communications. [Includes workbook]

Woititz, J. G. (1984). *Adult children of alcoholics.* Pompano Beach, FL: Health Communications.

ADOPTION

Krementz, J. (1988). *How it feels to be adopted.* New York: Knopf. [Interviews with adopted children]

Lifton, B. J. (1979). *Twice born: Memoirs of an adopted daughter.* New York: McGraw-Hill.

McKuen, R. (1976). *Finding my father: One man's search for identity*. Los Angeles: Cheval Books.

Schaeffer, J., & Lindstrom, C. (1989). *How to raise an adopted child*. New York: Crown Publishing.

CHILDREN WITH SPECIAL NEEDS

Brown, H. (1976). *Yesterday's child*. New York: New American Library.

Brutten, M., Richardson, S., & Mangel, C. (1973). *Something's wrong with my child*. New York: Harcourt Brace Jovanovich. [Mental retardation]

Featherstone, H. (1980). *A difference in the family: Living with a disabled child*. New York: Basic Books. [Written by a parent of child with special needs who is also a professional]

Fowler, M.C. (1990). *Maybe you know my kid: A parent's guide to identifying, understanding and helping your child with attention deficit hyperactivity disorder*. New York: Birch Lane Press.

Gordon, S. (1975). *Living fully: A guide for young people with a handicap, their parents, their teachers and professionals*. New York: John Day.

Greenfield, J. (1973). *A child called Noah*. New York: Warner Paperback. [Autism]

Killilea, M. L. (1975). *Karen*. Englewood Cliffs, NJ: Prentice-Hall. [Physical handicaps]

Lord, J.H. (1990). *Beyond sympathy: What to say and do for someone suffering an injury, illness or loss*. Ventura, CA: Pathfinder Publishers.

MacCracken, M. (1986). *Turnabout children*. New York: Signet. [Dyslexia, learning disabilities]

Osman, B. R. (1979). *Learning disabilities: A family affair*. New York: Random House.

Popp, R. A. (1983). Learning about disabilities. *Teaching Exceptional Children, 15*(2), 78–81. [Lessons for primary-level students]

Segal, M. (1983). *In time and with love*. New York: Newmarket Press. [Written by a psychologist and mother of a child with developmental delays]

Williams-Wilson, M.J. (1989). *Help for children: A national directory of hotlines, organizations, resources*. Shepherdstown, WV: Rocky River Publishers.

DIVORCE AND REMARRIAGE

Cunningham, C. (1988). *All kinds of separation*. Mount Dora, FL: Kidsrights. [Coloring and drawing book; primary grades; covers divorce, hospitalization, jail]

Fassler, D. (1988). *Changing families: A guide for kids and grownups*. Burlington, VT: Waterfront Books. [Workbook, ages 7-12]

Gardner, R. A. (1970). *The boys' and girls' book about divorce*. New York: Bantam Books. [All ages]

Gardner, R. A. (1970). *The parent's book about divorce*. New York: Bantam Books. [For parents to read and share with their children]

Gardner, R. A. (1973). *The boys' and girls' book about one-parent families*. New York: Bantam Books. [All ages]

Gardner, R. A. (1974). *The boys' and girls' book about stepfamilies*. New York: Bantam Books. [All ages]

Getzoff, A., & McClenahan, C. (1984). *Stepkids: A survival guide for teenagers in stepfamilies*. New York: Walker & Co.

Kransny-Brown, L., & Brown, M. (1986). *Dinosaurs divorce: A guide for changing families*. Boston: Little Brown.

Krement, J. (1988). *How it feels when parents divorce*. New York: Knopf. [Interviews with children with divorced parents]

Larson, J. H., Anderson, J. O., & Morgan, T. (1984). *Workshops models for family life education: Effective stepparenting*. New York: Family Service America.

Lindsay, J.W. (1982). *Do I have a daddy? A story about a single parent child*. Buena Park, CA: Morning Glory Press.

Wallerstein, J. S., & Blakeslee, S. (1990). *Second chances: Men, women, and children a decade after divorce: Who wins, who loses—and why*. New York: Ticknor & Fields.

ETHNICITY

Cardenai, L. (1970). *Return to Ramos*. New York: Hill and Wang.

Carter, F. (1976). *The education of little tree*. Alburquerque: University of New Mexico Press.

Carter, M.K. (1970). *On to freedom*. New York: Hill and Wang.

Figueroa, J. (1970). *Antonio's world.* New York: Hill and Wang.

Rose, P.I. (1964). *They and we.* New York: Random House.

Wyatt, E. (1952). *Geronimo.* New York: McGraw-Hill

Wyatt, E. (1953). *Cochise.* New York: McGraw Hill.

GENERAL

Bradshaw, J. (1990). *Homecoming: Reclaiming and championing your inner child.* New York: Bantam Books.

Clark, A., Clemes, H., & Bean, R. (1980). *How to raise teenagers' self-esteem.* Los Angeles: Enrich. [For parents and school professionals]

Clarke, J. I. (1980). *Self-esteem: A family affair.* New York: Harper and Row.

Clemes, H., & Bean, R. (1980). *How to raise children's self-esteem.* Los Angeles: Enrich. [For parents and school professionals]

Crary, E. (1983). *My name is not dummy: A child's problem solving book.* Seattle, WA: Parenting Press.

Landy, L. (1990). *Child support through small group counseling.* Mount Dora, FL: Kidsrights.

Schmitz, C., & Hipp, E. (1987). *A teachers guide to fighting invisible tigers: A 12-part course in lifeskills development.* Minneapolis, MN: Free Spirit Publishers.

Sheneve, S. (1979). *Family secrets: Five very important stories.* New York: Alfred A. Knopf. [Primary grades; stories about death, incest, divorce]

Vernon, A. (1989). *Thinking, feeling, behaving: An emotional educational curriculum for children grades 1-6.* Champaign, IL: Research Press.

SIBLINGS

Cleary, M. E. (1976). Helping children understand the child with special needs. *Children Today,* 5(4), 6-10.

Lasker, J. (1974). *He's my brother.* New York: Albert Whitman & Company.

Meyer, D. J., Vadasy, P. F., & Fewell, R. R. (1985). *Sibshops: A handbook for implementing workshops for siblings of children with special needs.* Seattle: University of Washington Press.

Sobol, H. L. (1977). *My Brother Steven is Retarded.* New York: Macmillan.

RESOURCES C

ABUSE AND ADDICTIONS

Local Resources (Local Telephone Directory)
Adult Children of Alcoholics
Al-Anon
Al-Ateen
Alcoholics Anonymous
Gamblers Anonymous
Narcotics Anonymous
Overeaters Anonymous
Sex Addicts Anonymous
Sex and Love Addicts Anonymous
Women for Sobriety

National Resources
Addiction Research Foundation Dept.
c/o Marketing Services
33 Russell St.
Toronto, Ontario, Canada M55 2S1

Adult Children of Alcoholics
PO Box 3216
Torrance, CA 90510
(213) 534-1815

Al-Anon/Al-Ateen Family Group Headquarters
PO Box 182
Madison Square Garden
New York, NY 10010

Alcoholics Anonymous World Services
PO Box 459
Grand Central Station
New York, NY 10163
(212) 686-1100

Drug Abuse Council
1828 L St., NW
Washington, DC 20036

Drug Enforcement Administration
1405 Eye St., NW
Washington, DC 20537

Nar-Anon Family Group Headquarters Inc.
PO Box 2562
Palos Verdes, CA 90274-0119
(213) 547-5800

Narcotics Anonymous
PO Box 9999
Van Nuys, CA 91409
(818) 780-3951

National Association for Children of Alcoholics
35182 Coast Hwy., Suite B
South Laguna, CA 92677
(714) 499-3889

National Center for Alcohol Education
1901 N Moore St.
Arlington, VA 22209

National Clearinghouse for Alcohol Information
PO Box 2345
Rockville, MD 20852
(301) 468-2600

National Coordinating Council of Drug Education
1526 18th St., NW
Washington, DC 20036

National Council on Alcoholism
2 Park Ave.
New York, NY 10016

National Council on Alcoholism and Drug Dependency, Inc.
12 W 21st St.
New York, NY 10010
(800) NCA-CALL

National Institute of Drug Abuse
11400 Rockville Pl.
Rockville, MD 20852

National Institute on Alcohol Abuse and Alcoholism
5600 Fishers Lane
Rockville, MD 20857

Overeaters Anonymous
4025 Spencer St., Suite 203
Torrance, CA 90503
Mail Address: PO Box 92870
Los Angeles, CA 90009
(213) 618-8835

Rational Recovery
5540 Davie Rd.
Davie, FL 33314-6066
(800) 328-4402
(305) 791-0298

Rutgers Center of Alcohol Studies
PO Box 969
Pitscataway, NJ 08903

Talking about Alcohol: A Program for Parents of Preteens
PO Box 1799
Ridgely, MD 21681
(800) 732-4726

Innovative Alcohol Abuse Education
Drug Free Schools and Communities
U.S. Department of Education
400 Maryland Ave., SW
Washington, DC 20202-6439
Donna Marie Marlowe
(202) 401-1258

CHILD ABUSE AND NEGLECT

National Resources

National Center for the Prevention and Treatment of Child Abuse and Neglect
University of Colorado Medical Center
1205 Onedia St.
Denver, CO 80220

National Center on Child Abuse and Neglect
PO Box 1182
Washington, DC 20213

National Committee for Prevention of Child Abuse
111 E Wacker Dr., Suite 510
Chicago, IL 60601

Parents Anonymous
2810 Artesia Blvd.
Redondo Beach, CA 90278

CHILDREN WITH SPECIAL NEEDS

National Resources—Physical Handicaps

Arthritis Foundation
115 E 18th St.
New York, NY 10003

International Center for the Disabled
Rehabilitation and Research Center
340 E 24th St.
New York, NY 10010

National Easter Seal Society for Crippled Children and Adults
2023 W Ogden Ave.
Chicago, IL 60612

United Cerebral Palsy Association, Inc.
66 E 34th St.
New York, NY 10016

National Resources—Sensory Handicaps

Alexander Graham Bell Association for the Deaf
3417 Volta Pl., NW
Washington, DC 20007

American Foundation for the Blind
15 W 16th St.
New York, NY 10011

Association for Education of the Visually Handicapped
206 N Washington St.
Alexandria, VA 22314

National Association for the Deaf
814 Thayer Ave.
Silver Springs, MD 20910

National Association for the Visually Handicapped
305 E 24th St.
New York, NY 10010

National Resources—Chronic Illness

American Cancer Society
1599 Clifton Rd., NE
Atlanta, GA 30379
(800) ACS-2345

American Diabetes Association
2 Park Ave.
New York, NY 10016

American Heart Association
1615 Stemmons Fwy.
Dallas, TX 75207

Epilepsy Foundation of America
4351 Garden City Dr., Suite 406
Landover, MD 20785

Leukemia Society of America
800 Second Ave.
New York, NY 10017

Make Today Count
1017 S Union St.
Alexandria, VA 22314
(703) 548-9674

Muscular Dystrophy Association of America
810 Seventh Ave.
New York, NY 10019

National Multiple Sclerosis Society
205 E 42nd St., 3rd Floor
New York, NY 10017

National Resources—Learning Disabilities

Association for Children with Learning Disabilities
4156 Library Rd.
Pittsburgh, PA 15234

National Network of Learning Disabled Adults
PO Box 3130
Richardson, TX 75080

National Resources—Emotional and Behavioral Disorders

National Institute of Mental Health
5600 Fishers Lane, Suite 15C17
Rockville, MD 20857

Research and Training Center to Improve Services for Seriously Emotionally
    Handicapped Children and Their Families
Regional Research Institute for Human Services
PO Box 751
Portland State University
Portland, OR 97207-0751

National Resources—Mental and Cognitive Handicaps

American Association on Mental Deficiency
5101 Wisconsin Ave., NW, Suite 405
Washington, DC 20016

National Association for Retarded Citizens
2501 Ave. J
Arlington, TX 76011

National Society for Children and Adults with Autism
1234 Massachusetts Ave., NW, Suite 1017
Washington, DC 20005-4599

National Resources—Multicultural

Mexican-American Legal Defense Fund
28 Geary St.
San Francisco, CA 94108

Multicultural Resource Center
8443 Crenshaw Blvd.
Englewood, CA 90305

Native American Rights Fund
1506 Broadway
Boulder, CO 80302
(303) 447-8760

National Resources—Miscellaneous

American Association for Gifted Children
15 Gramercy Park
New York, NY 10003

Association for the Care of Children's Health
3615 Wisconsin Ave., NW
Washington, DC 20016
(202) 244-1801

Children's Behavioral Services
6171 W Charleston
Las Vegas, NV 89158

Closer Look
Parents' Campaign for Handicapped Children and Youth
PO Box 1492
Washington, DC 20013

Compassionate Friends
PO Box 3696
Oak Brook, IL 60522-3696
(708) 990-0010

Council for Exceptional Children
1920 Association Dr.
Reston, VA 22091

Divorce Anonymous
2600 Colorado Ave., Suite 270
Santa Monica, CA 90404
(213) 315-6538

Health Services and Mental Health Administration
Maternal and Child Health Services
Parklawn Bldg., Suite 739
5600 Fishers Lane
Rockville, MD 20852

National Information Center for Children and Youth with Handicaps (NICHCY)
PO Box 1492
Washington, DC 20013
(800) 999-5599

Sibling Information Network
Connecticut's University Affiliated Program on Developmental Disabilities
991 Main St.
East Hartford, CT 06108
(203) 282-7050

THEOS (Loss of Spouse)
1301 Clark Bldg.
717 Liberty Ave.
Pittsburg, PA 15222-3510
(412) 471-7779

Tough Love
PO Box 1069
Doylestown, PA 18901
(800) 333-1069
(215) 348-7090

CRIME VICTIMS

National Resources

National Organization for Victim Assistance
1757 Park Road, NW
Washington, DC 20010
(202) 232-6682

National Victim Center
307 W Seventh St., Suite 1001
Forth Worth, TX 76102
(817) 877-3355

Victim Services
(212) 577-7777 (Hotline)
(212) 577-7700

SEXUAL ABUSE

Local Resources (local telephone directory)

Incest Survivors Anonymous
Survivors of Incest Anonymous

National Resources

AMACU Coordinator
c/o Parents United
232 E Gish Rd., 1st Floor
San Jose, CA 95112
(408) 453-7616

Incest Resources
Women's Center
46 Pleasant St.
Cambridge, MA 02139
(617) 492-1818

Incest Survivors Anonymous
PO Box 5613
Long Beach, CA 90805-0613

Looking Up
PO Box K
Augusta, ME 04330
(207) 626-3402

SARAH, Inc.
PO Box 20353
Bradenton, FL 34203
(813) 746-9114

Survivors of Incest Anonymous
PO Box 21817
Baltimore, MD 21222
(301) 282-3400 or 433-2365

VOICES in Action, Inc.
PO Box 148309
Chicago, IL 60614
(312) 327-1500

REFERENCES

Abbott, D. A., & Meridith, W. H. (1986). Strengths of parents with retarded children. *Family Relations, 35*, 371–375.

Abi-Nader, J. (1991). Creating a vision of the future: Strategies for motivating minority students. *Phi Delta Kappan, 72*, 546–549.

Abramovitch, R., Corter, D., & Lando, B. (1979). Sibling interaction in the home. *Child Development, 50*, 997–1003.

Abramovitch, R., & Strayer, F. F. (1977). Preschool social organization: Agonistic, spacing and attentional behaviors. In P. Pliner, T. Kramer, & T. Alloway (Eds.), *Recent advances in the study of communication and affect* (Vol. 6). New York: Academic Press.

Abrams, J. C., & Kaslow, F. (1977). Family systems and the learning disabled child: Intervention and treatment. *Journal of Learning Disabilities, 10*, 86–90.

Ackerman, R. J. (1983). *Children of alcoholics: A guidebook for educators, therapists, and parents* (2nd ed.). Holmes Beach, FL: Learning Publications.

Adkins, P.G., & Young, R.G. (1976). Cultural perceptions in the treatment of handicapped school children of Mexican-American parentage. *Journal of Research and Development in Education, 9*(4), 83-90.

Adler, A. (1959). *Understanding human nature*. New York: Fawcett.

Affleck, J., Madge, S., Adams, A., & Lowenbraun, S. (1988). Integrated classroom versus resource model: Academic viability and effectiveness. *Exceptional Children, 54*, 339–348.

Aldous, J. (1978). *Family careers: Developmental change in families*. New York: John Wiley.

Alexander, C., & Strain, P. S. (1978). A review of educators' attitudes toward handicapped children and the concept of mainstreaming. *Psychology in the Schools, 15*, 390–396.

Amerikaner, M. J., & Omizo, M. M. (1984). Family interaction and learning disabilities. *Journal of Learning Disabilities, 17*, 540-543.

Anderson, H., & Goolishian, H. (1986). Systems consultation with agencies dealing with domestic violence. In L. C. Wynne, S. H. McDaniel, & T. T. Weber (Eds.), *Systems consultation: A new perspective for family therapy*. (pp. 284–299). New York: Guilford Press.

Anderson, J.A. (1988). Cognitive styles and multicultural populations. *Journal of Teacher Education, 29* (1), 2–9.

Aponte, H.J. (1976a). The family–school interview: An eco-structural approach. *Family Process, 15*, 303–311.

Aponte, H.J. (1976b). Underorganization in the poor family. In P. Guerin (Ed.), *Family therapy: Theory and practice* (pp. 432–448). New York: Gardner Press.

Aponte, H. J., & Hoffman, L. (1973). The open door: A structural approach to a family with an anorectic child. *Family Process, 12*(1), 1–44.

Aponte, H. J., & Van Deusen, J. M. (1981). Structural family therapy. In A.S. Gurman & D. P. Kniskern (Eds.), *Handbook of family therapy* (pp. 310–361). New York: Brunner/Mazel.

Arends, R. I. (1990). Connecting the university to the school. In B. Joyce (Ed.), *Changing school culture through staff development*. Alexandria, VA: Association for Supervision and Curriculum Development.

Arnstein, H. S. (1979). *Brothers and sisters/sisters and brothers*. New York: E. P. Dutton.

Atkins, D. V. (1987). Siblings of the hearing impaired: Perspectives for parents. *Volta Review, 89*(5), 32–45.

Attneave, C. L., & Verhulst, J. (1986). Teaching mental health professionals to see family strengths: Core network interventions in a hospital setting. In M. Karpel (Ed.), *Family resources* (pp. 259–271). New York: Guilford Press.

Bailey, D. (1984). A triaxial model of the interdisciplinary team and group process. *Exceptional Children, 51*, 17–25.

Bailey, D. B., Jr., Simeonsson, R. J., Isbell, P., Huntington, G. S., Winton, P., Comfort, M., & Helm, J. (1988). Inservice training in family assessment and goal-setting for early interventionists: Outcomes and issues. *Journal of the Division for Early Childhood, 12*, 126–136.

Bailey, D. B., Simeonsson, R. J., Winton, P., Huntington, G., Comfort, M., Isbell, P., O'Donnell, K., & Helm, J. (1986). Family-focused intervention: A functional model for planning, implementing, and evaluating individualized family services in early intervention. *Journal of the Division for Early Childhood, 10*, 156–171.

Bailey, D. B., & Winton, P. J. (1987). Stability and change in parents' expectations about mainstreaming. *Topics in Early Childhood Special Education, 7*(1), 73–88.

Baldridge, V., & Deal, T. (Eds.). (1983). *The dynamics of organizational change.* Boston: Addison-Wesley.

Bandler, R., & Grinder, J. (1979). *Frogs into princes: Neurolinguistic programming.* Moab, UT: Real People Press.

Bandler, R., & Grinder, J. (1982). *Reframing: Neurolinguistic programming and the transformation of meaning.* Moab, UT: Real People Press.

Bank, S. P., & Kahn, M. D. (1975). Sisterhood-brotherhood is powerful: Sibling subsystems and family therapy. *Family Process, 14*, 311–337.

Bank, S. P., & Kahn, M. D. (1982). *The sibling bond.* New York: Basic Books.

Barney, J. (1990). Stepfamilies: Second chance or second-rate? *Phil Delta Kappan, 72*, 144–148.

Barnhill, L. R., & Longo, D. (1978). Fixation and regression in the family life cycle. *Family Process, 17*, 469–478.

Barth, R. P., & Berry, M. (1988). *Adoption and disruption. Rates, risks, and responses.* New York: Aldine de Gruyter.

Bateson, G. (1972). *Steps to an ecology of the mind.* New York: Ballantine Books.

Beal, E. W., & Hochman, G. (1991). *Adult children of divorce.* New York: Delacorte Press.

Beattie, M. (1987). *Codependent no more.* New York: Harper/Hazelden.

Beavers, J., Hampson, R. B., Hulgus, Y. F., & Beavers, W. R. (1986). Coping in families with a retarded child. *Family Process, 25*, 365–378.

Beckman, P. J. (1983). Influence of selected child characteristics on stress in families of handicapped infants. *American Journal of Mental Deficiency, 88*, 150–156.

Beckman-Bell, P. (1981). Child-related stress in families of handicapped children. *Topics in Early Childhood Special Education, 1*(3), 45–53.

Benne, K. D., & Sheats, P. (1948). Functional roles of group members. *Journal of Social Issues, 2*, 42–47.

Bennett, C.I. (1990). *Comprehensive multicultural education: Theory and practice.* Boston: Allyn and Bacon.

Bennett, F. (1982). The pediatrician and the interdisciplinary process. *Exceptional Children, 48*, 306–314.

Bennett, L. A., Wolin, S. J., Reiss, D., & Teitelbaum, M. A. (1987). Couples at risk for transmission of alcoholism: Protective influences. *Family Process, 26*, 111–129.

Berardo, F. M. (1980). Decade preview: Some trends and directions for family research and theory in the 1980s. *Journal of Marriage and the Family, 42*, 723–728.

Berger, A. (1985). Characteristics of abusing families. In L. L'Abate (Ed.), *The handbook of family psychology and therapy* (Vol. II, pp. 900–936). Homewood, IL: Dorsey Press.

Berger, M. (1984a). Social network interventions for families that have a handicapped child. In J. Hansen & E.I. Coopersmith (Eds.), *Families with handicapped members* (pp. 127–136). Rockville, MD: Aspen Systems.

Berger, M. (1984b). Special Education Programs. In M. Berger & G. J. Jurkovic (Eds.), *Practicing family therapy in diverse settings* (pp. 142–179). San Fransisco: Jossey-Bass.

Berger, M., & Jurkovic, G. (Eds.). (1984). *Family therapy in context: The practice of systemic therapy in community settings.* San Francisco: Jossey-Bass.

Berman, W. H., & Turk, D. C. (1981). Adaptation to divorce: Problems and coping strategies. *Journal of Marriage and the Family, 27*, 179–189.

Blacher, J. (1984). Sequential stages of parental adjustment to the birth of a child with handicaps: Fact or artifact? *Mental Retardation, 22*(2), 55–68.

Bluhm, H. P., Egan, M. W., & Perry, M. L. (1981). The training and evaluation of preservice multidisciplinary teams. *Teacher Education and Special Education, 4*(1), 18–24.

Blumberg, B. D., Lewis, M. J., & Susman, E. J. (1984). Adolescence: A time of transition. In M. Eisenberg, L. Sutkin, & M. Jansen (Eds.), *Chronic illness and disability through the life span: Effects on self and family* (pp. 133–149). New York: Springer Publishing.

Boszormenyi-Nagy, I., & Spark, G. M. (1973). *Invisible loyalties.* New York: Harper and Row.

Bowen, M. (1966). The use of family theory in clinical practice. *Comprehensive Psychiatry, 7,* 345–374.

Bowen, M. (1976). Theory in the practice of psychotherapy. In P. J. Guerin, Jr. (Ed.), *Family therapy: Theory and practice* (pp. 42–90). New York: Garden Press.

Bowen, M. (1978). *Family therapy in clinical practice.* Northvale, NJ: Jason Aranson.

Bowen, M. (1985). *Family therapy in clinical practice* (3rd ed.). Northvale, NJ: Jason Aranson.

Bowman, P., & Goldberg, M. (1983). "Reframing": A tool for the school psychologist. *Psychology in the Schools, 20,* 210–214.

Bradt, J. (1980). *The family diagram.* Washington, DC: Groome Center.

Brendtro, L., Brokenleg, M., & Van Bockern, S. (1990). *Reclaiming youth at risk: Our hope for the future* Bloomington, IN: National Educational Service.

Breslau, N. (1982). Siblings of disabled children: Birth order and age-spacing effects. *Journal of Abnormal Child Psychology, 10*(1), 85–96.

Brody, E. M. (1974). Aging and family personality: A developmental view. *Family Process, 13*(1), 23–37.

Brody, G. H., & Stoneman, Z. (1983). *Contextual issues in the study of sibling socialization.* Paper presented at the NICHD Conference on Research on Families with Retarded Persons, September, Baltimore, MD.

Brodzinsky, D. M. (1990). A stress and coping model of adoption adjustment. In D. M. Brodzinsky & M. D. Schechter (Eds.), *The psychology of adoption.* New York: Oxford University Press.

Bronfenbrenner, U. (1979). *The ecology of human development.* Cambridge: Harvard University Press.

Buktenica, N. A. (1981). Multidisciplinary training teams: A transactional approach to training and service. *Teacher Education and Special Education, 4*(1), 31–38.

Burgess, R. S., & Conger, R. D. (1977). Family interaction patterns related to child abuse and neglect: Some preliminary findings. *Child Abuse and Neglect, 1,* 269–277.

Buscaglia, L. (1983). *The disabled and their parents: A counseling challenge.* (rev. ed.). Thorofare, NJ: Charles Slack.

Byers, P. (1992). The spiritual in the classroom. *Holistic Education Review, 5*(1), 6–11.

Calof, D. L. (1988). *Adult children of incest and child abuse.* Workshop publication. Seattle: Family Psychotherapy Practice of Seattle.

Carter, E. A., & McGoldrick, M. (1980). *The family life cycle: A framework for family therapy.* New York: Gardner Press.

Carter, J., & Sugai, G. (1989). Survey on prereferral practices: Responses from state departments of education. *Exceptional Children, 55,* 298–302.

Chalfant, J. C., Pysh, M., & Moultrie, R. (1979). Teacher Assistance Teams: A model for within-building problem solving. *Learning Disability Quarterly, 2,* 85–96.

Christensen, H.T. (1964). Development of the family field of study. *Handbook of marriage and the family.* Chicago: Rand McNally and Company.

Cicirelli, V. G. (1972). The effect of sibling relationships on concept learning of young children taught by child teachers. *Child Development, 43,* 282–287.

Cleveland, D. W., & Miller, N. (1977). Attitudes and life commitments of older siblings of mentally retarded adults: An exploratory study. *Mental Retardation, 15* (3), 38–41.

Coates, D. L. (1990). Social network analysis as mental health intervention with African-American adolescents. In F. C. Serafica, A. I. Schwebel, R. K. Russell, P. D. Isaac, & L. B. Myers (Eds.), *Mental health of ethnic minorities* (pp. 230–253). New York: Praeger.

Cobb, S. (1976). Social support as a moderator of life stress. *Psychosomatic Medicine, 38,* 301–314.

Cohen, R. (1969). Conceptual styles, culture conflict, and nonverbal tests of intelligence. *American Anthropologist, 71,* 828–856.

Colapinto, J. (1982). Structural family therapy. In A. Horne & B. Ohlsen (Eds.), *Family counseling and therapy* (pp. 112–140). Itasca, IL: F.E. Peacock.

Coleman, S. B., Kaplan, J. D., & Downing, R. W. (1986). Life cycle and loss—The spiritual vacuum of heroin addiction. *Family Process, 25,* 5–23.

Combrinck-Graham, L. (1983). The family life cycle and families with young children. In J. Hansen & H. Liddle (Eds.), *Clinical implications of the family life cycle.* Rockville, MD: Aspen.

Conoley, J. C., & Conoley, C. W. (1982). *School consultation: A guide to practice and training*. New York: Pergamon Press.

Coopersmith, E. I. (1983). The family and public service systems: An assessment method. In J. Hansen & E. Keeney (Eds.), *Diagnosis and assessment in family therapy* (pp. 83–100). Rockville, MD: Aspen.

Corbett, H. D., Firestone, W. A., & Rossman, G. B. (1987). Resistance to planned change and the sacred in school cultures. *Educational Administration Quarterly, 33*(4), 36–59.

Corrales, R. G., Kostoryz, J., Ro-Trock, L., & Smith, B. (1983). Family therapy with developmentally delayed children: An ecosystemic approach. In D. Bagarozzi, A. Jurich, & R. Jackson (Eds.), *Marital and family therapy: New perspectives in theory, research, and practice* (pp. 137–164). New York: Human Sciences Press.

Council for Exceptional Children (1979). *We can help*. Reston, VA: Author.

Courtnage, L., & Healy, H. (1984). Interdisciplinary team training. *Teacher Education and Special Education, 7*, 3–11.

Courtnage, L., & Smith-Davis, J. (1987). Interdisciplinary team training: A national survey of special education teacher training programs. *Exceptional Children, 53*, 451–458.

Courtois, C. A. (1988). *Healing the incest wound: Adult survivors in therapy*. New York: W. W. Norton.

Coyne, A., & Brown, M. E. (1985). Developmentally disabled children can be adopted. *Child Welfare, 64*, 607–615.

Crisler, J. (1979). Utilization of a team approach in implementing Public Law 94-142. *Journal of Research and Development in Education, 12*, 101–108.

Cuban, L. (1989). The "at-risk" label and the problem of urban school reform. *Phi Delta Kappan, 70*, 780–784.

Cummins, J. (1989). A theoretical framework for bilingual special education. *Exceptional Children, 56*, 111–119.

Daniels-Mohring, D. (1986). *Sibling relationships with an older sibling as identified patient*. Unpublished manuscript, Georgia State University, Atlanta.

Delaney, A. J. (Ed.). (1979). *Black task force report: Project on ethnicity*. New York: Family Service Association of America.

delCarmen, R. (1990). Assessment of Asian-Americans for family therapy. In F. C. Serafica, A. I. Schwebel, R. K. Russell, P. D. Isaac, & L. B. Myers (Eds.), *Mental health of ethnic minorities* (pp. 24–68). New York: Praeger.

Dudley, J. (1983). *Living with stigma: The plight of the people who we label mentally retarded*. Springfield, IL: Charles C Thomas.

Dunlap, W. R., & Hollinsworth, J. S. (1977). How does a handicapped child affect the family? Implications for practitioners. *The Family Coordinator, 26*, 286–293.

Dunn, J., & Kendrick, C. (1982). *Siblings*. Cambridge: Harvard University Press.

Dunn, L. (1968). Special education for the mildly retarded: Is much of it justifiable? *Exceptional Children, 35*, 5–22.

Dunst, C. J., Trivette, C. M., & Cross, A. H. (1986). Mediating influences of social support: Personal, family, and child outcomes. *American Journal of Mental Deficiency, 90*, 403–417.

Duvall, E. M. (1977). *Marriage and family development (5th ed.)*. Philadelphia: Lippincott.

Dyson, L., & Fewell, R. R. (1985). Stress and adaptation in parents of young handicapped and nonhandicapped children: A comparative study. *Journal of the Division for Early Childhood, 10*, 25–34.

Edgar, E., Singer, T., Ritchie, C., & Heggelund, M. (1981). Parents as facilitators in developing an individual approach to parent involvement. *Behavioral Disorders, 6*, 122–127.

Eheart, B. K., & Ciccone, J. (1982). Special needs of low-income mothers of developmentally delayed children. *American Journal of Mental Deficiency, 87*(1), 26–33.

Erikson, E. (1963). *Childhood and society*. New York: W. W. Norton.

Farber, B. (1963). Interaction with retarded siblings and life goals of children. *Marriage and Family Living, 25*, 96–98.

Featherstone, H. (1980). *A difference in the family*. New York: Basics.

Feiring, C., & Lewis, M. (1985). Changing characteristics of the U.S. family. In M. Lewis (Ed.), *Beyond the dyad* (pp. 59–90). New York: Plenum Press.

Ferrari, M. (1984). Chronic illness: Psychosocial effects on siblings—I. Chronically ill boys. *Journal of Child Psychology and Psychiatry, 25*, 459–476.

Ferrari, M., Matthews, W. S., & Barabas, G. (1983). The family and the child with epilepsy. *Family Process, 22,* 53–59.

Figley, C., & McCubbin, H. (1983). *Stress and the family: Vol. 2: Coping with catastrophe.* New York: Brunner/Mazel.

Fischer, J., & Roberts, S. C. (1983). The effect of the mentally retarded child on his siblings. *Education, 103,* 399–401.

Fischgrund, J. E., Cohen, O. P., & Clarkson, R. L. (1987). Hearing-impaired children in Black and Hispanic families. *Volta Review, 89*(5), 59–67.

Fisher, B. A. (1980). *Small group decision making* (2nd ed.). New York: McGraw-Hill.

Fogarty, T. (1976). On emptiness and closeness, Part II. *The family, 3*(2), 3–17.

Fordyce, W. (1981). On interdisciplinary peers. *Archives of Physical Medicine, 62*(2), 51–53.

Forman, R. (1987, July-August.). Circle of care, Confronting the alcoholic's denial. *Family Therapy Networker,* pp. 35–41.

Foster, M. (1986). Families with young disabled children in family therapy. In J.C. Hansen & L. Combrinck-Graham (Eds.), *Treating young children in family therapy* (pp. 62–72). Rockville, MD: Aspen Systems.

Foster, M., Berger, M., & McLean, M. (1981). Rethinking a good idea: A reassessment of parent involvement. *Topics in Early Childhood Special Education, 1*(3), 56–65.

Fowle, C. M. (1968). The effect of the severely mentally retarded child on his family. *American Journal of Mental Deficiency, 73,* 468–473.

Fox, J., & Savelle, S. (1987). Social interaction research and families of behaviorally disordered children: A critical review and forward look. *Behavioral Disorders, 12,* 276–291.

Framo, J. L. (1981a). The integration of marital thrapy with sessions with family of origin. In A. S. Gurman & D. P. Kniskern (Eds.), *Handbook of family therapy* (pp. 133–158). New York: Bruner/Mazel.

Framo, M. D. (1981b). Common issues in recoupled families and therapy interventions. In A. S. Gurman (Ed.), *Questions and answers in the practice of family therapy* (pp. 333–337). New York: Brunner/Mazel.

Friedman, E. H. (1986). Emotional process in the market place: The family therapist as consultant to work systems. In L. C. Wynne, S. H. McDaniel, & T. T. Weber (Eds.), *Systems consultation: A new perspective for family therapy* (pp. 398–422). New York: Guilford Press.

Friedman, L. J. (1981). Common problems in stepfamilies. In A. S. Gurman (Ed.), *Questions and answers in the practice of family therapy* (pp. 329–332). New York: Brunner/Mazel.

Friedrich, W. N. (1979). Predictors of the coping behavior of mothers of handicapped children. *Journal of Consulting and Clinical Psychology, 47,* 1140–1141.

Friedrich, W. N., & Friedrich, W. L. (1981). Psychosocial assets of parents of handicapped and nonhandicapped children. *American Journal of Mental Deficiency, 85,* 551–553.

Friedrich, W. N., Wilturner, L. G., & Cohen, D. S. (1985). Coping resources and parenting mentally retarded children. *American Journal of Mental Deficiency, 90,* 130–139.

Friend, M. (1984). Consultation skills for resource teachers. *Learning Disability Quarterly, 7,* 246–250.

Frymier, J., & Gansneder, B. (1989). The *Phi Delta Kappan* study of students at risk. *Phi Delta Kappan, 71,* 142–146.

Fuchs, D., Fuchs, L., & Bahr, M. (1990). Mainstream assistance teams: A scientific basis for the art of consultation. *Exceptional Children, 57,* 128–139.

Fuchs, D., Fuchs, L., Bahr, M., Fernstrom, P., & Stecker, P. (1990). Prereferral intervention: A prescriptive approach. *Exceptional Children, 56,* 493–513.

Fullan, M. (1982). *The meaning of educational change.* New York: Teachers College Press.

Fuqua, R. W., Hegland, S. M., & Karas, S. C. (1985). Processes influencing linkages between preschool handicap classrooms and homes. *Exceptional Children, 51,* 307–314.

Furstenberg, F. F. (1988). Child care after divorce and remarriage. In E. M. Hetherington & J. D. Arasteh (Eds.), *Impact of divorce, single parenting, and stepparenting on children.* Hillsdale, NJ: Lawrence Erlbaum Associates, Inc.

Gabel, H., & Kotsch, L. S. (1981). Extended families and young handicapped children. *Topics in Early Childhood Special Education, 1*(3), 29–35.

Gallagher, J. J., Beckman, P., & Cross, A. H. (1983). Families of handicapped children: Sources of stress and its amelioration. *Exceptional Children, 50,* 10–19.

Gallagher, J. J., Cross, A., & Scharfman, W. (1981). Paternal adaptation to a young handicapped child: The father's role. *Journal of the Division for Early Childhood, 3*, 3–14.

Garcia-Preto, N. (1982). Puerto Rican families. In M. McGoldrick, J. Pearce, & J. Giordano (Eds.), *Ethnicity and family therapy* (pp. 164–186). New York: Guilford Press.

Gesell, A., Ilg, F. L., & Ames, L. B. (1974). *Infant and child in the culture of today* (rev. ed.). New York: Harper and Row.

Gibran, K. (1923). *The prophet.* New York: Alfred E. Knopf.

Gilliam, J. (1979). Contributions and status rankings of educational planning committee participants. *Exceptional Children, 45,* 466–468.

Glidden, L. M. (1989). *Parents for children, children for parents: The adoption alternative.* Washington, DC: American Association on Mental Retardation.

Goffman, E. (1963). *Stigma: Notes on the management of spoiled identity.* Englewood Cliffs, NJ: Prentice-Hall.

Goldstein, S., Strickland, B., Turnbull, A. P., & Curry, L. (1980). An observational analysis of the IEP conference. *Exceptional Children, 46,* 278–286.

Golin, A. K., & Ducanis, A. J. (1981). Preparation for teamwork: A model for interdisciplinary education. *Teacher Education and Special Education, 4*(1), 25–30.

Gould, J. (1970). The phases of adult life: A study in developmental psychology. *American Journal of Psychiatry, 129*(5), 35–79.

Graden, J. (1989). Redefining "prereferral" intervention as intervention assistance: Collaboration between general and special education. *Exceptional Children, 56,* 227–231.

Graden, J., Casey, A., & Christenson, S. (1985). Implementing a prereferral intervention system: Part I. The model. *Exceptional Children, 51,* 377–384.

Greer, J. (1989). Another perspective and some immoderate proposals on "teacher empowerment." *Exceptional Children, 55,* 294–297.

Grossman, F. (1972). *Brothers and sisters of retarded children: An exploratory study.* Syracuse, NY: Syracuse University Press.

Guerin, P. J. (1976). *Family therapy: Theory and practice.* New York: Gardner Press.

Guidubaldi, J., & Cleminshaw, H. (1985). Divorce, family health, and child adjustment. *Family Relations, 34,* 35–41.

Guidubaldi, J., Cleminshaw, H. K., Perry, J. D., & McLoughlin, C. S. (1973). The implications of parental divorce on children: Report of a nationwide NASP study. *School Psychology Review, 12,* 30–323.

Guskey, T. (1986). Staff development and the process of teacher change. *Educational Researcher, 15*(5), 5–12.

Gutkin, T. B., & Curtis, M. J. (1982). School-based consultation. In C.R. Reynolds & T.B. Gutkin (Eds.), *The handbook of school psychology* (pp. 796–828). New York: John Wiley.

Hadley, T., Jacob, T., Miliones, J., Caplan, J., & Spitz, D. (1974). The relationship between family developmental crisis and the appearance of symptoms in a family member. *Family Process, 13,* 207–214.

Hale, J. (1981). Black children: Their roots, culture, and learning styles. *Young Children, 36,* 37–50.

Hale-Benson, J. E. (1982). Black children. *Their roots, culture, and learning styles* (rev. ed.). Baltimore: Johns Hopkins University Press.

Haley, J. (1973). *Problem-solving therapy.* San Francisco: Jossey-Bass.

Haley, J. (1980). *Leaving home: The therapy of disturbed young people.* New York: McGraw-Hill.

Haley, J. (1985). (Ed.). *Changing individuals: Conversations with Milton H. Erickson, M.D.* (Vol. 1). New York: Triangle Press.

Haley, J., & Hoffman, L. (1967). *Techniques of family therapy.* New York: Basic Books.

Hall, C. S., & Lindzey, G. (1978). *Theories of personality* (3rd ed.). New York: John Wiley.

Hall, G. E., & Hord, S. M. (1987). *Change in schools: Facilitating the process.* Albany: State University of New York Press.

Hall, G. E., Wallace, R. C., Jr., & Dossett, W. (1973). *A developmental conceptualization of the adoption process within educational institutions.* Austin: The University of Texas at Austin, Research and Development Center for Teacher Education. (ERIC Document Reproduction Service No. ED 095 126)

Hall, J., & Taylor, K. (1971). The emergence of Eric: Co-therapy in the treatment of a family with a disabled child. *Family Process, 10*(1), 85–96.

Hansen, J., & Falicov, C. J. (Eds.). (1983). *Cultural perspectives in family therapy.* Rockville, MD: Aspen.

Hansen, J., & Imber-Coopersmith, E. (Eds.). (1984). *Families with handicapped members*. Rockville, MD: Aspen.

Hansen, J., & Keeney, B. (Eds.). (1983). *Diagnosis and assessment in family therapy*. Rockville, MD: Aspen.

Hansen, J., & Liddle, H. (Eds.). (1983). *Clinical implications of the family life cycle*. Rockville, MD: Aspen .

Harrington, R., & Gibson, E. (1986). Preassessment procedures for learning disabled children: Are they effective? *Journal of Learning Disabilities, 19*(9), 538–541.

Harvey, D. H., & Greenway, A. P. (1984). The self-concept of physically handicapped children and their non-handicapped siblings: An empirical investigation. *Journal of Child Psychology and Psychiatry, 25*, 273–284.

Hauser, S. T., Jacobson, A. M., Wertlieb, D., Brink, S., & Wentworth, S. (1985). The contribution of family environment to perceived competence and illness adjustment in diabetic and acutely ill adolescents. *Family Relations, 34*, 99–108.

"He pits Jane and me against each other!": Conflicting family styles. (1988). *Exceptional Parent, 18*(3), 62–68.

Helge, D. (1981). Multidisciplinary personnel preparation: A successful model of preservice team training for service delivery. *Teacher Education and Special Education, 4*(1), 13–17.

Hendrick, J. (1984). *The whole child: Early education for the eighties*. St. Louis: C. V. Mosby.

Hess, B. B., & Waring, J. M. (1978). Parent and child in later life: Rethinking the relationship. In R. Lerner & G. Spanier (Eds.), *Child influences on marital and family interaction: A life-span perspective* (pp. 241–275). New York: Academic Press.

Hesse-Biber, S., & Williamson, J. (1984). Resource theory and power in families: Life cycle considerations. *Family Process, 23*, 261–278.

Hines, P. M., & Boyd-Franklin, N. (1982). Black families. In M. McGoldrick, J. Pearce, & G. Giordano (Eds.), *Ethnicity and family therapy* (pp. 84–107). New York: Guilford Press.

Hoffman, L. (1981). *Foundations of family therapy*. New York: Basic Books.

Holman, T. B., & Burr, W. R. (1980). Beyond the beyond: The growth of family theories in the 1970s. *Journal of Marriage and the Family, 42*, 729–740.

Hoopes, J. L. (1990). Adoption and identity formation. In D. M. Brodzinsky & M. D. Schechter (Eds.), *The psychology of adoption*. New York: Oxford University Press.

Howard, J. (1978). The influence of children's developmental dysfunctions on marital quality and family interaction. In R. Lerner & G. Spanier (Eds.), *Child influences on marital and family interaction: A life-span perspective* (pp. 275–298). New York: Academic Press.

Huberman, M., & Miles, M. (1984). *Innovation up close*. New York: Plenum.

Hughes, S. F., Berger, M., & Wright, L. (1978, October). The family life cycle and clinical intervention. *Journal of Marriage and Family Counseling*, 33–40.

Idol, L., Paolucci-Whitcomb, P., & Nevin, A. (1986). *Collaborative consultation*. Rockville, MD: Aspen.

Idol-Maestes, L. (1983). *Special educator's consultation handbook*. Rockville, MD: Aspen.

I'm not going to be John's babysitter forever: Siblings, planning and the disabled child. (1987). *The Exceptional Parent, 17*(8), 60–68.

Imber-Black, E. (1986). Toward a resource model in systemic family therapy. In M. Karpel (Ed.), *Family resources: The hidden partner in family therapy* (pp. 148–174). New York: Guilford Press.

Intagliata, J., & Doyle, N. (1984). Enhancing social support for parents of developmentally disabled children: Training in interpersonal problem solving skills. *Mental Retardation, 22*(1), 4–11.

Jackson, D. (1957). The question of family homeostasis. *Psychiatric Quarterly Supplement, 31*, Part 1, 79–90.

Jalali, B. (1982). Iranian families. In M. McGoldrick, J. Pearce, & G. Giordano (Eds.), *Ethnicity and family therapy* (pp. 289–309). New York: Guilford Press.

Jenkins, J., & Heinen, A. (1989). Students' preferences for service delivery: Pull-out, in-class, or integrated models. *Exceptional Children, 55*, 516–523.

Joel, B. (1983). *An innocent man*. New York: Columbia Records.

Johnson, C. L. (1982). Sibling solidarity: Its origin and functioning in Italian-American families. *Journal of Marriage and the Family, 44*, 155–167.

Johnston, J. C., & Zemitzsch, A. (1988). Family power: An intervention beyond the classroom. *Behavioral Disorders, 14*, 69–79.

Kahn, M. D. (1986). The sibling system: Bonds of intensity, loyalty, and endurance. In M. Karpel (Ed.), *Family resources: The hidden partner in family therapy* (pp. 235–258). New York: Guilford Press.

Kalter, N., Riemer, B., Brichman, A., & Woo Chen, J. (1985). Implications of parental divorce for female development. *Journal of the American Academy of Child Psychiatry, 24*, 538–544.

Kantor, D. (1983). The structural-analytic approach to the treatment of family developmental crisis. In J. Hansen & H. Liddle (Eds.), *Clinical implications of the family life cycle* (pp. 12–34). Rockville, MD: Aspen.

Karpel, M. (Ed.). (1986a). *Family resources: The hidden partner in family therapy.* New York: Guilford Press.

Karpel, M. (1986b). Testing, promoting, and preserving family resources: Beyond pathology and power. In M. Karpel (Ed.), *Family resources: The hidden partner in family therapy* (pp. 174–234). New York: Guilford Press.

Kazak, A. E. (1987). Families with disabled children: Stress and social networks in three samples. *Journal of Abnormal Child Psychology, 15*, 137–146.

Kazak, A. E., & Marvin, R. S. (1984). Differences, difficulties and adaptation: Stress and social networks in families with a handicapped child. *Family Relations, 33*, 66–77.

Kazak, A.E., & Wilcox, B. (1984). The structure and function of social support networks in families with handicapped children. *American Journal of Community Psychology, 12*, 645–661.

Kelso, D. R., & Attneave, C. L. (1981). *Bibliography of North American Indian mental health.* Westport, CT: Greenwood Press.

Kerr, M. (1981). Family systems theory and therapy. In A.S. Gurman & D.P. Kniskern (Eds.), *Handbook of family therapy* (pp. 226–264). New York: Brunner/Mazel.

Kerr, M. (1988, September). Chronic anxiety and defining a self. *The Atlantic Monthly*, pp. 35–58.

Kerr, M., & Bowen, M. (1988). *Family evaluation: An approach based on Bowen theory.* New York: W.W. Norton.

Kew, S. (1975). *Handicap and family crisis: A study of the siblings of handicapped children.* London: Pitman Publishing.

Koch, A. (1985). "If only it could be me": The families of pediatric cancer patients. *Family Relations, 34*, 63–70.

Komoski, P. K. (1990). Needed: A whole-curriculum approach. *Educational Leadership, 47*(5), 72–78.

Krauss, M. W. (1990). New precedent in family policy: Individualized Family Service Plan. *Exceptional Children, 56*, 388–395.

Kroth, R. (1972). Facilitating educational progress by improving parent conferences. *Focus on Exceptional Children, 4*(7), 1–10.

Kroth, R. (1975). *Communicating with parents of exceptional children.* Denver: Love Publishing.

Kroth, R. L. (1987). Mixed or missed messages between parents and professionals. *Volta Review, 89*(5), 1–10.

Kroth, R., & Simpson, R. (1977). *Parent conferences as a teaching strategy.* Denver: Love Publishing.

Kuo, W. (1984). Prevalence of depression among Asian Americans. *Journal of Nervous and Mental Diseases, 172*, 449–457.

Lambert, N. (1988). Perspectives on eligibility for and placement in special education programs. *Exceptional Children, 54*, 297–301.

Lambie, R. (1983). *Project CRITERIA: The final report of the REGI grant project CRITERIA, 1980–1983.* (ERIC Document Reproduction Service No. ED 244 479)

Lambie, R. (1986, March). Eight training problems...and some solutions. *The Developer*, pp. 2, 6–7.

Lambie, R. (1987a). Local heroes. *Style Weekly, 5*(35), 27.

Lambie, R. (1987b). *Working with families of children with handicaps.* Richmond: Virginia Department of Education.

Lambie, R., & Scearce, C. (1982, December). The multiplier effect in inservice education. *The Developer*, pp. 14–19.

Landerholm, E. (1990). The transdisciplinary team approach. *Teaching Exceptional Children*, 66–70.

Larson, J. H., Anderson, J. O., & Morgan, A. (1984). *Workshop models for family life education: Effective stepparenting.* New York: Family Service America.

Leigh, I. W. (1987). Parenting and the hearing impaired: Attachment and coping. *Volta Review, 89*(5), 11–21.

Levine, M. (1982). The child with school problems: An analysis of physician participation. *Exceptional Children, 48*, 296–304.

Lin, K. M., Inui, T. S., Kleinman, A. M., & Womack, W. M. (1982). Sociocultural determinants of the helpseeking behavior of patients with mental illness. *Journal of Nervous and Mental Disease, 170*, 78–84.

Longo, D. C., & Bond, L. (1984). Families of the handicapped child: Research and practice. *Family Relations, 33*, 57–65.

Losen, S., & Losen, J. (1985). The special education team. Boston: Allyn & Bacon.

Love, H. D. (1973). *The mentally retarded child and his family.* Springfield, IL: Charles C Thomas.

Lowe, J. I., & Herranen, M. (1981). Understanding teamwork: Another look at the concepts. *Social Work in Health Care, 7*(2), 1–10.

Lusthaus, C., Lusthaus, E., & Gibbs, H. (1981). Parents' role in the decision process. *Exceptional Children, 48,* 256–257.

Lynch, E. W., & Stein, R. C. (1987). Parent participation by ethnicity: A comparison of Hispanic, Black, and Anglo families. *Exceptional Children, 54,* 105–111.

Lyon, S., & Lyon, G. (1980). Team functioning and staff development: A role release approach to providing integrated educational services for severely handicapped students. *Journal of the Association for the Severely Handicapped, 5,* 250–263.

Machotka, P., Pittman, F. S., III, & Flomenhaft, K. (1967). Incest as a family affair. *Family Process, 6,* 98–116.

Mack, C.C., Jr. (1981). Racism, educational models, and black children. In D. Claerbaut (Ed.), *New directions in ethnic studies: Minorities in America* (pp. 84–94). Saratoga, CA: Century Twenty-One.

Margalit, M., & Raviv, A. (1983). Mothers' perceptions of family climate in families with a retarded child. *The Exceptional Child, 30,* 163–169.

Margolis, H., & Branningan, G. G. (1986). Relating to angry parents. *Academic Therapy, 21,* 343–346.

Martin, H. P. (1980). Working with parents of abused and neglected children. In R. R. Abidin (Ed.), *Parent education and intervention handbook* (pp. 252–271). Springfield, IL: Charles C Thomas.

Maslow, A. (1970). *Motivation and personality.* New York: Harper and Row.

McCubbin, H. I., & Patterson, J. (1982). Family adaptation to crises. In H. McCubbin, A. Cauble, & J. Patterson (Eds.), *Family stress, coping and social support.* Springfield, IL: Charles C Thomas.

McFadden, V. M., & Doub, G. (1983). The therapist's new role: Training families for healthy survival. In J. Hansen & H. Liddle (Eds.), *Clinical implications of the family life cycle* (pp. 134–160). Rockville, MD: Aspen.

McGill, D., & Pearce, J. (1982). British American families. In M. McGoldrick, J. Pearce, & G. Giordano (Eds.), *Ethnicity and family therapy* (pp. 457–482). New York: Guilford Press.

McGoldrick, M., & Gerson, R. (1985). *Genograms in family assessment.* New York: W.W. Norton.

McGoldrick, M., Pearce, J., & Giordano, J. (Eds.). (1982). *Ethnicity and family therapy.* New York: Guilford Press.

McHale, S. M., Sloan, J., & Simeonsson, R. J. (1986). Sibling relationships of children with autistic, mentally retarded, and nonhandicapped brothers and sisters. *Journal of Autism and Developmental Disorders, 16,* 399–413.

McKeever, P. (1982). Siblings of chronically ill children: A literature review with implications for research and practice. *American Journal of Orthopsychiatry, 53,* 209–218.

McLoughlin, J. A. (1981). Training together to work together. *Teacher Education and Special Education, 4*(4), 45–54.

McLuhan, M. (1967). *The medium is the message.* New York: Touchstone.

McMillan, D. L., & Turnbull, A. P. (1983). Parent involvement with special education. *Education and Training of the Mentally Retarded, 18*(1), 5–9.

Meier, J. H., & Sloan, M. P. (1984). The severely handicapped and child abuse. In J. Blacher (Ed.), *Severely handicapped young children and their families* (pp. 247–274). New York: Academic Press.

Meyer, D. J., Vadasy, P. F., & Fewell, R. R. (1985). *Sibshops: A handbook for implementing workshops for siblings of children with special needs.* Seattle: University of Washington Press.

Mills, J., & Crowley, R. (1986). *Therapeutic metaphors for children and the child within.* New York: Brunner/ Mazel.

Miner, R. A. (1981). Single parenthood and child management problems. In A. S. Gurman (Ed.), *Questions and answers in the practice of family therapy* (pp. 318–321). New York: Brunner/Mazel.

Mink, I. T., Meyers, C. E., & Nihira, K. (1984). Taxonomy of family life styles: II. Homes with slow-learning children. *American Journal of Mental Deficiency, 89,* 111–123.

Minuchin, S. (1974). *Families and family therapy.* Cambridge: Harvard University Press.

Minuchin, S., & Fishman, H. (1981). *Family therapy techniques.* Cambridge: Harvard University Press.

Minuchin, S., Montalvo, B., Guerney, B.G., Jr., Rosman, B.L., & Schumer, F. (1967). *Families of the slums.* New York: Basic Books.

Minuchin, S., Rosman, B., & Baker, L. (1978). *Psychosomatic families: Anorexia nervosa in context.* Cambridge: Harvard University Press.

Momeni, J. A. (1984). (Ed.). *Demography of racial and ethnic minorities in the United States.* Westport, CT: Greenwood Press.

Montalvo, B., & Guitierrez, M. (1983). A perspective for the use of the cultural dimension in family therapy. In J. C. Hansen & C. J. Falicov (Eds.), *Cultural perspectives in family therapy* (pp. 15–32). Rockville, MD: Aspen.

Montgomery, R., Gonyea, J., & Hooyman, N. (1985). Caregiving and the experience of subjective and objective burden. *Family Relations, 34,* 19–26.

Moran, M. (1978). *Assessment of the exceptional learner in the regular classroom.* Denver: Love Publishing.

Mullins, J. B. (1983). The uses of bibliotherapy in counseling families confronted with handicaps. In M. Seligman (Ed.), *The family with a handicapped child: Understanding and treatment* (pp. 235–260). New York: Grune & Stratton.

Nazzaro, J. N. (Ed.). (1981). *Culturally diverse exceptional children in school.* Washington, DC: National Institute of Education.

Niels, J. B. (1980). *A study of birth order and family constellation among high school and delinquent students.* Ann Arbor, MI: Xerox University Microfilms.

Nihira, K., Meyers, C. E., & Mink, I. T. (1983). Reciprocal relationship between home environment and development of TMR adolescents. *American Journal of Mental Deficiency, 88,* 139–149.

Nihira, K., Mink, I. T., & Meyers, C. E. (1981). Relationship between home environment and school adjustment of TMR children. *American Journal of Mental Deficiency, 86*(1), 8–15.

Nihira, K., Mink, I. T., & Meyers, C. E. (1985). Home environment and development of slow-learning adolescents: Reciprocal relations. *Developmental Psychology, 21,* 784–794.

Olson, D., McCubbin, H., Barnes, H., Larsen, A., Muxen, M., & Wilson, M. 1983. *Families: What makes them work.* Beverly Hills, CA: Sage Publications.

Orelove, F., & Sobsey, D. (1991). *Educating children with multiple disabilities: A transdisciplinary approach* (2nd ed.). Baltimore: Paul H. Brookes.

Otto, M. L., & Smith, D. G. (1980). Child abuse: A cognitive behavioral intervention model. *Journal of Marital and Family Therapy, 6,* 425–430.

Our son has had trouble at school for a long time: Learning disabilities and delinquency. (1986). *The Exceptional Parent, 16*(5), 48–54.

Palazzoli, S. M., Boscolo, L., Cecchin, G. F., & Prata, G. (1980). The problem of the referring person. *Journal of Marital and Family Therapy, 6,* 3–9.

Patterson, J. M. (1985). Critical factors affecting family compliance with home treatment for children with cystic fibrosis. *Family Relations, 34,* 79–89.

Patterson, J. M., & McCubbin, H. I. (1983). Chronic illness: Family stress and coping. In C. Figley & H. McCubbin (Eds.), *Stress and the family: Vol. II: Coping with catastrophe* (pp. 21–36). New York: Brunner/Mazel.

Pedersen, F. A. (1983). Differentiation of the father's role in the infancy period. In J. Vincent (Ed.), *Advances in family intervention, assessment, and theory* (Vol. 3, pp. 185–208). New York: JAI Press.

Perkins, T. F., & Kahan, J. P. (1979). An empirical comparison of natural-father and stepfather family systems. *Family Process, 18,* 175–183.

Perosa, L. M., & Perosa, S. L. (1981). The school counselor's use of structural family therapy with learning disabled students. *The School Counselor, 29,* 152–155.

Peschley, D. J. (1988). Minority MMR overrepresentation and special education reform. *Exceptional Children, 54,* 316–323.

Peterson, E. T., & Kunz, P. R. (1975). Parental control over adolescents according to family size. *Adolescence, 10,* 419–427.

Pfeiffer, S. (1980). The school-based interprofessional team: Recurring problems and some possible solutions. *Journal of School Psychology, 18,* 388–394.

Pfeiffer, S. I., & Tittler, B. I. (1983). Utilizing the multidisciplinary team to facilitate a school family systems orientation. *School Psychology Review, 12,* 169–173.

Phillips, V., & McCullough, L. (1990). Consultation-based programming: Instituting the collaborative ethic in schools. *Exceptional Children, 56,* 291–304.

Piaget, J. (1952). *The origins of intelligence in children.* New York: International Universities Press.

Piaget, J., & Inhelder, B. (1958). *The growth of logical thinking from childhood to adolescence* (A. Parsons & S.

Milgram, Trans.). New York: Basic Books.

Piaget, J., & Inhelder, B. (1969). *The psychology of the child.* New York: Basic Books.

Pinkney, A. (1975). *Black Americans.* Englewood Cliffs, NJ: Prentice-Hall.

Price, M., & Goodman, L. (1980). Individualized Education Programs: A cost study. *Exceptional Children, 46,* 446–458.

Pugach, M., & Johnson, L. (1988). Rethinking the relationship between consultation and collaborative problem-solving. *Focus on Exceptional Children, 21*(4), 1–8.

Quinn, W. H., Newfield, N. A., & Protinsky, H. O. (1985). Rites of passage in families with adolescents. *Family Process, 24,* 101–111.

Ralph, J. (1989). Improving education for the disadvantaged: Do we know whom to help? *Phi Delta Kappan, 70,* 385–401.

Raynes, M., Snell, M., & Sailor, W. (1991). A fresh look at categorical programs for children with special needs. *Phi Delta Kappan, 73,* 326–331.

Raynor, L. (1980). *The adopted child comes of age.* London: George Allen & Unwin.

Reece, B. L., & Brandt, R. (1987). *Effective human relations in organizations* (3rd ed.). Boston: Houghton Mifflin.

Reed, D.F. (1992). Culturally diverse students. In J. Wood (Ed.), *Mainstreaming: A practical approach for teachers.* Columbus, OH: Merrill.

Reinsmith, W.A. (1989). The whole in every part: Steiner and Waldrof schooling. *Educational Forum, 54,* 79–91.

Reisberg, L., & Wolf, R. (1986). Developing a consulting program in special education: Implementation and interventions. *Focus on Exceptional Children, 19*(3), 1–14.

Reiss, D., & Oliveri, M. E. (1980). Family paradigm and family coping: A proposal for linking the family's intrinsic adaptive capacities to its responses to stress. *Family Relations, 29,* 431–444.

Rich, S. (1986, November 12). Parental fighting hurts even after divorce. *The Washington Post,* p. H-12

Roit, M., & Pfohl, W. (1984). The readability of P.L. 94-142 parent materials: Are parents truly informed? *Exceptional Children, 50,* 496–505.

Rollins, B. C., & Galligan, R. (1978). The developing child and marital satisfaction of parents. In R. Lerner & G. Spanier (Eds.), *Child influences on marital and family interaction: A life-span perspective* (pp. 71–106). New York: Academic Press.

Rotunno, M., & McGoldrick, M. (1982). Italian families. In M. McGoldrick, J. Pearce, & G. Giordano (Eds.), *Ethnicity and family therapy* (pp. 340–363). New York: Guilford Press.

Rubin, K. H. (1985). Socially withdrawn children: An "at risk" population? In B. H. Schneider, K. H. Rubin & J. E. Kedingham (Eds.), *Children's peer relations: Issues in assessment and intervention* (pp. 125–140). New York: Springer-Verlag.

Rucker, C. N., & Vautour, J. A. (1981). The child study team training program: Research and development. *Teacher Education and Special Education, 4*(1), 5–12.

Rueveni, U. (1979). *Networking families in crisis: Intervention strategies with families and social networks.* New York: Human Sciences Press.

Safer, D. J. (1966). Family therapy for children with behavior disorders. *Family Process, 5,* 243–255.

Samuels, S. C. (1990). *Ideal adoption. A comprehensive guide to forming an adoptive family.* New York: Plenum Press.

Sarason, S. (1982). *The culture of the school and the problem of change* (2nd ed.). Boston: Allyn & Bacon.

Satir, V. (1972). *Peoplemaking.* Palo Alto, CA: Science and Behavior Books.

Satir, V. (1978). *Your many faces.* Millbrae, CA: Celestial Arts.

Satir, V. (1983a). *AVANTA Process Community III. The Third international Summer Institute.* Crested Butte, CO: AVANTA Process Community.

Satir, V. (1983b). *Conjoint family therapy* (3rd ed.). Palo Alto, CA: Science and Behavior Books.

Satir, V. (1988). *The new peoplemaking.* Mountain View, CA: Science and Behavior Books.

Satir, V., & Baldwin, M. (1983). *Satir step by step.* Palo Alto, CA: Science and Behavior Books.

Satir, V., Stachowiak, J., & Taschman, H. (1975). *Helping families to change.* New York: Jason Aronson.

Schaefer, C., Briesmeister, J., & Fitton, M. (1984). *Family therapy techniques for problem behaviors of children and teenagers.* San Francisco: Jossey-Bass.

Schell, G. (1981). The young handicapped child: A family perspective. *Topics in Early Childhood Special Education, 1*(3), 21–27.

Schniedewind, N., & Davidson, E. (1983). *Open minds to equality*. Englewood Cliffs, NJ: Prentice-Hall.

Schulman, G. L. (1984). Transitions in family structure. In C. E. Schaefer, J. M. Briesmeister, & M. E. Fitton (Eds.), *Family therapy techniques for problem behaviors of children and teenagers*. San Francisco: Jossey-Bass.

Schvaneveldt, J. D., & Ihinger, M. (1979). Sibling relationships in the family. In W. R. Burr, R. Hill, F. J. Nye, & I. L. Reiss (Eds.), *Contemporary theories about the family* (Vol. 1, pp. 96–97). New York: Free Press.

Seligman, M. (1979). *Strategies for helping parents of exceptional children*. New York: Free Press.

Seligman, M. (1983). Understanding and communicating with families of handicapped children. In S. G. Garwood (Ed.), *Educating young handicapped children: A developmental approach* (2nd ed., pp. 435–473). Rockville, MD: Aspen.

Seligman, M. (1983). *The family with a handicapped child: Understanding and treatment*. New York: Grune & Stratton.

Serafica, F. C. (1990). Counseling Asian-American parents: A cultural-developmental approach. In F. C. Serafica, A. I. Schwebel, R. K. Russell, P. D. Isaac, & L. B. Myers (Eds.), *Mental health of ethnic minorities*. New York: Praeger.

Sevcik, B., & Ysseldyke, J. (1986). An analysis of teachers' prereferral interventions for students exhibiting behavioral problems. *Behavioral Disorders, 11,* 109–117.

Shapiro, J. (1983). Family reactions and coping strategies in response to the physically ill or handicapped child: A review. *Social Science Medicine, 17,* 913–931.

Sheehy, G. (1976). *Passages: Predictable crises of adult life*. New York: Dutton.

Showers, B., Joyce, B., & Bennett, B. (1987). Synthesis of research on self-development: A framework for future study and a state-of-the-art analysis. *Educational Leadership, 45*(3), 77–87.

Shulman, B., & Mosak, H. H. (1977). Birth order and ordinal position: Two Adlerian views. *Journal of Individual Psychology, 33,* 114–121.

Silver, L. B. (1984). *The misunderstood child. A guide for parents of learning disabled children*. New York: McGraw-Hill.

Simon, S. B., Howe, L. W., & Kirschenbaum, H. (1978). *Values clarification*. New York: Dodd, Mead.

Simpson, R. (1982). *Conferencing parents of exceptional children*. Rockville, MD: Aspen.

Skrtic, T. (1991). *Behind special education: A critical analysis of professional culture and school organization*. Denver: Love Publishing.

Slavin, R., & Madden, N. (1989). What works for student at risk: A research synthesis. *Educational Leadership, 46*(5), 4–13.

Sloman, L., & Konstantareas, M. M. (1990). Why families of children with biological deficits require a systems approach. *Family Process, 29,* 417–432.

Sluckin, A., & Smith, P. (1977). Two approaches to the concept of dominance in preschool children. *Child Development, 48,* 911–923.

Smith, A. H. (1978). Encountering the family system in school-related behavior problems. *Psychology in the Schools, 15,* 379–386.

Smith, S. L. (1981). *No easy answers: The learning disabled child at home and at school*. New York: Bantam Books.

Smith, S. W. (1990). Individualized Education Programs (IEPs) in special education—From intent to acquiescence. *Exceptional Children, 57*(1), 6–14.

Somers, M. N. (1987). Parenting in the 1980s: Programming perspectives and issues. *Volta Review, 89*(5), 68–77.

Sonnier, I. L. (1985). *Methods and techniques of holistic education*. Springfield, IL: Charles C Thomas.

Spark, G. M., & Brody, E. M. (1970). The aged are family members. *Family Process, 9,* 195–210.

Spitz, R. A. (1946). Hospitalism: An inquiry into the genesis of psychiatric conditioning in early childhood. In D. Fenschel (Ed.), *Psychoanalytic studies of the child* (Vol. 1). New York: International Press.

Stanton, M. D., Todd, T. C., & Assoc. (1982). *The family therapy of drug abuse and addiction*. New York: Guilford Press.

Stewart, J. (1986). *Counseling parents of exceptional children* (2nd ed.). Columbus, OH: Merrill.

Strickland, B., & Turnbull, A. (1990). *Developing and implementing Individualized Education Programs* (3rd ed.). Columbus, OH: Merrill.

Strom, R., Rees, R., Slaughter, H., & Wurster, S. (1981). Child rearing expectations of families with atypical children. *American Journal of Orthopsychiatry, 51,* 285–296.

Suelzle, M., & Keenan, V. (1981). Changes in family support networks over the life cycle of mentally retarded persons. *American Journal of Mental Deficiency, 86,* 267–274.

Tashima, N. (1981). Asian Americans in psychiatric systems. In D. Claerbaut (Ed.), *New directions in ethnic studies: Minorities in America* (pp. 95–106). Saratoga, CA: Century Twenty One.

Tavormina, J. B., Boll, T. J., Dunn, N. J., Luscomb, R. L., & Taylor, J. R. (1981). Psychosocial effects on parents of raising a physically handicapped child. *Journal of Abnormal Child Psychology, 9*(1), 121–131.

Tew, B. J., Lawrence, K. M., Payne, H., & Rawnsley, K. (1977). Marital stability following the birth of a child with spina bifida. *British Journal of Psychiatry, 131,* 79–82.

Thaxton, L. (1985). Wife abuse. In L. L'Abate (Ed.), *The handbook of family psychology and therapy,* (Vol. 2, pp. 876–899). Homewood, IL: Dorsey Press.

Tindal, G., Shinn, M., & Rodden-Nord, K. (1990). Contextually based school consultation: Influential variables. *Exceptional Children, 56,* 324–336

Tittler, B., Friedman, S., Blotcky, A., & Stedrak, J. (1982). The influence of family variables on an ecologically-based treatment program for emotionally disturbed children. *American Journal of Orthopsychiatry, 52,* 123–130.

Toman, W. (1976). *Family constellation* (2nd ed.). New York: Springer Publishing.

Trailor, C. B. (1982). Role clarification and participation in child study teams. *Exceptional Children, 48,* 529–530.

Treadway, D. (1987, July/August). The ties that bind: Both alcoholics and their families are bound to the bottle. *Family Networker,* pp. 17–23.

Trevino, F. (1979, October). Siblings of handicapped children: Identifying those at risk. *Social Casework,* pp. 488–493.

Trout, M. D. (1983). Birth of a sick or handicapped infant: Impact on the family. *Child Welfare, 62,* 337–347.

Tseng, W., & McDermott, J. (1979). Triaxial family classification. *Journal of the American Academy of Child Psychiatry, 18,* 22–43.

Turnbull, A. P., & Turnbull, H. R. (1982). Parent involvement in the education of handicapped children: A critique. *Mental Retardation, 20*(3), 115–122.

Turnbull, A. P., & Turnbull, H, R. (1986). *Families, professionals, and exceptionality: A special partnership.* Columbus, OH: Merrill.

Turnbull, A. P., & Turnbull, H. R. (1990). *Families, professionals, and exceptionality: A special partnership* (2nd ed.). Columbus, OH: Merrill.

Turner, A. L. (1980) Therapy with families of a mentally retarded child. *Journal of Marital and Family Therapy,* 167–170.

Turner, R. (1981). Social support as a contingency in psychological well-being. *Journal of Health and Social Behavior, 22,* 357–367.

Vadasy, P. F., Fewell, R. R., Meyer, D. J., & Schell, G. (1984). Siblings of handicapped children: A developmental perspective on family interactions. *Family Relations, 33,* 155–167.

Vaillant, G. E. (1983). *The natural history of alcoholism: Causes, patterns, and paths to recovery.* Cambridge: Harvard University Press.

Visher, E. B., & Visher, J. S. (1979). *Stepfamilies: A guide to working with stepparents and stepchildren.* New York: Brunner/Mazel.

Wahler, R. G. (1980). The insular mother: Her problems in parent-child treatment. *Journal of Applied Behavior Analysis, 13,* 207–219.

Wald, E. (1981). *The remarried family: Challenge and promise.* New York: Family Service Association of America.

Wallerstein, J. S. (1983). Children of divorce: The psychological tasks of the child. *American Journal of Orthopsychiatry, 53,* 230–243.

Wallerstein, J. S., & Blakeslee, S. (1990). *Second chances.* New York: Ticknor and Fields.

Wallerstein, J. S., & Kelly, J. B. (1980). Divorce counseling: A community service for families in the midst of divorce. In R. R. Abidin (Ed.), *Parent education and intervention handbook* (pp. 272–298). Springfield, IL: Charles C Thomas.

Walsh, F. (1982). *Normal family processes.* New York: Guilford Press.

Walsh, F. (1983). The timing of symptoms and critical events in the family life cycle. In J. Hansen & H. Liddle (Eds.), *Clinical implications of the family life cycle* (pp. 120–132). Rockville, MD: Aspen.

Walters, M. (1972). We became family therapists. In A. Ferber, M. Mendelsohn, & A. Napier (Eds.), *Book of family therapy* (pp. 118–120). New York: Science House.

Wang, M., & Birch, J. (1984). Effective special education in regular classes. *Exceptional Children, 50*, 391–397.

Watzlawick, P. (1976). The psychotherapeutic technique of "reframing." In J. Claghorn (Ed.), *Successful psychotherapy* (pp. 119–127). New York: Brunner/Mazel.

Watzlawick, P., Weakland, J. H., & Fisch, R. (1974). *Change: Principles of problem formation and problem resolution.* New York: W.W. Norton.

Weber, J. L., & Stoneman, Z. (1986). Parental nonparticipation in program planning for mentally retarded children. An empirical investigation. *Applied Research in Mental Retardation, 7*, 359–369.

Wegscheider-Cruise, S. (1985). *Choicemaking.* Pompano Beach, FL: Health Communications.

Weinberg, R. B., & Mauksch, L. B. (1991). Examining family-of-origin influences in life at work. *Journal of Marital and Family Therapy, 17*, 233–242.

Weisner, T. S. (1982). Sibling interdependence and child caretaking: A cross-cultural view. In M. E. Lamb & B. Sutton-Smith (Eds.), *Sibling relationships* (pp. 305–328). Hillsdale, NJ: Lawrence Erlbaum.

Wendell, H. V., & Leoni, D. (1986). *Multiethnic/multicultural materials.* Richmond: Virginia State Department of Education.

West, J., & Idol, L. (1987). School consultation (Part I): An interdisciplinary perspective on theory, models, and research. *Journal of Learning Disabilities, 20*, 388–408.

Whiteside, M. F. (1983). Families of remarriage: The weaving of many life cycle threads. In J. Hansen & H. Liddle (Eds.), *Clinical implications of the family life cycle* (pp. 100–119). Rockville, MD: Aspen.

Wikler, L. (1981). Chronic stresses of families of mentally retarded children. *Family Relations, 30*, 281–288.

Wikler, L., Wasow, M., & Hatfield, E. (1981). Chronic sorrow revisited: Parent vs. professional depiction of the adjustment of parents of mentally retarded children. *American Journal of Orthopsychiatry, 51*(1), 63–70.

Wilchesky, M., & Reynolds, T. (1986). The socially deficient LD child in context: A systems approach to assessment and treatment. *Journal of Learning Disabilities, 19*, 411–415.

Will, M. (1986). Educating children with learning problems: A shared responsibility. *Exceptional Children, 52*, 411–415.

Wilson, W. J. (1982). The declining significance of race. In N. R. Yetman & C.H. Steele (Eds.), *Majority and minority: The dynamics of race and ethnicity in American life* (3rd ed., pp. 385–392). Boston: Allyn & Bacon.

Winton, P. J., & Turnbull, A. P. (1981). Parent involvement as viewed by parents of preschool handicapped children. *Topics in Early Childhood Special Education, 1*(3), 11–19.

Wodarski, J. S. (1984). A comprehensive treatment program for abusive parents. In C. E. Schaefer, J. M. Briesmeister, & M. E. Fitton (Eds.), *Family therapy techniques for problem behaviors of children and teenagers* (pp. 365–367). San Francisco: Jossey-Bass.

Wright, L. S., Matlock, K. S., & Matlock, D. T. (1985). Parents of handicapped children: Their self-ratings, life satisfactions and parental adequacy. *The Exceptional Child, 32*(1), 37–40.

Yanok, J., & Derubertis, D. (1989). Comparative study of parental participation in regular and special education programs. *Exceptional Children, 56*, 195–199.

Yoshida, R., Fenton, K., Maxwell, J., & Kaufman, M. (1978). Group decision making in the planning team process: Myth or reality? *Journal of School Psychology, 16*, 237–244.

Youngstrom, N. (1990, October). Therapy in the schools aids children of divorce. *APA Monitor*, p. 22.

Ysseldyke, J. E. (1979). Issues in psychoeducational assessment. In D. Reschly & G. Phye (Eds.), *School psychology: Methods and roles* (pp. 87–122). New York: Academic Press.

Ysseldyke, J. E., & Algozzine, B. (1983). LD or not LD: That's not the question. *Journal of Learning Disabilities, 16*, 29–31.

Ysseldyke, J., Algozzine, B., & Allen, D. (1982). Participation of regular education teachers in special education team decision making. *Exceptional Children, 48*, 365–367.

Ysseldyke, J. E., Algozzine, B., & Epps, S. (1983). A logical and empirical analysis of current practice in classifying students as handicapped. *Exceptional Children, 50*, 160–166.

Ysseldyke, J., Algozzine, B., Richey, L., & Graden, J. (1982). Declaring students eligible for learning disability services: Why bother with the data? *Learning Disability Quarterly, 5*(1), 37–44.

Zetlin, A. G. (1985). Mentally retarded teenagers: Adolescent behavior disturbance and its relation to family environment. *Child Psychiatry and Human Development, 15*, 243–254.

Zins, J. E., Curtis, M. J., Graden, J. L., & Ponti, C. R. (1988). *Helping students succeed in the regular classroom.* San Francisco: Jossey-Bass.

INDEX